IN YOUR LIGHT WE SEE LIGHT

A Reformed Theology of Divine Illumination

STUDIES IN HISTORICAL
& SYSTEMATIC THEOLOGY
H
S
S
T

"Like the apostle, Paul Uyen is not content to explain the theology of illumination. He writes to help us feel the light that has set his own heart on fire. Here is an exercise in Reformed catholicity that stretches mind and heart, a work of theological retrieval that revives the soul."

Justin Ariel Bailey, dean of chapel and
professor of theology, Dordt University, Iowa

"As this carefully researched and well-argued work exhibits, union with Christ is inseparable from illumination from the Father, in the Son, by the Spirit. Joining the great conversation across Christian traditions and eras, Uyen pushes us into the deep end to reawaken our interest in this crucial reality. It's not only intellectually stimulating but spiritually edifying—indeed, illuminating!"

Michael Horton, professor, Westminster Seminary California

"Union with Christ is the greatest truth of the Gospel story. Paul Uyen, in this wonderful book, has demonstrated how true it really is! By elucidating the doctrine of illumination in relation to being united to Christ, he has opened up yet another rich, biblical avenue to this glorious truth. I am so glad this book now exists, and I hope it is read far and wide."

Marcus Johnson, professor of theology, Moody Bible Institute;
senior pastor, Calvary Lutheran Church, Brookfield, Wisconsin

"What a rich historical and theological treatment of illumination. Through both a creative employment of participation and by being genuinely Trinitarian in orientation—and not relegating illumination merely to the Spirit—Paul C. Uyen has offered us a real treat in this volume. I know much good will be generated as a result of his valuable contribution."

Kelly M. Kapic, professor of theological studies, Covenant College, Georgia

"Dr. Uyen's theology of divine illumination contains astonishing learning, and it is that as the fruit of wisdom, humility, and sincerity. Uyen reads the Scriptures attentively, competently, and submissively from within the reality of which he writes, and he listens with charity and understanding to the broad assembly of illumined believers across the church. Beyond exegesis and retrieval, he proffers a Reformed dogmatic account of the economy of illumination. This is a work to be read more than once."

Jon C. Laansma, Gerald F. Hawthorne Professor of
New Testament Greek and Exegesis, Wheaton College, Illinois

"This is a beautiful book. Paul C. Uyen's *In Your Light We See Light* is a standard-bearer on theological retrieval in service of positive, dogmatic construal. Uyen draws deeply from the waters of Eastern Orthodoxy, Roman Catholicism, and the Reformed tradition on the economy of divine illumination to set forth a truly catholic and truly Reformed doctrine. Not only is this work a real triumph of scholarship, it is also profoundly edifying."

Samuel G. Parkison, associate professor of theological studies,
Gulf Theological Seminary, United Arab Emirates

"This is a remarkable and wide-ranging study of the triune God's abundantly gracious act of illumination, which unites persons with Christ and communion with God. Paul Uyen brings together a close reading of the Bible and a generously ecumenical explication of Christian tradition in service of a lively dogmatic account of the 'economy of illumination.' He ably guides the reader towards a deeper understanding of God's illumination that transforms the minds and hearts of Christian disciples. This wise and insightful study enlightens our doctrinal understanding and in so doing leads us to live before God with deeper prayer, devotion, and obedience."

David Lauber, dean of humanities and theological studies and professor of theology, Wheaton College, Illinois

"The doctrine of illumination is frequently reduced in its scope to a narrow set of epistemological and hermeneutical concerns. Paul Uyen convincingly demonstrates to the contrary that illumination is a unifying theme of redemptive history and thus a vital locus of Christian theology."

David Luy, associate professor of systematic theology, North American Lutheran Seminary, Pennsylvania

"What does it mean to participate in God? Uyen addresses this important question through a wide-ranging study of the way in which divine illumination has been conceived in the Bible and several key theological traditions. A truly valuable overview of the doctrine and an innovative study of its relevance to Christian life and thought today."

Lydia Schumacher, professor of historical and philosophical theology, King's College London

"Paul Uyen has done a great service by offering a fully Trinitarian theology of God's illumination of those he calls to faith in Jesus. What a privilege and blessing is communion with the Lord. And what a blessing to be reminded in this marvelous monograph of the ways in which God's people are enabled to walk in the light of God himself in Christ by the power of the Spirit."

Douglas A. Sweeney, dean and professor of divinity, Beeson Divinity School, Alabama

"Paul Uyen's thorough study of the economy of illumination pulses with joy. He enriches evangelical understanding by connecting illumination more organically to inseparable Trinitarian operations, to participation in Christ, to varied traditions and practices—and ultimately to the heart and the body along with the mind."

Daniel J. Treier, Knoedler Professor of Theology, Wheaton College, Illinois

"In In Your Light We See Light, Dr. Uyen richly incorporates the doctrine of illumination with participation in Christ. The reader will benefit greatly not only from the content itself but also by observing the erudite integration of biblical, historical, and dogmatic theology. This work, with a winsome wisdom and depth, invites all those who are 'in Christ' to 'gaze upon the beauty of the Lord' (Ps 27:4)."

Brian H. Tung, assistant professor of theology, California Baptist University

IN YOUR LIGHT WE SEE LIGHT

A Reformed Theology of Divine Illumination

PAUL C. UYEN

STUDIES IN HISTORICAL AND SYSTEMATIC THEOLOGY

In Your Light We See Light: A Reformed Theology of Divine Illumination
Studies in Historical and Systematic Theology

Lexham Academic, an imprint of Lexham Press
1313 Bay St, Bellingham, WA 98225
LexhamPress.com

Print ISBN 9781683598329
Digital ISBN 9781683598336
Library of Congress Control Number 2025937903

Lexham Editorial: Todd R. Hains, Zachary Gordon, James Spinti
Cover Design: Fanny Palacios
Typesetting: Justin Marr

25 26 27 28 29 30 31 / US / 12 11 10 9 8 7 6 5 4 3 2 1

For my wife, Christine, and our children,

Eden, Saige, Violet, Callum, and Elliot

CONTENTS

PRAYER FOR THE LIGHT OF THE LORD

—

In the name of the Father and of the Son and of the Holy Spirit. Amen.

The LORD is God,
  and he has made his light to shine upon us. *Ps 118:27*
    Your word is a lamp to my feet
  and a light to my path. *Ps 119:105*
    Make your face shine upon your servant,
  and teach me your statutes. *Ps 119:135*
    Restore us, O LORD God of hosts!
  Let your face shine, that we may be saved! *Ps 80:19*

Merciful Lord, cast the bright beams of your light upon your church, that being enlightened by the doctrine of your blessed and holy word we may walk in the light of your truth and attain to the light of everlasting life; through Jesus Christ our Lord, who lives and reigns with you and the Holy Spirit, one God, now and forever. Amen.

FOREWORD

The Psalmist says, "in your light do we see light" (Ps 36:9), a line that, because "God is light" (1 John 1:5), has launched a thousand ships – and not a few theological dissertations. The book you are about to read did begin its life as a doctoral thesis, but make no mistake: while it may resemble academic theology, it's made of sterner stuff, woven from real life. It is a dogmatic account of the awful (in the sense of awe-inspiring) process of conversion, which includes crucifying the old self in order to bring forth the glorious new.

I never met Dr. Paul Uyen's old self, but I heard about him, not in detail, but in rough outline. *Rough* is the operative term. For, once upon a time, he was a gang member, hardly the worst of sinners (that prize goes to his namesake, the apostle, according to 1 Tim 1:15) yet "alienated and hostile in mind, doing evil deeds" (Col 1:21), like the rest of us when we were sinners. I first met Paul in the fall of 2009, when he was an MA student at Wheaton College. Truth be told, he did not have a strong background in theology; however, he had a burning desire to make theology a means to growing mature disciples of Jesus Christ, and an indefatigable determination to make up for lost (study) time. The quality of the thesis he eventually produced surprised me. If there had been a Most Improved Student Award, Paul would have deserved it. It was largely on the strength of his work at Wheaton that Paul was admitted to the PhD program at Trinity Evangelical Divinity School (to which I had by then returned), where I continued to serve as his supervisor.

Paul's is not a rags to riches but a gang- to faculty-member story. It brings to mind the not dissimilar life-story of John Newton, who in 1772 wrote a hymn about his personal conversion experience: "Amazing Grace." As a troubled young man lacking religious conviction, Newton served in the Royal Navy and later got involved in the slave trade. It was during a violent storm at sea that he eventually cried out to God for mercy. He finally left the slave trade, began studying theology with an aim to ordination, and ultimately became both an Anglican curate and an abolitionist. The lines from "Amazing Grace" that bear most directly on Paul's thesis is this:

I once was lost, but now am found
Was blind but now I see.

Paul has written not a hymn to illumination, but a theological treatise, a patient and thorough answer to the question occasioned by radical conversions such as Newton's, Paul's own, and anyone else's: *What just happened?* The book you are about to read gives a three-part answer to the salvific mystery of amazing grace that draws on biblical, historical, and dogmatic resources and, for that reason, is a theological education in its own right.

In Dr. Uyen's hands, the "economy of illumination" – the way the God who is eternal light shines forth in time – is the all-encompassing framework that traces how the Father of lights sheds the light of the Son (the Son's knowledge of his Father, the knowledge of God made flesh) into human hearts through the Spirit's effectual ministry of the gospel of Jesus Christ. Many contemporary treatments of the doctrine of illumination focus on the work of the Spirit in ministering understanding of Scripture, but Dr. Uyen, appealing to the doctrine of inseparable operations, argues for a recovery of the Father's and Son's activity in illumination as well.

In Your Light We See Light is a veritable parade of theological disciplines. As already mentioned, Dr. Uyen's tripartite approach provides a biblical, historical, and dogmatic account of light-giving Trinitarian operations. Along the way, he builds two important bridges. The first, which takes up most of Part 2, is a kind of "mere Christian" integration of Eastern Orthodox, Roman Catholic, and Reformed accounts of illumination spanning two millennia. His purpose is not to dilute the doctrine into some facile common denominator but, on the contrary, to let each tradition make its own distinct contribution. The net result is a thick description of illumination in which Trinitarian enlightening produces both cognitive and cardiac effects, renewing darkened minds and hardened hearts, the human person as a whole. Even natural light does more than enable us to see things; it is also a necessary condition for plant, animal, and human life.

The second bridge, under construction throughout Part 3, spans what has become an ugly ditch: a dichotomizing of (intellectual) illumination by the Spirit from (existential) participation in Christ. The historic traditions surveyed in Part 2 disagree not only about illumination, but also about participation in Christ, as do the contemporary theologians Dr. Uyen examines in Part 3. In the most general (and inadequate) of terms: Orthodoxy emphasizes theosis and liturgical participation; Roman Catholicism emphasizes transforming grace and sacramental participation; Radical Orthodoxy appeals to Platonism to fund an ontological participation; Barth appeals to Christ's being humanity's elected representative in order to set forth a peculiarly christological kind of ontological participation. What aggravates this intramural disagreement even more is that contemporary theologies of participation typically fail to mention, and thus profit from, earlier discussions of illumination.

Dr. Uyen wants to retrieve, and restore the integrity of, these two themes that modern theologians have put asunder – participation in Christ and illumination by the Spirit – and to coordinate them via his expanded triune economy of illumination. Doing so clarifies both participation (the believer's sharing in the light and love that characterizes the relationship of Father and Son) and illumination (the means, manner, and mark of the Spirit-enabled participation in the love and light of that Father-Son relationship).

The purpose of this impressive and wide-reaching dogmatic exercise, though scholarly, is far from being simply academic. *In Your Light We See Light* is a serious attempt to help disciples appreciate, and grow into, all the spiritual blessings signaled by Dr. Uyen's namesake, the apostle Paul, and his notion of being "in Christ." Like all good theology, the proper end of reflection on this topic, union with Christ, is at once doctrinal and devotional: deeper communion with God. The ultimate goal of *both* Pauls, the apostle and my former student, is that their readers, having the eyes of their minds and hearts enlightened, may know "what are the riches of [Christ's] glorious inheritance in the saints" (Eph. 1:18).

Kevin J. Vanhoozer

ACKNOWLEDGMENTS

The book you have in your hand came out of my dissertation at Trinity Evangelical Divinity School (TEDS), where I devoted my study to the economy of illumination. The seed of this study was sown from my desire to understand my new life in Christ, the light for the study came from Kevin Vahoozer's Advanced Theological Prolegomena class at TEDS, when I wrote my paper on illumination in the hospital awaiting the birth of my firstborn, Eden, and the study was finally conceived through Scott Manetsch's class on John Calvin and an independent study with Douglas Sweeney on Jonathan Edwards, as it suddenly dawned on me that to be illumined is a mode of being in union with Christ because it is in his light that we see light (Ps 36:9).

The love, sacrifices, and friendships of the following people are the fruits that tender the seed for this study. Without words, my father, Quan Chuoc Uyen†, and my mother, Thau Tu Lai†, taught me how to be humble, honest, and work hard with their lives. I want to thank my brothers, Fred, Steven, and Dee†, and my sisters, Diana, Lanna, Lannie, Lynda, and Jennie, for showing me Jesus Christ's long-suffering and kindness on the cross, which eventually led me to repentance. I am humbled and overwhelmed by God's goodness by you. I'm also grateful to my wife's family: mom, dad, Tommy, Monique, and especially Lisa who offered a helping hand during my homestretch to the dissertation defense. Tom Chau, Bumble, and Jennie Ho have taught me in Christ and encouraged me to make every effort to present myself approved to God, a workman who rightly handles the word of truth (2 Tim 2:15). They probably didn't know that they were the catalysts to my academic journey. From my undergraduate to the completion of my dissertation, the prayers from the First Chinese Baptist Church at Fountain Valley, Vietnamese Alliance Church at Midway, Vietnamese Alliance Church of Wheaton, and especially Long Nguyen have sustained me daily. During my PhD program and the process of writing this book, my family grew from 2 to 7, and God has provided for us abundantly through Jill Carr, Bob Norris, and Leon, Angela, and Christopher Yuan. I saw God's hand through you. Now, if I did not remember to thank God for my friends, Huy Ha, Dennis Tran, Khoa Ha, Phillip Duong, Ha Diep, Donald Le, Tri Luong, Tony Nguyen, Leroy Le, and all our friends in the old neighborhood, I would have forgotten who I am because the experiences and memories that we shared have shaped me into who I am now in Jesus Christ.

I also want to thank those who have made this book a reality. During my research, George Hunsinger and Kelly Kapic have kindly replied to my inquiries of Karl Barth and John Owen respectively to help me wrap my head around these two theologians. Ben Dally, Daniel Bair, Sylvie Chau, and Stephen Dowell have read what I wrote and provided helpful inputs along the way. Eric Tully, the program director for my dissertation, helped me think more clearly about the nature of the economy of illumination. The kind words of David Luy, my second reader, have encouraged me to pour more into this book as an offering to God and his Church. Matthew Levering, my external reader, sacrificed his time to meet with me on several occasions to hammer out what it means to participate in God. I may not agree with him in every area, but I treasure his word in my heart dearly because our life with God is not a cold concept for Professor Levering but a reality he warmly expressed with tears. Todd Hains and his team at Lexham Press were wonderful to work with, making the publication process a worshipful one to our God and Savior. I see their motto, "Love the Word, Love the Faith, and Love the Church," on full display in their willingness to help and guide. Last but not least, I want to thank God for his goodness and steadfast love in Kevin Vanhoozer, my Doktorvater. Like the apostle Paul who said, "Follow my example, as I follow the example of Christ" (1 Cor 11:1 NIV), the way Professor Vanhoozer lives and gives his time and energy also bids me to come and follow as he follows Christ, our Lord. He has read more drafts than I can remember to provide invaluable instructions, encouragement, and inspiration to improve this book and shape me as a Christian. May God bless you, Dr. Vanhoozer, as he has used you to bless me so richly.

Finally, my life together with my wife, Christine, and our children, Eden, Saige, Violet, Callum, and Elliot, have offered a glimpse into our life with God—the Father, Son, and Spirit, who are in subsistent relation. My children prayed for me each night before bed to finish my dissertation. They write me notes, light up my day with their smiles and hugs, and bless me profoundly as they run and ride their bikes to see me off when I go to work and study. God, you have used them to teach, love, and cheer me on to completion. I have also found favor with you, Lord, in my wife, Christine. She waited for me to come home each day with a hot meal, taught the children to honor and love me, and quietly and patiently gave herself to me and our call to you, O Lord. As you have used her to show me your care and faithfulness, may your goodness and love now overwhelm her with joy and peace unspeakable.

In all things, I thank you, God, Father, Son, and Holy Spirit, from whom all blessings flow. "Now to the King eternal, immortal, invisible, the only God, be honor and glory for ever and ever. Amen" (1 Tim 1:17 ESV).

ABBREVIATIONS

AB	Anchor Bible
ACW	Ancient Christian Writers
ANF	*Ante-Nicene Fathers*
AYBD	*Anchor Yale Bible Dictionary*
BDAG	*Greek-English Lexicon of the New Testament and Other Early Christian Literature* (Danker-Bauer-Arndt-Gingrich)
BECNT	Baker Exegetical Commentary on the New Testament
BCOT	Baker Commentary on the Old Testament
BNP	*Brill's New Pauly: Encyclopaedia of the Ancient World*
CCSL	Corpus Christianorum: Series Latina
COS	*The Context of Scripture*
DCH	*Dictionary of Classical Hebrew*
ECC	Eerdmans Critical Commentary
FC	Fathers of the Church
GCS	Die griechischen christlichen Schriftsteller der ersten [drei] Jahrhunderte
HALOT	*The Hebrew and Aramaic Lexicon of the Old Testament*
IBC	Interpretation: A Bible Commentary for Teaching and Preaching
ICC	International Critical Commentary
JRT	*Journal of Religious Thought*
JSFSC	*Journal of Spiritual Formation and Soul Care*
LCL	Loeb Classical Library
NBf	*New Blackfriars*
NDBT	*New Dictionary of Biblical Theology*
NICNT	New International Biblical Commentary on the New Testament
NICOT	New International Biblical Commentary on the Old Testament
NIDNTT	*New International Dictionary of New Testament Theology*
NIDOTTE	*New International Dictionary of Old Testament Theology and Exegesis*
NIGTC	New International Greek Testament Commentary

NIVAC	NIV Application Commentary
NPNF	*Nicene and Post-Nicene Fathers*
NSBT	New Studies in Biblical Theology
OCD	*Oxford Classical Dictionary*
OTL	Old Testament Library
PNTC	Plllar New Testament Commentary
SC	Sources chrétiennes
TCNT	Twentieth Century New Testament
TDNT	*Theological Dictionary of the New Testament*
TLNT	*Theological Lexicon of the New Testament*
TNTC	Tyndale New Testament Commentaries
TOTC	Tyndale Old Testament Commentaries
WBC	Word Biblical Commentary
WMANT	Wissenschaftliche Monographien zum Alten und Neuen Testament
WUNT	Wissenschaftliche Untersuchungen zum Neuen Testament
ZECNT	Zondervan Exegetical Commentary on the New Testament

INTRODUCTION

For with you is the fountain of life; in your light do we see light.

—Ps 36:9

For God, who said, 'Let light shine out of darkness,' has shone in our hearts to give the light of the knowledge of the glory of God in the face of Jesus Christ.

—2 Cor 4:6

As the sun rises and brings the world into light, God shines light into our hearts to draw us into light, so we may see him—light.[1] If God is light and outside of him is darkness, then how can we participate in God apart from being illumined by God? The relationship between participation and illumination is clear, but contemporary theology has divorced the two. Discussion on illumination now limits itself to the interpretation of Scripture. This makes Ike Miller's book, *Seeing by the Light*, unique. In his book, he argues, "*illumination is human participation in the Son's knowledge of the Father by the power of the Holy Spirit.*"[2] Participation, for Miller, is "the means of illumination"

1. "God is light," so those in him are in light and see light (1 John 1:5–6; Ps 36:9). God is light because light represents all that God is: holy (Isa 6:3; 10:17), glorious (Isa 60:1–3, 19–20; Rev 21:23), truth (Ps 43:3; John 3:21), perfect (Jas 1:17), life (Ps 36:9; Job 33:30; John 1:4), and salvation (Ps 27:1; cf. 18:28; 44:3). Light was also the epithet of gods in the ancient Near East (see "The Cylinders of Gudea," translated by Richard E. Averbeck [*COS* 2:155:417–33] and "Letter of the Ruler of Gezer (Gazru)," translated by William Moran [*COS* 3.92C-D:239–242]). If God's light is shone into the heart, then God's presence has manifested itself inside a person rather than outside in the world (e.g., burning bush, pillar of fire, filling the temple with smoke and his glory, and the incarnation of the Son). Kevin Vanhoozer also writes, "'Light' implies knowledge. The main function of light is to illuminate; when light is shed on something, it reveals and makes it known." Kevin J. Vanhoozer, *Remythologizing Theology: Divine Action, Passion, and Authorship* (Cambridge: Cambridge University Press, 2010), 249.

2. Ike Miller, *Seeing by the Light: Illumination in Augustine's and Barth's Reading of John* (Downers Grove, IL: IVP Academic, 2020), 3 (emphasis original).

because we come to know the Father in the Son's knowledge.[3] But how do we participate in the Son's knowledge without being illumined? Since "no one knows the Son except the Father, and no one knows the Father except the Son" (Matt 11:27; cf. Luke 10:22; John 10:15), Jesus said, "[n]o one can come to me unless the Father who sent me draws him," but "[e]veryone who has heard and learned from the Father comes to me" (John 6:44–45). Illumination is also a means and mode of participation because we come to faith and participate in union with Christ through being "taught by God," participating in the Father's knowledge of the Son through the Spirit (John 6:45a).

Discussion on participation has mounted up in monographs and articles for the last four decades,[4] but we can hardly find any material relating it to illumination.[5] Consequently, discussion on what happens and what a person receives in union with Christ has flourished but talk of what it means to participate in the *person* of Christ himself has stammered a bit. According to John Calvin, from whom Protestants get our concept of union with Christ, Jesus

3. Miller, *Seeing*, 187.

4. According to Bruce McCormack, "There is no theme enjoying greater popularity currently than the ancient soteriological theme of 'deification' ... accompanied by a strong emphasis on the theme of 'union with Christ'" because of "a longing for theologies of human transformation capable of competing with options provided by a surrounding culture that is increasingly religious and therapeutic." Bruce L. McCormack, *Orthodox and Modern: Studies in the Theology of Karl Barth* (Grand Rapids: Baker Academic, 2008), 236. Here is a small sample of the growing literature on the theme of participation: E. P. Sanders, *Paul and Palestinian Judaism: A Comparison of Patterns of Religion* (Philadelphia: Fortress, 1977); A. N. William, *The Ground of Union: Deification in Aquinas and Palamas* (New York: Oxford University Press, 1999); Michael Horton, *Covenant and Salvation: Union with Christ* (Louisville: Westminster John Knox, 2007); J. Todd Billings, *Calvin, Participation, and the Gift: The Activity of Believers in Union with Christ* (Oxford: Oxford University Press, 2007); Hans Burger, *Being in Christ: A Biblical and Systematic Investigation in a Reformed Perspective* (Eugene, OR: Wipf & Stock, 2009); Julie Canlis, *Calvin's Ladder: A Spiritual Theology of Ascent and Ascension* (Grand Rapids: Eerdmans, 2010); Robert Letham, *Union with Christ: In Scripture, History, and Theology* (Phillipsburg, N.J.: P & R, 2011); Constantine R. Campbell, *Paul and Union with Christ: An Exegetical and Theological Study* (Grand Rapids: Zondervan, 2012); Michael J. Tate, Kevin J. Vanhoozer, and Constantine R. Campbell, eds., *'In Christ' in Paul: Exploration in Paul's Theology of Union and Participation* (Tübingen: Mohr Siebeck, 2014); Athanasios Despotis, ed., *Participation, Justification, and Conversion: Eastern Orthodox Interpretation of Paul and the Debate between Old and New Perspective on Paul* (Tübingen: Mohr Siebeck, 2017); Andrew Davison, *Participation in God: A Study in Christian Doctrine and Metaphysics* (Cambridge: Cambridge University Press, 2019); Grant Macaskill, *Living in Union with Christ: Paul's Gospel and Christian Moral Identity* (Grand Rapids: Baker Academic, 2019); and Khaled Anatolios, *Deification through the Cross: An Eastern Christian Theology of Salvation* (Grand Rapids: Eerdmans, 2020).

5. Through his reading of Athanasius, Grant Macaskill touches on this relationship between participation and illumination in passing. Grant Macaskill, *Union with Christ in the New Testament* (Oxford: Oxford University Press, 2013), 68–69, 296.

has made us "participants not only in all his benefits but also in himself."[6] To have union with another *person* is to share his heart and mind. Without a grasp of participation in relation to illumination, how can we understand what it means to share the heart and mind of Christ who is truly man and truly God, transcending our creaturely reality? In this study, I hope to join what contemporary theology has put asunder. My twofold aim is to enrich the discussion on participation with illumination and explain the doctrine of illumination in relation to union with Christ for communion with God.

PROJECT'S AIM

By bringing illumination in the discussion with participation, I hope to enrich the doctrine of participation in three ways: (1) demonstrate how God turns the gospel call into an effectual call to bring a person in Adam into union with Christ; (2) denote the link between union with Christ in the eternal decree of God (Eph 1:4–6) and union with Christ in the history of believers (Eph 1:7–10); and (3) detail the way union with Christ offers a person ongoing access to communion with God from glory to glory. Calvin said, "as long as Christ remains outside of us, and we are separated from him, all that he has suffered and done for the salvation of the human race remains useless and of no value for us" (*Inst.* 3.1.1). So how does God draw us into union with Christ to apply what Christ has accomplished for us? I will use the term the *economy of illumination* in this study to speak of the landscape of how the redemption accomplished in Jesus Christ is *applied* to the church in union with Christ for communion with God. The economy of illumination, in other words, is the catch-all term for the process by which God shines the light of his eternal intention, actualized in the person and work of Christ in time, into the heart and mind of the church by making the gospel call effective through the Spirit to form and perfect her into the image of Christ through beholding him in the mirror dimly until seeing him face to face.

In relating the economy of illumination to participation in God, I want to highlight four features that are often missed in the contemporary discussion of illumination. First, the economy of illumination is not the individual

6. John Calvin, *Institutes of Christian Religion*, trans. Ford Lewis Battles, ed. John T. McNeill (Philadelphia: Westminster John Knox, 1960), 570. Hereafter cited as *Inst.* 3.2.24

operation of the Spirit, but the trinitarian operations of the Father, Son, and Spirit that makes a person's heart alight with the knowledge of God's glory in the face of Jesus as reflected in the mirror of Scripture.[7] Second, the economy of illumination not only affects the mind as a "cognitive process," but also the heart as a "cardiac process," turning a heart of stone to a heart of flesh to respond and know God as covenant Lord.[8] Third, we are not passive in God's economy of illumination but are called to participatory action in the process of divine lighting. Like the middle voice in Greek, our participatory actions allow us to participate in the result of God's concerted action of lighting.[9] To listen and perform God's word in the economy of illumination, for instance, is to hear and be formed by God who speaks and works in us both to act and to will (Phil 2:13). Fourth, the body is as vital as the mind in being illumined. Knowing how to live with God in covenant fellowship is like knowing a craft because we know by feeling, doing, and forming habits with our bodies through following the example of a master. To follow Christ, our Master, we also need

---

7. If we think of the economy of God as God actualizing his eternal plan (οἰκονομίαν) in the history of redemption (Eph 1:10–13), then we can view the economy of illumination as the ordered process by which the triune God brings to light (φωτίζει) his eternal plan (οἰκονομία) in Christ, making his revelatory light in the Son alight in our heart and mind through the indwelling Spirit (Eph 3:9). I use the economy of illumination to make a distinction from the economy of revelation. These two economies form the two sides of the economy of light because the economy of revelation concerns the objective light of the knowledge of God and the economy of illumination refers to the subjective light of the knowledge of God within the believer. According to Vanhoozer, "The economy of light refers to the work of the Father, Son and Spirit alike in communicating the knowledge of glory of the God of the gospel. ... light proceeds from the Father, proceeds through the Son and is perfected by the Spirit. God is the agent, act and effect of his self-communication: light, lighting and enlightenment." Kevin J. Vanhoozer and Daniel J. Treier, *Theology and the Mirror of Scripture: A Mere Evangelical Account* (Downers Grove, IL: IVP Academic, 2015), 89.

8. Because the economy of illumination involves a transformative knowledge of God, I refer to God's mode of imparting knowledge as a cognitive process and God's mode of transforming us as a cardiac process. Since the heart is the core of our being and the source of our action (Matt 15:18–20; Mark 7:21), change begins with our heart and, from there, our whole being because our thought and action come from our heart. A heart affected by the love of God turns the mind to God to know him more intimately and fully with the body (Eph 4:17–18), which is offered up to God as an "reasonable worship" (τὴν λογικὴν λατρείαν, Rom 12:1 KJV).

9. Eugene Peterson writes: "When I speak in the middle voice, I actively participate in the results of an action that another initiates: 'I take counsel'" because in the middle voice, "two wills operate, neither to the exclusion of the other, neither canceling out the other, each respecting the other." Eugene H. Peterson, *The Contemplative Pastor: Returning to the Art of Spiritual Direction* (Grand Rapids: Eerdmans, 1993), 103.

our bodies to conform our lives and actions to his, so we may know "the truth that is in Christ" personally and tacitly (Eph 4:21; Col 3:10).[10]

THESIS

A thesis is now in order. The economy of illumination is the trinitarian operation of God, the Father, Son, and Spirit, to make their knowledge ours, transforming and perfecting us with the knowledge of God's glory in union with Christ for communion with God. As we will discover in John Owen, communion with God can only transpire through union with Christ. To know and commune with God, we need a new heart and mind *in* Christ because, *in* Adam, our hearts are hard, and our minds are veiled from the light of God. We are in the dark and can no longer respond to God, so we are alienated from God. So to restore our communion with God, the economy of illumination involves both a cardiac and cognitive process, which are integral to fellowship with God, and an initial and ongoing lighting that not only brings us into covenant union with Christ (2 Cor 4:6) but also draws us into contemplative union with Christ for communion with God from glory to glory (2 Cor 3:18).

The initial lighting of the economy of illumination brings us in covenant union with Christ, the head of new humanity, by awakening our faith to the light of God's glory in the face of his Son (2 Cor 4:6) that enables us, on the one hand, to receive Christ into our hearts and minds as the object of faith and love (Eph 3:17; Col 3:16) and, on the other hand, to share the heart and mind of Christ through the presence of the Spirit to know and respond to God in new covenant fellowship (1 Cor 2:16). The ongoing lighting of the economy of illumination stretches us into ever-increasing closeness with God in contemplative union with Christ. In this union, we are united to Christ as we are joined to the object of our sight by *seeing*. As object, light, and sight are three distinct, but inseparable components of seeing, the ongoing process of light from the Father, Son, and Spirit are three distinct, but inseparable flashes of light in contemplative union because we behold God in Christ, the *image*

10. R. McL. Wilson, *A Critical and Exegetical Commentary on Colossians and Philemon*, ICC (London: T & T Clark, 2005), 252, offers an apt comment on the inner renewal via knowledge, which requires obedience: "This new man is being renewed εἰς ἐπίγνωσιν, literally 'into knowledge'. ... Knowledge of God's will is of no avail without obedience. In the same way, knowledge of the mystery which is Christ entails a recognition of his supreme place in the ordering of things, and again obedience." See also Peter T. O'Brien, *Colossians-Philemon*, WBC 44 (Nashville: Thomas Nelson, 1982), 191, who refers to it as an inward renewal from life in Adam to life in Christ.

of light, through the Spirit, the *presence* of light, from the perspective of the Father, the *sight* of light. In contemplative union, we participate in the Son's knowledge of the Father and the Father's knowledge of the Son through the Spirit from glory to glory (Matt 11:27; Luke 10:22; John 10:15).

KEY TERMS

The following terms will parse my thesis on the economy of illumination and guide readers to the following study. "Light" is the essence of God and the activity of God to impart knowledge of God because God acts according to who he is. "Darkness" is what is not God, the ignorance of God, and the domain hostile to God (Col 1:13). "Union with Christ" refers to the reality of the church's whole existence in the person of the Son from the decree of God in eternity to her glorification with Christ for eternity (Rom 8:28–30; cf. Eph 1:3–14). "Participation" in union with Christ concerns having Christ dwell in our hearts by faith (Eph 3:17), sharing his heart and mind (1 Cor 2:16), and receiving spiritual blessings in him (namely, forgiveness, adoption, redemption, regeneration, justification, sanctification, and glorification) for communion with God. "Communion" or "new covenant fellowship with God" is the sharing of light (knowledge) and love (will) between the Father and the Son in the Spirit that the church enjoys in union with Christ because she communicates with the Father in the Son who is with him in heaven, and the Father communicates with her in the Son who dwells in her heart and mind through the Holy Spirit. The *heart* is the "center and source of the whole inner life," encompassing our "thinking, feeling, and volition."[11] In relation to God, the heart is the "centre of spiritual life"; that is to say, the "heart is that in man which is addressed by God. It is the seat of doubt and hardness as well as faith and obedience."[12] The mind (νοῦς) is the eye (ὀφθαλμός) of the heart (Eph 1:18) because our minds allow our hearts to see and understand God.[13]

---

11. καρδία, BDAG, 508.

12. Theo Sorg, "Heart," *NIDNTT* 2:182. The heart is the place of faith, where God's truth is embraced (Rom 10:9–10), and it enables the person to discern what is right and wrong (1 Kgs 3:9, 12). See also Richard E. Averbeck, "Spirit, Community, and Mission: A Biblical Theology for Spiritual Formation," *JSFSC* 1.1 (2008): 33.

13. The eye (ὀφθαλμός) is at times a metaphor of our "mental and spiritual understanding" BDAG, 744.

THE APPROACH TO THE STUDY

With these definitions in place, I turn to the approach for my dogmatic account of the economy of illumination. By dogmatic account, I have in mind an account of the economy of illumination rooted in and shaped by the life and work of the triune God revealed in Scripture to and through the church, the community of the redeemed who live in the "domain of the Word."[14] To reflect critically on what it means to confess that God has shone his light into the darkness of our hearts and minds to bring us into light, I construct my dogmatic account in three parts, or moments—a biblical, retrieval, and constructive moment.

Part I presents a biblical sketch of the economy of illumination. Part II thickens the sketch by retrieving the trinitarian operation of illumination from the Orthodox, Roman Catholic, and Reformed traditions. These three theological traditions function as paradigms, offering three configurations of the different parts of illumination from their vantage points. The three theological configurations of illumination not only save me from reinventing the wheel, but also locate areas of tension (from where they diverge) that call for an extended dogmatic analysis in Part III.[15]

Part III fleshes out the biblical outline of the economy of illumination in Part I dogmatically with the theological materials, principles, and interpretations drawn from the three traditions in Part II. I retrieve from the Orthodox and Roman Catholic traditions to refine my Reformed understanding of the economy of illumination.[16] In reading Scripture with leading theologians from these traditions, I do not want to add to what Scripture

14. "That domain is constituted by the communicative presence of the risen and ascended Son of God who governs all things. His governance includes his rule over creaturely intelligence: he is Lord and therefore teacher." John Webster, *Domain of the Word: Scripture and Theological Reason* (London: T & T Clark, 2012), 3.

15. Similarly, in scientific advancement, Thomas S. Kuhn, *The Essential Tension* (Chicago: University of Chicago Press, 1977), 226–27, argues that convergent thinking is just as essential as divergent thinking. He saw that scientific revolution is not something that takes place outside of the tradition but begins in the tradition and *breaks* away from it: this is what he means by "essential tension." Kuhn writes, "only investigations firmly rooted in the contemporary scientific tradition are likely to break that tradition and give rise to a new one. That is why I speak of an 'essential tension' implicit in scientific research" (Kuhn, *Essential Tension*, 227).

16. It is in a sense an exercise in "Reformed catholicity," which can be described as "an exercise in theological remembrance and retrieval, seeking to recover the habits of theological thought and argumentation belonging to an older confessional dogmatics, and to the broad churchly tradition of biblical interpretation that lies both behind and beside it, for the sake of contemporary theological renewal" (Michael Allen and Scott R. Swain, *Reformed*

has revealed but I seek to understand more fully what Scripture teaches through the theological categories and concepts that I find in these theologians concerning what it means to proclaim that God shines light into our hearts to bring us into light.[17]

THE CONTOUR OF THE STUDY

Regarding the contour of the study, Part I consists of two chapters. Chapter 1 narrates how human beings made for God who is light ended up outside of God in darkness. Chapter 2 presents a biblical sketch of the economy of illumination as both the initial lighting of God to return us to light in covenant union with Christ (2 Cor 4:6) and the ongoing process of lighting, by which God draws us in contemplative union with Christ for covenant fellowship with God from glory to glory (2 Cor 3:18).

I divide Part II into four chapters. The idea of this retrieval moment is to read key theologians before, during, and after Nicaea descriptively, to tender three theological configurations of the economy of illumination from the Orthodox, Roman Catholic, and Reformed traditions. These three theological configurations offer three paradigms of the economy of illumination as a means, manner, and mark of participation in God, which I will draw from in Part III, to expand my biblical sketch of the economy of illumination in the first moment. Chapter 3 begins with the reading of ante-Nicene theologians (Irenaeus of Lyons, Clement of Alexandria, Tertullian, and Origen) to show, on the one hand, how the relationship between illumination and participation was vital in the early church's understanding of life with God and to establish, on the other hand, the theological foundation to follow the way theologians in the next three chapters employ and develop the ante-Nicene fathers' account of the economy of illumination as participation in God.

Catholicity: The Promise of Retrieval for Theology and Biblical Interpretation [Grand Rapids: Baker Academic, 2015], 96).

17. In his introduction to Athanasius's *On the Incarnation*, for example, C. S. Lewis advises readers to read books from the past because they allow us to see our blind spots: "Every age has its own outlook. It is specially good at seeing certain truths and specially liable to make certain mistakes. We all, therefore, need the books [from the past] that will correct the characteristic mistakes of our own period" (Athanasius, *On the Incarnation*, trans. and ed. C.S.M.V. [Crestwood, NY: St. Vladimir's Seminary Press, 1996], 4).

Chapter 4 turns to the Orthodox tradition, which views the economy of illumination as the process of participation and transformation (or deification) in the uncreated energy, ἐνέργεια, or hypostatic light (φῶς ἐνυποστάτως) of God from the writings of Athanasius, the Cappadocian fathers, Cyril of Alexandria, Gregory Palamas, and Dumitru Staniloae. From the works of Augustine, Thomas Aquinas, Bonaventure, and Hans Urs von Balthasar, chapter 5 offers a Roman Catholic configuration of illumination as participation in God himself through the person of Christ, our inner light and Teacher, and the person of the Spirit, the love of God in our hearts.[18] Chapter 6 closes

18. Since the East-West Schism between the Roman Catholic Church and Orthodox Church did not occur until 1054, some justification is due at this point for my selection and placement of certain theologians. I am not insisting here that during the patristic era the East and the West diverged on their approach and configuration of the dogma of the Trinity, the East beginning with the distinct persons and the West with the unity of the divine nature of God, which became the prominent view in patristic studies after the publication of Théodore de Régnon's first volume, Études de théologie positive sur la Sainté Trinité, in 1892. What I am insisting instead is that the theological configurations (traditions) as we have now from the Orthodox and Roman Catholic traditions are profoundly shaped by these pro-Nicene theologians and their successors. If we speak of theology as a conversation, then my claim is the theological conversation of Orthodox tradition generally begins with Athanasius and the Cappadocian fathers and the one from the Roman Catholic tradition commences with Augustine. For a historical account of how Régnon's work influenced and evolved in the landscape of French and English scholarship, see Michel René Barnes, "De Régnon Reconsidered," *Augustinian Studies* 26–2 [1995]: 51–79. Barnes clarifies that although Régnon argues "that patristic trinitarian theology, as represented by the Cappadocians, proceeds from the diversity of persons while scholastic trinitarian theology, as represented by Augustine, proceeds from the unity of nature" [Barnes, "De Régnon," 51], he "never limits the emphasis on person over nature to Greek theology" and "never reads pre-Augustinian Latins out of this patristic emphasis on the individual persons. Nevertheless, the popular understanding of the categories that de Régnon called patristic and scholastic has identified them with Greek and Latin theologies respectively" [Barnes, "De Régnon," 54]). For examples of this view, see Henry Chadwick, *East and West: The Making of a Rift in the Church: From Apostolic Times until the Council of Florence* (Oxford: Oxford University Press, 2003), 28 and Timothy Ware, *The Orthodox Church: An Introduction to Eastern Christianity*, 3rd ed. (London: Penguin, 2015), 46. Those who hold this view have come to understand the Eastern concept of person "in the categories of 'relation[ship]' or 'consciousness'" and the Western concept in the category of individualism (Michel René Barnes, "Divine Unity and the Divided Self: Gregory of Nyssa's Trinitarian Theology in its Psychological Context," in *Re-Thinking Gregory of Nyssa*, ed. Sarah Coakley [Malden, MA: Blackwell, 2003], 45). John Zizioulas, for instance, believes that this overemphasis on individualism from Boethius and Augustine "'accounts for the impossibility of real communion, because it implies distance and hence division instead of difference,'" but the concept of person in the East, represented by the Cappadocian fathers, is concerned with relationship and communion (Lucian Turcescu, "'Person' versus 'Individual', and Other Modern Misreadings of Gregory of Nyssa," in *Re-Thinking Gregory of Nyssa*, ed. Sarah Coakley [Malden, MA: Blackwell, 2003], 99). On the contrary, Lucian Turcescu argues that Zizioulas's account of personhood is more in line with what Martin Buber put forth in *I and Thou*, which claimed that a person appears in relationship, than with what Gregory had understood a person to be because, in *Ad Graecos* 23.8, Gregory himself wrote, "'the individual ... is the person (ἄτομον, ὅπερ ἐστὶ πρόσωπον)" (Turcescu, "'Person' versus 'Individual'," 104; for Turcescu's lengthier discussion

the retrieval moment with the Reformed tradition through the teachings of John Calvin, John Owen, Jonathan Edwards, and Karl Barth, which present a communicative and redemptive model of participation in God. Because of the Reformed stance on sola Scriptura, the gospel and the Spirit have a prominent place in the economy of illumination for this tradition.

Funded by basic principles, theological interpretations, and vantage points from the three Christian traditions in the retrieval moment, Part III constructs a Reformed dogmatic account of the economy of illumination in three chapters. Unlike the Roman Catholic and Orthodox traditions,

---

on Gregory of Nyssa's concept of personhood, see idem, *Gregory of Nyssa and the Concept of Divine Persons* [Oxford: Oxford University Press, 2005]). Other revisionary accounts like Turcescu's continue to challenge this longstanding view in patristic studies, arguing that the division between the East and the West is largely a caricature that overlooks the pro-Nicene stance that the East and the West affirm. Barnes, a leading revisionist, makes this point: "the standard division of trinitarian theologies ... ignores the close affiliation that flourished between Alexandrian ('Greek) and Roman ('Latin') the theologies a generation earlier. The more one tends to speak of a real division between Greek and Latin trinitarian theologies in the late-fourth and early-fifth centuries, the more one must acknowledge and explain a fundamental shift away from the mid-fourth-century synthetic theology of Alexandria and Rome. The more one postulates a turn-of-the-century opposition between Greek and Latin theologies, the more one implicitly claims the loss of the prior consensus, and a dominant consensus at that, found in the theologies of Rome and Alexandria, a consensus that was above all 'Nicene'" (Michel René Barnes, "Augustine in Contemporary Trinitarian Theology," *Theological Studies* 56 [1995]: 240). According to Chadwick, however, the Nicene Creed had "little currency in the Latin west" because Hilary of Poitier's statement in *Synod* 91 shows that he "could be bishop for some years before hearing about it [Nicene creed]" (Chadwick, *East and West*, 14). Lewis Ayres, another revisionist voice, suggests that a more plausible reading of Hilary's statement in *Synod* 91 is that, before his exile to Milan, Hilary "had not heard of the creed recited in a public context as an authoritative statement of faith" (Lewis Ayres, *Nicaea and Its Legacy: An Approach to Fourth-Century Trinitarian Theology* [Oxford: Oxford University Press, 2004], 137). Thus, similarly to Barnes, Ayres concludes that the traditional division between the East, proceeding from the three-ness of God, and the West, proceeding from the one-ness of God, is "unsustainable" because "they 'begin' ... at the same point" (Ayres, *Nicaea*, 300–301). Both pro-Nicene theologians from the East and the West begin with the simplicity and unity of the triune God, the mystery of the "irreducible unity of the three irreducible divine persons" (Ayres, *Nicaea*, 278). In the East, for example, Basil the Great and Gregory of Nyssa always "insist that the grammar of simple and indivisible divinity is the context for all talk of differentiation: it is this combination that marks the real if subtle advance of pro-Nicene theology" (Lewis Ayres, "On Not Three People: The Fundamental Themes of Gregory of Nyssa's Trinitarian Theology as Seen in *To Ablabius: On Not Three Gods*," in *Re-Thinking Gregory of Nyssa*, ed. Sarah Coakley [Malden, MA: Blackwell, 2003], 20). Furthermore, Barnes points out that, while Gregory of Nyssa's psychology, which focused on the divine will, has been employed to draw out the "personal relationship" within the triune God, it was intended by Gregory to reveal the perfect unity within the Godhead. "'For the *community of nature* [φύσεως κοινωνία] gives us warrant that the will of the Father, of the Son, and of the Holy Spirit is one, and thus, if the Holy Spirit wills that which seems good to the Son, the community of will [ἡ κοινωνία τοῦ θελήματος] clearly points to *unity of essence* [τῆς οὐσίας ἑνότητα]'" (Barnes, "Divine Unity," 59 [emphasis his]).

Reformed theology holds tightly to sola Scriptura in its account of illumination because illumination neither adds to the revelation in Scripture nor opens us to truth in Christ outside of Scripture. Chapter 7 begins my account with the nature, source, and substance of our communion with God in union with Christ, which John Murray teaches is a truth in God's mind for the elect before time begins.[19] Chapter 8 sheds light on how the economy of illumination brings us into union with Christ by fleshing out the outline of the initial lighting of the economy of illumination in the biblical moment dogmatically with theological materials and interpretation from the retrieval moment. It presents the economy of illumination as both a cardiac and cognitive process, involving knowledge and transformation to bring a person into covenant union with Christ, who is life and light (John 1:4), to enjoy communion with God, the knowledge and love between the Father and the Son in the Spirit from eternity, opened now to us through the gospel. Chapter 9 concludes the constructive moment by putting dogmatic flesh on the biblical outline of the ongoing lighting in the economy of illumination, which draws us into contemplative union with Christ. The ongoing lighting in the economy of illumination, I argue, involves both God's concerted action and our participatory actions of reading, praying, obeying, partaking, and singing Scripture. Our participatory actions in God's concerted action of lighting allow the truth of the gospel to burn more deeply in our hearts, minds, and lives, so we may reflect God's marvelous light more brightly and warmly to the world. The economy of illumination, in other words, entails a knowledge of God that is both given by God and acquired by us in Christ through the habits and obedience of faith from the power of the Holy Spirit.

Now as we move together through this study, my prayer is that we may recall the way the triune God has transferred us from darkness to light with his light, so we may enter all the more deeply into his triune life of light and love, which never ends. God is light (1 John 1:5), and in his light, we see light (Ps 36:9). Outside of God, there is only darkness (Col 1:13). So whenever and wherever we see God, we are in God—illumined.

19. John Murray, *Redemption, Accomplished, and Applied* (Grand Rapids: Eerdmans, 1955), 172, for example, writes, "[t]he foundation of salvation itself in the eternal election of the Father is 'in Christ.'"

Part 1

—

ECONOMY OF ILLUMINATION: A BIBLICAL ACCOUNT

1

THE REASON AND PURPOSE OF ILLUMINATION

How did human beings whom God has made for himself in light end up outside him in darkness? And how does this new mode of being in darkness affect human knowledge and fellowship with God? Without a grasp of this, we would not understand how illumination from God restores the knowledge of God to those in darkness. To grasp this, the present chapter begins with the way darkness entered the world that God has made "very good" (Gen 1:31), explains the noetic effects of sin and darkness, and concludes with God speaking into darkness, but those in darkness cannot comprehend because darkness and light are incommensurable. Before the fall, Adam and Eve did not need illumination as we do now because knowledge of God was instinctual for the couple. After the fall, however, human beings in Adam no longer saw God, reality, or themselves in God, but outside of God, from their own eyes, the domain of darkness.[1]

THE KNOWLEDGE OF GOD AND THE TREE OF KNOWLEDGE

The contrast between light and darkness is the contrast between wisdom from above and wisdom from below. Wisdom from God is covenantal knowledge, life with God. "And this is eternal life, that they may know you, the only

1. To be in light is to know God in covenant (1 John 1:5–7) because to live in light is to abide in the covenantal agreement to act, love, and live as children of light (Eph 5:8; 1 Thess 5:5). John said that to be in the light is to live as God lives, which is in truth and love: "If we say that we have fellowship with Him and *yet* walk in the darkness, we lie and do not practice the truth" (1 John 1:6), and "[t]he one who says he is in the Light and *yet* hates his brother is in the darkness until now. The one who loves his brother abides in the Light" (1 John 2:9–10). See John R. W. Stott, *The Letter of John: An Introduction and Commentary*, TNTC 19 (Downers Grove, IL: InterVarsity Press, 1988), 74–77. So, to be in darkness is to be outside of God, without knowledge and fellowship. Speaking of those outside the covenant, Paul wrote, "They are darkened in their understanding, alienated from the life of God because of their ignorance and hardness of heart" (Eph 4:18 NRSV).

true God, and Jesus Christ whom you have sent" (John 17:3 NRSV).[2] Wisdom from God begins with faith and the fear of the Lord—perceiving reality and discerning good from evil not according to what is right in our own eyes, but what is right in God's sight (Prov 3:5–7).[3] If wisdom from above is life, then wisdom from below, of "those who are wise in their own eyes and clever in their own sight" (Isa 5:21 NIV), is death.

What makes the wisdom of God and the wisdom of the world incommensurable and distinct in nature (light and darkness) and terminus (life and death) are their sources, the former purifying, renewing, and enlightening the heart and mind, the latter polluting, corrupting, and darkening the heart and mind. The source of wisdom leading to the life is God, the fountain of life, in whose light, we see light (Ps 36:9; Prov 2:6).[4] The way of this wisdom is the fear of the Lord, which turns us from sin (Prov 8:13; 16:6). The means by which God imparts wisdom are his presence, speech, and creation (Gen 2:15–17).

Before the fall, creation pointed Adam and Eve to God instead of distracting them from him (Rom 1:20–23). Adam and Eve neither needed a mediator, as Israel would in Moses (Exod 20:18–19), nor their eyes to be opened to understand God's law (Gen 2:16–17), as the psalmist would pray after the fall: "Open my eyes, that I may behold wondrous things out of your law" (Ps 119:18). God spoke to the first humans directly (Gen 1:28; 2:16–17). What Adam saw as good and not good was in accordance with what God saw. Adam knew no other reality than the one God has made and revealed. In fact, Adam could neither conceive nor imagine any other reality, since it neither existed nor was there any category for it in his mind and experience.[5] What Adam saw, sensed, and

---

2. According to George Beasley-Murray, "Such knowledge advances beyond the intellect to include relationship and communion; its revelation by the Son entails entry into the *koinonia* (fellowship) of the Father and the Son, which is the heart of life in the saving sovereignty, (cf Rev 21:3; 22:3–5)." George R. Beasley-Murray, *John*, WBC 36 (Waco: Word Books, 1987), 297. "In examining the concept of knowledge of God, which is eternal life," C. H. Dodd writes, "we found that at a certain point this concept passed into a further idea of the relation between God and men, which may be define as one of reciprocal or mutual immanence." C. H. Dodd, *The Interpretation of the Fourth Gospel* (Cambridge: Cambridge University Press, 1953), 187.

3. In Prov 1:7 and 9:10, "knowledge" (דַּעַת) and "wisdom" (חָכְמָה) are used interchangeably. See Roland E. Murphy, *Proverbs*, WBC 22 (Grand Rapids: Zondervan, 1998), 5. See Derek Kidner, *Proverbs: An Introduction and Commentary*, TOTC 17 (Downers Grove, IL: InterVarsity Press, 1964), 56.

4. See E. J. Schnabel, "Wisdom," in *NDBT* (Downers Grove, IL: InterVarsity Press, 2000), 843–48.

5. Ingrid Faro writes that Adam and Eve "could neither imagine nor have the visceral or experiential knowledge of pain, trouble, hardship, suffering, conflict, illness, grief, violence, or sorrow. These things were *bad*. These define *evil*" (emphasis hers). Ingrid Faro, "A Lexical,

experienced was in harmony with what God saw—everything as very good (Gen 1:31). Adam saw everything in God's light because God was Adam's source of knowledge, the one who formed and shaped Adam's perception of reality. If Adam continued to listen and live by God's word, then he would continue to enjoy life with God and see God's goodness (Mark 10:18; Jas 1:17), truth (Isa 65:16; John 3:33), and beauty everywhere he turned (Ps 27:4; 96:6).

Knowledge of God refers to covenantal knowledge that requires Adam, God's covenant partner, to trust and obey.[6] Obeying God shaped and formed the way Adam saw and existed in the world. Obedience leads to a deeper covenant fellowship with God, enjoying God and all that he offers in covenant fellowship. This knowledge came unhindered from God to Adam through God's word and creation before the fall. All this, however, changed after the fall: an additional mediating light from God was required because of sin (Rom 1:21; Eph 4:18). Moreover, the prince of darkness would blind the minds of those in Adam from "the light of the glory of the gospel of Christ" (2 Cor 4:4; cf. Acts 26:18; 1 John 5:19; Eph 2:2).

The tree of knowledge of good and evil is the source of knowledge that led the world into darkness (Gen 2:9). The tree is not a true source, but a quasi-one, since it was created and placed there in the garden by God.[7] The purpose for the placement of the tree is debated. Since everything was created good, John Walton believes the tree had a future purpose: it was placed there for Adam and Eve to partake once the time was ripe.[8] However, this interpretation finds support neither from the immediate context nor the linguistic evidence of Gen 2:17, which highlights instead the certainty of death, once Adam and Eve disobey. For example, we can observe this demonstrated

---

Exegetical, Conceptual, and Theological Study of Evil in Genesis" (PhD diss., Trinity Evangelical Divinity School, 2013), 145.

6. Adam was the head of the covenant of creation (Hos 6:7). See Thomas R. Schreiner, *Covenant and God's Purpose for the World* (Wheaton: Crossway, 2017), 22; Peter J. Gentry and Stephen J. Wellum, *Kingdom through Covenant: A Biblical-Theological Understanding of the Covenants* (Wheaton, IL: Crossway, 2012), 117–221; 611–28. In general, a covenant between God and his people, according to Paul Williamson, "may be defined as the solemn ratification of an existing elective relationship involving promises or obligations that are sealed with an oath." Paul R. Williamson, *Sealed with an Oath: Covenant in God's Unfolding Purpose*, NSBT 23 (Downers Grove, IL: InterVarsity, 2007), 43. The main obligations for God's covenant partners are faithfulness and obedience to God, their covenant Lord.

7. Besides, no knowledge could completely be apart from God because all things find their meaning and purpose in God, the Creator.

8. John Walton, *Genesis*, NIVAC (Grand Rapids: Zondervan, 2001), 205–6.

linguistically with the infinitive absolute construct מוֹת תָּמוּת ("will surely die")[9] and the temporal marker בְּיוֹם ("in the day").[10] In light of the covenant context of God's command (Gen 2:16–17), the placement of the two trees sets before Adam and Eve blessing and cursing, life and death (cf. Deut 28; 30:15; Prov 6:23; Hos 6:7).[11] The two trees, in other words, offered an opportunity for Adam and Eve to say "Yes" or "No" to God with their whole being. Adam's "No" would alter the nature of human knowledge: human beings would experience and relate to knowledge in a new but distorted way because sin would corrupt their newly acquired ability from the tree of knowledge of good and evil.[12]

In the temptation, the "serpent was leading them to see: to look at the physical world around them with new eyes."[13] The serpent, in other words, was tempting the couple to see reality apart from what God saw. Ingrid Faro detects, for example, a parallel between what God saw in creation, וַיַּרְא אֱלֹהִים כִּי־טוֹב ("And God saw that it was good" [Gen 1:4, 10, 12, 18, 21, 25, 31]), and what Eve saw in the forbidden fruit as she fell into temptation, וַתֵּרֶא הָאִשָּׁה כִּי טוֹב הָעֵץ לְמַאֲכָל ("the woman saw that the tree was good for food" [Gen 3:6]).[14] This

9. According to E. Kautzsch, ed., and A. E. Cowley, the infinitive construct emphasizes "either the certainty (especially in the case of threats) or the forcibleness and completeness of an occurrence." E. Kautzch, ed., and A. E. Cowley trans., *Gesenius' Hebrew Grammar*, 2nd ed. (Oxford: Oxford, 1910), 342.

10. Similar to Gen 3:5 "כִּי בְּיוֹם אֲכָלְכֶם מִמֶּנּוּ וְנִפְקְחוּ עֵינֵיכֶם" ("when you eat from it your eyes will be opened" [Gen 3:5 NIV]), the temporal construct in Gen 2:17 "כִּי בְּיוֹם אֲכָלְךָ מִמֶּנּוּ מוֹת תָּמוּת" ("when you eat from it you will certainly die" [Gen 2:17 NIV]) marks "an actual time" of the main verb (for discussion on the temporal function of בְּ, see Bruce K. Waltke and Michael P. O'Connor, An Introduction to Biblical Hebrew Syntax, [Winona Lake, Ind.: Eisenbrauns, 1990], 196).

11. In a similar way, Philo interpreted the two trees allegorically as two roads, one leading to virtue and life and the other leading to vice and death: "For they say that in the Paradise there were plants in no respect similar to those which exist among us; but they speak of trees of life, trees of immortality, trees of knowledge, of comprehension, of understanding; trees of the knowledge of good and evil. Now these cannot have been trees of the land, but must indisputably have been plants of a rational soil, which was a road to travel along, leading to virtue, and having for its end life and immortality; and another road leading to vice, having for its end the loss of life and immortality, that is to say, death" (*Planter* 1:36–37).

12. "In the biblical text," Faro writes, "reference to the Tree of Knowledge does not specify the content or type of knowledge, but 'the nature of the knowledge,' the opportunity to become like God by being the One who knows, the possessor and arbitrator of knowledge." Faro, "Evil," 148.

13. Faro, "Evil," 152. The subtle shift from *hearing* to *sight* in the fall narrative highlights the shift in the way Adam and Eve experienced and knew the world. Before the fall, what Adam and Eve knew derived from *hearing* God's word (Gen 1:22, 28; 2:15–17). The serpent tempted them away from God's word with a wager: "You surely will not die! For God knows that in the day you eat from it your eyes will be opened, and you will be like God, knowing good and evil" (Gen 3:4–5 NASB).

14. Faro, "Evil," 152.

parallel highlights the way Eve was turning from what God deemed as good (in his provision of all the "trees that were pleasing to the eye and good for food" [2:9 ,כָּל־עֵץ נֶחְמָד לְמַרְאֶה וְטוֹב לְמַאֲכָל]) to what she now saw as "good for food ... and pleasing to the eye" in the forbidden fruit (Gen 3:6 NIV). Once Adam and Eve gave in to the temptation and ate, they turned from God's word (Gen 2:16–17) and so from God, the source of life and light. Turning from God, they also turned from themselves. Like a person who looks into the mirror and forgets who he is after he turns away (Jas 1:23–24), they forgot who they were and what they were called to do after they turned from the mirror of God's word. Human beings called by God to work (עבד) and care (שמר) for the world would now objectify, exploit, and desecrate it and one another (Gen 2:15). The lie of the serpent's temptation, which reversed what God had said, also reversed what God had created the world to be into what it is not: darkness, chaos, and death (Jer 4:23; cf. Isa 5:30).[15] Consequently, human beings would experience knowledge of the world in a whole new way; they would now know through experience not only what is good, but also what is not good.[16]

The serpent's temptation was not simply a lie. There were some truths in what the serpent said because the eyes of Adam and Eve were indeed opened (Gen 3:7), and they now knew good and evil like God (Gen 3:22). The tree of knowledge did impart something to the couple.[17] What exactly the tree of

---

15. The temptation was a lie, saying something about nothing, because what was said, "You surely will not die!" (Gen 3:4 NASB), did not correspond with reality, with what God had said: "in the day that you eat from it you will certainly die" (Gen 2:17 NASB). Although a lie, the temptation would affect the way Eve saw the world and unravel the fabric of reality back into darkness and chaos once she falls into its lie.

16. According to Walter Vogels, the tree of knowledge of good and evil is a "symbol of having the experience (yadaʿ) of what is good and bad, beautiful and ugly, of happiness and misery, harmony and disharmony." Walter Vogels, "Like One of Us, Knowing Ṭôḇ and Raʿ (Gen 3:22)" *Semeia* 81 (1998): 149.

17. Gordon Wenham, argues, "As the tree of life offered immortality, so this tree offered knowledge appropriate only to the divine (3:5, 22)." Gordon J. Wenham, *Genesis 1–15*, WBC 1 (Grand Rapids: Zondervan, 1987), 63. There are three other clues that support this reading. First, the moment before Eve took and ate, the temptation narrative climaxed with the phrase וְנֶחְמָד הָעֵץ לְהַשְׂכִּיל ("the tree was desirable to make *one* wise" [Gen 3:6 NASB]). The verb, שׂכל, is referring to the autonomous insight that Eve desired "to achieve success" apart from God's word. Second, in the aftermath of eating from the tree, "the eyes of both of them were opened" (Gen 3:7). Opening of the eyes is the ability to judge, analogous to the ability that God bestows to make proper judgment of his law: "Open my eyes, that I may behold Wonderful things from Your law" (Ps 119:18 NASB). Third, Psalm 19 alludes to the tree of knowledge in Genesis 2–3 to "assert the superiority of the law to the tree of knowledge as a means of obtaining wisdom," insinuating that the tree is an alterative source of wisdom to the law. For more discussion concerning the

knowledge imparted is difficult to say.[18] Commentators are divided, construing knowledge of good and evil as (1) moral discernment, (2) sexual knowledge, (3) omniscience, or (4) wisdom. Since Adam and Eve would have had a degree of moral discernment to obey God (Gen 2:15–17) and an awareness of their sexuality to fulfill God's command to "be fruitful and multiply" (Gen 1:22, 28), and since they were not omniscient after they ate the fruit, we could narrow it down to some sort of wisdom. The merismic structure of "good and evil" (טוֹב וָרָע),[19] in association with דַּעַת ("knowledge" or "ability"),[20] indicates that the wisdom imparted by the tree is the ability to discern and arbitrate what is good and bad for human flourishing *apart* from God (Gen 2:9, 17; 3:5, 22).[21] It is the ability to perceive and judge what is good and not good in accordance with one's own eyes, as their own gods.

---

parallel between the tree of knowledge and the law of God, see David J. A. Clines, "The Tree of Knowledge and the Law of Yahweh (Psalm XIX)," *Vestus Testamentum* 24 (1974): 8–14. The law is not only superior to the tree, but also reverses the effect of the tree that made Adam and Eve wise in their own eyes and of the sin that brought death into the world because it revives the soul, makes "wise the simple" (Ps 19:7), and "enlightens the eyes" to live in God's wisdom (Ps 19:8).

18. While the tree of life finds parallels in the Epic of Gilgamesh and other places in the Bible (Gen 2:9; 3:22, 24; Prov 3:18; 11:30; 13:12; 15:4; Rev 2:7; 22:2, 14, 19), the tree of knowledge of good and evil only appears in Gen 2 and finds no ancient Near East parallels of which scholars are presently aware that could provide any background to its possible meaning.

19. The following survey of the merismic structure of good and bad in Scripture suggests that the tree imparted an ability to formulate and make judgments concerning what is good (conducive) and bad (harmful) for human flourishing. According to Isa 7:15–16, the ability to judge what is good and evil is not something that children naturally possess (cf. Deut 1:39); it is rather something that they acquire through experience and in maturity (Umberto Cassuto, *A Commentary on the Book of Genesis I - V18: Part I From Adam to Noah* [Jerusalem: Magnes, 1961] 112–13). In 2 Samuel, the woman from Tekoa flattered David: "My lord the king is like an angel of God in discerning good and evil" (2 Sam 14:17), and then finished by saying, "My lord has wisdom like that of an angel of God—he knows everything that happens in the land" (2 Sam 14:20). What her flattery implied was not that David knew everything, but that he had the ability to arbitrate what is good and bad for the welfare of Israel (Howard M. Wallace, *The Eden Narrative* [Atlanta: Scholars Press, 1985], 121). This was also the ability that Solomon beseeched God for when he became king, in order "to judge" (שׁ
פט) over Israel (1 Kgs 3:9; cf. 2 Chr 1:10). Simon John De Vries writes, "It is precisely the ability to distinguish good from evil, truth from falsehood, that is indispensable in the administration of justice." Simon John De Vries, *1 Kings*, WBC 12 (Grand Rapids: Zondervan, 1985), 52.

20. The word could also denote "ability" (Exod 31:3; 35:31; 1 Kgs 7:14); see "דַּעַת," *HALOT*, 1:229.

21. According to "רַע רָע," *HALOT*, 3:1252, for example, "what is meant by טוֹב וָרָע associated with יָדַע is a comprehensive knowledge which relates concretely to humanity; thus what is meant is not what is good and evil in itself, but what is good (or evil) for humanity, i.e. 'what is necessary and what is harmful.'" Bruce Waltke and Cathi J. Fredricks write, "The knowledge of good and evil represents wisdom and discernment to decide and affect 'good' (i.e., what advances life) and 'evil' (i.e., what hinders it). Unless we know everything, we only know relatively; unless we know comprehensively, we cannot know absolutely. Therefore, only God in heaven, who transcends time and space, has the prerogative to know truly what is good and

THE EFFECTS OF SIN: A HARDENED HEART AND DARKENED MIND

Sin, the act of turning from God's word to a lie,[22] would affect the couple's newly acquired ability, twisting their judgment so that they saw good as evil and evil as good (Isa 5:20; cf. Job 17:12; Amos 5:7), by preventing them from seeing themselves and the world in proper relationship to God. For instance, after the couple turned away from God, "the eyes of both were opened" to their nakedness (Gen 3:7). The point here is not that they were now aware of their physical nudity, but their fallenness.[23] They perceived themselves apart from God, in their own impurity.[24] Apart from God, they saw their lack, shame,[25] and vulnerability, so they covered themselves.[26] Their eyes were now opened to the "domain of darkness" (τῆς ἐξουσίας τοῦ σκότους, Col 1:13), the sphere of sin and rebellion (Rom 6:12–14), over which the god of this world reigns and blinds those who are perishing from the light of the knowledge

---

bad for life. Thus, the tree represents knowledge and power appropriate only to God (Gen. 3:5, 22). Human beings, by contrast, must depend upon a revelation from the only one who truly knows good and evil (Prov. 30:1–6), but humanity's temptation is to seize this prerogative independently from God (see 3:7)." Bruce Waltke and Cathi J. Fredricks, *Genesis: A Commentary* (Grand Rapids: Zondervan, 2001), 86. See also Nahum M. Sarna, who construes this wisdom likewise as "the capacity to make independent judgments concerning human welfare" or the "capacity to make judgments as to [one's] own welfare independently of God." Nahum M. Sarna *Genesis* (Philadelphia: JPS, 1989), 19, 25.

22. According to Henri Blocher, "Sin, according to the classical definition, is lack of conformity to the law of God. The testimony of Scripture, as a whole, confirms this definition." Henri A. G. Blocher, "Sin," in *NDBT* (Downers Grove, IL: InterVarsity Press, 2000), 783. The purpose of my definition above is to underscore the aspect of sin within the activity of the human heart and mind in order to draw out the noetic effect of sin.

23. There is a drastic shift in how Adam and Eve saw themselves before and after the fall. Before they ate of the fruit, they were "naked" (עָרוֹם), completely exposed to each other—yet without shame (Gen 2:25). After the fall, they lost their innocence and were conscious of their shame and evil.

24. For example, Paul wrote: "To the pure, all things are pure, but to the defiled and unbelieving, nothing is pure; but both their minds and their consciences are defiled" (Titus 1:15). Nakedness will have a different meaning from this point forward throughout Scripture (Gen 9:22–23; Exod 20:26; 1 Sam 20:30; Lam 1:8; Ezek 22:10; Mic 1:11; Rev 3:18; 16:15). According to Victor P. Hamilton, "With the exception of this verse [Gen 2:25], nakedness in the OT is always connected with some form of humiliation." Victor P. Hamilton, *The Book of Genesis Chapters 1–17*, NICOT (Grand Rapids: Eerdmans, 1990), 181. Nakedness also has a sense of defeat (Isa 20:4–5). Perhaps, the couple may also sense defeat after falling into temptation.

25. They feel shame because their own conscience indicted them before God: "'I heard ... , I was afraid ... , I was naked; I hid. ... I ate' (Gen 3:10–13)" (Walter Brueggemann, *Genesis*, IBC [Atlanta: John Knox Press, 1982], 49).

26. Waltke suggests that they felt vulnerable from "being defenseless, weak, or humiliated (Deut. 28:48; Job 1:21; Isa 58:7)". Waltke and Fredricks, *Gen*, 92.

of the glory of God (2 Cor 4:4; Luke 22:53; John 12:31; Acts 26:18; Eph 2:2; Heb 2:14–15; 1 John 5:19; cf. 1QS 2:4–5; 1QM 1:1–11; 4:2; 13:2). Similar to Isaiah's hearers, Adam and Eve hoped "for light, and behold, darkness" (Isa 59:9). They saw reality within the purview of the father of lies.

Another way the Bible depicts sin's effect is the darkening of the mind and hardening of the heart (Rom 1:21; Eph 4:17–18; Ps 69:22–23). The biblical concept of heart and mind overlap in function, but the heart generally refers to the core (the seat of faith,[27] the volition, emotion, and intellect) of the inner person,[28] whereas the mind has more to do with the intellect.[29] In light of Eph 1:18, I think we can interpret our mind more precisely as the eyes of our heart because our mind is similar to physical eyes in the way it allows our heart to sense spiritual and intellectual things, but our heart is in the driver seat, directing our mind to the object of its desire. So, the darkened mind, which refers to spiritual ignorance, is due to the hardening of the heart, a kind of numbness toward God's word. For example, Paul exhorted the church of Ephesus to walk no longer as "Gentiles do, in the futility of their minds," because gentiles "are darkened in their understanding, alienated from the life of God because of the ignorance that is in them, due to their hardness of heart. They have become callous and have given themselves up to sensuality, greedy to practice every kind of impurity" (Eph 4:17–19). Frank Thielman notes that Paul describes here the conditions of gentiles "who have not experienced union with Christ."[30] Life outside of God is futile, a chasing after the

---

27. James D. G. Dunn, *Romans 9–16*, WBC 38B (Dallas: Word Books, 1988), 616: "To talk of the 'heart' is to talk of faith; faith operates at and from the level of the heart."

28. James D. G. Dunn draws out the broad reference of the biblical concept of the heart within the person, "*καρδία* had a broader use than its modern equivalent ('heart'), denoting the seat of the inner life, the inner experiencing 'I,' but not only in reference to emotions, wishes, or desires (eg, 1:24; 9:2), but also in reference to the will and decision making (eg, 2 Cor 9:7) and to the faculty of thought and understanding." James D. G. Dunn, *Romans 1–8*, WBC 38A (Dallas: Word Books, 1988), 60. The heart is the place where the purpose and intention of the person derives (Exod 10:10). It directs the person's path of life (Ps 139:23–24; Prov 4:23; Matt 12:34–35; Luke 6:45; Rom 8:5–8). It is the storehouse of memory, which forms personal identity (Isa 65:17; Jer 3:16).

29. At times, the Bible uses them interchangeably, but other times for their particular emphasis. For example, LXX translation of the Hebrew Bible used "*διάνοια*" ("mind," e.g., Gen 8:21; 17:17; 27:41; Exod 28:3; Deut 4:39; 7:17; 28:28; 29:17; Josh 5:1; Isa 14:13; 35:4; 57:11; Jer 38:33) or "*νοῦς*" ("mind," Exod 7:23; Josh 14:7; Job 7:17, 20; 33:16; 36:19; Isa 10:7, 12) as well as *καρδία* ("heart" [e.g., Gen 20:5–6; 42:28; 50:21; Exod 4:21; 7:3; 8:11; 9:7; Lev 26:36; Deut 1:28; Ruth 2:13; Prov 3:5; Isa 6:10; 66:14; Jer 3:10, 15–16]) to translate לֵב. In 1 Kgs 3:9, 12, for example, English translators go back and forth on translating לֵב as either "heart" (NASB, NIV, and NKJV) or "mind" (ESV, NET, and NRSV).

30. Frank Thielman, *Ephesians*, BECNT (Grand Rapids: Baker Academic, 2010), 296.

wind (Eph 4:17; cf. Eccl 2:26), and it is also darkness because the light of the knowledge of God has been "blacked out" from the mind (Eph 4:17a).[31] A darkened mind refers to the inability to think God's thoughts, seeing God and all things as God sees (Rom 11:10), and to love what God loves, relating to God and other people as God does (1 John 1:5–8; 2:8–11). To be in the dark is then to be outside of God, alienated from the life of God, to be denied a share in the "life and light" of the Father and Son in the Spirit.[32]

If knowledge of God is life with God (John 17:3), then the reason why those outside of Christ are alienated from this life is because of their ignorance (ἄγνοιαν) of God (Eph 4:18). Their ignorance is not simply an intellectual oversight of who God is, but a rebellion, a refusal of God with their whole being.[33] This refusal of God comes from "their hardened heart" (τὴν πώρωσιν τῆς καρδίας αὐτῶν, Eph 4:18),[34] which denotes numbness toward God.[35] It is an inability to sense, know, and respond to God, even as God speaks and reveals himself to us every moment through creation and his word (Ps 19).[36] It is similar to having a stubborn (Jer 7:24; 11:8; 13:10; 23:17; cf. Ps 81:12), uncircumcised (Lev 26:41; Acts 7:51), and stony heart (Ezek 11:19; 36:26) because it is to be set in our ways, walking in accordance to the counsel of our own hearts, which are wicked and deceitful above all things (Jer 17:9). Sin envelops us in the domain of darkness, enslaving our hearts with our own pride and lust and

---

31. Markus Barth, *Ephesians: Translation and Commentary on Chapters 4–6*, AB (Garden City, NY: Doubleday, 1974), 500.

32. Barth argues, "The term 'life of God' is in 4:18 a circumscription of that life and light which according to John 1:4 is in God, and which following John 17:3 is experienced where there is knowledge of God and of his Anointed One. In Rom 8:2, 10 the Spirit is identified with this life." Barth, *Ephesians*, 502.

33. For example, "just as in biblical terminology 'knowledge' transcends a mere intellectual process or possession, and means existential acknowledgement and recognition (that is, honor, obedience, acceptance shown to a partner), so also ignorance is frequently a stance of the total man that includes his emotion, will, and action. Not to know the Lord is as much as to ignore him." Barth, *Ephesians*, 500–501.

34. Barth notes that the relationship between ignorance and hardening is one of cause or effect in Eph 4:18: "In the Greek wording 'petrifaction' may be the cause or effect of the 'refusal to know,' rather than only the accompaniment of the latter" as the NRSV translation renders it (Barth, *Ephesians*, 502). Ignorance and hardening of the heart mutually enforce each other. The refusal of God hardens a person's heart, and the person's heart hardened causes him or her to further refuse and ignore God.

35. Thielman, *Ephesians*, 298.

36. The refusal to acknowledge God as God is universal to all humanity outside of Christ because God has revealed himself to all in creation (Rom 1:18–23).

distorting our minds from what it means to flourish in the world that God has made. Perhaps that is why Paul in 2 Cor 3:14–4:4 described humanity as bound, rather than free. They are separated from a communicative relation with God because their minds are callous (2 Cor 3:14), and their hearts are veiled (2 Cor 3:15), and "blinded" by "the god of this world" from the light of the gospel of Jesus Christ (2 Cor 4:4).[37]

The domain of darkness and light of the gospel are incommensurable and cannot coexist because they oppose one another, operating from different logics, value systems, and points of view.[38] They are contrasting modes of being. To be in the light of the gospel is to be in God, enjoying a fellowship of knowledge and love and doing what is right in God's sight (1 John 1:6; 2:9–11). To be in the domain of darkness is to live in a lie, opposed to God who is truth. So, a mind and heart darkened and hardened by sin cannot accept God's truth (1 Cor 2:14), but suppresses it in unrighteousness (Rom 1:18), trading it for a lie (Rom 1:25).[39] The more people suppress God's truth the further God hands them over to their undoing, so they go further into a lie—darkness—because they go further away from the purpose and truth for which they were made (Rom 1:24–28). Faith is the way back from darkness to light because it is "embracing the divine truth," seeing reality from God's perspective, in his truth.[40] But how is faith awakened?

REVELATION: GOD SPEAKS INTO DARKNESS

Faith comes from hearing God speak (Rom 10:16). As mentioned, God speaks through creation (Ps 19:1).[41] The form and order of creation reveal God's splendor as Creator and Sustainer. If creation is God's word put into creative form

---

37. See Blocher, "Sin," 786. Blocher also points out the following: "Through the infection of the 'flesh', sin makes the human person a slave. ... Slavery to sin signals that sin is alienation, estrangement from the life of God (Eph. 4:18; *cf.* 2:12)," and "[t]wo enslaving agencies are identified in addition to the flesh: the world and the devil."

38. See Karen H. Jobes, *1, 2, and 3 John*, ZECNT (Grand Rapids: Zondervan, 2014), 63.

39. As a consequence of the fall, people worship created things rather than the Creator. Dunn writes, "Man the creature is bound by his very nature to worship and serve something beyond himself. So that if he rejects the only one worthy of his worship and service, it is inevitable that he will direct that basic drive toward an inferior object and thus reduce his own stature in consequence." Dunn, *Romans 1–8*, 73.

40. Craig S. Keener, *The Mind of the Spirit: Paul's Approach to Transformed Thinking* (Grand Rapids: Baker Academic, 2016), 5.

41. Robert Yarbrough puts it nicely: "The things God has created, as people live in symbiotic dependence on them, reveal God's being and even aspects of his nature." Robert W. Yarbrough,

(Gen 1:3) and "upheld" (φέρω) by the power of God's word (Heb 1:3), then observing its form and order would reveal God's thought. Jesus, for instance, pointed to the birds of the air and the lilies of the field to awaken listeners to observe God's providential care and kindness in creation (Matt 6:26; Luke 12:6, 27–31). God speaks also in the events of salvation history. God acted in the event of the exodus to reveal his identity as YHWH (Exod 3:15; 7:14–11:10; 14:21). God speaks finally and definitively in the Son (Heb 1:2) and him crucified (1 Cor 1:23; 2:2). The cross is the hour of glory for Jesus's ministry on earth (John 17:1)[42] because it is the climax of Jesus's revelation to the fullness of God's grace and truth (John 1:14).[43]

The cross is the core of the gospel message, which God has put into the written form of Scripture (1 Cor 1:24; 2:5).[44] "[K]now this first of all," said Peter, "that no prophecy of Scripture becomes *a matter* of *someone's* own interpretation [ἐπιλύσεως], for no prophecy was ever made by an act of human will, but men moved by the Holy Spirit spoke from God" (2 Pet 1:20–21 NASB).[45] The word, ἐπίλυσις, here refers to "the act or process of explaining."[46] Scripture explains the event of the cross not from the perspective of men, but from the perspective of the Spirit who knows the mind and intention of God in sending the Son to the cross (1 Cor 2:11).[47] The message of the cross comes "not in words taught by human wisdom, but in those taught by the Spirit,

---

"Revelation," in *NDBT* (Downers Grove, IL: InterVarsity Press, 2000), 732.

42. According to Raymond Brown, "'Glory' has two aspects: it is the *visible* manifestation of majesty through *acts of power*." But the power that Jesus manifested is not the kind of power we find in explosives or anything in this world for that matter, it is the power of God for salvation. Raymond E. Brown, *The Gospel According to John II, 13–21*, AB (Garden City, NY: Doubleday, 1970), 751.

43. Anthony Hanson argues that the glory of Jesus (i.e., "full of grace and truth") in John 1:14 is a reference to Exod 33:7–34:7. Anthony T. Hanson, "John 1.14–18 and Exodus 34," in *The New Testament Interpretation of Scripture* (London: SPCK, 1980), 97–109.

44. David Garland puts it this way: "Spiritual subjects—namely, the things that God has graciously given, such as Christ's sacrificial death on the cross—require spiritual expression, 'words taught by the Spirit." David E. Garland, *1 Corinthians*, BECNT (Grand Rapids: Baker Academic, 2003), 100.

45. Concerning these verses, Richard Bauckham explains, "The Holy Spirit of God inspired not only the prophets' dreams and visions, but also their interpretations of them, so that when they spoke the prophecies recorded in Scripture they were spokesmen for God himself." Richard J. Bauckham, *Jude, 2 Peter*, WBC 50 (Waco: Word Books, 1983), 235.

46. "ἐπίλυσις," BDAG, 375.

47. To be sure, "Jesus is the supreme revelation of God to men; there can be no witness to the world other than the witness he bore. All other witness by the Paraclete through the disciples simply interprets that" (Brown, *John*, 701).

combining (συγκρίνοντες) spiritual thoughts with spiritual words" (1 Cor 2:13 NASB).[48] Scripture is the interpretive word of the Spirit (2 Pet 3:15–16), where the Spirit combined the thought of God with the words of human writers, "giving spiritual truth a spiritual form."[49] The Spirit guided (ὁδηγέω) these writers of Scripture into all truth concerning Jesus and moved them (John 16:13),[50] as the wind blows the sail and moves the boat on its course, to write God's truth in their own particular personalities, experiences, and styles of writing (2 Tim 3:16; 2 Pet 1:21), so what they wrote in their own unique way is God's word—"thus saith the Lord" (Jer 9:22 KJV).[51] Through the biblical writers, the Holy Spirit put all God's act in creation and history into a coherent biblical account with Jesus and the cross as the climax and key to unlock the intention of all that God has said and done at different times and in various ways (Heb 1:1–3).

Though God finally spoke in the Son and the cross, his glory and wisdom remained hidden from the world.[52] The cross of Jesus Christ was where God

48. See Peter Stuhlmacher, *Biblische Theologie und Evangelium* (Tübingen: Mohr Siebeck, 2002), 158. Stuhlmacher interprets Paul's message of the cross as words given and taught by the Spirit concerning God's will for people who have received the Spirit: "[1Kor] 2,1–5 zeigen, was Paul meint: Seine Lehre vom Gekreuzigten in Korinth was Deutung von geistlichen Tatbeständen für geisterfüllte Menschen in Worten, die der Geist gelehrt hat, und was der Apostel jetzt in 2,6–16 schreibt, setzt seine frühere Lehre fort und vertieft sie." Like the prophets in the OT, God endowed Paul with the Spirit, so that what he wrote revealed the mind of God. According to G. F. Hawthorne, "It was the Spirit that gave [the prophets] their prophetic immediacy of insight into the will of God so that their hearers recognized in their message an authority unlike that of their merely human advisers or teachers—a message that in reality was the revelation of the mind of God to their minds by persons especially endowed with the Spirit." G. F. Hawthorne, "Prophets, Prophecy," in *Dictionary of Jesus and the Gospels* (Downers Grove, IL: InterVarsity Press, 1992), 637.

49. "συγκρίνω," BDAG, 953.

50. To be guided into truth is to understand truth. For example, when Philip asked the Ethiopian eunuch if he understood what he read in Isaiah, he asked Philip with a rhetorical question: "How can I, unless someone guides (ὁδηγέω) me" (Acts 8:31 NRSV)?

51. The word of Scripture is the word of God, breathed-out by the Spirit of God who sets apart, moves, and guides the biblical writers to write and reveal God's truth. Inspiration refers to the divine origin of Scripture, and revelation is the purpose of inspiration. God purposed Scripture to make himself known to his covenant partners.

52. C. S. Lewis wrote that for us to know God is similar to Hamlet finding Shakespeare, which is an impossible feat because Shakespeare exists outside of Hamlet's universe. "[I]f Shakespeare and Hamlet could ever meet, it must be Shakespeare's doing" (C. S. Lewis, *Surprised by Joy: The Shape of My Early Life* [Orlando: Harcourt, 1955], 227). Shakespeare would have to write himself into Hamlet's story. But the cross of Jesus Christ throws a curve ball to this analogy because the Son of God came, but those who searched Scripture for eternal life with God rejected him (John 5:39–40) and nailed him to the cross (John 19:6, 15). The cross demonstrates that God's knowledge is outside of human reach, foolishness.

revealed himself in his hiddenness. It spoke "God's wisdom in a mystery, the hidden wisdom which God predestined before the ages to our glory; the wisdom which none of the rulers of this age has understood; for if they had understood it they would not have crucified the Lord of glory" (1 Cor 2:7–8 NKJV).[53] The glory of the cross was hidden from the wisdom of the world because it revealed the logic of God's wisdom (1 Cor 2:13): "The last will be first" (Matt 20:16); the greatest of all is the servant of all (Matt 23:11; cf. 20:26; Luke 9:48);[54] and God's power for salvation is made perfect in human weakness (2 Cor 12:9). This wisdom is illogical and foolishness to the perspective and value system of the world (1 Cor 1:23). The wisdom of the world is incommensurable with the wisdom of God.[55]

CONCLUSION

God spoke in creation, the Son, and the gospel, but those in darkness did not comprehend light (John 1:5). They saw reality only in the domain of darkness, from the purview of the father of lies who blinded them from the light of the gospel (2 Cor 4:4). Though the gospel revealed the glory and wisdom of God on the cross, the gospel was foolishness to them because the wisdom of the gospel was from the perspective of God (1 Cor 2:14). God's perspective was incommensurable with their perspective because they judged what is good and not good outside of God, from their own eyes, so they did not see what God saw as good and not good (Judg 17:6; 21:25).

53. Markus Bockmuehl states, "This hidden divine wisdom is expressed chiefly … in the cross. … Moreover God's wisdom and His corresponding plan of salvation are concealed from the 'wise' and the 'rulers' of this world. Indeed this hiddenness continues in the present era." Markus N. A. Bockmuehl, *Revelation and Mystery in Ancient Judaism and Pauline Christianity* (Tübingen: Mohr Siebeck, 1990), 165.

54. According to Stuhlmacher, only those who have died to their own worldly view of the cross and receive the gift of the Spirit could understand the rich revelation of God's glory in the cross: "Den Reichtum der Offenbarung von Gottes Herrlichkeit im gekreuzigten Christus könne nur Menschen wahrnehmen, die vor Gott mit ihrem selbstmächtigen Wissen und Willen zunichte geworden und durch den Geist mit geistlichem Verständnis beschenkt worden sind." Stuhlmacher, *Biblische Theologie*, 159.

55. In other words, "the person who lives on an entirely human level rejects them [things of the Spirit]. They are rejected because within the prior horizons of these preexisting interests and concerns the message of the cross and the things of the Spirit find no desired relevance or credibility; they are folly unless or until the Spirit moves or expounds those horizons" Anthony C. Thiselton, *The First Epistle to the Corinthians: A Commentary on the Greek Text*, NIGTC (Grand Rapids: Eerdmans, 2000), 270.

To be in light and see as God sees, a new heart and mind is required for those in darkness (Ezek 36:26; cf. 1 Cor 2:16) because their hearts and minds are hardened and darkened, neither willing nor able to acknowledge God's truth or think God's thoughts. They need illumination like Saul, a persecutor of the church, who became Paul, the apostle to the gentiles (2 Cor 4:6). The function and purpose of illumination is to enable hardened hearts and darkened minds to see what God sees in the Son through the Spirit who knows the deep things of God (1 Cor 2:10) and makes them known to us in union with the Son (John 14:25; 16:13–14).

2

THE BIBLICAL CONCEPT OF ILLUMINATION

To present a biblical concept of illumination, I trace the concept from the promise of the new covenant in the Old Testament (OT) to its fulfillment in Jesus Christ through the New Testament (NT).[1] I begin the chapter with the metaphors of illumination in the OT. Then I read the OT metaphors from the promise of the new covenant in light of their fulfillment in Jesus Christ who has become the head of the new covenant for the new creation. So, whoever is in him is a new creation (2 Cor 5:17). They see all things, especially Christ, no longer according to the flesh (2 Cor 5:16). This shift in perspective takes place in the process that I will call, "the economy of illumination," God imparting knowledge promised to his people in the new covenant (Jer 24:7; 31:34; Isa 11:9; 54:13; John 6:45; 1 John 2:20; 5:20). The economy of illumination, I will argue, involves both an initial lighting to bring us into covenant union with Christ (2 Cor 4:6) and ongoing lighting to unveil us deeper and deeper into contemplative union with Christ from glory to glory (2 Cor 3:18).

OLD TESTAMENT METAPHORS OF ILLUMINATION

Light, which represents God's nature (1 John 1:5), deliverance (Ps 27:1), goodness (Jas 1:17), life (Ps 36:9), and presence (Pss 89:15; 90:8), is one of the key metaphors of illumination in the OT. The psalmist, for example, uses the

1. In the OT, a covenant (בְּרִית) is "a solemn commitment, guaranteeing promises or obligations undertaken by one or both covenanting parties" (Paul R. Williamson, "Covenant," in *NDBT* [Downers Grove, IL: InterVarsity Press, 2000], 420). The promise and obligations of the new covenant is established and fulfilled first and foremost by God. The obedience of the human covenant partners is the fruit of what God has established and fulfilled in the promise of the new covenant.

verb אוֹר, which means "to light" or "to shine," to denote the act of illumination. God is the agent (MT Ps 13:3; 13:4) and the means by which he illumines is his word (MT 19:8; 19:9; cf. 119:130). In Psalm 19, God's word is not only a superior source of wisdom to the tree of knowledge of good and evil,[2] but also counteracts the wisdom from the tree (Ps 19:7). God's word illumines people to their hidden sin (Ps 19:12) and the snares of the wicked to deliver them from "great transgression" (Ps 19:13) so they may enjoy deeper covenant fellowship with God (v. MT 14; cf. 13:3; 13:4).[3] Without natural light, the physical eye cannot see and enjoy the world. Likewise, without divine light from God's word, the mind's eye cannot see and enjoy God.

Another metaphor for illumination in the OT is the "opening of the eye."[4] Numbers 22–24 tells a story of a "heathen seer" named Balaam, whom Balak, the king of Moab, hired to curse Israel, but instead had to bless Israel with four oracles.[5] The narrative begins with the seer's spiritual blindness. When Balaam ventured off with the leaders of Moab, God sent an angel to stand in his way (Num 22:21–22). Ironically, the donkey saw the angel, but the seer did not until God opened his eyes (Num 22:28–31).[6] After Balaam's eyes were opened,[7] God puts in his mouth four oracles. Balaam's third and fourth oracles

---

2. David J. A. Cline, "The Tree of Knowledge and the Law of Yahweh (Psalm XIX)," *Vestus Testamentum* 24 (1974): 8–14.

3. On the psalmist's prayer in MT Ps 13:4, Peter Craigie points out, "There is more than a prayer for physical health in the psalmist's plea; at a deeper level, he desires to return to close fellowship with the Lord." Peter C. Craigie, *Psalms 1–50*, WBC 19 (Grand Rapids: Zondervan, 1983), 142.

4. For example, God opened Hagar's eyes to the well (Gen 21:19; cf. 2 Kgs 6:17). We see similar thing happening in God's provision of the ram for Abraham to sacrifice, though the narrative did not explicitly mention that God opened Abraham's eyes to see the ram, which was probably there all along (Gen 22:13).

5. See especially Gordon J. Wenham, *Numbers: An Introduction and Commentary*, TOTC 4 (Downers Grove, IL: InterVarsity Press, 1981), 185–90. Though Balaam "preferred money to serving God (31:8–16; Deut. 23:4–5; 2 Pet. 2:15; Jude 11; Rev. 2:14)" (Wenham, *Numbers*, 188), he could only do, even if reluctantly, what God said, demonstrating that God's promise to bless Abraham and his descendants will not be void (Gen 12:1–3; 15:18; 17:2). For an opposing view, which interprets Balaam as a virtuous hero, see Rolf P. Knierim and George W. Coats, *Numbers*, Forms of Old Testament Literature 4 (Grand Rapids: Eerdmans, 2005), 252–62.

6. It is like what Elisha's servant experienced, when he beheld the army of angels (2 Kgs 6:17).

7. According to Wenham, this insinuates Balaam's spiritual blindness: "Up to this point Balaam has been portrayed as a man of great spiritual stature, who can meet with God when he wants and whose words have tremendous effects on the fate of nations. Here his spiritual blindness and powerlessness are disclosed. He cannot see the angel of the LORD standing in his path, though his donkey can" (Wenham, *Numbers*, 192). If this is the case, then God was opening more than Balaam's physical eye.

offer the pattern of being illumined to give God's oracle.[8] In both of these oracles, Balaam identified himself as "the man whose eye is opened [שְׁתֻם]" and "uncovered [גְּלוּי]" (Num 24:3–4 ESV; cf. Num 24:15–16).[9] The third oracle, in particular, points out that the opening of Balaam's eyes occurred after the "Spirit of God ... came upon" him (Num 24:2; cf. Num 11:17; Judg 14:6; 1 Sam 10:10; 11:6).[10] The presence of the Spirit opened Balaam's inner eye, tuning his thoughts to God's thoughts to present God's oracle.

Psalm 119 offers the metaphor of opening the eyes in connection to reading Scripture. Throughout this Psalm, the psalmist prayed that God would "teach" him God's "statute."[11] God's word is something that the psalmist has tasted: "How sweet are your words to my taste, sweeter than honey to my mouth" (Ps 119:103 NRSV)! So he desired another taste: "Open [גַּל] my eyes, so that I may behold wondrous things out of your law" (Ps 119:18 NRSV).[12] The wonders (פלא), which the psalmist desired to behold, are God's wondrous deeds in delivering Israel[13] and the wonderful things hidden in God's word.[14] The psalmist was praying essentially to experience (1) "the saving, miraculous power of Torah" in retelling God's deeds and (2) a deeper "insight into

8. Timothy Ashley observes that Balaam received revelation in his third and fourth oracles differently than the first two because the words were not placed in his "mouth" by God (Num 23:5, 16), but are described as coming by the presence of the Spirit. Timothy R. Ashley, *The Book of Numbers*, NICOT (Grand Rapids: Eerdmans, 1993), 487.

9. The expression of having eyes opened and unveiled is not referring so much to Balaam's physical eyes as his inner eyes. Jacob Milgrom suggests that Balaam "was figuratively 'enlightened'; that is, he saw with his inner eyes." Jacob Milgrom, *Numbers* (Philadelphia: JPS, 1990), 203. For more discussion on the meaning of the expression in Num 24:3–4, 15–16, see Ashley, *Numbers*, 488–89.

10. Milgrom writes, "Balaam introduces himself—now that he is invested with the divine spirit—as one who is privy to God's direct revelation." Or as Ashley, *Numbers*, 488, puts it, "Balaam's inner perception has been tuned to understand and communicate what Yahweh wants." Milgrom, *Numbers*, 202.

11. "לַמְּדֵנִי חֻקֶּיךָ," MT Ps 119:12, 26, 64, 68, 124, 135, 171 or "*δίδαξόν με τὰ δικαιώματά σου*," LXX 118:12, 26, 64, 68, 124, 135, 171.

12. The word, גלה, is the same word used in Num 24:4, 16. The Greek translation of Ps 119:18 (or LXX 118:18) also used *ἀποκαλύπτω*, which often means to "reveal" or "make known" in the NT (Matt 11:25; Luke 10:21; 1 Cor 2:10; Eph 3:5; Gal 1:16), to render גַּל.

13. See "פלא," *HALOT*, 3:927.

14. John Goldingay thinks the wonders of God's word is more in line with what the psalmist had in mind because it fits better with the overall theme of God's word in the psalm. But the immediate context (e.g., Ps 119:17–24) suggests a longing to experience God's salvation in God's word, especially here: "Even though princes sit plotting against me, your servant will meditate on your statutes" (Ps 119:23). See John Goldingay, *Psalms*, BCOT (Grand Rapids: Baker Academic, 2008), 3:389–90.

the mystery of Torah as the medium for beholding God himself."[15] God's word is wonderful because it gives light, direction, and guidance for life in a world full of darkness (Ps 119:105)[16] and offers the "key ... to good fortune (Ps 119:1–2), honor (Ps 119:6) and life (Ps 119:17)."[17] The wonder of God's word is the basis for the psalmist's obedience: "Your testimonies are wonderful [פְּלָאוֹת]; therefore my soul keeps them" (Ps 119:129).[18] That is why the psalmist's desire to "live and keep [God's] word" (Ps 119:17) is followed by his prayer to have his eyes opened to God's word (Ps 119:18). To taste and behold God and the wonder of God's word through illumination enlarged and freed the psalmist's heart to obey God more deeply as his covenant God (Ps 119:32).

The metaphors of light and the opening of the eyes demonstrate that illumination enables the person to see and experience what otherwise would not be possible on the person's own ability. It enabled the psalmist to experience God's truth subjectively and existentially, moving him to obey and conform his life to the truth that God's word reveals. The metaphors also imply that sin blinds people from God's word, act, and splendor in history and creation. These two OT metaphors of illumination offer glimpses into how God frees people from darkness with light, so they may see and obey God who is light.

THE NEW COVENANT PROMISE OF ILLUMINATION

The new covenant promise foresees a climax in illumination, where participants from the least to the greatest will all know (Jer 31:34) and be taught directly by God (Isa 54:13). The term "new covenant" (בְּרִית חֲדָשָׁה) is unique to Jeremiah in the OT (Jer 31:31), but the concept already exists in Deuteronomy,

---

15. Frank-Lothar Hossfeld and Erich Zenger, *Psalms: A Commentary on Psalms 101–150*, trans. Linda M. Maloney, Hermeneia (Minneapolis: Fortress, 2011), 3:268.

16. The comment of Goldingay on Ps 119:105 draws out the value of God's word for the life of faith in the fallen world: "In literal darkness we can lose our way or lose our footing and stumble, perhaps with fatal results. In a metaphorical darkness the same is true; one might not realize (or might not face the fact) that certain sorts of offerings or certain forms of sexual activity are wrong, and might end up losing one's religious or moral footing, with fatal results (as Prov. 1–9 points out with regard to the latter)." Goldingay, *Psalms*, 421.

17. Goldingay, *Psalms*, 390.

18. In v. 129, the noun פֶּלֶא, instead of the verb "פלא," is used, which means "something unusual" or a "miracle" ("פֶּלֶא," *HALOT*, 3:928). The עַל־כֵּן clause tells us that the wonder of God's word is the basis for the inference of obedience.

Isaiah, and Ezekiel as we will see. While the metaphors of light and opening of eyes appear in Isaiah's account of the new covenant, Deuteronomy, Jeremiah, and Ezekiel employ other metaphors to similar effect.

In Deuteronomy, we see that the law written on stones was unable to produce the obedience that Israel would need to enjoy and live with God in the Promise Land (Gen 12:1–7). After the requirement of the law was laid out (Deut 10:12–13), for example, Moses admonished Israel: "Circumcise, then, the foreskin of your heart, and do not be stubborn any longer" (Deut 10:16 NRSV). To circumcise one's heart is to commit oneself to God.[19] But Israel was not able to do it. So, Moses prophesied their exile (Deut 28:15–68) and their future transformation thereafter:[20] "the LORD your God will circumcise your heart and the heart of your descendants, so that you will love the LORD your God with all your heart and with all your soul, in order that you may live" (Deut 30:6 NRSV). This surgical metaphor, Daniel Block points out, "refers to removing all psychological, moral, and spiritual barriers to true devotion to Yahweh, resulting in undivided love and obedience."[21] According to Paul, believers are circumcised in the heart by faith in Christ's circumcision, his death on the cross (Col 2:11). Since faith comes through illumination, there is a connection between illumination and the surgical procedure for renewing the heart, so the person may enjoy covenantal life with God. The connection becomes clearer when we come to the fulfillment of the new covenant in 2 Corinthians 3–4.

Jeremiah's account of the new covenant picks up on the concept of the circumcised heart (Jer 4:4; 9:25),[22] rewording it as an inscription of God's law within the heart.[23] Jeremiah (c. 640–587 BC), a prophet on the brink of Israel's exile, underscored forgiveness of sin as the basis of the new covenant[24] that

---

19. See Jack R. Lundbom, *Deuteronomy: A Commentary* (Grand Rapids: Eerdmans, 2013), 818.

20. According to Alex Luc, "the 'heart' is the primary locus of divine evaluation of people's spiritual state." Alex Luc, "לֵב לֵבָב לְבַב," *NIDOTTE*, 2:744.

21. Daniel I. Block, *Deuteronomy*, NIVAC (Grand Rapids: Zondervan, 2012), 697.

22. See Lundbom, *Deuteronomy*, 818–20.

23. Block believes, "Although Jeremiah does not refer to the circumcision of the heart, his understanding of the divine inscription of the Torah on the hearts of the people and his vision for all Israel participating in the new order fall within the same theological field." Block, *Deuteronomy*, 701.

24. This is indicated by the causal כִּי in Jer 31:34. For the function of כִּי, which marks forgiveness of sin as the basis of the new covenant, see "כִּי," *HALOT*, 2:470.

removes the barrier of sin and produces the fruit of obedience, in order to know God in new covenant fellowship.[25]

> The days are surely coming, says the LORD, when I will make a new covenant [בְּרִית חֲדָשָׁה] with the house of Israel and the house of Judah. It will not be like the covenant that I made with their ancestors when I took them by the hand to bring them out of the land of Egypt—a covenant that they broke, though I was their husband, says the LORD. But this is the covenant that I will make with the house of Israel after those days, says the LORD: I will put my law within them, and I will write it on their hearts; and I will be their God, and they shall be my people. No longer shall they teach one another, or say to each other, "Know the LORD," for they shall all know me, from the least of them to the greatest, says the LORD; for [כִּי] I will forgive their iniquity, and remember their sin no more. (Jer 31:31–34 NRSV)

As I've mentioned, sin darkens the mind and hardens the heart, causing people to be unperceptive and unresponsive to God's word. The new covenant overcomes the effect and consequence of sin with forgiveness. Forgiveness reestablishes fellowship, so God may insert and write his law on the new heart, which he promised to give (Jer 24:7; 32:39).[26] The new heart is the new disposition to obey God's word. With a proclivity for obedience, God is able then to write his word on their heart, attuning their thought, will, and affection to his word. As we will see in Ezekiel's prophecy, the new heart and attunement come from the Spirit who affects and

25. So what is *new* about this covenant? According to William Dumbrell, "It will not be new because of new conditions which Yahweh will attach to it, nor because it is the product of a new historical epoch, nor because it will contain different promises, for indeed those attached to the Sinai covenant could hardly have been more comprehensive, but what will make it new is that in the new age *both* partners will keep it." In other words, "Nothing short of an inward and transforming arrangement, to which Jeremiah will now refer in vv. 33–34, will guarantee continued human fidelity within the new arrangement." William J. Dumbrell, *Covenant and Creation: A Theology of the OT Covenants* (Grand Rapids: Baker, 1984), 178.

26. According to Keown, Scalise, and Smothers, "Divine action upon the human heart, understood to be the corporal site of the mind in its capacity to reason, will, decide, make commitments, and control actions, enables people to fulfill God's call upon their lives (eg, Saul in 1 Sam 10:9 and Solomon in 1 Kgs 3:9, 12; 10:24)." Gerald L. Keown, Pamela J. Scalise, and Thomas G. Smothers, *Jeremiah 26–52*, WBC 27 (Grand Rapids: Zondervan, 1995), 160.

internalizes God's truth in the person.[27] Those attuned to God's word are able to know God covenantally,[28] because they trust God with all their hearts (Prov 3:5–7; cf. Jer 24:7; 32:39).[29]

The book of Isaiah adds another layer to the promise of the new covenant with the agency of the servant. It was written by Isaiah (the son of Amoz), whose prophetic ministry in Israel spanned from the death of king Uzziah (740/39 BC) to the reign of king Hezekiah (716/15–687/86 BC). As the Babylonian exile loomed over Israel, Isaiah offered a glimmer of light from God: "I will give you [i.e., the servant] as a covenant for the people, a light for the nations, to open the eyes that are blind, to bring out the prisoners from the dungeon, from the prison those who sit in darkness" (Isa 42:6–7; cf. Isa 49:6, 8–9). The servant is God's covenant[30] because he will establish in himself God's "covenant of peace" (בְּרִית שְׁלוֹם, Isa 54:10),[31] bringing peace and healing from sin through the sacrifice of himself (Isa 53:5); and he is God's light[32] because he will deliver people from the darkness of idolatry (Isa

27. It is similar to what Paul said of having the eyes of our hearts illumined (πεφωτισμένους) to know the hope of our calling (Eph 1:18).

28. Thomas McComiskey argues that Jeremiah "is not speaking of theoretical knowledge but of the inward, personal relationship with God inherent in the word *know*." Thomas E. McComiskey, *The Covenants of Promise: A Theology of the Old Testament Covenants* (Grand Rapids: Baker, 1985), 87.

29. William Holladay sees a close parallel between the imperative "to know the Lord" in Jer 31:4 and the imperative "to trust" and "in all your ways *know* him" in Prov 3:6. It implies a personal knowing based on trust. The torah, written on tablet of stone, will be internalized, written on human hearts. William L. Holladay, *Jeremiah 2*, Hermeneia (Minneapolis: Fortress, 1989), 198. Bruce Waltke, who also compares Jer 31:31–34 to Prov 3:5–6, offers a helpful explanation of knowledge in v. 6: "'To know' … means personal knowledge, intimate experience with a person's reality." It is to experience God's presence so deeply that his will penetrates deeply into the core of the person's being. Bruce Waltke, *The Book of Proverbs: Chapter 1–15*, NICOT (Grand Rapids: Eerdmans, 2004), 244. According to J. A. Thompson, "The verb *know* here probably carries its most profound connotation, the intimate personal knowledge which arises between two persons who are committed wholly to one another in a relationship that touches mind, emotion, and will. In such a relationship the past is forgiven and forgotten." The struggle in the human heart to obey God will be dealt with in the new covenant. J. A. Thompson, *The Book of Jeremiah*, NICOT (Grand Rapids: Eerdmans, 1980), 581.

30. J. Alec Motyer, *The Prophecy of Isaiah: An Introduction and Commentary* (Downers Grove, IL: InterVarsity Press, 1993), 322, puts it succinctly: "The servant will *be a covenant*, i.e. the means through whom people will come into a covenant relation with the Lord."

31. Covenant of peace is another term for the new covenant (Ezek 34:25; 37:26).

32. Shalom M. Paul, *Isaiah 40–66: Translation and Commentary*, ECC (Grand Rapids: Eerdmans, 2012), 189, renders בְּרִית עָם as "a people of the covenant," thus arguing that the servant has two missions, the "first mission is a national one, to be a 'covenant people'" and the second mission is to be a light to the nations. John Goldingay and David Payne, *Isaiah 40–55*, ICC (London: T&T Clark, 2006), 1:228, argue that the covenant in Isa 42:6 should be understood as "divine

42:7). Those who worship idols become like the idols they worship, deaf and blind to the light of God's word (Isa 42:17–20; cf. Isa 6:8–10). The imagery of the servant setting captives free[33] and opening their eyes paints a picture of the agency of the servant in illumination—bringing people from the darkness of ignorance to the light of knowledge in new covenant fellowship with God.[34] In the servant, God's covenant and light, people are unshackled from darkness to participate in fellowship with God. I will flesh this reading out theologically in chapter 7.

The chiastic structure of Ezek 11:19 and 36:26 introduces the agency of the Spirit in transforming people's hearts and minds so that God may write his law on their hearts to know him covenantally.[35]

MT Ezek 11:19	Ezek 11:19
A. וְנָתַתִּי לָהֶם	A. I will give to them
B. לֵב אֶחָד	B. one heart
B'. וְרוּחַ חֲדָשָׁה	B'. a new spirit
A'. אֶתֵּן בְּקִרְבְּכֶם	A'. I will put inside of them
MT Ezek 36:26	**Ezek 36:26**
A. וְנָתַתִּי לָכֶם	A. I will give to you
B. לֵב חָדָשׁ	B. a new heart
B'. וְרוּחַ חֲדָשָׁה	B'. and a new spirit
A'. אֶתֵּן בְּקִרְבְּכֶם	A'. I will put inside of you

During the time of the Babylonian exile (c. 593–571 BC), Ezekiel revealed that God promised to replace the people's "heart of stone" in the future with the

commitment along the lines of the covenant with all living things in Gen 9.8–17." Seeing the parallel between "people" (עָם) and "nations" (גּוֹיִם) in Isa 42:6, Brevard S. Childs, *Isaiah*, OTL (Louisville: Westminster John Knox, 2001), 326, argues that the covenant carries a "universal scope. ... Moreover, the one commissioned does not form a covenant, but rather embodies a covenantal relationship with the nations."

33. Goldingay and Payne, *Isaiah 40–55*, 1:230, suggest, "Blindness and imprisonment extends to people's attitude to God."

34. The act of the first couple eating from the tree of knowledge to gain the ability to make judgment from their own perspective and to be their own has placed all humanity in the domain of darkness. John N. Oswalt, *The Book of Isaiah: Chapters 40–66*, NICOT (Grand Rapids: Eerdmans, 1998), 118.

35. According to Daniel I. Block, *The Book of Ezekiel: Chapters 1–24*, NICOT (Grand Rapids: Eerdmans, 1997), 354.

"heart of flesh" (Ezek 11:19b; 36:26b)[36] through his Spirit:[37] "I will put my Spirit within you; I will take the initiative and you will obey my statutes and carefully observe my regulations" (Ezek 36:27 NASB). The agency of the Spirit transforms the heart of God's covenant partners, so they may have a single-hearted devotion (e.g., "one heart" [לֵב אֶחָד], Ezek 11:19–20; cf. Jer 32:39) to their covenant Lord by conforming their thought, affection, and will to God's.[38]

The new covenant promise is God's solemn oath to establish covenant fellowship with a new people whom he will create for his praise (Isa 43:21), a people who will know and obey him as their covenant Lord, on the basis of the forgiveness of sin and as a result of the transformation of the heart (Jer 31:34). The servant is light, and his sacrifice is the means to establish the forgiveness of sin for new covenant fellowship. The transformation of the heart comes from the gift of the Spirit, who replaces the heart of stone with the heart of flesh—a heart that is compliant and responsive to God. It is not clear at this point how the agencies of God, the servant, and the Holy Spirit are related to one another in restoring covenantal knowledge of God after the fall or how a person is to become a participant of the new covenant in the servant through the Spirit. In chapter 8, I will clarify this relationship between the servant (or the Son) and the Spirit in the economy of illumination.

THE FULFILLMENT OF THE NEW COVENANT PROMISE IN CHRIST

Second Corinthians 3:1–5:17 provides a fulcrum, from which we can build on the biblical passages above and connect other pertinent texts, to conceptualize the economy of illumination as a process by which God imparts his knowledge

36. Israel's heart of stone denotes an unwillingness to respond and acknowledge the word of God. The heart of flesh, on the other hand, denotes a heart responsive and compliant to God's word.

37. Daniel I. Block, *The Book of Ezekiel: Chapters 25–48*, NICOT (Grand Rapids: Eerdmans, 1998), 356, argues, "the new spirit placed inside Israel is identified as Yahweh's *rûaḥ* (v. 27), which animates and vivifies the recipients."

38. See Leslie C. Allen, *Ezekiel 1–19*, WBC 28 (Dallas: Word Books, 1994), 165. The Qumran community also saw God's Spirit as the agent that purifies people for new covenant fellowship with God: "By His truth God shall then purify all human deeds, and refine some of humanity so as to extinguish every perverse spirit from the inward parts of the flesh, cleansing from every wicked deed by a holy spirit. Like purifying waters, He shall sprinkle each with a spirit of truth, effectual against all the abominations of lying and sullying by an unclean spirit. Thereby He shall give the upright insight into the knowledge of the Most High and the wisdom of the angels, making wise those following the perfect way. Indeed, God has chosen them for an eternal covenant" (1QS 4:20–22).

promised in the new covenant. Paul wrote 2 Corinthians to defend his office as a minister of the new covenant to the church that he had founded in his second missionary journey (ca. AD 51 [Acts 18]).[39] After Paul wrote his first letter, intruders infiltrated Corinth:[40] these Judaizers were not so much concerned with circumcision or the observance of the law as they were "with prestige and power in accord with the contemporary values of Corinthian society."[41] So the "devastating effects of" Paul's sufferings on his body (being beaten, stoned, imprisoned, and shipwrecked had taken a toll on Paul's body [2 Cor 11:25]) "were taken as proof positive that Paul was far from the God-appointed mediator of the life-giving Spirit that he claimed to be."[42] Paul turns their argument on its head, demonstrating that his suffering and weakness are actually *signa* to the *res*, the glory of God in the cross of Jesus Christ. The message of the cross was preached not only through Paul's words but also with his body (σώματι, 2 Cor 4:7–18).[43] So Paul's weakness, suffering, and hardship did not discredit him as a minister of the new covenant (2 Cor 7:5–6; 11:23–33), but they were what God used to make him sufficient (2 Cor 12:1–10; cf. 2 Cor 1:9–10; 3:6) to proclaim the gospel (2 Cor 2:14). For what Paul proclaimed and therefore embodied was the gospel of Christ, the Suffering Servant—and him crucified (1 Cor 2:2). Paul's whole life spoke "in the sight of God ... in Christ" (ἐν Χριστῷ, 2 Cor 2:17) with "words ... taught by the Spirit" (1 Cor 2:13). So, the message of Paul's cruciform life should make sense to those who have experienced the new covenant fulfilled in Christ through the Spirit.

In 2 Cor 3:1–4:6, Paul strings together the metaphors of the new covenant from Isaiah ("light," 2 Cor 4:6; cf. Isa 42:6), Jeremiah (the torah "writing on

---

39. After the second Macedonian War (200–197 BC), Corinth became the center for the final resistance against Rome. As an object lesson, the Romans decimated Corinth in 146 B.C. (Yves Lafond, "Corinthus/Corinth," *BNP* 3:798–804). Julius Caesar reestablished Corinth as a Roman colony in 44 BC. "By the late 1st cent. AD the colony was a flourishing centre of commerce, administration, the imperial cult, and entertainment" (Antony J. S. Spawforth, "Corinth," *OCD* 390–91). When Paul came to Corinth, the city was one of the most magnificent cities in the Greco-Roman world.

40. Scott J. Hafemann, *Suffering and the Spirit: An Exegetical Study of II Cor. 2:14–3:3 within the Context of the Corinthians Correspondence* WUNT 19 (Tübingen: Mohr Siebeck, 1986), 67. Cf. Dieter Georgi, *Die Gegner des Paulus im 2. Korintherbrief: Studien zur Religiösen Propaganda in der Spätantike* WMANT (Neukirchen-Vluyn: Neukirchener Verlag, 1964).

41. D.A. Carson and Douglas Moo, *An Introduction to the New Testament*, 2nd ed. (Grand Rapids: Zondervan, 2005), 447.

42. The clarification (Paul) is a modification of the quotation in James M. Scott, *2 Corinthians* New International Biblical Commentay 8 (Peabody, MA: Hendrickson, 1998), 2.

43. Scott, *2 Corinthians*, 112.

the heart," 2 Cor 3:2–3; cf. Jer 31:31–34),[44] and Ezekiel ("Spirit," and a "heart of flesh" in contrast to a "heart of stone," 2 Cor 3:3, 15–17; cf. Ezek 11:19; 36:25–27) to communicate the nature of his ministry. He was a minister of the new covenant, so those who received him and his message were participants of the new covenant fulfilled in Christ. Contrary to the intruders who required letters of recommendation (2 Cor 3:1), Paul said that the church of Corinth is his "letter [of recommendation, v. 2] from Christ [ἐπιστολὴ Χριστοῦ] delivered by [him], written not with ink but with the Spirit of the living God, not on tablets of stone but on tablets of the human heart" (v. 3). In other words, Paul's office as a minister of the new covenant was confirmed by these Corinthians who have experienced the fulfillment of the new covenant through his gospel.

THE ECONOMY OF ILLUMINATION AND COVENANT UNION WITH CHRIST

Let us turn now to the part of Paul's apologia that relates the economy of illumination to covenant union with Christ, i.e., the transfer of a person from the headship of Adam who led the world into the domain of darkness to the headship of Christ who inaugurated the new covenant and new creation in his death and resurrection. In 2 Cor 4:6, Paul wrote, "For God, who said, 'Let light shine out of darkness,' has shone in our hearts to give the light of the knowledge of the glory of God in the face of Jesus Christ" (ἐν προσώπῳ ['Ιησοῦ] Χριστοῦ, 2 Cor 4:6). Here, Paul is referring to the initial shining of the economy of illumination that brings a person from darkness to light in covenant union with Christ.[45] The "economy of God" (οἰκονομίαν θεοῦ, 1 Tim 1:4) refers

44. N. T. Wright, *Resurrection and the Son of God* (Minneapolis: Fortress, 2003), 303, writes, "when the Spirit writes in people's hearts, this can only mean that Jeremiah 31 and Ezekiel 35 are being fulfilled."

45. Similarly, John's account of the paternal act of illumination invokes the imagery of creation with "Ἐν ἀρχῇ" (John 1:1a; cf. LXX Gen 1:1a), but for John, the Father's act of shining forth his light is the act of sending forth His Word (in whom the Father gave the Spirit "without measure" to speak his word [John 3:34]) into darkness (John 1:5)—the "true light, which enlightens all men" (τὸ φῶς τὸ ἀληθινόν, ὃ φωτίζει πάντα ἄνθρωπον, John 1:9, cf. 1:5, 14–18; 3:17). The Father then sends the Spirit, after the Son's glorification, to indwell Jesus' disciples (John 14:16–17), to teach them all things and bring to remembrance everything that Jesus was sent by the Father to say (14:26), to bear witness to Jesus and transform disciples into Jesus' witnesses (John 15:26–27), to convict the world of sin, a false sense of righteousness, and blind judgment of Jesus (John 16:8–11; See D. A. Carson, "The Function of the Paraclete in John 16:7–11," *JBL* 98/4 [1979]: 547–66), and to lead his disciples into all truth to glorify Jesus (13–14), so that people may be illuminated by the Father to come to the Son: "Everyone who has heard and learned from the Father comes to me" (John 6:45 NRSV; cf. 1 John 2:20, 27). F. F. Bruce, *The Gospel of John: Introduction, Exposition and Notes*

to God's "plan of salvation, i.e., arrangements for redemption of humans."[46] It is the execution of the eternal plan of the Father "in the mission of the Son, who accomplishes salvation, and in the mission of the Spirit, who applies salvation by relating believers to Christ (Jn 14–16)."[47] The economy of illumination refers to the interior process of the Father shining "the long awaited light of the eschaton, heralding a new creation" in Christ through the Spirit, into the hearts and minds of those in darkness.[48]

In this initial lighting, God awakens the person from her spiritual slumber to the light of new creation in covenant union with Christ for new covenant fellowship with God: "Awake, O sleeper, and arise from the dead, and Christ will shine on you" (Eph 5:14). In the light of new creation, participants receive a new heart and mind in Christ, the head of new humanity, to know and respond to God in new covenant fellowship. In contrast to darkness, which symbolizes spiritual ignorance, the sin of unbelief, and judgment,[49] the light of new creation refers to the new covenant knowledge that God has promised through the prophets for those in union with Christ because this light concerns the reality of new creation that Christ has established in himself through the cross and resurrection. The gospel is the instrument of this light in Christ (2 Cor 4:4),[50] and the lighting is the act of God to cause the heart of those in darkness to light up with the knowledge of God's glory in the "face (or person) of Christ" (προσώπῳ ... Χριστοῦ, v. 6).

In 2 Cor 5:16–17, Paul said that to receive this light in the person of Christ is to behold Christ, the cross, and all things new.[51] Those in Christ no longer

---

(Grand Rapids: Eerdmans, 1983), 157, puts it thus: "Those who receive this divine illumination and respond to it show by their coming to Christ that they are children and citizens of the new Jerusalem, as the prophet foretold [in Isa 54:13]." So the Father illuminates with the light of the Son and the enlightenment of the Spirit.

46. "οἰκονομία," BDAG, 697.

47. Leland Ryken, James C. Wilhoit, and Tremper Longman III, eds., *Dictionary of Biblical Imagery* (Downers Grove: IVP Academic, 1998), 754.

48. Timothy B. Savage, *Power through Weakness: Paul's Understanding of the Christian Ministry in 2 Corinthians* (Cambridge: Cambridge University Press, 1996), 126.

49. As Paul understands the background of the OT, he also uses the concept of darkness from the OT, which symbolizes God's judgment (Exod 10:21–22; Prov 13:9; Job 12:25; 18:5–6; Jer 4:23; Lam 3:2; Amos 5:18–20; Zech 14:6–7).

50. Murray J. Harris, *The Second Epistle to the Corinthians*, NIGTC (Grand Rapids: Eerdmans, 2005), 330.

51. Grant Macaskill, *Union with Christ in the New Testament* (Oxford: Oxford University Press, 2013), 235, writes, for example: "What is striking here is the noetic thrust of Paul's account of

see Christ according to the flesh and the cross as folly, but with new heart and mind they see the crucified One as "the power of God and the wisdom of God" (1 Cor 1:24). In 1 Cor 2:10–11, Paul said that only the Spirit can allow the person to behold Christ in this way because the Spirit knows what is in the mind of the Father concerning his Son. The Spirit enables the person to see what the Father has revealed definitively in the person and work of Christ and perpetually in the "gospel of the glory of Christ" (2 Cor 4:4). In John 6:45, Jesus asserted that those who come to see him by faith have experienced the fulfillment of the new covenant promise: "It is written in the Prophets, 'And they will all be taught by God.' Everyone who has heard and learned from the Father comes to me."[52]

In the new covenant, God made a solemn promise not only to be faithful, but also to make his people faithful by transforming their hearts and minds through the gift of the Spirit, so they may enjoy new covenant life with him as their God (Ezek 11:20; 36:27). For new covenant fellowship with God to take place, participants need to be made new in covenant union with Christ, the head of new humanity, because those in Adam no longer can know and obey God due to the hardness of their hearts and minds. "But their minds were hardened," Paul said, "for until this very day at the reading of the old covenant the same veil remains unlifted, because it is removed in Christ [ἐν Χριστῷ]" (2 Cor 3:14 NASB).

THE ECONOMY OF ILLUMINATION AND CONTEMPLATIVE UNION WITH CHRIST

The ongoing process of beholding God from glory to glory comes through the unveiling of the Spirit in contemplative union with Christ (2 Cor 3:14–18). "And all of us, with unveiled faces, seeing the glory of the Lord as though reflected in a mirror, are being transformed into the same image from one degree of

---

new creation in 2 Cor 5:16–17: in Christ, the old having passed and the new having come, reality is understood and evaluated differently." Harris, *Corinthians*, 433–34, adds that in 2 Cor 5:17 the "old," which passes away, so the new can come "refers to the whole set of conditions and relationships that marked believers in their unregenerate state when they behaved *κατὰ σάρκα*, that is, they were governed in thought and action by the desires of *σάρξ* (cf. Rom. 8:2, 4; Eph. 2:3) and so were under the dominion of sin and death (cf. Rom. 8:2), and when they made value judgments *κατὰ σάρκα* (cf. Rom 5:16), that is, assessed others by external and worldly standards." In chapter 9, I will touch on the relationship between regeneration and faith in the process of illumination.

52. Concerning John 6:45, see D. A. Carson, *The Gospel According to John*, PNTC (Grand Rapids: Eerdmans, 1991), 293–94, who connects divine illumination to the experience of new covenant.

glory to another; for this comes from the Lord, the Spirit" (2 Cor 3:18 NRSV). Outside of Christ, the veil remains.[53] When a person turns from sin to the Spirit, the veil is removed (2 Cor 3:16–17).[54] The Spirit removes the veil in Christ (ἐν Χριστῷ, 2 Cor 3:14)[55] because the presence of the Spirit makes Christ present to the person's heart.[56] In John 14:17–18, for example, the parallel between the coming of the Spirit (John 14:17) and the coming of Jesus after his glorification (John 14:18),[57] according to Raymond Brown, is "John's way of telling the reader that the presence of Jesus after his return to the Father is accomplished in and through the Paraclete."[58] The indwelling of the Spirit unveils the person to Christ because the presence of the Spirit makes Christ present within the core of the person's consciousness, unveiling the eyes of the person's heart to behold Christ, so Christ may dwell there richly by faith (Eph 3:16–17; Col 3:16).[59]

With the barrier symbolized by the veil removed through the Spirit in contemplative union with Christ, the person beholds the glory of God and is

---

53. The veil, which symbolize the barrier for communion between God and his covenant partners, is not only the inability to respond to God and understand the purpose of the law (v. 13), but also divine judgment due to the sin of unbelief (Exod 4:21; 7:3; Josh 11:20; Isa 6:9–10; 29:10; John 12:40). So Edward P. Meadors, *Idolatry and the Hardening of the Heart: A Study in Biblical Theology* (New York: T & T Clark, 2006), ix, argues, "The hardening of the heart is most often quite simply God's disciplinary punishment for the specific sin of idolatry. As idols have eyes but cannot see and ears but cannot hear, so idolaters lose their sensory faculties as they conform to created, inanimate objects."

54. Harris, *Corinthians*, 307, states that the modification from εἰσεπορεύετο (LXX Exod 34:34) to ἐπιστρέψῃ πρὸς (v. 16) "was doubtless prompted by Paul's desire to express spiritual rather than physical movement ... a spiritual 'turning to the Lord' (or, to God) in heartfelt repentance (e.g., 1 Kgdms. 7:3; Hos. 5:4; 6:1; Amos 4:6)."

55. According to Harris, *Corinthians*, 304, the phrase, ἐν Χριστῷ, could be render as "'in union with Christ' (TCNT), 'through union with Christ' (Goodspeed), 'within the Christian community' (Thrall), or 'by being in Christ' (cf. ἐν Χριστῷ Ἰησοῦ in Gal. 3:28)." The parallel between ἐν Χριστῷ and the presence of the Spirit seems to suggest that the veil was removed through union with Christ by the bond of the Spirit. For a different view of the function of ἐν Χριστῷ in 2 Cor 3:14, see Constantine R. Campbell, *Paul and Union with Christ: An Exegetical and Theological Study* (Grand Rapids: Zondervan, 2012).

56. See James D. G. Dunn, *The Theology of Paul the Apostle* (Grand Rapids: Eerdmans, 1998), 264, who suggests that "believer and Lord in union of commitment are one Spirit (1 Cor. 6.17). The Spirit is the medium of Christ's union with his own."

57. The presence of Jesus with the Father there in heaven was with the disciples here on earth by the indwelling of the Spirit. The "*promised Spirit ... will mediate the presence and self-revelation of Father and Son*" (Max Turner, "Holy Spirit," in *NDBT* [Downers Grove, IL: InterVarsity Press, 2000], 556; emphasis his).

58. Raymond E. Brown, *The Gospel According to John II, 13–21*, AB (Garden City, NY: Doubleday, 1970), 645.

59. Macaskill, *Union with Christ*, 300, argues similarly: "As the gift of the new covenant, the Spirit makes real to (and in) believers 'the truth as it is in Jesus.' ... This is not simply formal but real, because of the Spirit's presence."

transformed into the image of God in Christ from glory to glory (2 Cor 3:16–18). As Moses unveiled his face to come into God's presence, God now unveils his new covenant partner through the Spirit in contemplative union with Christ to behold and be transformed into his image (2 Cor 3:14). The Spirit unites the person to Christ as a beholder is united to the object beheld by beholding and becoming like it.[60] In contemplative union with Christ, knowledge (i.e., beholding as in a mirror) and transformation in the image (εἰκών) of Christ are in a reciprocal relationship.[61] On the one hand, transformation in Christlikeness is the result of being renewed in the knowledge of God (Rom 12:2). On the other hand, our transformation or renewal "is *to result* in the true knowledge of God" (Col 3:10).[62] So transformation and knowledge of Christ mutually affect one another in the journey from faith to sight. To know God is to become more like him and to become more like God enables us to know him more deeply. Knowledge and transformation through the economy of illumination go hand in hand in bringing us to see Christ in a mirror dimly until face to face (1 Cor 13:12).[63] In chapter 9, I will put dogmatic flesh to the cognitive (knowledge) and cardiac (transformation) process in the economy

60. Whereas "[a]n unremoved veil prevents recognition of glory of the new covenant," "[a] removed veil not only guarantees recognition of that glory but also enables participation in that glory" (Harris, *Corinthians*, 313–14).

61. Norbert Hugedé, *La métaphore du miroir dans les épîtres de saint Paul aux Corinthiens* (Neuchâtel: Delachaux & Niestlé, 1957), 29, points out that we are being transformed "'en la même image,'" rather than "en la même gloire." The accusative "τὴν αὐτὴν εἰκόνα" with the passive "μεταμορφούμεθα" indicates an "accusative of the thing" function (F. Blass, A. Debrunner, and R. W. Funk, *A Greek Grammar of the New Testament and Other Early Christian Literature* [Chicago: University of Chicago Press, 1961], 87), denoting the "image" as the object, into which the process of transformation is undergoing as a result of beholding (κατοπτριζόμενοι) as in a mirror the Lord's glory (τὴν δόξαν κυρίου). In his commentary on 1 John 3:2, B. F. Westcott, *The Epistles of St. John* (1883; repr., Grand Rapids: Eerdmans, 1966), 99, also observes the reciprocal relationship of knowledge and transformation, "The likeness to God may be either (1) the necessary condition, or (2) the actual consequence of the Divine Vision. The argument may be: We shall see God, and therefore, since this is possible, we must be like Him; or, We shall see God, and in that Presence we shall reflect His glory and be transformed into His likeness. Both thoughts are scriptural; and perhaps the two thoughts are not very sharply distinguished here. It is true that likeness is, in this case, the condition of vision; and it is true also that likeness is the consequence of vision. We see that which we have the sympathetic power of seeing and we gain greater power of seeing, that is greater sympathy with the object of sight, by exercise of the power which we have."

62. N. T. Wright, *Colossians and Philemon: An Introduction and Commentary*, TNTC 12 (Downers Grove, IL: InterVarsity Press, 1986), 143. See also Douglas J. Moo, *The Letters to the Colossians and to Philemon*, PNTC (Grand Rapids: Eerdmans, 2008), 268.

63. "As in 1 John, the transforming work of God takes place through the knowledge imparted by the Son and applied by the Spirit to the heart of believers. This knowledge is not merely intellectual, but involves the establishment of an eternal relationship with God as Trinity" (David G.

of illumination that draws us into communion with God through contemplative union with Christ from glory to glory.

CONCLUSION

Sin has hardened and darkened the heart and mind of those in Adam, causing them to be unresponsive to God. To know God, those in Adam are required to have a new heart and mind in Christ. This knowledge promised by the new covenant comes through the economy of illumination—the process by which God shines the light of new creation to make the person's heart alight with the knowledge of God's glory in the face of Jesus Christ. The economy of illumination is not only an initial lighting by which God brings a person into covenant union with Christ, but also the ongoing lighting through which God unveils her through the Spirit in contemplative union with Christ as beholder is united to the object beheld in beholding and being transformed to the image of the object. This lighting process from God in the heart draws the person into ever-increasing closeness with God. God makes himself known to the person's innermost being through the presence of the Spirit who unites her to Christ, making Christ present in her heart as the object of knowledge and love, so the person can become cognizant of the Father and respond to him in the Son through the Spirit.

Peterson, *Transformed by God: New Covenant Life and Ministry* [Downers Grove, IL: InterVarsity, 2012], 182–83).

Part 2

—

ECONOMY OF ILLUMINATION: A RETRIEVAL ACCOUNT

3

THE ECONOMY OF ILLUMINATION IN THE ANTE-NICENE FATHERS

Part II of this study aims to retrieve the Trinitarian framework, theological interpretation, categories, and key components of illumination from the Orthodox, Roman Catholic, and Reformed traditions, in order to fund my account of the economy of illumination in Part III, where I seek to put dogmatic flesh on my biblical sketch from Part I. The present chapter begins the retrieval moment with four ante-Nicene theologians, Irenaeus of Lyon, Clement of Alexandria, Tertullian, and Origen, to offer an early Christian account of how illumination is a mode of participation with God. This move lays the theological groundwork to understand the development of the economy of illumination from the theologians in the East and West for the chapters that ensue,[1] and to thicken my interpretation of 2 Cor 3:14–4:6 by reading it with our ante-Nicene fathers.

Before we delve into the writings of our theologians, provisional definitions of the following terms may help us understand their works. First, "light" refers in general to the knowledge of God and in particular to the capacity or the revelation that God bestows on a person to know God. Second, the "economy of God" is concerned with the ordered process of the three persons of God in executing their eternal plan to unite all things in Christ (Eph 1:9–10). Theologians distinguish the economy of God from the being of God in himself and describe the economy of God as the work of God's "two hands" (the Son and the Spirit), the "outflow" of God's being, or the "missions" of God in the world. Third, the "economy of illumination" is my term for the patristic conception of the way the Father brings

1. Pro-Nicene theologians from the East and the West learned how to speak well of God not only from Scripture, but also from the teaching of ante-Nicene theologians.

those in the darkness of ignorance into the light of fellowship in the Son through the Spirit. This Trinitarian operation is both a means and a mode of participation—a means because it is what God does to bring us into his life of light, and a mode because it is the spiritual sight to enjoy contemplative union with God from faith to beatific sight. With these definitions in place, let us turn to our theologians.

IRENAEUS OF LYONS (C. 130–200)

Our first theologian, Irenaeus, was the bishop of Lyons in the last quarter of the second century.[2] During this time, the church experienced not only external persecutions from the Roman Empire, but also doctrinal attacks from the Gnostic movement within the church. "For the gnostics, there is no 'participation' but only a unique spirit-nature. The Gnostic conception of 'natures' excludes the economy of grace: there is neither gift nor participation."[3] For Irenaeus, however, we were made to participate in God. And to participate in "fellowship with God [*participatio autem Dei*] is to know God, and to enjoy His goodness" (*Haer.* 4.20.5).[4] In fellowship with God, the whole person matures into what God has created her to become in body and soul after his image and likeness (*Haer.* 3.18.7; 5.12.2).[5] Because to participate in God is to know and enjoy God, the economy of illumination is vital.

---

2. For a brief look at Irenaeus's life and works, see either Eric Osborn, *Irenaeus of Lyons* (Cambridge: Cambridge University Press, 2001), 1–7 or Robert M. Grant, *Irenaeus of Lyons* (London: Routledge, 1997), 1–10. Unless noted otherwise, the English translation of Irenaeus's works is as follows: *Adversus haereses* (*Haer.*) 1–3 will be from St. Irenaeus of Lyons, *Against the Heresies, Book* 1, trans. D. J. Unger, ACW 55 (New York: Newman Press, 1992); idem, *Against the Heresies, Book* 2, trans. D. J. Unger, ACW 65 (New York: Newman Press, 2012); and idem, *Against the Heresies, Book* 3, trans. D. J. Unger, ACW 64 (New York: Newman Press, 2012); *Haer.* 4–5 will be from Irenaeus of Lyon, *Against Heresies* 4–5, trans. A. Roberts and J. W. H. Rambaut, ANF 1 (1887; repr., Peabody, MA: Hendrickson, 2004), with exception of *Haer.* 4.38–39, which will be from J. Patout Burns, trans. and ed., *Theological Anthropology* (Philadelphia: Fortress, 1981); and *Epideixis tou apostolikou karygmatos* (*Epid.*) will be St. Irenaeus, *Proof of the Apostolic Preaching*, trans. Joseph P. Smith (New York: Newman Press, 1952).

3. Ysabel de Andia, *Homo vivens* (Paris: Études augustinennes, 1986), 223, translated and quoted by Julie Canlis, *Calvin's Ladder: A Spiritual Theology of Ascent and Ascension* (Grand Rapids: Eerdmans, 2010), 173.

4. See A. N. Williams, *The Divine Sense: The Intellect in Patristic Theology* (Cambridge: Cambridge University Press, 2007), 34.

5. See John Behr, *Asceticism and Anthropology in Irenaeus and Clement* (Oxford: Oxford University Press, 2000), 86–92, who interprets the image as the form of the human body after the Son, and the likeness as the freedom and the intellect of human beings through the presence of the Spirit.

Irenaeus's account adds another wrinkle to the sketch of the economy of illumination from the previous chapter. It fleshes out how God who dwells in unapproachable light, immortal, and invisible uses his "two hands," the Son and the Spirit, to make himself visible and to show us that the way to become gods is to obey like the Son who became man.[6] Irenaeus's concept of *theosis* offers another way to understand the transformation of the person into Christlikeness and the active role of participants in the economy of illumination, which will become clearer when we get to chapter 9. For Irenaeus, to see God involves more than an intellectual knowledge of God, but a personal and tacit knowledge of God acquired through the practice and habits of faith in illumination.

HUMAN BEINGS: BEINGS IN BECOMING

In his account of human maturation, Irenaeus links the economy of God in creation (*Epid.* 5)[7] to redemption (*Epid.* 7).[8] The Son and the Spirit, God's "two hands" that formed us in our immature state in creation are the same two hands that will bring us to perfection, communion with God in the end (*Haer.* 4.praef.4; 4.7.4; 4.20.1; 4.39.2–3; 5.1.3; 5.5.1; 5.6.1; 5.28.4; *Epid.* 11).[9] This process of maturation is one of the earliest pictures of

---

6. To become divine does not mean we become like God in our "essence," but to partake and share in God's "properties," holiness, love, incorruptibility, etc. (Norman Russell, *The Doctrine of Deification in Greek Patristic Tradition* [Oxford: Oxford University Press, 2004], 108).

7. The roles of the three persons of the triune God in creation are as follows: "the Father is creator, the Word the means of which the Father creates, and the Spirit is the adorner of that creation wrought by the Father through the Word" (M. C. Steenberg, *Irenaeus on Creation* [Leiden, Brill, 2008], 64–65).

8. The Father is the orchestrator of the divine economy of salvation because it is based on his "good pleasure" (*Haer.* 3.23.1). "The Father decided and commanded; the Son molded and shaped; the Spirit nourished and developed" (*Haer.* 4. 38.3). For a recent discussion on Irenaeus's Trinitarian theology and the cooperative work of the Trinity in the economy of creation and salvation, see Jackson Lashier, *Irenaeus on the Trinity* (Leiden: Brill, 2014), 212–26.

9. "[I]n [the times of] the end, the Word of the Father and the Spirit of God, having become united with the ancient substance of Adam's formation, rendered man living and perfect, receptive of the perfect Father, in order that as in the natural [Adam] we all were dead, so in the spiritual we may all be made alive. For never at any time did Adam escape the *hands* of God, to whom the Father speaking, said, 'Let Us make man in Our image, after Our likeness.' And for this reason in the last times (*fine*), not by the will of the flesh, nor by the will of man, but by the good pleasure of the Father, His hands formed a living man, in order that Adam might be created [again] after the image and likeness of God" (*Haer.* 5.1.3 [ANF]). For discussion on Irenaeus's concept of the two hands, see Anthony Briggman, *Irenaeus of Lyons and the Theology of the Holy Spirit* (Oxford: Oxford Univeristy Press, 2012), 104–107.

theosis: God made us first as human beings in his image and likeness, so we may become gods.[10] God made our body in the "image of the as yet invisible Son"[11] (*Epid.* 22) because through our body we image the Son in obedience to God.[12] The likeness of God in our soul (or mind)[13] comes through the Holy Spirit who enables us to be holy (*Epid.* 14) and free like God (*Haer.* 5.6.1; 5.11.2; 5.16.2; *Epid.* 11). The mind is our point of contact (*Anknüpfungspunkt*) with God in the Spirit.

We mature from being humans to gods,[14] in body and mind, through participating in God's incorruptibility, which has the sense of both God's everlasting and moral attributes. While human beings participate in the strength of God's uncreated glory, they remain created beings. The creature-Creator distinction is never blurred.[15] "Though as created, they are not uncreated; still since they continue for long ages, they will take on the strength of the uncreated. God will give them everlasting endurance" (*Haer.* 4.38.3). Theologians in the East will later refer to this strength as the uncreated energy of God. We partake in the strength of God's incorruptibility through seeing God. The vision of God matures us from being humans by faith to gods by sight:

---

10. As we mature physically from infancy to adulthood, we mature spiritually "first [as] human and then divine" (*Haer.* 4.38.4).

11. Russell, *Deification*, 107.

12. In gnostic thought, "[t]he expulsion of Sophia, or erring wisdom, from this commonwealth ['of aeons which make up the *plêrôma*, or fullness, of divine hypostases'] precipitates the creation of the material world, which is characterized initially only by its *husterêma*, or defect (*Gospel of Truth* 35.25f)" (Mark Edwards, "Growing Like God: Some Thoughts on Irenaeus of Lyons," in *Visions of God and Ideas on Deification in Patristic Thought*, ed. Mark Edwards and Elena Ene D-Vasilescu [London: Routledge, 2017], 40–41). This was how they explained why there is corruption in the material world and how the material world is irredeemable. Contrary to the gnostic who did not believe that God redeemed the body, Irenaeus argued that both body and soul must be redeemed (*Haer.* 5.14.1–4) because human beings are made both of body and soul (*Haer.* 4.praef.4).

13. Unlike Tertullian, Irenaeus conflated the mind and soul: "For the intellect of man—his mind, thought, mental intention, and such like—is nothing else than his soul" (*Haer.* 2.29.3).

14. According to Gustaf Wingren, *Man and the Incarnation: A Study in the Biblical Theology of Irenaeus*, trans. Ross Mackenzie (Edinburgh: Oliver & Boyd, 1959), 92, "God fashioned psychic man (Adam) as one who was to obtain his salvation in the spiritual Man (Christ) (cf. 1 Cor. XV.45–49). 'For since salvation existed beforehand, it was necessary that there should be created that which was to be saved, that salvation should not lack anything.' From this point of view man's history becomes quite secondary. The only reality of any significance is the Son."

15. Russell, *Deification*, 105. To see an illustration of the different models of deification, see Ben C. Blackwell, *Christosis: Pauline Soteriology in Light of Deification in Irenaeus and Cyril of Alexandria* (Tübingen: Mohr Siebeck, 2011), 103.

> It was therefore appropriate for humanity first to be made, being made to grow, having grown to be strengthened, being stronger to multiply, having multiplied to recover from illness, having recovered to be glorified, and once glorified to see its Lord. God is the one who is going to be seen; the vision of God produces incorruptibility [*visio autem Dei efficax est incorruptelae* or ὅρασις δὲ Θεοῦ περιποιητικὴ ἀφθαρσίας]; incorruptibility makes a person approach God. (*Haer.* 4.38.3)[16]

The *visio Dei* is "an epistemological rendering of the general emphasis on divine immediacy as self-mediation" from the Son and the Spirit.[17] Knowledge of God produces incorruptibility because to see God is to be in communion with God and share in his light and life (*Haer.* 4.20.5). This is the *telos* for which God made us.

THE FALL: THE BARRIER TO MATURATION AND PERFECTION

Though God is the one who perfects us because we can only see God through God alone (*Haer.* 4.6.3–4; cf. 4.20.5; 4.5.1; 3.38.3), we actively mature into God's image and likeness by acknowledging and submitting to the truth that the God who formed us in the beginning is also the one who is deifying and perfecting us in the end. In this way, God has set the nature of our maturation that by acknowledging our finitude and dependency on God we receive God's incorruptibility to mature into what we are to become as gods (*Haer.* 4.38.2–4; cf. 4.39.2; Ps 82:6).

In the garden of Eden, however, the serpent deceived our first parents about this truth. Since the mind is our "point of contact to God,"[18] he attacked them there with a lie (*Haer.* 3.23.1–2; 5.21.1),[19] causing them to become "irrational" because they "override the law of human nature;

---

16. The vision of God, for Irenaeus, generally means the knowledge of God, but in this passage, it refers to what is known as the "beatific vision," the face-to-face knowledge of God in the end. There are many "steps," however, along the way until the person is fully mature (*Haer.* 4.9.3).

17. Khaled Anatolios, "The Immediately Triune God: A Patristic Response to Schleiermacher," *Pro Ecclesia* 10 (2001): 168. The reason why the Son and the Spirit make the presence of God immediate to us for communion with God is because they "are themselves *immediately* related to the divine realm" (Anatolios, "Immediately Triune God," 169).

18. Williams, *Divine Sense*, 35.

19. The mind is the part of the person that allows her to behold the vision of God, which produces incorruptibility and directs and sustains the person's service to God (*Epid.* 3). Once the mind is overcome, it is impossible for the person to mature into what God had intended her to be.

they already want to be like God the Creator before they even become human beings. They want to do away with all the difference between the uncreated God and created humans" (*Haer.* 4.38.4). Since it is precisely in acknowledging the creature-Creator distinction and growing in understanding that the power of God is made perfect in their creaturely weakness that they would mature (*Haer.* 5.3.1),[20] it was impossible for them "to refashion [themselves] and obtain the prize of victory" after they lost sight of God and themselves (*Haer.* 3.18.2). They corrupted their divine image, bringing death to their body (*Haer.* 3.23.6), and lost their likeness of divine "freedom," which implies they lost the Holy Spirit,[21] becoming the devil's captives (*Haer.* 3.23.1; *Haer* 3.18.1; *Epid.* 11).[22]

THE ECONOMY OF ILLUMINATION IN THE RENEWAL OF HUMAN BEINGS

Like the "freedom" from the Spirit that we read in 2 Cor 3:17, Irenaeus saw the economy of illumination as the process by which God frees and renews us from the consequence of the fall because "the knowledge of God renews man" (*Haer.* 5.12.4). The economy of illumination is a vital part of salvation[23] because to see the light of the Son in Scripture through the Spirit is to partake in communion with God, from whom comes "life and light" (*Haer.* 5.27.2).[24]

---

20. Understanding the creature-Creator distinction is a part of the process of maturation because it enables us to see things as they are (*Haer.* 5.2.3) and receive God's goodness with gratitude. Irenaeus believes that we become gods by participating in the attributes of God, namely incorruptibility.

21. According to Ireneaus: if the Spirit is not united to the soul, then the person is only the image of God rather than the likeness of God because the likeness of God comes through the Spirit: "... if the Spirit be wanting to the soul, he who is such is indeed of an animal nature, and being left carnal, shall be an imperfect being, possessing indeed the image [of God] in his formation (*in plasmate*), but not receiving the similitude through the Spirit; and thus is this being imperfect" (*Haer.* 5.6.1).

22. Though we suffer the consequence of Adam's sin ever since the fall, it actually worked out for our "advantage" in the end. The fall "enables us to gain a deeper understanding of good through experience of the contrary, and also teaches us the limitations of our nature and thus the 'true comprehension of existent things, that is, of God and man' (*AH* 5.2.3)" (Russell, *Deification*, 108)

23. According to Behr, *Irenaeus and Clement*, 86, the economy of salvation "is directed towards the becoming truly human of both God and human beings, first realized 'in the last times' in Jesus Christ, and to be fully realized for the adopted sons of God in the eschaton."

24. Irenaeus's concept of knowing God as having life with God echoes John 17:3: "And this is eternal life, that they know you, the only true God, and Jesus Christ whom you have sent."

> For as those who see the light [*lumen*] are within the light [*intra lumen*], and partake [*percipiunt*] of its brilliancy; even so, those who see God are in God, and receive of His splendour. But [His] splendour vivifies them; those, therefore, who see God, do receive life. And for this reason, He, [although] beyond comprehension, and boundless and invisible, rendered Himself visible, and comprehensible, and within the capacity of those who believe, that He might vivify those who receive and behold Him through faith. For as His greatness is past finding out, so also His goodness is beyond expression; by which having been seen, He bestows life upon those who see Him. It is not possible to live apart from life, and the means of life is found in fellowship with God [*Dei participatione*]; but fellowship with God [*participatio autem Dei*] is to know God, and to enjoy His goodness. (*Haer.* 4.20.5; cf. 4.39.4)[25]

The economy of illumination, for Irenaeus, is how God opens our "mind's eye" with his two hands, the Son and the Spirit, to see God and ourselves truly,[26] and to guide us in discerning good from evil, so we may choose the good, obedience to God (*Haer.* 4.39.1), to regain the glory lost in Adam (*Haer.* 3.18.1).

Although God is invisible and unknowable in his essence and greatness, he has made himself visible to us in his love through the light of his Son (*Haer.* 4.20.1–4; cf. 3.24.2; 4.5.1; 4.6.5, 7) and the presence of his Spirit (*Haer.* 4.33.7).

> For God is powerful in all things, having been seen ... prophetically through the Spirit, and seen, too, adoptively through the Son; and He shall also be seen paternally in the kingdom of heaven, the Spirit truly preparing man in the Son of God, and the Son leading him to the Father, while the Father, too, confers [upon him]

25. The Latin text is from Irénée de Lyon, *Contre les* heresies, *Livre* 4, eds. A. Rousseau and L. Doutreleau, SC 100 (Paris: Les Éditions du Cerf, 1965).

26. Irenaeus pointed to Paul as an example of our need for illumination to see God: "his [Paul's] former ignorance being driven out by his subsequent knowledge: just as the blind men whom the Lord healed did certainly lose their blindness, but received the substance of their eyes perfect, and obtained the power of vision in the very same eyes with which they formerly did not see; the darkness being merely driven away by the power of vision, while the substance of the eyes was retained, in order that, by means of those eyes through which they had not seen, exercising again the visual power, they might give thanks to Him who had restored them again to sight" (*Haer.* 5.12.5).

> incorruption for eternal life, which comes to every one from the fact of his seeing God. (*Haer.* 4.20.5)

In the economy of illumination, the Son and the Spirit, God's two hands, work alongside one another to illuminate us to the vision of God. The Son is the "*true Light who enlightens* [*illuminans* or φωτίζον] *every man*" (*Haer*. 1.9.2; emphasis original).[27] In the advent of the Son, "the paternal light" comes "to us from His resplendent flesh," so we may "attain ... immortality, having been invested with the paternal light" (*Haer.* 4.20.2). As sunlight illuminates our eyes to the physical world, the light of the Son in the incarnation illumines our mind's eye to the knowledge and love of God.[28] Jesus' incarnation is likened to a kind of synesthesia, where what the physical eyes see in the life and suffering of Jesus awakens the mind's eye to see the love of God. In this way, Jesus prepares us for God and God for us[29] by nurturing us with spiritual milk "to make us accustomed to eat and drink the Word of God, so that we would be able to hold in ourselves the one who is the bread of immortality, the Spirit of the Father" (*Haer.* 4.38.1).[30]

The Spirit, in turn, opens our mind's eye to see the light and Word of God in Scripture, that "the treasure hid in the Scriptures is Christ" (*Haer.* 4:26.1; cf. 4.20.4–5; 4.29.1; 3.6.4; *Epid.* 5), because "without the Spirit there is no seeing the Word of God, and without the Son there is no approaching the Father; for the Son is the knowledge of the Father and the knowledge of the Son is through the Holy Spirit" (*Epid.* 7). And as "the ladder of ascent to God," the Spirit leads us up to God in the Son (*Haer.* 3.24.1), so we may enjoy communion with God as his children by grace (*Haer.* 4.20.5;

27. For the Greek and Latin text, see Irénée de Lyon, *Contre les* heresies, *Livre* 1, eds. A. Rousseau and L. Doutreleau, SC 264 (Paris: Les Éditions du Cerf, 2008).

28. For Irenaeus, light means at least two things: (1) the person of Jesus Christ who is light from light (*Haer*. 1.8.5; 4.14.1) and (2) the knowledge of God in Jesus through Scripture (*Haer*. 4.29.1; cf. 2 Cor 4:4).

29. "He was the Word of God who dwelt in humanity, and was made the Son of Man in order that He might accustom humankind to receive God, and accustom God to dwell in humanity according to the Father's good pleasure" (*Haer*. 3.20.2; cf. 5.16.2). Or as Réal Tremblay, *La manifestation et la vision de Dieu selon saint Irénée de Lyon* (Münster: Aschendorff, 1978), 176, writes that without the incarnation of Christ, "le Père ne peut s'approcher de l'homme et l'homme ne peut s'approcher du Père."

30. See John Eifion Morgna-Wynne, *Holy Spirit and Religious Experience in Christian Literature ca. AD 90–200* (Waynesboro, GA: Paternoster, 2006), 197.

5.36.2).[31] "For, in what way could we be partakers of filial adoption, unless we had received through the Son participation in Himself; unless His Word, having become flesh, had granted us communion in God" (*Haer.* 3.18.7)?[32] The Spirit, whom we receive from God in baptism (*Haer.* 3.17.2; *Epid.* 6; 42),[33] cleanses and illumines our soul to the truth of faith,[34] that we are contingent on God, our Creator,[35] to perfect us through Christ in communion with him (*Haer.* 1.10.1–2; *Epid.* 2–3).

Irenaeus's account offers the practical side of beholding and being transformed by God in 2 Cor 3:18. God renews us in his image by guiding us in the incarnate light of the Son so we may enact truth and regain the glory that we have lost in Adam by following Jesus in God's service because "the glory of man [is] to continue and remain in the service of God" (*Haer.* 4.14.1). To follow Jesus is to conform our image, our bodily form of life, to his and experience greater illumination from God: "to those who believe in Him and follow Him, He grants a fuller and greater illumination of mind" (*Haer.* 4.29.1; 4.20.5; 4.38.3) because "to follow the light is to perceive the light" (*Haer.* 4.14.1). In following Jesus, God illuminates our minds to see by personal experience that his power is also made perfect in our weakness (*Haer.* 4.37.7; 5.2.3; 5.3.1).[36] It is by understanding that we are weak that we are made strong, and it is by humbling ourselves before God as human beings that God makes us gods—his likeness. That is why God sent "the only true and steadfast Teacher, the Word of God, our Lord Jesus Christ, who did, through His transcendent love,

31. Andia, *Homo vivens*, 225–33.

32. Communion with God or the vision of God always comes in the light of the Son through the presence of the Spirit. As Irenaeus wrote, "Men therefore shall see God, that they may live, being made immortal by that sight, and attaining even unto God; which, as I have already said, was declared figuratively by the prophets, that God should be seen by men who bear His Spirit [in them], and do always wait patiently for His coming" (*Haer.* 4.20.6).

33. See Everett Ferguson, *Baptism in the Early Church: History, Theology, and Liturgy in the First Five Centuries* (Grand Rapids: Eerdmans, 2009), 306.

34. For discussion on adoption through the Spirit's indwelling presence, see Briggman, *Holy Spirit*, 151–64. For a slightly more nuanced view, see Behr, *Irenaeus and Clement*, 96–107, who argues that the presence of the Spirit is in all humanity, but those who are adopted are the ones who receive "communion with the Spirit."

35. Understanding the creature-Creator distinction is a part of the process of maturation because it allows us to draw strength from God in our weakness (*Haer.* 5.2.3).

36. In Jesus' obedience and ultimately in his death, God reveals that his power is made perfect in weakness. Jesus teaches us from the cross how to serve God in humility, long-suffering, and obedience (*Haer.* 3.18.6).

become what we are, that He might bring us to be even what He is Himself" (*Haer.* 5.Praef.).[37] So, the knowledge of God through illumination is not merely intellectual, but tacit and personal, a knowledge that is acquired through obeying and following the Son. To put it another way, knowledge of God restores both our body and mind to the image and likeness of God by following and embodying the light of the Son.[38]

Irenaeus' insight on the vital role of the Spirit for freedom with God in Eden and the loss of the Spirit after the fall will be picked up in the next chapter by Athanasius who will argue that the incarnate Word enabled the Spirit, whom Adam lost, to indwell Christians permanently after the fall. In chapters 8 and 9, I will develop Irenaeus' insight on the integral relationship between knowing God and becoming like God and the role of the body in being illumined by God.

CLEMENT OF ALEXANDRIA (C. 150–215)

Similar to the idea of contemplative union with Christ in chapter 2, Clement of Alexandria believed faith leads us to contemplation with Christ for communion with God (2 Cor 3:18). We will also find a similar movement from Augustine in chapter 6, a movement from faith to contemplation in Christ, our Teacher, "in whom are hidden all the treasures of wisdom and knowledge" (Col 2:3 ESV). Concerning 2 Cor 4:6, Clement wrote: "But it is the truth, I say, which cries, 'Light shall shine out of darkness.' Let the light then shine in the hidden part of man, in his heart; and let the rays of knowledge rise, revealing and illuminating the hidden man within, the disciple of light, friend of Christ and joint-heir with Him" (*Protr.* 11.89).[39] Clement was pleading with those whom he described as having no "sense and sight ... in darkness ... and falling to pieces through corruption" to heed the cry of "truth" and come into "light."

37. "The 'exchange,'" suggests Russell, *Deification*, 108, "signifies precisely that: an exchange of properties, not the establishment of an identity of essence."

38. "[S]ince man is an animal made up of soul and body," God restores and matures both our body and soul through the knowledge of God (*Epid.* 2). Therefore, "in Christ Jesus we ... receive what we had lost in Adam, namely, to be according to the image and likeness of God" (*Haer* 3.18.1). "For these two [cognition of God and good works]," Irenaeus said, "rejoice in each other's company, and agree together and fight side by side to set man in the presence of God" (*Epid.* 2).

39. English translation is from Clement of Alexandria, *Christ the Educator*, trans. Simon Wood, FC 23 (Washington: Catholic University of America Press, 1953).

Let us reflect now on Clement's understanding of the way the Son through the Spirit return us to communion with God in the economy of illumination.

Like Irenaeus, Clement believed we were created to mature into God's likeness by following Christ.[40] Sin is a barrier to maturation, a disease that leaves us like "beasts" in our passion (*Paed.* 1.13.101–102). To bring us back to health, Jesus came to offer us "remedies of reason to effect understanding and salvation ... to those who are sick" (*Paed.* 1.12.100), so we "may come to a full knowledge of the truth" and be perfect (*Paed.* 1.1.3).[41] The economy of illumination is the means through which God perfects us because it is God's process of emitting the light of his knowledge to bring us from faith to sight, everlasting contemplation (θεωρία) of God (*Protr.* 10.80). "This act of *theoria*," Andrew Louth writes, "is not simply consideration or understanding; it is union with, participation in, the true objects of true knowledge. It bespeaks, as Festugière says again and again, 'un sentiment de présence'—a feeling of presence, of immediacy."[42] To contemplate God is to participate in God who made himself present in our minds as the inner Teacher.

---

40. Cf.: "It seems to me that the reason that He formed man from dust with His own hands, gave him a second birth through water, increase through the Spirit, education by the Word, thereby guiding him surely to the adoption of sons and to salvation with holy precepts, was precisely that He might transform an earth-born man into a holy and heavenly creature by His coming, and accomplish the original divine command: 'Let us make mankind in our image and likeness.' It is Christ, in fact, who is, in all its perfection, what God then commanded; other men are so only by a certain image" (*Paed.* 1.12.98). Unless noted otherwise, the English translation of *Paedagogus* (*Paed.*) 1–3 will also be from Wood's translation, and for the Greek text of book 1, see Clément d'Alexandrie, *le Pédagogue, livre 1*, ed. and trans. Henri-Irénée Marrou and Marguerite Harl, SC 70 (Paris: Les Éditions du Cerf, 1960); the English translation and Greek text for *Protrepticus* (*Protr.*) will be from Clement of Alexandria, *Exhortation to the Greeks, The Rich Man's Salvation*, and *To the Newly Baptized*, trans. G. W. Butterworth, LCL 92 (Cambridge, MA: Harvard University Press, 1919); *Stromata* (*Strom.*) 1–3 will be from Clement of Alexandria, *Stromateis: Books One to Three*, trans. John Ferguson, FC 85 (Washington: Catholic University of America Press, 1991); *Strom.* 4–6, 8 will be from idem., *The Stromata, or Miscellanies*, trans. W. Wilson, ANF 2 (1885; repr., Peabody, MA: Hendrickson, 2004); and *Strom.* 7 will be from John E. L. Oulton and Henry Chadwick, trans. and eds., *Alexandrian Christianity* (Philadelphia: Westminster Press, 1954).

41. According to Peter (Panayiotis) Karavites, *Evil, Freedom, and the Road to Perfection in Clement of Alexandria* (Leiden: Brill, 1999), 15, Clement believed that "[t]he knowledge of God is so important that if it were to be separated from salvation and one had to choose between the two, he should definitely decide in favor of knowledge (Protr. 68.4)." But this is hypothetically speaking because, similar to Irenaeus, Clement thought that our salvation or perfection comes from knowing God (See Russell, *Deification*, 121–40). Those who know God are perfect, "for what more does he need who possesses the knowledge of God" (*Paed.* 1.6.26)? The person who knows God has God and becomes like God, so he is complete.

42. See Andrew Louth, *The Origins of the Christian Mystical Tradition: From Plato to Denys*, 2nd ed. (Oxford: Oxford University Press, 2007), 3.

JESUS CHRIST: THE DIVINE EDUCATOR AND TEACHER

In *Protr.* 11.87, Clement used φωτίζω and καταυγάζω, which can both be translated as "to illuminate" or "to enlighten," for the work of Christ and Scripture in making God known within the person's "soul" or "consciousness" (ψυχῆς). Clement also described illumination as divine instruction (*Paed.* 1.12.99), teaching (*Paed.* 1.13.102), spiritual cleansing from sin (*Paed.* 1.6.28), and the spiritual sight from being born again (*Paed.* 1.6.25, 27). Together, these descriptions illustrate how God emits the light of Jesus Christ into our hearts (*Protr.* 11.89). While Clement shared many affinities with Irenaeus concerning the agency of Jesus in the economy of illumination, he differed from the bishop of Lyons on the light of Jesus because Jesus' light is the power of sight rather than the resplendent flesh of Christ that makes the invisible and unapproachable light of the Father visible to our hearts and minds.

Clement also depicted a more nuanced picture than Irenaeus of the way Jesus, as the divine "Teacher" (διδασκαλικός) and "Educator" (παιδαγωγός) (*Paed.* 1.1.1–2), illumines and perfects us in the knowledge (γνῶσιν) and communion with God. "As Teacher, He explains and reveals through instruction, but as Educator He is practical" (*Paed.* 1.1.2). For instance, Jesus' "leadership enlightens and educates" us in the way of "poverty and humility," so we may "become like God by a likeness of virtue" (*Paed.* 1.12.99).[43] So while the knowledge that Jesus imparts as Teacher is contemplative, the knowledge that Jesus instills as Educator is tacit: "He persuades men to form habits of life, then He encourages them to fulfill their duties by laying down clear-cut counsels and by holding up, for us who follow, examples" (*Paed.* 1.1.2; cf. 1.12.99).[44] Through

---

43. We become more like God by following Jesus because our "Educator ... resembles His Father, ... God immaculate in form of man, accomplishing His Father's will" (*Paed.* 1.2.1). Moreover, by following Jesus in the "obedience" of "faith," we fulfill our "duty" and become virtuous (*Paed.* 1.13.101). While the Stoics refers to "virtue" as "the dutiful and the fitting" (προσῆκον καὶ καθῆκον), Clement argued that that which "is a duty is also fitting," so "that which is done properly in the service of God fulfills in deeds the duty imposed on it" (*Paed.* 1.13.102).

44. As it is with Irenaeus, being and knowing are connected because to know God requires us to be right with God and to be cured of being "hard of heart," which in turn allows us to become more responsive to God (*Paed.* 1.5.19) and "come to the full knowledge of truth" (*Paed.* 1.1.3). Like Christ whose life and teaching are in sync with one another, our faith and reason must also be in agreement: "the Educator and His precepts are worthy of one another and adapted one to the other. In keeping with such a model, we ought also to adapt ourselves to our Educator, conform our deeds to the Word, and then we will truly live" (*Paed.* 1.12.100). In other words, "the deed of a Christian soul is the work of its reason accomplished by means of its friend and companion, the body, obeying the dictate of an educated judgment and of a desire for the truth" (*Paed.* 1.13.102).

the instrumental means of Scripture, Christ, as our Educator, brings us to the knowledge of God in contemplation as the divine Teacher (*Strom.* 7.10.55; *Paed.* 1.2.5; 1.13.103; 2.1.1).

Contrary to Tertullian who considered philosophy to be "the mother of all heresy" (cf. *Nat.* 2.1.7; *An.* 3.1),[45] Clement believed that it can be a preparatory way for faith to attain γνῶσιν ("knowledge," *Strom.* 1.20.99.1; cf. 1.6.33.1).[46] By γνῶσιν,[47] Clement meant the "knowledge" of God through Scripture and tradition[48] that perfects the γνωστικός ("gnostic," *Strom.* 7.1.1).[49] The true gnostics, for Clement, are not the few who attained a secret knowledge of God but all those who have "been illuminated" (κατηυγάθημεν) by the knowledge of God in the Son (*Protr.* 11.87). Through Scripture and tradition, the Son illumines

---

45. Clement compared the light of philosophy to a wick and the light of the gospel to the sun: "Whence the Hellenic philosophy is like the torch of wick which men kindle, artificially stealing the light from the sun. But on the proclamation of the Word all that holy light shone forth. Then in houses by night the stolen light is useful; but by day the fire blazes, and all the night is illuminated by such a sun of intellectual light" (*Strom.* 5.5 ANF).

46. See Behr, *Irenaeus and Clement*, 19, and Eric Osborn, *Clement of Alexandria* (Cambridge: Cambridge University Press, 2005), 199.

47. According to Piotr Ashwin-Siejkowski, *Clement of Alexandria: A Project of Christian Perfection* (London: T & T Clark, 2008), 144, "Γνῶσιν was for Clement of Alexandria a very valuable, desirable and achievable state. It was an 'illumination' that had the potential to change a person's existence, self-understanding and relationship with the divine."

48. Clement used tradition in several ways, but here I am referring to his understanding of tradition as the "interpretation" of Scripture or the "teaching of the Lord and apostle. ... Here practice (8.) is included in the tradition. This tradition from the Lord and the apostles is the church's tradition and is identified with truth" (Everett Ferguson, "Paradosis and Traditio: A Word Study," in *Tradition and the Rule of Faith in the Early Church: Essays in Honor of Joseph T. Lienhard* [Washington: Catholic University of America Press, 2010], 14).

49. Clement employed the word gnostic (γνωστικός) as a way to criticize the gnostic movement of his day, which saw matter as evil and so rejected the humanity of Jesus and His bodily resurrection, by showing that a true gnostic is one who is saved by "revealed knowledge" (γνῶσιν) that is freely spreading to all the world through His disciples because of the incarnation and resurrection of Jesus Christ (*Protr.* 11.87; *Paed.* 1.5.20). The true gnostic is one whose "soul dwells with the Lord, continues as his familiar friend, shares the same hearth, bears the cross with the savior, and even becomes the Holy of Holies itself" (Andrew C. Itter, *Esoteric Teaching in the Stromateis of Clement of Alexandria* [Leiden: Brill, 2009], 204). Another way of putting it is the gnostic is one who is illuminated by God to receive Gnosis, the knowledge of God that perfects (*Paed.* 1.6.31). Salvatore R. C. Lilla, *Clement of Alexandria: A Study in Christian Platonism and Gnosticism* (Oxford: Oxford University Press, 1971), 142, divides γνῶσιν into two stages: "In Clement's conception of *gnosis* it is possible to distinguish two different stages. *Gnosis* can already be attained by man to some extent during his stay on earth; but it reaches its climax after the death of the body, when the soul of the γνωστικός is allowed to fly back to its original place where, after becoming a god, it can enjoy, in a complete and perpetual rest, the contemplation of the highest divinity 'face to face,' together with the other θεοί." So although the "gnostic ... is already holy and divine, carrying God within him and being carried by God" (*Strom.* 7.82.2), he is not complete until he sees Christ as he is.

us in himself, to light up "God for us" (*Protr.* 10.86) and to guide our whole existence to God (*Protr.* 11.87), "transplanting corruption to the soil of incorruption" (*Protr.* 11.114), because his "light is life eternal, and whatsoever things partake of it, live" (*Protr.* 11.88).

BAPTISM: "BATHING IN LIGHT"

In Clement's writing on baptism, we find a clear example of his understanding of illumination as participation in Christ for communion with God. "When we are baptized, we are enlightened" (Βαπτιζόμενοι φωτιζόμεθα, *Paed.* 1.6.26).[50] By being "baptized into Christ" (εἰς Χριστὸν ἐβαπτίςθητε, *Paed.* 1.6.31),[51] "we behold the wonderful holy light of salvation, that is, it enables us to see God clearly" (*Paed.* 1.6.26). Clement compared being baptized in light to waking up from a deep sleep and receiving sight after being blind.

> It is just like men who shake off sleep and then are wide-awake interiorly; or, better, like those suffering from some blinding eye-disease who meanwhile receive no light from the outside and have none themselves, but must first remove the impediment from their eyes before they can have clear vision. In the same way, those who are baptized are cleansed of the sins which like a mist overcloud their divine spirit and then acquire a spiritual sight which is clear and unimpeded and lightsome [φωτεινόν], the sort of sight [ὄμμα] which alone enables us to behold [ἐποπτεύομεν] divinity, with the help of the Holy Spirit who is poured forth from heaven upon us. This is an admixture [κρᾶμα] of eternal sunlight, giving us the power to see the eternal light [ἀίδιον φῶς]. Like indeed attracts like; so it is that

50. The early church commonly referred to illumination as baptism. This practice goes back as far as Justin Martyr, c. 100–165, who writes, "'this washing is called illumination [φωτισμός], as those who learn these things are illumined [φωτιζομένων] in the mind. And he who is illuminated is washed in the name of Jesus Christ'" (*1 Apol.* 61.9–14; 34–39, quoted in Timothy P. McConnell, *Illumination in Basil of Caesarea's Doctrine of the Holy Spirit* [Minneapolis: Fortress, 2014], 15). In fact, an unknown Christian inserted "in the Jewish *Sibylline Oracles* 1, dated about 150, in recounting the incarnation and life of Christ refers to John the Baptist, a 'voice ... through the desert land.' It describes baptism in Christian terms: 'That every human person be illumined by waters, so that, being born from above, they may no longer in any respect at all transgress justice' [*Sib. Or.* 1.339–341]" (Ferguson, *Baptism*, 108).

51. According to Williams, *Divine Sense*, 72, "The sanctification that comes with the Spirit's descent in baptism bestows illumination perfection, making illumination the immediate effect of baptism, which leads in turn to adoption, perfection and, ultimately, immortality."

> what is holy attracts Him who is the source of holiness, who properly speaking is called Light. "For you once were darkness, but now light in the Lord." That is why, I believe, the ancients once called man by a name that means light [φῶτα]. (*Paed.* 1.6.28; cf. 2.9.79)

To know God is to be born again in baptism. Clement wrote, "though a man receives nothing more than this rebirth, still, because he is by that fact enlightened, he is straightway rid of darkness, as the name itself suggests, and automatically receives light" (*Paed.* 1.6.27).

In baptism, a person has gone from blindness to sight in Christ (cf. Eph 5:14).[52] This sight from new birth is described as full of light (φωτεινὸν)[53] because it is the power to see God (*Protr.* 11.87; *Paed.* 1.6.28). The light, illumining the soul's eyes to God, is the Son because he enables us to see the Father.[54] The Spirit is the other agent of illumination (*Strom.* 4.17) because the Spirit clears the "impediment" of sin from the mind's eye by "bathing the mind in light"—a "baptism in the Word" (*Paed.* 1.6.29–30). The cleansing of water through the Spirit enables us to receive and partake in the light of Jesus Christ. Those who participate in the Son through the Spirit receive divine "power"[55] that unites "the soul with light, through unbroken love, which is God-bearing and God-borne" (*Strom.* 6.12; cf. 6.16).[56]

---

52. Clement seemed to be following Philo's use of ὄμμα for the "sight" of the soul that beholds (ἐποπτεύομεν) God. Philo often uses ὄμμα to refer to transcendental knowledge (*Opif* 1:71; *Sacr.* 1:36, 69, 78; *Det.* 1:22; *Post.* 1:8; *Plant.* 1:21–22; *Ebr.* 1:44; *Sobr.* 1:3; *Migr.* 1:39, 48, 165). Clement of Rome similarly wrote, "Let us behold him with our mind and consider with the eyes of our soul his long-suffering will; let us perceive how he is without wrath toward all his creation" (1 *Clem.* 19.3; translation mine).

53. Jesus uses the same word, φωτεινός, to describe the "body" or life of his followers, which is "full of light" (Matt 6:22; Luke 11:34, 36).

54. Jesus is light because the truth of God is in him, and it is in his light that we see the light of God's truth (*Paed.* 1.10.93; cf. 1.5.20). Clement also referred to the Spirit at times as "light of truth—a light true, casting no shadow. ... By following Him [i.e., the Spirit], therefore, through our whole life, we become impossible; and this is to rest" (*Strom.* 6.16).

55. Elsewhere, Clement said that the gnostic who responds to the Master's call is "being joined with Christ there, to make himself worthy from his purity to receive by inward union the power of God which is supplied through Christ" (*Storm.* 7.12.79).

56. Clement compared the engrafting of the gnostic into Christ to a "form of engrafting called budding," where a "bud (eye) ... is cut out of a trunk of a good sort" and placed on a new trunk that "is stripped, to suit the eye, over an equal circumference. And so the graft is inserted" (*Strom.* 6.15). He goes on to say, "This mode is the style of gnostic teaching, which is capable of looking into things themselves. This mode is, in truth, of most service in the case of cultivated trees. And 'the engrafting into the good olive' mentioned by the apostle, may be

To be in union with Christ by the Spirit, then, is to "receive power to see; receive thy light" (*Protr*. 11.87),[57] to see God and his will through Scripture and tradition (*Protr.* 11.87–88; *Paed.* 1.12.98; *Strom.* 5.10; 7.10.55).[58] It is to receive γνῶσις, "revealed knowledge," the knowledge "of being itself" (*Strom.* 2.17.76.3). To have this knowledge is to partake in the reality that it communicates, namely God, and to become virtuous (*Paed.* 1.12.99; *Strom.* 6.12.99) and incorruptible like God (*Paed.* 1.5.20–21).[59]

THE LIGHT FOR THE ROAD FROM FAITH TO SIGHT

Illumination sets us on the journey to the *visio Dei*, which begins by faith until it reaches sight in the heavenly rest, eternally contemplating God with Christ (*Paed.* 1.6.29). "When the soul rises above earthly experience, finds itself alone, and consorts with ideas, it is similar to the Coryphaeus in [Plato's] Theaetetus, becoming now like an angel; *it is with Christ*, being

---

[engrafting into] Christ Himself; the uncultivated and unbelieving nature being transplanted into Christ—that is, in the case of those who believe in Christ. But it is better [to understand it] of the engrafting of each one's faith in the soul itself. For also the Holy Spirit is thus somehow transplanted by distribution, according to the circumscribed capacity of each one, but without being circumscribed" (*Strom.* 6.15). Clement, however, was not as clear on the relationship between the Son and Spirit in believers' union with Christ as Calvin was, who believed that believers are engrafted in Christ through the Spirit by faith. With this quote from Clement, we are left wondering if the Spirit was somehow transplanted after the believers' union with Christ, as a part of union, or as a means of union. But since Clement maintained that the agency of the Spirit is what awakens the faith of the gnostic in baptism (*Paed.* 1.6.30), we could conjecture that the Spirit is the one who unites the gnostic to Christ by faith. The Spirit is also given in greater portion or comes closer to the gnostic as he becomes more virtuous. Clement, for instance, wrote, "For the Scripture somewhere says, 'The Spirit of the Lord is a lamp, searching the recesses of the belly.' And the more of a Gnostic a man becomes by doing right, the nearer is the illuminating Spirit to him" (*Strom.* 4.17).

57. For Clement, to be illuminated and to follow Jesus go hand in hand: "Let us make room in our hearts for the light and become the Lord's disciples" (my translation of "χωρήσωμεν τὸ φῶς καὶ μαθητεύσωμεν τῷ κυρίῳ." *Protr.* 11.87).

58. Clement equated the teaching of Scripture and tradition to Christ's teaching, so anyone who turns from the teaching of Scripture and tradition is a heretic and does not belong to Christ (*Paed.* 1.5.18). To be illuminated by Christ through Scripture requires us to search Scripture. Clements wrote that the "gift of the God-given knowledge" of Scripture comes "through the true illumination of logical investigation" (*Strom.* 8.1).

59. Since God is holy, "he who knows God is holy and pious" (*Strom.* 7.7.47). Like Irenaeus, Clement argues that we don't partake in God's essence but in his virtue and quality. For example, Clement maintains that those who know truth are united to truth and enjoy the eternal quality of God's truth: "For, those who have partaken of the new Word must themselves be new. But whatever partakes of eternity assumes, by that very fact, the qualities of the incorruptible; therefore, the name 'childhood' is for us a life-long springtime, because the truth abiding in us is ageless and our being, made to overflow with that truth, is ageless, too" (*Paed.* 1.5.20–21).

contemplative, constantly contemplating the will of God" (*Strom.* 4.25.155).[60] Illumination is a means of communion with God because it is the light needed for the contemplative journey (*Strom.* 7.11.68).

In the beginning, God made us in the image and likeness of his Son, "for the contemplation [θέαν] of heaven ... to come to the knowledge of God" and "to be in close fellowship with God" (*Protr.* 10.80; cf. 4.55; Cicero, *Nat. d.* 2.140; Ovid, *Metam.* 1.85–86). Unlike Irenaeus, Clement understood the *imago Dei* as our "mind" (*Protr.* 10.79; *Strom.* 2.19.102.6), which allows us to contemplate God because "God ... is perceived not by the sense but by the mind" (*Protr.* 4.45; cf. *Paed.* 1.3.7). The likeness of God, on the other hand, is something that we obtain in the end by conforming our minds to the "mind of the Master" (*Strom.* 6.15; *Paed.* 1.12.99–100).[61] Our "duty" (καθῆκον), to this end,

> is to cultivate a will [βούλημα] that is in conformity and united [ἕν] throughout [our] life to God and Christ, properly directed to eternal life. Indeed, the life of the Christian, in which we are now being educated, is a united whole made up of deeds controlled by reason; that is, it is the persevering accomplishment of the truths taught by reason, or rather, the Word, an accomplishment which we call fidelity [πίστιν]" (*Paed.* 1.13.102).

Clement referred to faith (πίστιν) as an "accomplishment of truths" because faith is conforming our will to "reason, or the Word" through obedience (*Paed.* 1.13.101).

Faith unites and directs us to God to become *like* God (*Paed.* 1.6.28). In his interpretation of Gal 3:23–25, for instance, Clement wrote, "faith is salvation reaching the whole of mankind, and that it is an impartial share of union [κοινωνία] with the just and loving God, given to all" (*Paed.* 1.6.30).[62] However, anything done apart from faith is sin (Rom 14:23), which severs

---

60. My translation seeks to draw out the contemplative aspect of this passage: ""Οταν γὰρ ψυχὴ γενέσεως ὑπεξαναβᾶσα καθ' ἑαυτήν τε ᾖ καί ὁμιλῇ τοῖς εἴδεσιν, οἷός ἐστιν ὁ ἐν τῷ Θεαιτήτῳ κορυφαῖος, οἷον ἄγγελος ἤδη γενόμενος · σὺν Χριστῷ τε ἔσται, θεωρητικὸς ὤν, ἀεὶ τὸ βούλημα τοῦ θεοῦ σκοπῶν"). The Greek text is from Clément d'Alexandrie, *les Stromates IV*, ed. and trans. Annewies van den Hoek and Claude Mondésert, SC 463 (Paris: Les Éditions du Cerf, 2001), 316.

61. See P. Augustinus Mayer, *Das Gottesbild im Menschen: Nach Clemens von Alexandrien* (Rome: Pontificium Institutum S. Anselmi, 1942), 32–36.

62. Those who come to know God by faith through illumination experience initial perfection. "For we were enlightened, that is, we came to the knowledge of God. Certainly, he who possesses knowledge of the Perfect Being is not imperfect" (*Paed.* 1.6.25).

us from God and causes us to become like "beasts" because it is contrary to God and "right reason" (*Paed.* 1.13.101).[63]

Since we have all followed Adam and become like beasts,[64] we need illumination[65] because it gives rise to faith to set us on the path to perfection. The Spirit awakens faith with the light of the knowledge of God in baptism[66] because, without knowledge, there would be no faith,[67] and faith, in turn, leads us to the contemplation of God. We see this movement from faith to contemplation in how Clement positioned the role of Christ as Educator before his role as Teacher. "Just as our body needs a physician when it is sick, so, too, when we are weak, our soul needs the Educator to cure its ills. Only then does it need the Teacher to guide it and develop its capacity to know, once it is made pure and capable of retaining the revelation of the Word" (*Paed.* 1.1.3). Christ, our Educator, brings us to health by evoking faith (*Paed.* 1.3.8), so that Christ, our Teacher, can bring us into contemplation of God through Scripture (*Paed.* 3.12.87, 97).[68]

---

63. Concerning the unitive force of faith, Clement wrote, "Wherefore also to believe in Him, and by Him, is to become a unit, being indissolubly united in Him; and to disbelieve is to be separated, disjoined, divided" (*Strom.* 4.25).

64. Clement saw Adam's story as the "story of 'everyman'; it is a story that is true of each one of us" (Andrew Louth, *Introducing Eastern Orthodox Theology* [Downers Grove, IL: IVP Academic, 2013], 72). See *Protr.* 11.86.

65. If ignorance is darkness, which causes us to be blind to truth and fall into sin (*Paed.* 1.6.29; cf. *Strom.* 3.43.1–2; *Protr.* 83.1–2), then the knowledge of God in Christ is "light, for it dispels the darkness of ignorance and endows us with keenness of vision" (*Paed.* 1.6.29).

66. "For instruction [κατήχησις] leads us to faith, but faith is established and developed [παιδεύεται] by the Spirit at the time of holy baptism" (*Paed.* 1.6.30). My translation here of πίστις δὲ ἅμα βαπτίσματι ἁγίῳ παιδεύεται πνεύματι seeks to draw out the permissive function of παιδεύεται (which is a 3rd person singular present passive [or middle] indicative of παιδεύω) to highlight that faith comes from the Spirit's illumination in baptism. For the permissive function of the middle voice, see Daniel B. Wallace, *Greek Grammar Beyond the Basics: An Exegetical Syntax of the New Testament* (Grand Rapids: Zondervan, 1996), 425. The reference of κατήχησις (instruction) is most likely the law from the Old Testament (OT) and philosophy, which lead the person to faith but do not give them faith. That is probably why Clement, who was a convert to Christianity from Greek philosophy instead of the OT law, wrote, "we who were uninstructed [i.e., by the OT law] but were learning [i.e., philosophy], heard that knowledge is engendered together with enlightenment, bathing the mind in light" (*Paed.* 1.6.30). In baptism, the Spirit establishes and develops our faith through the knowledge of Christ (Karavites, *Perfection*, 144).

67. Faith derives from the knowledge of God. See Osborn, *Clement*, 162.

68. Faith, in other words, sets the gnostic on the quest for deeper contemplation of truth: "Starting with that admiration for the creation which he brings with him as an evidence of his capacity to receive knowledge, he becomes an eager disciple of the Lord, and the moment he hears of God and Providence, his admiration prompts him to believe. Proceeding from this point

The obedience of faith through the body not only sets "strong foundations" for knowledge of God to flourish (*Strom.* 2.2.9.3; 7.11.60.1),[69] but also purifies the soul's eye to contemplate God more purely (*Paed.* 2.1.1) because it attunes and conforms the "disposition of [our] soul" to the disposition of Christ through obedience, so we may see what he sees (*Paed.* 1.13.101; *Strom.* 2.2.8.). Faith allows the person's mind to unite to Christ by assimilating his disposition to Christ's.

Prayer is required on faith's quest to the face-to-face vision of God because prayer rightly relates us to God, who supplies us with light on the way to "eternal rest" (*Paed.* 1.13.102).[70] So we are constantly to strive "to be united with God in prayer" (*Strom.* 7.7.40), praying for the light or "power of contemplation" to increase in contemplating God on earth (*Strom.* 7.7.46) as we will in heaven (*Strom.* 7.10.56). Our communion with God by faith through illumination on earth culminates in our communion with God by love through vision in heaven (*Strom.* 7.3.13), a worshipful communion of "loving God and being loved by him" (*Strom.* 7.1.2).[71]

In Clement's concept of baptism as illumination, we have another way to look at the relationship between Jesus and the Spirit for my concept of contemplative union from 2 Cor 3:18. Clement likened the unveiling of our face in Paul's epistle to the removal of the impediment of sin from our minds through the washing of the Spirit to behold the light that is in Christ. This light is not only the object of illumination, but also the capacity of illumination, the power to behold God. To behold God, the obedience of faith is required. Since like attracts like, the beholder must be made holy through faith by conforming to Christ, the Educator, to contemplate God who is holy in Christ, the Teacher. The beholder is united to Christ by assimilating his mind, disposition, and life to Christ's, so he may contemplate what Christ contemplates for all eternity, namely his Father.

---

he does his best to learn in every way, employing every means to obtain the knowledge of those things which he longs for (and longing joined with seeking arises as faith increases), that is, to be made worthy of such high and glorious contemplation" (*Strom.* 7.11.60.1).

69. Osborn, *Clement*, 167–169. Clement's view of knowledge on the basis of faith comes from his reading of the LXX Isa 7:9: "*καὶ ἐὰν μὴ πιστεύσητε, οὐδὲ μὴ συνῆτε*" (*Strom.* 2.2.8.2).

70. Osborn, *Clement*, 272–73.

71. Karavites, *Perfection*, 59.

TERTULLIAN (C. 155–220)[72]

Like Irenaeus and Clement, Tertullian maintained that we could only know God in Christ, "the Enlightener and Guide of the human race" (*Apol.* 21.7), and know Christ through the Spirit:[73] "For by whom has truth ever been discovered without God? By whom has God ever been found without Christ? By whom has Christ ever been explored without the Holy Spirit? By whom has the Holy Spirit ever been attained without the mysterious gift of faith" (*An.* 1.4)? But we find in Tertullian the two natures and Trinitarian account of the soul, the simple and immaterial substance of a person that consists of the abilities to think and to feel (*An.* 14.1; 18.8). His concept of the "psychological image of the divine Trinity" in the soul may have been the precursor to Augustine's in *De Trinitate* 15.11–19 (*Prax.* 5).[74] Tertullian's account offers insight into how our mind is illumined through our senses in baptism, communion, and the reading of Scripture.

---

72. Unless otherwise noted, the English translations of Tertullian's works are as follows: *De anima* (*An.*), *Apologeticus* (*Apol.*), and *De testimonio animae* (*Test.*) will be from Rudolph Arbesmann, Emily Joseph Daly, and Edwin A. Quain, trans., *Tertullian: Apologetical Works*, FC 10 (Washington: Catholic University of America Press, 1950); *De baptismo* (*Bapt.*) will be from Ernest Evans, *Tertullian's Homily on Baptism* (London: SPCK, 1964); *Adversus Marcionem* (*Marc.*) will be from Tertullian, *The Five Books against Marcion*, trans. Peter Holmes, ANF 3 (1885; repr., Peabody, MA: Hendrickson, 2004); *De resurrectione carnis* (*Res.*) will be from Ernest Evans, *Tertullian's Treatise on the Resurrection* (London: SPCK, 1960), which also includes the Latin text; and *De virginibus velandis* (*Virg.*) will be from Geoffrey D. Dunn, *Tertullian* (London: Routledge, 2004), which also presents a concise introduction of the life, thoughts, and works of Tertullian.

73. Born in Carthage c. 155 to a Roman centurion, Tertullian was converted to Christianity c. 193 and pioneered "the writing of Latin theology" (Henry Chadwick, *East and West: The Making of a Rift in the Church: From Apostolic Times until the Council of Florence* [Oxford: Oxford University Press, 2003], 8). Modern scholarship on Tertullian has argued that Tertullian converted to Montanism c. 206. In the last few decades, however, scholars have come to a more nuanced position. Eric Osborn, *Tertullian: First Theologian of the West* (Cambridge: Cambridge University Press, 1997), 176, argues that Tertullian "remained within the catholic church, despite ... his allegiance to the New Prophecy." David E. Wilhite, "The Spirit of Prophecy: Tertullian's Pauline Pneumatology," in *Tertullian and Paul*, ed. Todd D. Still and David E. Wilhite (New York: Bloomsbury, 2013), 68, goes further and argues instead that the New Prophecy, which Tertullian referred to, was the prophecy of the New Testament: "The 'New Prophets' (*De pud.* 21.7) are not the Phrygian prophets [i.e., those who broke from the church], who are nowhere named or referenced in this text (contra Barnes, *Tertullian*, 44), but the Christian prophets from the New Testament (*De pud.* 12.1), such as Peter (*De pud.* 21.9). They stand in contrast only with the 'old prophets' of the Old Testament (*De pud.* 6.2; 7.9, 18; 18.4; 21.5)." Wilhite believes that Tertullian never left his Carthaginian church to join the Montanist sect, and if there were any signs of "Montanist thinking" in his writings, then it was probably a view that the community in Carthage also accepted (Wilhite, "Spirit of Prophecy," 47). If Wilhite is right, then there is no real shift in Tertullian's writings after 206, but more likely a further development of his earlier works. My account of Tertullian's concept of illumination will consist of both his earlier and later works.

74. Williams, *Divine Sense*, 39.

THE RATIONAL AND IRRATIONAL NATURES OF THE SOUL

Tertullian believed that without the divine light found in the person and work of Jesus Christ (*Apol.* 21.7–28; *Marc.* 4.25) the soul is blind to the things of God (*Paen.* 1). The soul's blindness is caused by its "irrational element" (*An.* 16.1), which leads to passions, desires, and emotions that are contrary to reason or nature (*An.* 16.7). However, the soul by nature is "rational" because the God who made it is "rational" (*An.* 16.1; cf. *Marc.* 1.3). The rational nature of our soul reflects the relationship between the Father and the Son in the Spirit from eternity:

> Observe, then, that when you are silently conversing with yourself, this very process is carried on within you by your reason, which meets you with a word at every movement of your thought, at every impulse of your conception. Whatever you think, there is a word; whatever you conceive, there is reason. You must needs speak it in your mind; and while you are speaking, you admit speech as an interlocutor with you, involved in which there is this very reason, whereby, while in thought by means of that converse with your word. Thus, in a certain sense, the word is a second *person* within you, through which in thinking you utter speech, and through which also, (by reciprocity of process,) in uttering speech you generate thought. The word is itself a different thing from yourself. Now how much more fully is all this transacted in God, whose image and likeness even you are regarded as being, inasmuch as He has reason within Himself even while He is silent, and involved in that Reason His Word! (*Prax.* 5)[75]

Similar to the dialogue between the Father and the Son, the rational element of our soul naturally reasons and testifies to us about God, but God is the chief Teacher who guides our soul to himself.[76] "The irrational element, however, must be thought to have come later, resulting from the suggestion of the serpent and producing the very act of the first transgression. ... The distinction, then, between

75. The Spirit is not mentioned explicitly, but the Spirit is the conversation, the reciprocal or reasoning process between the Word and God's self in uttering speech and generating thought. In *Apol.* 21.12, Tertullian wrote concerning the relationship of the Spirit and the Son: "in Spirit giving utterance, there would be the Word."

76. "Nature," Tertullian said, "is the teacher; the soul is the pupil. Whatever either the one has taught or the other has learned has come from God, that is, the Teacher of the teacher. What the soul can divine with regard to its chief teacher, you are able to judge from that which is within you. Learn to perceive that which makes you perceive" (*Test.* 5).

these two elements of the soul arises from the difference of their authors" (*An.* 16.1–2). So human beings in a sense have two natures, the first is the rational nature from the Father of light, and "the corruption of nature is a second nature, one which has its own god and father, namely, the author of all corruption" (*An.* 41.1).

THE TESTIMONY OF THE SOUL

The first nature of the soul is corrupted, but not destroyed by sin (*An.* 41.2). When the soul is revived and awakened to the consciousness of "its divine origin and native goodness" (*An.* 41.3–4), it testifies about God:

> The soul, though it be repressed by the prison house of the body, though it be circumscribed by base institutions, weakened by lust and concupiscence, and enslaved to false gods, yet, when it revives, as from intoxication or sleep or some sickness and enjoys health again, names 'God' with this name alone because, properly speaking, He alone is true. 'God God!' 'God will reward me.' O testimony of the soul, which is by natural instinct Christian [*testimonium animae naturaliter christianae*]. ... It knows the abode of the living God; from Him and from there it has come. (*Apol.* 17.5–6)

While the testimony from the rational nature of the soul "is by natural instinct Christian" (*Apol.* 17.6; cf. *Test.* 5), it is, nevertheless, "made a Christian, not born one" (*Apol.* 18.4).[77] No one is a Christian by birth because "[e]very soul is considered as having been born in Adam until it has been reborn in Christ" (*An.* 40.1, 4). We become Christians when we are born again in Christ through the water of baptism by faith, a baptism that illumines us to God "as one already known" (*An.* 41.4).[78] Faith is the "recollection of things past," recollecting the One from whom and for whom we were made.[79]

THE RELATIONSHIP OF THE BODY AND SOUL IN BAPTISMAL LIGHT

Like Clement, Tertullian believed that when a person is baptized, he experiences a "cleansing in Christ [his] light" (*Marc.* 4.9).[80] When the veil of corruption and irrationality is uncovered from the soul in baptism, a person

77. My paraphrase of "*fiunt non nascuntur christiani.*"

78. Osborn, *Tertullian*, 83.

79. Osborn, *Tertullian*, 83.

80. To be a Christian is to be "in God's light" (*Pud.* 7).

"perceives the full glory of the light" of the Son and is "welcomed by the Holy Spirit as, at its physical birth, it was met by the evil spirit" (*An.* 41.4; cf. *Bapt.* 1). But what is distinct in Tertullian's account from Clement is the whole person, body and soul, is renewed in baptism. And what is done to the body physically also affects the soul spiritually in baptism.

> For example, the flesh is washed that the soul may be made spotless: To such a degree is the flesh the pivot of salvation, that since by it the soul becomes *linked* with God, it is the flesh which makes possible the soul's election by God. For example, the flesh is washed that the soul may be made spotless: the flesh is anointed that the soul may be consecrated: the flesh is signed [with the cross] that the soul too may be protected: the flesh is overshadowed by the imposition of hands that the soul may be illumined by the Spirit [*anima spiritu illuminetur*]. (*Res.* 8; emphasis mine)[81]

A look at the relationship between the body and the soul in knowing God will shed light on the way the Spirit enables the soul through the body to approach and be united to God.

In *De anima*, Tertullian taught that while the soul is a "simple" substance,[82] its "powers" or "functions" are complex because "the power of the soul is intellectual as well as sensual" (*An.* 18.8). Although sensation takes place in the soul, the body is required as an instrumental means by which the mind (the "innate faculty of the soul" [*An.* 12.1; 18.5]) senses and perceives the physical world (*An.* 14.3; 12.1; 17.5, 11; 18.5).[83] The senses

81. A reason that Tertullian gave for this is that from a biblical perspective "no soul can ever obtain salvation unless while it is in the flesh it has become a believer" (*Res.* 8). Similarly to Irenaeus, Tertullian believed that our body is made in the image of God (*Res.* 40). So a person's salvation must consist of both body and soul. But Tertullian wanted to go further to safeguard the doctrine of the resurrection from Gnostics who argue for the "salvation of the soul ... but destruction to the flesh" by arguing that the soul cannot be saved without or outside of the flesh.

82. The soul is simple because it is immortal. "For, to be divided is to be dissolved and to be dissolved is to die" (*An.* 14.1).

83. The sense is the power of the soul that allows the mind, the innate faculty of the soul, to know: "The sense of man have been given the mastery over all God's creation that by them we might understand, inhabit, dispose of, and enjoy His goodness. ... Is not all life dependent upon the senses? Are not our senses the second source of knowledge with which we are endowed? ... Without his senses, man's life would be deprived of all joy and satisfaction, the only rational being in creation would thus be incapable of intelligence or learning, or even of founding an Academy!" (*An.* 17.11).

and intellect are *indistinguishable*[84] operations (or "powers") within the soul, mutually affecting one another in the way the soul perceives the world and God.[85] On the one hand, the soul cannot understand something without sensing it because "thought begins in the senses" (*An.* 17.5).[86] But on the other hand, "if there is no understanding, there is no sensation" (*An.* 18.8) because sensation is the "perception of the thing felt" (*An.* 18.7). For example, to know the sweetness of honey, we must taste honey, but to taste the sweetness of honey, we must know what we are tasting. Our senses and intellect always operate together for our souls to know. The two "come under the soul for the purpose of being at its service; thus, the soul perceives corporeal things with the help of the body and spiritual things by means of the mind, since the soul is really exercising sensation when it is thinking. ... to feel is to understand and to think is to have sensation" (*An.* 18.6–7). While the intellect is what allows the soul to understand spiritual things, which are by nature invisible and intangible, the intellect depends on the senses to perceive spiritual things through the body because God has made it thus, making known his invisible attributes through visible things (Rom 1:20).[87]

The person and work of Jesus Christ, the image of the invisible God, is the prime example of how the invisible is revealed through the visible (*Prax.* 24). "[L]isten," exhorted Tertullian, "to the word of St. John: 'What we have seen, and heard, perceived with our eyes, what our hands have handled of the word of life'" (*An.* 17.14). The divinity that the eternal Word shares with the Father is revealed to our *senses* in the person and work of the incarnated

84. Tertullian's rationale behind this is that if they were distinguishable, then they could be separated. So he wanted to emphasize how difficult it is to pinpoint exactly what their operations are from each other within the soul.

85. But "[i]f we must say that corporeal things are 'sensed' and spiritual things are 'understood,' it is the nature *of those objects* which causes distinction and not the abode of sensation and understanding, that is, the soul and the mind" (*An.* 18.8).

86. "Where," Tertullian asked, "does the mind get the idea the tower is really round, unless from the senses" (*An.* 17.5)?

87. Tertullian wrote, "We know that truth is apprehended by means of visible images, that is, the invisible through the visible. St. Paul tells us: 'The invisible attributes of God from the creation of the world are understood from the things that are made'" (*An.* 18.12). And as a literalist in his interpretation of Scripture, he also pointed to the example of Christ who saw the devil falling down from heaven to demonstrate that knowledge of spiritual reality comes through our senses of the physical world (*An.* 17.13). Moreover, the beauty and order of the universe that we see open to us God's "mind" (Williams, *Divine Sense*, 37).

Word to illuminate and give us access to the Father who dwells in unapproachable light (*Prax.* 15; *Apol.* 21.3; 1 Tim 6:16).[88]

Likewise, God illuminates us to see and partake in the spiritual reality of our union with Christ, in his death and resurrection, through baptismal water. The soul and the body work together not only to obey God's call to be baptized, but also to experience and receive spiritual cleansing through the washing of the water, so we may receive the Spirit and be united to Christ. For instance, it is through the body that the soul is able to respond to God's call to be baptized (*Bapt.* 13). But it is through the soul's directive that the body is able to experience God's will by being "spiritually cleansed" from sin and sanctified for God in the water of baptism (*Bapt.* 4).[89] The will of God is for us to be sanctified in body and soul, so we may become holy like God.

Taking a closer look at how the body and soul work together in baptism, we see the water, made holy by the Spirit (*Bapt.* 4), sanctifies the body through the soul's response to God's call by faith (*Bapt.* 13). The water at the same time allows the soul to sense through the body the spiritual reality of being "freed from sins" (*Bapt.* 7) and cleansed from the irrational effect of sin (*Marc.* 4.9). The body and soul are spiritually cleansed and enlivened by faith because both have been baptized into the death and resurrection of Jesus Christ through water (*Bapt.* 13), "neither can our death see dissolution except by the Lord's passion, nor our life be restored without His resurrection" (*Bapt.* 11).

Spiritual cleansing prepares the soul to receive the Spirit through the laying of hands on the body, which culminates in the baptismal ceremony (*Bapt.* 6). The Spirit that we receive by the imposition illumines us to Christ so we may be united to Christ by feeding on his body and blood in the Eucharist: "the flesh feeds on the Body and Blood of Christ so that the soul also may be replete with God" (*Res.* 8).[90] The Spirit illuminates us in baptism by (1) cleans-

88. Again, this accessible light is the revelation and knowledge of God radiated in the incarnation of the Son, divinity revealed in the form of a man (*Apol.* 21.7–28; *Marc.* 4.25).

89. As the body and soul of the person are both spiritually defiled in their act of sin because every act of sin is directed by the soul and enacted by the body, the soul and the body both need to be cleansed spiritually from their defilement (*Bapt.* 4). Tertullian also holds that the water is an instrumental means of sanctifying grace for both body and soul because it has been made holy by the Spirit.

90. The imposition and communion come right after baptism. Ferguson, *Baptism*, 348, writes, "[a]lthough Tertullian locates the coming of the Spirit at the postbaptismal imposition of hands (6; 8), he sometimes does not make this technical distinction and seems to imply the presence

ing us from the "sins of our original blindness," which blind us to God (*Bapt.* 1), (2) resurrecting our mind in Christ, in order to set our mind and body in a new trajectory toward God,[91] and (3) restoring the "likeness" of God that we lost when Adam lost the Holy Spirit by turning from God.[92] At each juncture of our Christian life, the Spirit leads us to Christ and through Christ to God.[93] Like John the Baptist from the Isenheim altarpiece who pointed to the crucified Lord with his Bible in hand, the Spirit prepares and perpetually points us to the truth of God "in the person of Christ" (*Res.* 44; cf. 8),[94] directing us to Christ initially in baptism and continually through the reading of Scripture (*Adv. Jud.* 9; *Val.* 3): "by clear lights upon words and meanings," the Spirit purges "the original documents of all darkness of ambiguity" (*Res.* 63).[95]

PARTICIPATION IN CHRIST: THE ILLUMINATION OF OUR SENSES AND INTELLECT

Zooming into Tertullian's commentary of 2 Cor 4:6 concerning illumination, we see how our body allows our soul to partake in Christ through our senses. The Father shines "in our hearts unto the illumination [*illuminationem*] of

---

of the Spirit in baptism. ... The distinction in *On Baptism* 6 seems to be Tertullian's own effort to rationalize the postbaptismal ceremonies."

91. Elsewhere, Tertullian argued that the act of faith in baptism regenerates the soul to see God: "when the soul embraces the faith, it is regenerated by this new birth in water and virtue celestial; the veil of its former corruption is removed and it at last perceives the full glory of the light" (*An.* 41.4).

92. Tertullian, for instance, wrote, "[i]n this way is man being restored to God, to the likeness of him who had aforetime been in God's image—the image had its actuality in the <man God> formed, the likeness <becomes actual> in eternity—for there is given back to him that spirit of God which of old he had received of God's breathing, but afterwards had lost through sin" (*Bapt.* 5).

93. We see God more clearly in the light of Christ as we grow in God's "likeness" (*similitudinem*), which is to become more "'holy' [*sancti*] just as Himself is 'holy' [*sanctus*]" (*Exh. cast.* 1), since without holiness, no one sees God (Heb 12:14; Matt 5:8).

94. "For, in Him [Christ] we perceive the rational, by which He taught, preached, and pointed out the way of salvation" (*An.* 16.4).

95. According to Wolfgand Bender, *Die Lehre über den heiligen Geist bei Tertullian* (Munich: Max Hueber Verlag, 1961), 115, Tertullian believed that the Spirit's work of illuminating and guiding us in faith today comes through the words of Scripture, which the Spirit taught and moved the apostles to write in the past: "Die eigentliche Aktivität des Geistes liegt für ihn zunächst mehr in der Vergangenheit, als er nämlich durch die Apostel lehrte. Was sie predigten, ist uns in der Heiligen Schrift überliefert. Durch die Worte der Schrift übt der Heilige Geist auch heute sein Amt als Hüter des Glaubens aus." According to Tertullian, "Only [the Paraclete] will both be called and revered as teacher by Christ. For [the Paraclete] speaks not from itself but the things commanded by Christ. [The Paraclete] is the only instructor, because [the Paraclete] alone is after Christ" (*Virg.* 1.7).

the knowledge of his glory in the person of Christ" by the Spirit through the reading and preaching of the gospel (*Res.* 44; cf. 2 Cor 4:3–6). Tertullian understood the "heart" (*cor*), where Christ dwells, as our physical organ.

> But the apostle would rather have "inner man" understood not as soul but as mind and intellect [*intellegi*], that is, not as the substance [*substantiam*] itself but as a flavor [*saporem*] of the substance: for in writing to the Ephesians that Christ should dwell in the inner man he meant that the Lord must be made intimate [*intimandum*] to their thoughts [or senses, *sensibus*]. In fact he added *By faith*, and *In your hearts*, and *In love*, setting down faith and love not as pertaining to the substance of the soul but to its content, while by saying *In your hearts* [*cordibus*], which are the substance of the flesh, he had already assigned even the inner man to the flesh by locating it in the heart. (*Res.* 40)[96]

The heart is the physical home of the soul (*An.* 15.4), where the soul's "directing faculty" or "ruling power" resides (*Res.* 40). While the body enables the soul to know and receive Christ through baptism and the word of Scripture, the intellect and the senses of the soul allow the light of God in Christ to come and dwell in the heart by faith. So the soul, on the one hand, participates in Christ and his suffering, "tribulations and distresses, tortures and executions," through the body (*Res.* 40), but the body, on the other hand, walks by the Spirit through the soul, which is renewed by the Spirit "in faith and doctrine from day to day" (*Res.* 40): "The flesh naturally follows the soul which is now wedded to the Spirit and, as part of the wedding dowry, it is no longer the slave of the soul but the servant of the Spirit" (*An.* 41.4).

In Tertullian's account, human beings are not either minds or bodies but embodied souls. So, we participate in God not only with our minds but also with our bodies. What the body undergoes *by* faith through baptism, communion, and reading Scripture also affects the way the mind knows and loves God. God illumines what we think and do in Christ, so we may know him personally and

96. In this passage, Tertullian was responding to the Gnostics who employed 2 Cor 4:16 to argue that the soul is saved, but the body is destroyed, so there is no resurrection of the body. Tertullian argues that Christ (the light that God shines) dwells in our hearts (*An.* 15.5). So he asks, "if that very light of God, that true light which is in the person of Christ, contains life in itself, and that life along with the light is deposited in flesh, is that flesh to perish in which life is deposited?" (*Res.* 44).

tacitly. Tertullian's take on the relationship of the body and mind will offer a way to reflect on our participatory actions in the economy illumination for chapter 9.

ORIGEN (c. 185–254)

According to Origen, the task of theology was only possible through illumination,[97] which sets the soul on the quest to God's likeness, a "contemplative communion" with God.[98] Similar to Clement, Origen believed that God gave us his image in the beginning, but we attain his likeness through contemplating God in the end.[99] Origen's view on contemplation adds another layer to our sketch of contemplative union thus far because it shows that our contemplative union with God flows from the Son's eternal contemplative union with the Father through the Spirit. Origen made a distinction between general illumination and special illumination that will allow us to compare the experience of illumination between the apostates and the church in chapter 9.[100] The church experiences special illumination initially

97. Contrary to Celsus, who argued that we could know God through logical deduction and analogy, Origen believed that we could know God through God alone (*Cels.* 7.44) because only God alone knows God (Williams, *Divine Sense*, 74). "The Father alone knows the Son, and the Son alone knows the Father (cf. Jn 10:15, 17:25), and the Holy Spirit alone searches out even the depths of God (cf. 1 Cor 2:10)" (*Princ.* 4.4.8). Henry Chadwick observes: "... for Origen Christianity was chiefly an illumination of the reason, which by itself and without revelation was incapable of knowing God, and growth in grace was a deeper and deeper apprehension of divine mysteries and of the Logos as he communicates himself more and more to the soul of man" (Oulton and Chadwick, *Alexandrian*, 185). While Origen acknowledged that Greek philosophy might give a glimpse of God, he confessed nevertheless: "We candidly admit that some Greek philosophers did know God, since 'God made it plain to them.' But they did not 'glorify Him as God or give thanks, but became vain in their reasonings, and professing themselves to be wise they became fools, and changed the glory of the incorruptible God for the likeness of an image of corruptible man, and of birds, and four-footed beasts, and creeping things" (*Cels.* 4.30). The English translation of *Contra Celsum* is from Oulton and Chadwick, *Alexandrian*, 185, and the Greek could be found in Origenes, *Contra Celsum*, ed. M. Marcovich (Leiden: Brill, 2001).

98. Peter W. Martens, *Origen and Scripture: The Contours of the Exegetical Life* (Oxford: Oxford University Press, 2012), 242.

99. Though it is "through the ceaseless work on our behalf of the Father, the Son and the Holy Spirit" that we are renewed "at every stage of our progress" to perfection, a face to face knowledge of God (*Princ.* 1.3.8), our "earnest efforts" are required (*Princ.* 3.6.1; English translation of *De principiis* [*Princ.*] is from Origen, *On First Principles*, trans. G. W. Butterworth [Notre Dame, IN: Ave Maria Press, 2013]). Origen went on to say, "while the possibility of attaining perfection was given to him in the beginning through the honor of the 'image,' he should in the end through the accomplishment of these works obtain for himself the perfect 'likeness'" (*Princ.* 3.6.1; cf. *Cels.* 4.30; *Comm. Rom.* 4.5).

100. General illumination gives all humanity the "possibility" to know God (*Princ.* 3.6.1; *Hom. Judic.* 1.1), but special illumination is only given to Christ's "Bride—that is to say, to the pure and perfect soul" (*Comm. Cant.* 1.1). Origen described special illumination as the "kisses of the Word of God Himself" or, more descriptively, as the Bride of Christ sharing his innermost thought in holy union: "So, when Christ leads a soul to understand His mind, she is said to be brought into

in baptism, when she receives the Spirit who sanctifies her to "become capable of receiving Christ afresh in his character of the righteousness of God" and sets her soul back on a journey to communion with God (*Princ.* 1.3.2–8).

ADAM'S SIN AND THE PROCESS TO PERFECTION

Humanity's journey to God took a detour when Adam sinned. His sin was not something that was passed on to us, but a "model" and "passage-way," in which "death" entered the world (*Comm. Rom.* 5.1.32; cf. *Comm. Jo.* 2.134).[101] Even after Adam's sin, we remain free to choose life with God or death, which is to live life apart from God (*Princ.* 1.5.5).[102] Origen personified death as a "tyrant" who (1) challenges the "rightful king" (Jesus) by infiltrating his kingdom via the "collusion" of the "first guard" (Adam) and (2) rules "over all those who had fallen away by a transgression similar to that of the first man" (*Comm. Rom.* 5.1.31). To follow the model of Adam is to dwell in the domain of death, separated from God,[103] but to follow the model of Christ in contemplating God is to partake in the domain of life with God (*Comm. Jo.* 2.18; *Comm. Rom.* 5.1.19–41; 5.5.3–9). This life leads to fellowship with the light of glory in the end, a perfect oneness with the Father like the Son in the Spirit.

DIVINE IMAGE AND LIKENESS

To understand this journey to perfection, we need to grasp what it means to be "according to the image and likeness of God" (κατ' εἰκόνα καὶ ὁμοίωσιν τοῦ θεοῦ or *ad imaginem et similitudinem dei*) is required (*Comm. Jo.* 2.148). Divine image and

---

the King's chamber, *in which are hid the treasures of His wisdom and knowledge*" (*Comm. Cant.* 1.5). All English translation of *Homiliae in Canticum* is from Origen, *The Song of Songs Commentary and Homilies*, trans. R. P. Lawson, ACW 26 (New York: Newman Press, 1956).

101. Origen, for example, wrote that the apostle Paul "has not said that sin came to all men, but 'into the world,' and death, on the other hand, not 'into the world,' but 'to all men,' and it did not 'come,' but 'passed through.' ... I think, therefore, that 'world' designates here certain earthly people, those who remain in an earthly way of life. On the other hand he calls 'men' those who are already beginning to know and understand that they have been made in the image of God. He says that sin had come into those who are called 'the world,' that is to say, those who are earthly" (*Comm. Rom.* 5.1.22). The English translation of *Commentarii in Romanos* is from Origen, *Commentary on the Epistle to the Romans Books 1–5*, trans. Thomas P. Scheck, FC 103 (Washington: Catholic University of America Press, 2001).

102. Human beings only have a potential to be good by virtue of their choice. Only God, the Father, Son, and Spirit, is essentially and perfectly good, holy, and wise, but all rational and created beings, whether humans or angels, are good, holy, and wise accidentally, in as far as they choose God, the source of all goodness, holiness, and wisdom (*Princ.* 1.6.2; 4.4.8).

103. Henri Crouzel, *Origen*, trans. A. S. Worrall (San Francisco: Harper & Row, 1989), 210.

likeness form the basis and *telos* for knowing God, which is "the same thing as union [with God] ... for knowledge is love."[104] Origen differentiated the image from the likeness of God in humanity (*Cels.* 4.30; cf. *Comm. Rom.* 4.5), the former being what we are endowed with in creation to know God and the latter being what we will become in the end through contemplating God (*Princ.* 3.6.1). "The way from the 'after-the-image' to the likeness is the road of spiritual progress."[105] Those who progress in the likeness of God are those who continuously follow Christ in contemplating God, but those who turn away from God are becoming what is contrary to nature, becoming like the "image of the devil" (*Hom. Gen.* 1.13). A closer look at this journey from being in God's image to his likeness will bring to light for us the two types of illumination and participation in Christ.

Origen argued that God not only created our minds in his image but "also continuously sustained the activity of thought."[106] Connecting general participation with general illumination,[107] Origen believed that, as we live and move and have our being in God, we think and have our every thought in the Word of God (Acts 17:28).

> That the activity of the Father and the Son is to be found both in saints and in sinners is clear from the fact that all rational beings are partakers of the word of God, that is, of reason, and so have implanted within them some seeds, as it were, of wisdom and righteousness, which is Christ. ... Christ is 'in the heart' of all men, in virtue of his being the word or reason, by sharing in which men are rational. (*Princ.* 1.3.6)

These "seeds ... of wisdom and righteousness" are what God has implanted in our soul when he created us in his image. For our mind to be made in his image is for it to be made to participate in Christ, the image of God, as a *word* (λογικός) of the Word (λόγου) of God (*Comm. Jo.* 2.114).[108]

---

104. Crouzel, *Origen*, 99.

105. Crouzel, *Origen*, 97.

106. Martens, *Origen*, 73.

107. In *Homiliae in Judices* 1.1, Origen preached that the light of Christ is distributed to all rational beings: "For the light of the world created by God is one, which shines for all in common and equally" (Origen, *Homilies on Judges*, trans. Elizabeth A. Dively Lauro, FC 119, (Washington: Catholic University of America Press, 2010). All rational beings are illuminated because they all participate in the Word: "God the Father bestows on all the gift of existence; and a participation in Christ, in virtue of his being the word or reason, makes them rational" (*Princ.* 1.3.8).

108. Our mind mirrors and resembles God's mind by virtue of our participation in Christ: "For as the word in us is the messenger of what the mind perceives, so the Word of God, since he

Origen was careful never to refer to humans as the image of God, but only "according to the image of God," because the Word alone is God's image. He illustrated this distinction with the two senses of image in ordinary speech: "Sometimes the term 'image' is applied to an object painted or carved on some material, such as wood or stone. Sometimes a child is said to be the image of its parent, when the likeness of the parent's features is in every respect faithfully reproduced in the child" (*Princ.* 1.2.6).[109] The first sense expresses the way the image of God is in us; the second is analogous to Christ because God's image in Christ "preserves the unity of nature and substance common to a father and a son" (*Princ.* 1.2.6).[110] However, the begetting of the Son is unique in that it "is an eternal and everlasting begetting, as brightness is begotten from light (cf. Wis 7:26; Heb 1:3). For [Jesus] does not become Son in an external way through the adoption of the Spirit (Rom 8:15), but is Son by nature" (*Princ.* 1.2.4).[111] Jesus is God's image by his divinity; we are God's image, insofar as we participate and reflect Christ.[112]

In contrast to Irenaeus' (*Epid.* 22), Origen follows Clement and believs that our "inner man, invisible, incorporeal, incorruptible, and immortal," rather than our bodily form, is created in the image of the λόγος (Word, *Comm. Jo.* 2.114; *Hom. Gen.* 1.13). Our inner man is our mind, our faculty of reasoning, which enables us to "perceive and understand God" in two ways (*Princ.* 4.4.9). First, since only like can know like, our mind (as created in God's image) is like God because it can reason and understand like God in a finite way (*Princ.*

has known the Father, reveals the Father whom he has known, because no creature can come into contact with him without a guide" (*Comm. Jo.* 1.277). Crouzel, *Origen*, 94, argues that being in God's image, for Origen, "is ... 'our principle substance', the very basis of our nature" because "man is defined, at the deepest level of his being, by his relation to God."

109. So participants share in the attributes of God, but remain distinct in their essence from God: "'Just as substance of ointment is one thing and its odour another, so Christ is one thing and his participants another' (*De Prin.* 2.6.6, GCS v. 146.2–3; cf. Plotinus, *Enn.* vi.4.13)" (Russell, *Deification*, 148; cf. 152).

110. The Son is the "image of God's substance" (*Princ.* 1.2.8). That is, the Father is light, and the "only-begotten Son ... is the brightness of this light, proceeding from God without separation, as brightness from light, and lightening the whole creation" (*Princ.* 1.2.7).

111. As the Father is light, the "only-begotten Son ... is the brightness of this light, proceeding from God without separation, as brightness from light, and lightening the whole creation" (*Princ.* 1.2.7). Contrary to Arius's reading of Origen, there was never a time that Christ was not. For example, Origen writes, "God was always the Father of his only-begotten Son, who was born indeed of him and draws his being from him, but is yet without any beginning" (*Princ.* 1.2.2), and "there was no time when the beginning was without the Word" (*Comm. Jo.* 2.130).

112. Similarly, Crouzel, *Origen*, 95, writes, "The 'after-the-image' is ... participation in the Son."

1.1.7; cf. Plato, *Phaed.* 78 B).[113] Like our bodily senses, which allow us to experience the physical world because its physical nature corresponds to the world, our mind is our "divine sense" (*sensum diuinum*, *Princ.* 1.1.9),[114] which enables us to sense God who is a "simple intellectual existence," without "any kind of body" or parts, but "Oneness throughout, and the mind and fount from which originates all intellectual existence or mind" (*Princ.* 1.1.6), because "there is a certain affinity between the [human] mind and God, of whom the mind is an intellectual image" (*Princ.* 1.1.7).

Second, God deposited his first light in our mind. We receive general illumination by virtue of being made in his image. Jesus is the light of God because he is the image of God by nature, light from light (*Princ.* 1.2.6). Since we are made in Christ, we have the first deposit of God's light in our very being.[115] Henri Crouzel, for instance, writes, "all knowledge of God is revelation, but the first of these revelations is the one God gave us when he created us in his image: in this 'after-the-image', which is the most profound element of our being, we find God."[116] Being created in God's image is that which connects us to God in general.[117]

The likeness of God is the purpose for which God has made us in his image. Similar to Tertullian (*Bapt.* 5), the "original likeness" does not refer to what humanity was originally, but what they were originally made to become: one with the Father and the Son in the Spirit. "For [Jesus] had already petitioned the Father for his disciples that the original likeness might be restored in them when he says: 'Father,' grant 'that just as you and I are one so also they may be one in us" (*Hom. Gen.* 1.13; cf. John 17:21).[118] From eternity, the Father

---

113. This is probably why, unlike Tertullian, Origen not only distinguished the bodily senses from the "sense of the mind" (*Princ.* 1.1.7), but also believed that the mind's senses and its subject matter (i.e., God) are superior to the bodily senses and its subject matters (i.e., material things).

114. The Latin text is from Origène, *Traité des principes*, *Livres* 1–2, ed. Henri Crouzel and Manlio Simonetti, SC 252 (Paris: Les Éditions du Cerf, 1978).

115. The Son is the image of the Father because the one who sees the Son sees the Father (*Hom. Gen.* 1.13; cf. John 14:9).

116. Crouzel, *Origen*, 96

117. If knowledge is "the same thing as union [with God] ... for knowledge is love" (Crouzel, *Origen*, 99), then this first revelation, which gives us the initial knowledge of God, is what enables us to commune with God.

118. The English translation of *Homiliae in Genesim* is from Origen, *Homilies on Genesis and Exodus*, trans. Ronald E. Heine, FC 71 (Washington: Catholic University of America Press, 1981). Similarly, Origen wrote, "the likeness of the Father and the Son has been promised to

and the Son are one in the Spirit, one in mind and will. The Father and Son, Origen wrote, "are two distinct existences, but one in mental unity, in agreement, and in identity of will" (*Cels.* 8.12).

On the one hand, the Son is the object of the Father's inmost thought and affection. The reason why the Son is the image of the Father in his substance and divinity is because he is eternally generated from the mind and will of the Father.

> For if 'all things that the Father doeth, these also doeth the Son likewise' (Jn 5:19), then in this very fact that the Son does all things just as the Father does, the Father's image is reproduced in the Son, whose birth from the Father is as it were an act of his will proceeding from the mind. And on this account my own opinion is that an act of the Father's will ought to be sufficient to ensure the existence of what he wills; for in willing he uses no other means than that which is produced by the deliberations of his will. It is in this way, then, that the existence of the Son also is begotten by him. (*Princ.* 1.2.6)

The Father, on the other hand, is the "sole object" of the Son's "desire and thought."[119] The reason why the Son is eternally one with the Father is because he ceaselessly contemplates the Father. "By being 'with *the* God' he always continues to be 'God.' But he would not have this if he were not with God, and he would not remain God if he did not continue in unceasing contemplation of the depth of the Father" (*Comm. Jo.* 2.18). In eternity, the Father and the Son were conscious of nothing else, but one another in the Spirit.

This contemplative communion of love and knowledge between the Father and the Son in the Spirit is what God invites and calls us to partake of in the end. It is reserved for the end when we shall be like Christ, who is one with the Father in the Spirit. We will become one with the Father in the Spirit because we will know and be known by the Father like the Son (*Princ.* 3.6.1; cf. John 17:21, 24). If being made in God's image is what causally connects us to God, our Creator, then becoming God's likeness is our eschatological oneness with God, our Father. Before moving to the final point of this

---

the saints, so that as the Father and the Son are one in themselves, so, too, the saints may be one in them" (*Princ.* 3.6.1).

119. Martens, *Origen*, 229.

section, it's important to note that whether it is general or special participation in Christ and through Christ with God, the creature-Creator distinction is never blurred: "'Just as substance of ointment is one thing and its odour another, so Christ is one thing and his participants another' (*De Prin.* 2.6.6, GCS v. 146.2–3; cf. Plotinus, *Enn.* 6.4.13)."[120] Our oneness with God is not by nature, but by grace, which perfects our nature.

SPECIAL LIGHT FOR THE JOURNEY TO LIKENESS

According to Peter Martens, Origen referred to this oneness with God at the end as our "original loving and contemplative communion with God," which we "fleetingly experienced in this life when [we] studied Scripture."[121] The study of Scripture allows us to contemplate God in the light of Christ through the Spirit until God is our all in all.

To contemplate is to fix our inner eye attentively on the person and works (*operum*) of the incarnate Son revealed in Scripture, rather than our feelings (*sensus*, *Princ.* 2.6.1), to train and strengthen our mind's eye to see God (*Comm. Cant.* 1.4; *Princ.* 1.2.7; *Cels.* 6.67). Similar to Jesus who eternally participates in communion with the Father through contemplation, we actively partake of this communion with God through contemplating him in the Son through Scripture (*Comm. Jo.* 2.18).[122] Our contemplation not only unites us to God, but also transforms us to his likeness because it is spiritual "food" (*cibus*) that nurtures our soul to grow into the likeness of God (*Princ.* 2.11.7).[123] As the saying goes, "you are what you eat," so in a spiritual sense, we become what we contemplate: "For if man, made according to the image of God, contrary to nature by beholding [*intuens*] the image of the devil has been

---

120. Russell, *Deification*, 148, cf. 152.

121. Martens, *Origen*, 242.

122. According to John Behr, *The Way to Nicaea*, vol. 1 of *Formation of Christian Theology* (Crestwood, NY: St. Vladimir's Seminary Press, 2001), 193, this communion through contemplation also extends to us through adoption: "The begetting of Wisdom by the Father is not a one-time act, somehow 'before' the beginning of time, but a continuous begetting, as it is also by the continuous contemplation of the Father that the Son participates in divinity (cf. *ComJn.* 2.18). It is also a relationship that extends beyond the Only-Begotten, who alone is Son by nature, to all those who receive the Spirit of adoption."

123. Even in the state of perfection, Origen believed we need the "food" of contemplation: "I think that the mind [*mentem*], when it has come to perfection, still feeds on appropriate and suitable food [*cibis*] in a measure which can neither admit of want nor of superfluity. But in all respects this food [*cibus*] must be understood to be the contemplation [*theoria*] and understanding of God [*intellectus dei*]" (*Princ.* 2.11.7).

made like him by sin, much more by beholding [*intuens*] the image of God, according to whose likeness he has been made by God, he will receive that form, which was given to him by nature, through the Word and his power" (*Hom. Gen.* 1.13).[124] The soul feasts on the Father through contemplating the Son in the Spirit. To contemplate God on earth is to set oneself on the journey to communion with God in heaven, until God is all in all—all that we contemplate and desire (*Princ.* 3.6.3).[125]

To contemplate God on the journey to his likeness is only possible through special illumination. Special illumination is a lamp unto our feet and a light onto our path to God. This "light" or "spiritual power," which enables us to "see clearly the truth of all things or to know God himself who is called the truth" (*Princ.* 1.1.1; 1.2.9), comes through participating in Jesus Christ (*Princ.* 1.1.1).[126] Outside of the special light of Christ, we would be in the dark to God's nature (*Cels.* 6.67; *Comm. Jo.* 161–62). Though it's true that all rational beings are created in the image of God, only those who are sanctified in the Spirit are truly rational (λογικός or *rationabilia*)[127] because they do "the works of light"

124. The Latin text of *Homiliae in Genesim* is found in Origène, *Homélies sur la Genèse*, ed. Louis Doutreleau, SC 7 bis (Paris: Les Éditions du Cerf, 2011).

125. Martens, *Origen*, 229. This journey of following Christ back to God is described "in terms of the doctrinal/ethical distinction" because "[i]t is necessary ... that among Christians be found 'not only the perfection of faith and knowledge, but also that of deeds and works'" (Martens, *Origen*, 214). The end of the journey is to behold God in the face to face encounter with Christ (Martens, *Origen*, 241).

126. It is through the Son's "brightness that the nature of the light itself is known and experienced" (*Princ.* 1.2.7). The Son is "the light of the spiritual world because he shines on those who are rational and intellectual, that their mind may see its proper visions" (*Comm. Jo.* 1.161). To see this light is to have the mind of Christ. "So, when Christ leads a soul to understand His mind, she is said to be brought into the King's chamber, *in which are hid the treasures of His wisdom and knowledge*" (*Comm. Cant.* 1.5). To have the mind of Christ or to hear the "mouth" of Christ speak to us directly is to be illumined. "And let us understand that by the 'mouth' of the Bridegroom is meant the power by which He enlightens the mind and, as by some word of love addressed to her—if so she deserve to experience the presence of power so great—makes plain whatever is unknown and dark to her. And this is the truer, closer, holier kiss, which is said to be granted by the Bridegroom-Word of God to the Bride—that is to say, to the pure and perfect soul; it is of this happening that the kiss, which we give one to another in church at the holy mysteries, is a figure" (*Comm. Cant.* 1.1).

127. This is a special participation in Christ that only the saints experience: "For if we think of the Word [λόγον] in the beginning, the Word [λόγον] who is with God, the Word [λόγον] who is God, perhaps we shall be able to say that he alone who participates in this Word [λόγον], insofar as he is such, is 'rational' [λογικόν]. Consequently, we could also say that the saint alone is rational [λογικός]" (*Comm. Jo.* 2.114; cf. 2.110–111; *Hom. Gen.* 1.13). The Greek text of *Commentarii in evangelium Joannis* is from Origène, *Commentaire sur saint Jean, Livre* 1–5, ed. Cécile Blanc, SC 120 (Paris: Les Éditions du Cerf, 1996).

(*Comm. Jo.* 2.158; 2.115) and participate in the life of Christ, which becomes in them the "foundation of the light of knowledge" (*Comm. Jo.* 2.156). This life leads us to be one with God because it is a life onto God (*Comm. Jo.* 2.115).

This life, Origen clarified, "is not that common to rational and irrational beings. It is instead the life which is added to the Word which is completed in us when a share from the first Word is received" (*Comm. Jo.* 2.156; cf. 2.128). It is added to the Word in the incarnation (*Comm. Jo.* 2.115; 20.369–370), when he emptied himself and took on flesh, no longer "dwell[ing] only in light unapproachable and abid[ing] in the form of God," so the soul may perceive and receive "the Word of God according to the measure of its capacity and faith" (*Comm. Cant.* 1.4). The life of the incarnate Word is "the light of men, which shines in the darkness" (*Comm. Jo.* 20.370). The soul receives this life in the incarnate Word, when the Spirit unveils the soul to the "fragrance" of the divine substance of Word in the written word of God.[128]

The illuminating work of the Spirit, unlike the Father and Son, takes place only in the saints (*Princ.* 1.3.5)—"the pure and perfect soul[s]" (*Comm. Cant.* 1.1).[129] A "share in the Holy Spirit is possessed ... by the saints alone" because "'[n]o man can say that Jesus is the Lord except in the Holy Spirit'" (*Princ.* 1.3.7). If general illumination is the means of general participation that rational beings have by virtue of being made in God's image, then special illumination comes from special participation in the Spirit and, through the Spirit, in Christ anew (*Princ.* 1.3.8).[130] We are born in the image of Christ, but only

128. In *Homiliae in Canticum* 1.4, Origen employed an example from the sense of taste and olfactory sense rather than the sense of sight to illustrate how the soul, when it is illumined, participates in the life of the Word: "when souls have thus drawn the Word of God to themselves, and have ingrafted Him into their minds and understanding, and have experienced the pleasantness of His sweetness and odour, when they have received the fragrance of His ointments and have grasped at last the reason for his coming, the motives of the Redemption and Passion, and the love whereby He, the Immortal, went *even to the death of the cross* for the salvation of all men, then these maiden souls, attracted by all this as by the odours of a divine and ineffable perfume and being filled with vigour and complete alacrity, run after Him and hasten to the odour of His sweetness, not at a slow pace, nor with lagging steps, but swiftly and with all the speed they can; even as did he who said: *I so run, that I may obtain.*" Elsewhere, he added, "people who are in Christ are a good odour of Christ in every place" (*Comm. Jo.* 20.415). Translation is from Origen, *Commentary on the Gospel of John Books 13–32*, trans. Ronald E. Heine, FC89 (Washington: Catholic University of America Press, 1993).

129. That is, the Spirit does not dwell "in all men, nor in those who are flesh, but in those whose 'earth has been renewed'" (*Princ.* 1.3.7).

130. Cf.: "For if, by participating in him, we arise and are enlightened, and perhaps also are shepherded or ruled, it is clear that we also become rational in a divine manner when he destroys in us all that is irrational and dead insofar as he is 'Word' and 'resurrection'" (*Comm. Jo.* 1.268).

mature into his likeness when we receive and participate in the sanctifying presence of the Spirit in baptism (*Princ.* 1.3.7). The Spirit sanctified us to receive "Christ afresh in his character of ... righteousness" and to "obtain in addition the gift of wisdom" to purge us from "all stains of pollution and ignorance," so we may be worthy of life with God (*Princ.* 1.3.8). Thus, "it is impossible to become partaker of the Father and the Son without the Holy Spirit" (*Princ.* 2.7.4). Unlike general illumination, those who are illuminated in Christ by participating in the sanctifying presence of the Spirit are the ones who perform "the works of light and know the light of knowledge" (*Comm. Jo.* 2.158). In special illumination, the progress in virtue and knowledge of God are inseparable (*Cels.* 6.369; 7.44).[131]

Scripture is vital for the soul on the journey to the likeness of God. To devote oneself to the study of Scripture is to turn the eyes of the soul from things below to things above.[132] In Scripture, the divine authors speak to the soul.[133] Through reading Scripture, the soul meets the Word (*Comm. Matt.* 12.37) and is united to the Word (*Hom. Gen.* 10.5), and through the Word, partakes in communion with the Father in the end.[134] But the soul is not able to hear and be united to the Word without the Spirit who removes the veil and the obstacles that harden our hearts to perceive the spiritual meaning of Scripture (*Comm. Jo.* 13.110). Thus, "all knowledge of the Father, when the Son reveals him, is made known to us through the Holy Spirit" (*Princ.* 1.3.4). The Spirit unveils the Word to us in the written word (*Comm. Cant.* 1.3; *Princ.* 1.1.2; 1.3.1), so the Word may shine "'in our hearts to illuminate the knowledge of his glory' (2 Cor 4.6)" (*Fr. Luc.* 151).[135] With unveiled face, we behold the glory of the Word and are transformed into his likeness from glory to glory (2 Cor 3:18). This journey from image to likeness begins in contemplating the Father in the light of the Son

131. Williams, *Divine Sense*, 75, writes, "there can be no progress apart from knowledge of God and purity of heart is the prerequisite of such knowledge."

132. Martens, *Origen*, 99–100.

133. Martens, *Origen*, 182–83.

134. Martens, *Origen*, 224–25.

135. Translation from Origen, *Homilies on Luke*, trans. Joseph T. Lienhard, FC 95 (Washington: Catholic University of America Press, 2009). As the Word of God, Christ illuminates us to the mind of God. "For as the word in us is the messenger of what the mind perceives, so the Word of God, since he has known the Father, reveals the Father whom he has known, because no creature can come into contact with him without a guide" (*Comm. Jo.* 1.277).

through the Spirit in reading Scripture until the soul reaches its terminus of contemplating God immediately in the face of the Son through the Spirit in eternity.

CONCLUSION

The ante-Nicene theologians filled my sketch of the economy of illumination from 2 Cor 3:14–4:6 with the nature of God, from which light flows and transfers us into light. God is light, intelligible, and communicative in nature, and the light of every mind, so it is in God that our mind moves, acts, and has its being. To participate in God is to share in the life, virtue, and mind of God and also in the incorruptibility, love, and knowledge between the Father and the Son in the Spirit. Participation in God always transpires in the Son through the Spirit because through his two hands, the Son and the Spirit, the Father baptizes us in light so we may see light. Our theologians uncovered an aspect of baptism that we may have missed in Scripture. In Eph 5:15, for example, Paul employed a "baptismal hymn" to suggest that illumination comes through baptism: "Awake, O sleeper, and arise from the dead, and Christ will shine on you" (ESV).[136] Baptism is illumination because it is where we receive the Spirit who cleanses, unveils, and enables us to participate in the light of the Son, light from light, for communion with the Father, the source of light.

Concerning the nature of light, our theologians diverged. Clement and Origen, on the one hand, viewed light as the power of sight. It is in his light that we see light: we see God in the presence and power of God (Ps 36:9). Irenaeus and Tertullian, on the other hand, understood light as the incarnation of the Son, the light that illuminates the world (John 1:9), because the humanity of the Son allows us to behold God. The Son is the self-manifestation of the Father's truth and love in bodily form. So, to see God's truth and love in the person and work of the incarnate Son is to be illumined by the Father through the Spirit (John 6:45).

However, our theologians can agree on the dictum that only like can know like because to see God we need to be like God.[137] They were not mindlessly

136. F. F. Bruce, *The Epistle to the Colossians, to Philemon, and to the Ephesians*, NICNT (Grand Rapids: Eerdmans, 1984), 376–377; Ferguson, *Baptism*, 316–317; and Andrew T. Lincoln, *Ephesians*, WBC 42 (Grand Rapids: Zondervan, 1990), 331–333.

137. "Like indeed attracts like; so it is that what is holy attracts Him who is the source of holiness, who properly speaking is called Light" (*Paed.* 6.1.28). What makes us holy, as God is

going with the Platonic trend of their day, but they employed it to draw out a truth revealed in Scripture—namely, knowing God requires us to be holy *like* God. For without holiness, no one can see God (Heb 12:14; Matt 5:8). To see God is to become like God in Christ through the Spirit because we have lost our divine likeness in Adam when he disobeyed and lost the Holy Spirit, but we are made holy and become like God again in Christ who restored the Spirit back to us. Knowledge and transformation to Christlikeness go hand in hand. In chapter 8, I will highlight this dual process, involving knowledge and transformation, in the economy of illumination because becoming like Christ is both the condition and the fruit of knowing God.

Irenaeus and Tertullian also opened us to the vital roles of the body and obedience in illumination, which I will apply to my idea of our "participatory actions" in the economy of illumination for chapter 9. Our embodiment of faith in everyday life illumines us to see and experience God's power and goodness *personally*. Our knowledge of God is not merely intellectual, but personal, covenantal, and tacit. It is a knowledge that we develop by our habits and practice of obedience. As the practice of sin and unbelief blinds us from truth, God illumines us to himself *in* our practice and habits of following Christ: "to follow the light is to perceive the light" (*Haer*. 4.14.1; cf. *Paed*. 1.1.2; 1.12.99; *Comm. Jo*. 2.158). And as we continue and remain in light, we will experience fuller and greater illumination (*Haer.* 4.29.1). We will know the truth, and the truth will set us free (John 8:32). The role of the body, for Tertullian, is *essential* for the mind to know and unite to Christ because the mind and body are two modes of being that work together to enable us to experience and know God in Christ. Tertullian also left insights to ponder on the way God opens our minds through the experience of reading and obeying Scripture and implications to why the body is necessary for the beatific vision because we will see Christ as he is with the eyes of our resurrected body (1 John 3:2).

---

holy, is the indwelling Spirit who purifies us from sin, gives us our second birth, and adopts us to become children of light (*Paed.* 6.1.26). Clement referred to the Spirit's presence in us as "an admixture of eternal sunlight, giving us the power to see the eternal light" (*Paed.* 6.1.28). The Spirit's baptism is "one grace of enlightenment, that we no longer are in the same state as before we were cleansed" (*Paed.* 6.1.30).

4

ECONOMY OF ILLUMINATION IN ORTHODOX TRADITION

"[I]n the eyes of many commentators, Orthodoxy quite simply *is* patristic Christianity."[1] For the Orthodox tradition, "the past constantly flows towards the future and, in so doing, lives in the present."[2] This means, Andrew Louth explains, the words of the patristics are living and "infallible authorities" for the Orthodox Church today.[3] Louth is well aware that the fathers "disagree with one another over all sorts of issues" but suggests, "we should beware of trying to iron out the differences between them. What we should hear from the chorus of the Fathers is a rich harmony, not a thin unison."[4] The present chapter will listen to some of the leading voices in this rich harmony, including Athanasius, the Cappadocian fathers, and Cyril of Alexandria, and then round it out with the retrieving echoes of Gregory of Palamas and Dumitru Staniloae. There is a thread from the ante-Nicene fathers (who viewed the economy of illumination as "the paternal light" shining in the "resplendent flesh" of the incarnate Son and through the "power of sight" from the Holy Spirit in contemplative union) running through our Nicene, medieval, and modern theologians from the East. Our theologians from the Orthodox tradition add to the account of the economy of illumination I have sketched thus far by including the inseparable operations of the triune God and the relationship between God *in se* (the being of God in himself) and God *pro nobis* (the activity of God in the world)

1. Augustine Casidy, "Church Fathers and the Shaping of Orthodox Theology," in *Cambridge Companion to Orthodox Christian Theology*, ed. Mary B. Cunningham and Elizabeth Theokritoff (Cambridge: Cambridge University Press, 2008), 167 (emphasis original).

2. Andrew Louth, *Introducing Eastern Orthodox Theology* (Downers Grove, IL: IVP Academic, 2013), 13.

3. Louth, *Orthodox Theology*, 13.

4. Louth, *Orthodox Theology*, 13.

because the economy of illumination is the inseparable operations of God that flow from the being of God to draw us from darkness to light.[5]

ATHANASIUS OF ALEXANDRIA (C. 297–373)

Scripture reveals God is one in three (Deut 6:4; Matt 28:19). How does the oneness of God correlate to the three operations of the persons of God in the economy of illumination? And why is communion with God in the Son permanent after the fall, but was not in Adam before the fall? Athanasius's account offers us implications to these questions. According to Khaled Anatolios, Athanasius viewed the relationship between God and creation in a "radical model of participation. God 'gives' by being participated in, so that all things subsist in him and through him, by partaking God."[6] This may at first sound like panentheism, which views the world to be "ontologically implicit in, and part of, the divine nature," turning *creatio ex nihilo* into *creatio ex Deo*.[7] If we follow Athanasius's train of thought, however, it is profoundly different. Anatolios explains, "Athanasius can rely precisely on his ontology to make the point that whereas our whole being is a participation in God, our nature is still absolutely distinct and 'external' to God, not because we have any 'structure' which is 'of itself' independent of God, but because we participate in God 'from nothing.'"[8] God has made us "out of nothing" (ἐξ οὐκ ὄντων); we have life and light from him, so when

5. Gregory Nazianzen had this to say of God's nature as light: "'God is light ... he is in the world of thought, what the sun is in the world of sense, presenting himself to our minds in proportion as we are cleansed ... himself contemplating and comprehending himself, and pouring himself out upon what is external to him. That light, I mean, which is contemplated in the Father and the Son and the Holy Spirit, whose riches is their unity of nature, and the one outleaping of their brightness'" (*Or.* 40.5 quoted in Lewis Ayres, *Nicaea and Its Legacy: An Approach to Fourth-Century Trinitarian Theology* [Oxford: Oxford University Press, 2004], 248. Cf. *Or.* 31.3); and Basil of Caesarea writes concerning the light of the Son, "'What the visible light is to the eye, God the Word is to the mind'" (*Eun.* 2.16.10–19 quoted in Timothy P. McConnell, *Illumination in Basil of Caesarea's Doctrine of the Holy Spirit* [Minneapolis: Fortress, 2014], 11).

6. Khaled Anatolios, "The Soteriological Significance of Christ's Humanity in St. Athanasius," *St. Vladimir's Theological Quarterly* 40:4 (1996): 272. Athanasius, for instance, wrote, "'there is nothing existing or created which did not come into being and subsist in him and through him (οὐδὲν ἐστι τῶν ὄντων καὶ γινομένων ὃ μὴ ἐν αὐτῷ καὶ δι' αὐτοῦ γέγονε καὶ ἕστηκεν)'" (*C. Gent.* 42 quoted by Anatolios, "Soteriological," 271–272).

7. John W. Cooper, *Panentheism: The Other God of the Philosophers* (Grand Rapids: Baker Academic, 2006), 63.

8. Khaled Anatolios, *Athanasius: The Coherence of His Thought* (New York: Routledge, 1998), 209; cf. 108. See also Andrew Louth, *The Origins of the Christian Mystical Tradition: From Plato to Denys*, 2nd ed. (Oxford: Oxford University Press, 2007), 73–74.

we turned from him, we return "to nothingness" (εἰς τὸ μὴ εἶναι [*Inc.* 4]) and "darkness" (σκότος [*C. Gent.* 7; cf. 9]). But out of his great love, God turns to us who turned from him to return us to his light (*Inc.* 54).[9] To return to light and be illumined is to receive and partake in the Son who secured for us the grace of the Spirit, which he received on our behalf as man, so he may give the Spirit permanently to us as God.[10]

CREATION AND PARTICIPATION IN LIGHT

On the doctrine of creation, we will find continuity and discontinuity between Athanasius and his Alexandrian predecessors. Athanasius follows Clement and Origen, who employed the platonic dictum that *only like can know like* (*Princ.* 1.1.7; cf. Plato, *Phaed.* 78 B), to establish that God made us in the image of his Son for Θεὸν θεωρίας, the contemplation of God (*Inc.* 4; *C. Gent.* 2; cf. *Protr.* 10.80; 4.55; cf. Cicero, *Nat. d.* 2.140; Ovid, *Metam.* 1.85–86).[11] Athanasius departed from them, however, with his doctrine of *creatio ex nihilo*, which was largely unknown at the time of Origen and "emerged only slowly and uncertainly in early Christian theology."[12] This doctrine allowed Athanasius to demonstrate how God is outside

---

9. Unless noted otherwise, the English translation and the Greek text for both *Contra Gentes* (*C. Gent.*) and *De Incarnatione* (*Inc.*) is from Athanasius, *Contra Gentes and De Incarnatione*, ed. and trans. Robert W. Thomson [London: Oxford University Press, 1971]).

10. Khaled Anatolios, *Retreiving Nicaea: The Development and Meaning of Trinitarian Doctrine* (Grand Rapids: Baker Academic, 2011), 136. Cf. Norman Russell, *The Doctrine of Deification in Greek Patristic Tradition* (Oxford: Oxford University Press, 2004), 172, 182.

11. Anatolios, *Retreiving Nicaea*, 102, writes, "The goal of human existence, achieved in Christ, is true knowledge (*gnōsis*) of God. See also idem, *Coherence*, 57. According to A. Louth, "The Concept of the Soul in Athanasius' Contra Gentes—De Incarnatione," *Studia Patristica* 13 (1975): 228, *De Incarnatione* and *Contra Gentes* offer two different perspectives of the fall and redemption: the former is "historical," but the later "gives an account of man's fall from a state of contemplation to a state subject to sensual pleasures. ... Redemption is likewise different: restoration of pure vision in *Contra Gentes* by purification (8, 34), salvation by the intervention of the Word incarnate in a world ruled by death and corruption in *De Incarnatione* (4, 6, 7, 13)." However, I believe the two works complement each other because one of the main points of *De Incarnatione* was to show that Jesus became man, in order to return us to the contemplation of God (*Inc.* 15–16; 54). See also the recent study by Kevin Douglas Hill, *Athanasius and the Holy Spirit: The Development of His Early Pneumatology* (Minneapolis: Fortress, 2016), 28–30, which notes the important parallel between the restoration of incorruptibility and the knowledge of God around the context of Athanasius' seminal statement, "αὐτὸς γὰρ ἐνανθρώπησεν, ἵνα ἡμεῖς θεοποιηθῶμεν" (*Inc.* 54).

12. Louth, *Mystical Tradition*, 73. Louth adds, "Neither for Plato nor for Origen were souls created: they were pre-existent and immortal" (Louth, *Mystical Tradition*, 74). For Origen, the soul was created before time (*Princ.* 2.1.1; 2.9.2). The doctrine of *creation ex nihilo*, however, may already have its inception in Christian thought as early as Tertullian who believed that the soul was given at conception (*An.* 11.6).

and inside creation simultaneously. Building on Irenaeus who argued that God is unknowable in his essence, but knowable in his love,[13] Athanasius held that God is outside of creation in his "essence," but present in his "power" (*Inc.* 17).[14]

The Son is the power of God, so all creation came into being by participating in the Son through the Spirit (*Ep. Serap.* 1.24; *C. Gent.* 2; 42; *Inc.* 1; 3).[15] Athanasius' view of participation consists of an asymmetrical relationship of giving and receiving between the Creator, who is partaken, and creation, which partakes.[16] Human beings, however, are unique among creation as they are "given a special order of grace, which is a rational participation in the Word."[17] Athanasius explains,

> And among these creatures, of all those on earth he had special pity for the human race, and seeing that by the definition of its own existence it would be unable to persist for ever, he gave it an added grace [χαριζόμενος], not simply creating men like all irrational animals on the earth, but making them in his own image and giving them also a share in the power of his own Word [μεταδοὺς αὐτοῖς καὶ τῆς τοῦ ἰδίου Λόγοθ δυνάμεως], so that having as it were shadows of the Word [Λόγου] and being made rational [λογικοί], they might be able to remain in felicity and live the true life in paradise, which is really that of the saints. (*Inc.* 3)

Athanasius understands "added grace" as "a share in the power of his own Word,"[18] that enables us to behold God (*Inc.* 3; cf. *C. Gent.* 2) because he follows Clement, who saw the power of Christ as the "power to see" God (*Protr.* 11.87).[19] "For [humanity] was created in order to see God and be enlight-

---

13. Athanasius also took this insight and developed it further to counter the Arians, who maintained that there was a time when the Son was not, by arguing that the very reason why the Son is able to make the Father known and present with us is because he shares in the realm of divinity (Anatolios, *Coherence*, 109–16).

14. Anatolios, *Coherence*, 46, 104.

15. See Anatolios, "Christ's Humanity," 270. However, if we must speak of the Son's participation in the Father, then it is in the "essence" of the Father that the Son participates (idem, *Coherence*, 105–6).

16. That is, God gives his grace by being partaken, and creation receives it by partaking the Son (*C. Gent.* 41–42). See Anatolios, *Coherence*, 156–61; and Hill, *Athanasius*, 191–94.

17. Anatolios, "Christ's Humanity," 275; and idem, *Coherence*, 55–58. Unique among all creation, we participate in τῷ λόγῳ (the Word) in such a way that we become λογικοί (rational [*Inc.* 3; *C. Gent.* 2]).

18. This power is also referred to as the "deifying and enlightening power of the Father" in Christ (*Syn.* 51).

19. See Anatolios, "Christ's Humanity," 272, who argues, "The crucial mediating term between God's beneficent perfection and creation's natural nothingness is therefore χάρις, understood as

ened by him" (*C. Gent.* 7). Rational participation, in other words, is divine illumination,[20] consisting of (1) God giving his "deifying and enlightening power" in the Son (*Syn.* 51) and (2) us receiving it by contemplating God in the Son. So, for humans, to live is to contemplate God because we do not live by bread alone, but by the Word of God (cf. Matt 4:4).[21]

THE FALL: AN INWARD TURN TO SELF

Since we possess a "greater grace" of rationality (λογικός),[22] we are responsible to remain (μένειν) consciously in the grace of God through contemplation and live (*C. Gent.* 31).[23] The fall marks our conscious turn from God to

---

participation in the power and providence of the Word." We could also see the parallel between "grace" and "power" by looking at the syntax of *C. Gent.* 2, for example, "having the grace of Him that gave it, having also God's own power from the Word of the Father, he might rejoice and have fellowship with the Deity, living the life of immortality unharmed and truly blessed" (ἔχων τὴν τοῦ δεδωκότος χάριν, ἔχων καὶ τὴν ἰδίαν ἐκ τοῦ πατρικοῦ Λόγου δύναμιν, ἀγάλληται καὶ συνομιλῇ τῷ Θείῳ, ζῶν τὸν ἀπήμονα καὶ μακάριον ὄντως ἀθάνατον βίον). The two ἔχων participles modifying the two verbs, ἀγάλληται καὶ συνομιλῇ ("might rejoice and have fellowship"), causally are paralleled to each other, suggesting that the phrase, "having the grace of Him that gave it" (ἔχων τὴν τοῦ δεδωκότος χάριν), is the same or similar to the phrase, "having also God's own power from the Word of the Father" (ἔχων καὶ τὴν ἰδίαν ἐκ τοῦ πατρικοῦ Λόγου δύναμιν). Thus, to have God's grace or power is what makes it possible for us to enjoy communion with God.

20. The syntax from *Contra Gentes*, for instance, draws out the parallel between participation and illumination: "... in order that creation, illuminated by the leadership, providence, and ordering of the Word, may be able to remain firm, since it shares in the Word who is truly from the Father and is aided by him to exist, and lest it suffer what would happen, I mean a relapse into non-existence, if it were not protected by the Word" (ἵνα τῇ τοῦ Λόγου ἡγεμονίᾳ καὶ διακοσμήσει φωτιζομένη ἡ κτίσις βεβαίως διαμένειν δυνηθῇ, ἅτε δὴ τοῦ ὄντος ἐκ Πατρὸς Λόγου μεταλαμβάνουσα καὶ βοηθουμένη δι' αὐτοῦ εἰς τὸ εἶναι. μὴ ἄρα πάθῃ ὅπερ ἂν ἔπαθεν, εἰ μὴ ὁ Λόγος αὐτὴν ἐτήρει). The adverbial participle φωτιζομένη (illuminated) is modifying the verb δυνηθῇ (may be able) either causally or as a means, and the causal clause ἅτε δὴ τοῦ ὄντος ἐκ Πατρὸς Λόγου μεταλαμβάνουσα (because it [creation] partakes in the Word who is from the Father) parallels the adverbial participle in explaining why creation is able to remain in existence. We could read them together as either "since it has been illuminated by ..., creation may be able ... because it [creation] partakes in the Word who is from the Father" or "through being illumination by ..., creation may be able ... because it [creation] partakes in the Word who is from the Father." In other words, illumination is an aspect of participation. Moreover, illumination and deification (which comes from participation) are closely associated with each other in such places as *Syn.* 51, e.g., "τὸ θεοποιὸν καὶ φωτιστικόν," in Athanasius' writings.

21. So "when they [human beings] lost the knowledge of God, they lost existence with it," but if a person "preserves that Likeness through constant contemplation, then his nature ... remains incorrupt" (*Inc.* 4; the English translation of *De incarnatione* (*Inc.*). St. Athanasius, *On the Incarnation*, trans. and ed. C. S. M. V. [Crestwood, NY: St. Vladimir's Seminary Press, 1996].

22. Because we participate in τῷ λόγῳ (the Word), we are λογικοί (rational [*Inc.* 3; *C. Gent.* 2]).

23. See Anatolios, "Christ's Humanity," 275; idem, *Athanasius* (London: Routledge, 2004), 42. Similarly, Athanasius wrote, "They are ... corruptible by nature, but by the grace [χάριτι] of the participation of the Word they could have escaped from the consequences of their nature if they had remained virtuous [μεμενήκεισαν καλοί]" (*Inc.* 5).

self—the descent from the mind to the body.[24] Our soul's descent from the mind (νοῦν) to the body (σώματος) is not a platonic concept of "estrangement from the true intelligible self," but a movement away from God.[25] Our "body, soul, and mind are hierarchically ordered within a continuum of self-transcending ascent" to God—the body as the point of departure, the soul as the intermediary, "orienting [the body] toward the divine contemplation whose locus is the 'mind,'" our point of contact with God.[26]

God has set us on the contemplative path of ascent with himself as the terminus, gradually uniting us to himself.[27] But we have inverted this path by our inward turn to self. We became captives to our own idolatrous imagination, shortsighted—no longer seeing the Creator as holy and created things as pointers to the Creator but as an end in themselves, turning created things into idols (*C. Gent.* 4).[28]

ON THE INCARNATION AND THE GIFT OF THE SPIRIT

Because of God's kindness, God cannot let us, whom he has made, turn to naught (*Inc.* 1; 4). So he sent his Son to be one with us, so we may be one with him (*Inc.* 15).[29] "For he became man, so we might become God" (αὐτὸς γὰρ ἐνανθρώπησεν,

---

24. Cf.: "So they turned their minds [νοῦν] away from intelligible reality [νοητῶν] and began to consider themselves. And by considering themselves and cleaving to the body [σώματος] and the other sense [ἄλλων αἰσθητῶν], deceived as it were in their own interests, they fell into selfish desires and preferred their own good to the contemplation of the divine [τὰ θεῖα θεωρίας]. Wasting their time thus and being unwilling to turn away from things close at hand, they imprisoned in the pleasures of the body their souls [ψυχήν] which had become disordered and defiled by all kinds of desires, and in the end they forgot the power they had received from God in the beginning" (*C. Gent.* 3; cf. *Inc.* 5).

25. Anatolios, *Athanasius*, 46.

26. Anatolios, *Athanasius*, 46.

27. Like Clement and Origen before him, Athanasius used the platonic concept of contemplation of his day in light of Scripture. For Plato, contemplation is more than an intellectual exercise, but a union with reality itself. For example, A. J. Festugière, *Contemplation et vie contemplative selon Platon*, 3rd ed. (Paris: Vrin, 1967), 5, writes, "La contemplation n'est pas consideration, ni intellection des essences ou des premiers principes. ... La θεωρία dit plus: ell dit un sentiment de presence, un contact avec l'Être saisi dans son existence."

28. God gave us physical eyes to see him in the "harmonious order" (τῆς παναρμονίου ... συντάξεως) of creation and a body to live unto him, but the soul turned from God and redirected "its bodily members in the opposite direction; and therefore it turned aside its eyes to desires instead of the contemplation of creation" (*C. Gent.* 4; 38; 40; 45). Man's inward turn to himself distorted his mind to see his own desire as the end of all good rather than God who is good (*C. Gent.* 4) and the "source of goodness" (*Inc.* 3).

29. "In the *De Incarnatione*," Anatolios, *Coherence*, 125, highlights, "Athanasius insists that only the real Image could renew the image of God within us, which is to say that our participation

ἵνα ἡμεῖς θεοποιηθῶμεν [*Inc.* 54]).[30] Jesus came to return us to God by remedying our failure to "remain" in God's grace, which is the Holy Spirit,[31] because Jesus secured the gift of the Spirit by receiving the Spirit on our behalf as one of us, flesh and bones. For "in no other way would we have partaken of the Spirit and been sanctified if it were not that the Giver of the Spirit, the Word himself, spoke of himself as anointed by the Spirit for our sakes. Therefore, we have received securely (*bebaiōs*) in that he is said to be anointed in the flesh" (*C. Ar.* 1.50).[32] By receiving the Spirit in his humanity, Jesus enabled the Spirit to remain permanently in us through baptism (*C. Ar.* 1.47–48; 2.41; *Decr.* 7.31; *Ep. Afr.* 11).[33]

The Spirit in turn *unites* us to Christ (*Ep. Serap.* 1.23.6–7) and *actualizes* for us what is in Christ,[34] actualizing the light of the knowledge of God in our hearts (*Ep. Serap.* 1.19.3–9).[35] So "when we are enlightened in the Spirit, it is Christ who enlightens us in him [τῷ δὲ πνεύματι φωτιζομένων ἡμῶν ὁ χριστός ἐστιν ὁ ἐν αὐτῷ φωτίζων].[36] For it says: '*He was the true Light who enlightens every human being coming into the world*'" (*Ep. Serap.* 1.19.4 emphasis original).[37] The Spirit enables us to contemplate the light of the Father in the radiance of the Son by sanctifying us from sin.[38] The three persons of God who are

in God (which constitutes our being 'in the image') can only be renewed from the divine side and not reconstructed from the creaturely side."

30. This English translation is mine. "As expressed here," Khaled Anatolios, "The Immediately Triune God: A Patristic Response to Schleiermacher," *Pro Ecclesia* 10 (2001): 172, helps us see, "the terminus of God's self-communication in Jesus Christ is not humanity but God; the terminus is humanity's return to the Father."

31. Anatolios, "Christ's Humanity," 269, argues, "Athanasius goes on to specify that the grace that is both given and received in Christ is the Holy Spirit, and that is how we are divinized as children of God."

32. English translation is from Anatolios, *Athanasius*, 108.

33. See Russell, *Deification*, 177, 183; and Hill, *Athanasius*, 248.

34. For discussion on the Spirit's "actualization of the content that is Christ," see Anatolios, *Retrieving Nicaea*, 143, 148; idem, *Athanasius*, 82–83; and *Ep. Serap.* 1.20.

35. Through the Spirit, we also receive divine presence (*Ep. Serap.* 1.19.7), power (*Ep. Serap.* 1.19.9), adoption (*Ep. Serap.* 1.19.5), and life in Christ (*Ep. Serap.* 1.19.8). The presence of the Spirit "provides creatures with participation in the Son," who "in turn, gives these creatures a participation in his sonship," making them "children of God by grace" and inheriting all the benefits of adoption (Hill, *Athanasius*, 234 [*C. Ar.* 1.37; 3.24]).

36. The Greek text is from Dietmar Wyrwa and Kyriakos Savvidis, eds., *Athanasius Werke 1.1, vol. 4: Die Dogmatischen Schriften: Epistulae I-IV ad Serapionem* (Berlin: Walter de Gruyter, 2010).

37. English translation of *Epistulae ad Serapionem* (*Ep. Serap.*) is from Athanasius the Great and Didymus the Blind, *Works on the Spirit*, trans. Mark DelCogliano, Andrew Radde-Gallwitz, and Lewis Ayres (Yonkers, NY: St. Vladimir's Seminary Press, 2011).

38. Only through sanctification can the soul contemplate God in the image of the Son: "So when the soul has put off every stain of sin with which it is tinged, and keeps pure only what

"indivisible" in essence are also "indivisible" in the *operatio* of turning us from darkness to light (*Ep. Serap.* 2.15.1–6). The Father shines his light in the radiance of the Son and the sanctifying presence of the Spirit to cleanse the mirror of our soul to reflect and contemplate his light in the Son, the radiance of his glory (*C. Gent.* 8; cf. Heb 1:2; John 1:14; 2 Cor 4:6; Col 1:15). The operations of the Trinity, in other words, are inseparable in the economy of illumination.

THE CAPPADOCIAN FATHERS

The Cappadocian fathers further fleshed out the inseparable operations of the three divine persons in the economy of illumination. For Basil of Caesarea, Gregory of Nazianzus, and Gregory of Nyssa, "Theology is not talking about God in his absence, but recognizing the work of God in one's life as God is present."[39] The Cappadocian fathers were devotees of Origen[40] and students of the ante-Nicene fathers because they believed their teachings were according to Scripture. "[A]s for us," Basil wrote, "what the Fathers said, we repeat. ... But we are not content simply because this is the tradition of the Fathers. What is important is that the Fathers followed the meaning of Scripture" (*Spir.* 7.16). The

is in the image, then when this shines forth, it can truly contemplate as in a mirror the Word [ὡς ἐν κατόπτρῳ θεωρεῖ], the image of the Father, and in him meditate on the Father, of whom the Saviour is the image" (*C. Gent.* 34; cf. 1 Cor 13:12; 2 Cor 3:18).

39. This comment by McConnell, *Illumination*, 217, concerns Basil, but as we will see, it is also true for Gregory of Nazianzus and Gregory of Nyssa. In *On the Holy Spirit* 2, for example, Basil entreated the "Holy Spirit to enlighten" him "to point out the direction" of his theological treatise on the divinity of the Spirit. Unless noted otherwise, the English translation will be from St. Basil the Great, *On the Holy Spirit*, trans. David Anderson (Crestwood, NY: St. Vladimir's Seminary Press, 1980), and the Greek text is from Basile de Césarée, *Sur le Saint-Esprit*, ed. Benoît Pruche, SC 17 (Paris: Les Éditions du Cerf, 2013).

40. Macrina senior, the grandmother of Basil and Gregory of Nyssa, was converted and received her theological training from Gregory of Thaumaturgus, who was himself "a pupil and convert of Origen ca. 233 at Caesarea, where Origen had spent the years from 231 subsequent to his departure from Alexandria" (Anthony Meredith, "Origen," in *The Brill Dictionary of Gregory of Nyssa*, eds. Lucas Francisco Mateo-Seco and Giulio Maspero [Leiden: Brill, 2010], 554). Through Macrina senior, the "influence of Gregory Thaumaturgus as well as of Origen, of whom Gregory was a fervent disciple, reached the family" (Lucas Francisco Mateo-Seco, "Macrina," in *The Brill Dictionary of Gregory of Nyssa*, ed. Lucas Francisco Mateo-Seco and Giulio Maspero [Leiden: Brill, 2010], 471). Basil who received his early theological education from his grandmother in turn trained his younger brother Gregory of Nyssa (Thomas Böhm, "Basil [of Caesarea]," in *The Brill Dictionary of Gregory of Nyssa*, ed. Lucas Francisco Mateo-Seco and Giulio Maspero [Leiden: Brill, 2010], 95). Together with Gregory of Nazianzus, Basil devoted a period of his life in solitude in Pontus (c. 358–359), where Macrina resided, to compile the *Philocalia* of Origen's texts (see Böhm, "Basil," and Jean Paul Lieggi, "Gregory Nazianzen," in *The Brill Dictionary of Gregory of Nyssa*, eds. Lucas Francisco Mateo-Seco and Giulio Maspero (Leiden: Brill, 2010), 377).

theology of the Cappadocians was a contextualization and development of the ante-Nicene fathers' teaching in their struggle to preserve orthodoxy from the doctrinal attack waged by various strands of heresy. The economy of illumination, interestingly, became a significant theme in their defense of orthodoxy.

BASIL OF CAESAREA (C. 330–379)

In his response to the Pneumatomachians (Spirit fighters),[41] Basil followed the principle of the fathers that only God can make himself known. So rather than stating that the Spirit is God, he shows how the Spirit is God by pointing to the activity of the Spirit in illumination.[42] In light of 2 Cor 3:17–18, Basil wrote, "he who fixes his gaze on the Spirit is transfigured to greater brightness, his heart illumined by the light of the Spirit's truth. Then the glory of the Spirit is changed into such a person's own glory, not stingily, or dimly, but with the abundance we would expect to find within someone who has been enlightened by the Spirit" (*Spir*. 21.52).[43] The Spirit can illumine us to God because he knows God's thoughts as our spirit knows ours, so it follows that the Spirit is one with the Father and Son as our spirit is one with us (1 Cor 2:11).[44] As we delve into his work, we will find that Basil's aim was not novelty but faithfulness to the tradition that was handed to him. What his work lacks in novelty it makes up in clarity, offering us a lucid patristic synthesis of illumination as participation: to be illumined is to be in God's presence.[45]

Following Irenaeus, Clement, and Origen, Basil views salvation as a process that culminates in the *visio Dei*. "For instance," he writes,

> wherever the Lord is called the *Way* [ὁδός], we should be raised to a higher meaning, and not to the common understanding of the word. We

---

41. Ayres, *Nicaea*, 215.

42. Basil wanted to highlight the divine "unity of activity and nature" (Ayres, *Nicaea*, 215), in order to show that the one who actively illumines us to God also "must be God" (Ayres, *Nicaea*, 219).

43. The English translation here is from St. Basil the Great, *On the Holy Spirit*, trans. Stephen Hildebrand (Yonkers, NY: St Vladimir Seminary Press).

44. Basil wrote, "the greatest proof that the Spirit is one with the Father and the Son is that He is said to have the same relationship to God as the spirit within us has to us: 'For what person knows a man's thoughts except the spirit of the man which is in him? So also no one comprehends the thoughts of God except the Spirit of God" (*Spir*. 40).

45. For Basil, McConnell, *Illumination*, 11–12, writes, "Illumination is an experience of the presence of God."

> understand the *Way* [ὁδός] to be the road to perfection, advancing in order step by step through the words of righteousness and the illumination of knowledge [τοῦ φωτισμοῦ τῆς γνώσεως], always yearning for that which lies ahead and straining toward the last mile, until we reach that blessed end [τὸ μακάριον τέλος], the knowledge of God [τὴν Θεοῦ κατανόησιν], with which the Lord blesses those who believe in Him. (*Spir.* 8.18)

Jesus is the Way because, in him, we behold God from glory to glory (*Spir.* 6.15). The world is our "training place [διδασκαλεῖον] ... and ... school [παιδευτήριον] for attaining the knowledge of God" (*Hex.* 1.6),[46] Scripture is a lamp, and "illumination" is the light to our path in the *Way* to the *visio Dei* (*Spir.* 8.18). To put it another way, if the world is "a book that proclaims the glory of God" (*Hex.* 11.4), then Scripture, "breathed out by God" (θεόπνευστον), is the lens that allows us to see the "meaning of the physical world,"[47] and illumination is the unveiling of our "face" to behold the glory of God in the Spirit *himself* (*Spir.* 21.52)[48] because "the illumination [the Holy Spirit] gives is Himself" (*Spir.* 9.22; 18.47).

The Spirit bring us into the light of God's knowledge through baptismal "regeneration" (παλιγγενεσίας, *Spir.* 10.26) because, unless one is born again, he cannot see God (cf. John 3:3–5). "In three immersions and in the same number of invocations, the great mystery of baptism is accomplished, in order that the type of death may be fully formed and the baptized be enlightened [φωτισθῶσιν] in their souls by the handing on [παραδόσει] of the knowledge of God" (*Spir.* 15.35).[49] The light of the knowledge of the Trinity in

46. So like Athanasius, Basil believed that the "purpose" (τέλος) of the world is to point us to God because "through visible and perceptible objects it provides guidance to the mind for the contemplation of the invisible" (*Hex.* 1.6). The English translation of *Homiliae in Hexaemeron* 1 (*Hex.*) is from Sister Agnes Clare Way, trans., *St. Basil: Exegetic Homilies*, FC 46 (Washington: Catholic University of America Press, 1963); *Hexaemeron* 11 is from St Basil the Great, *On the Human Condition*, trans. Nonna Verna Harrison (Crestwood, NY: St. Vladimir's Seminary Press, 2005), 51; and the Greek text of *Hexaemeron* is from Basile de Césarée, *Homélies sur l'Hexaéméron*, ed. Stanislas Giet, SC 26 (Paris: Les Éditions du Cerf, 1968).

47. Stephen M. Hildebrand, *Basil of Caesarea* (New York: Routledge, 2018), 30.

48. For discussion on the world and Scripture as the two books of revelation, see Stephen M. Hildebrand, *Basil of Caesarea* (Grand Rapids: Baker Academic, 2014), 37, who writes, "there are two books, two texts, that must be studied in order to read (if not decipher) the message that God wishes to communicate to us."

49. The use of παραδόσει is significant because it highlights that the Trinitarian faith in baptism is handed down by the fathers through the word of Scripture.

baptism is life with God: if "[i]gnorance of God is the death of the soul," then the "enlightenment" of baptism is new life with God (*Exh.* 1; cf. *Spir.* 15.35) because a "pure and heavenly light shines in the souls of those drawing near through faith in the Trinity" (*Exh.* 3).[50]

Basil views illumination as participation in the life of God because it takes place in the baptism of the Spirit, who is the luminous presence of God and who empowers us to see the Son in himself and the Father through the Son. The power of illumination, in other words, does not come from an "outside source," but from the Spirit *himself*, ἑαυτῷ:

> If we are illumined by divine power [διὰ δυνάμεως φωτιστικῆς], and fix our eyes on the beauty of the image of the invisible God, and through the image are led up to the indescribable beauty of its source, it is because we have been inseparably joined [πάρεστιν ἀχωρίστως] to the Spirit of knowledge. He gives those who love the vision of truth the power which enables them to see the image, and this power is Himself [ἑαυτῷ]. He does not reveal it to them from outside sources [ἔξωθεν], but leads them to knowledge personally [or in himself, ἐν ἑαυτῷ], "No one knows the Father except the Son," and "No one can say 'Jesus is Lord' except the Holy Spirit." Notice that it does not say *through* the Spirit, but *in* the Spirit [ἐν Πνεύματι]. It also says, "God is Spirit, and those who worship Him must worship in spirit and truth," and "in Thy light do we see light," through the illumination of the Holy Spirit, "the true light that enlightens every man that comes into the world." He [the Spirit] reveals the glory of the Only-Begotten in Himself [ἐν ἑαυτῷ], and He gives true worshippers the knowledge of God in Himself [ἐν ἑαυτῷ]. The way to divine knowledge ascends from one Spirit through the one Son to the one Father. (*Spir.* 18.47; cf. Eph 2:18)[51]

---

50. The English translation of *Exhortation* is from Everett Ferguson, *Baptism in the Early Church: History, Theology, and Liturgy in the First Five Centuries* (Grand Rapids: Eerdmans, 2009), 590.

51. From this passage, Timothy McConnell argues that there is a shift from the agency of Christ to the Spirit in illumination from Basil's work, *Against Eunomius*, ten years earlier (McConnell, *Illumination*, 11). But the context of *On the Holy Spirit* suggests otherwise. For instance, Basil wrote, "He [i.e., Jesus] enlightens those who are confined in the darkness of ignorance; therefore He is called the True light" (*Spir.* 8.19). It seems more accurate to see the shift in agency as Basil's aim to highlight the divinity of the Spirit and the relationship of the Son and the Spirit in illumination.

We cannot see God apart from God: it is only in the illuminating presence and power of the Spirit of God that we see the "Brightness of God's glory" in the Son (*Spir.* 26.64). As light and the object it illumines are inseparable to our sight, the Spirit, the light of God, and the Son, the image of God, are inseparable in illuminating us to God, the Father.

> We learn that just as the Father is made visible *in* the Son, so also the Son is recognized *in* the Spirit. To worship *in* the Spirit implies that our intelligence has been enlightened. ... If we say that worship offered *in* the Son (the Truth) is worship offered *in* the Father's image, we can say that the same about worship offered *in* the Spirit since the Spirit in Himself reveals the divinity of the Lord. The Holy Spirit cannot be divided from the Father and the Son in worship. If you remain outside the Spirit, you cannot worship at all, and if you are *in* Him you cannot separate Him from God. Light cannot be separated from what it makes visible, and it is impossible for you to recognize Christ, the Image of the invisible God, unless the Spirit enlightens you. Once you see the Image, you cannot ignore the light; you see the Light and Image simultaneously. It is fitting that when we see Christ, the Brightness of God's glory, it is always through the illumination of the Spirit. Through Christ the Image, may we be led to the Father, for He bears the seal of the Father's very likeness. (*Spir.* 26.64, emphasis original; cf. John 4:23–24)

The economy of illumination is the inseparable operations of the triune God who makes himself alight in our hearts with the image of the Son and the light of the Spirit, leading us into worship of the one God in three persons. Being illumined by the Trinity, we also illuminate others like a lantern, which the Spirit indwells and shines forth the Son, the glory of the Father (*Spir.* 9.23).

GREGORY OF NAZIANZUS (C. 329–389)

Gregory of Nazianzus explains the correlation between the immanent Trinity and the economy of the Trinity in illumination to build on Origen's idea of contemplative union with God, demonstrating how the triune God who is one in three distinct lights pours himself out in three inseparable operations of light to bring us into life with triune light. Gregory also follows Origen and maintains that God made our mind in his image (*Or.* 38.10), so our mind longs to return to him in and for whom it was created (*Or.* 28.17).[52]

While we are made to know God, God is not something that we can grasp as Eunomius, Gregory's Arian interlocutor, had claimed. To know God, for Gregory, is a gift we receive from God. Illumination is "God's gift of the saving knowledge of himself," which transforms and deifies us: "As the physical sun perfects our bodies, making them sunlike (ἡλιοειδεῖς), so God perfects our intellectual natures, making them godlike (θεοειδεῖς, 21.1)."[53] The knowledge of God through illumination not only transforms, but also requires our life to be pure.[54] The reason why "a radical change in one's character and way of life"[55] is necessary is because the knowledge of God is not an intellectual grasp or a philosophical abstraction, but a participation in the God who is light, with whom there is no variation or shadow of change (James 1:17). God's light is God's being *in se* and God's illuminating activity *ad extra*: God's illumination is an outflow of God's being (*Or.* 28.1).

As God's being is one and three (*Or.* 39.12), illumination is one and three because it is an outflow of his being (*Or.* 39.11), the inseparable operation of God to draw us into "communication" with God (*Or.* 38.13). God is light, "three in properties, or indeed in hypostases ... or ... 'persons' ... and one with regard to the concept of substance, or indeed divinity" (*Or.* 39.11; cf. 32.9), so illumination is "a flash of ... light which is both one and three" (*Or.* 39.11).[56] In his defense of the Spirit's divinity, for example, Gregory commenced his theological exposition by applying identical expressions [of illumination] to the Three:

---

52. The "image" is the "breath," which "Scripture understands to mean the intellectual soul, which is God's image" (*Or.* 38.11).

53. Christopher A. Beeley, *Gregory of Nazianzus on the Trinity and the Knowledge of God: In Your Light We Shall See Light* (Oxford: Oxford University Press, 2008), 104–105.

54. Our knowledge of God and our life before God are in reciprocal relationship. "In the *Theological Orations*, his most famous defense of Trinitarian doctrine," Christopher Beeley observes, "Gregory begins not with the ideas about God, Christ, or the Holy Spirit, but with a rhetorically charged prologue that focuses on the reader's own character and attitude toward God, in order to establish the human conditions for the possibility of knowing God" (Beeley, *Gregory of Nazianzus*, 65). We also find this parallel in Paul of "bearing fruit in every good work and increasing in the knowledge of God" (Col 1:10).

55. "For Gregory, 'purification' (κάθαρσις and its cognates) means first of all a radical change in one's character and way of life" (Beeley, *Gregory of Nazianzus*, 69; cf. *Or.* 38.6).

56. Unless indicated otherwise, the English translation of *Orations* 38–39 is from Brian E. Daley, *Gregory of Nazianzus* (New York: Routledge, 2006).

> "He was the true light that enlightens every man coming into the world"—yes, the Father. "He was the true light that enlightens every man coming into the world"—yes, the Son. "He was the true light that enlightens every man coming into the world"—yes, the Comforter. These are three subjects and three verbs—he was and he was and he was. But a single reality *was*. There are three predicates—light and light and light. But the light is one, God is one. This is the meaning of David's prophetic vision: "In your light we shall see light." We receive the Son's light from the Father's light in the light of the Spirit [ἐκ φωτὸς τοῦ Πατρὸς φῶς καταλαμβάνοντες τὸν Υἱὸν ἐν φωτὶ τῷ Πνεύματι]: that is what we ourselves have seen and what we now proclaim—it is the plain and simple explanation of the Trinity [Τριάδος]. (*Or.* 31.3).[57]

Divine illumination is God's "self-communication of pure goodness and truth,"[58] flowing from the Father through the Son in the Spirit to us (*Or.* 34.13; 60.34), "so the incomprehensible might be comprehended" (ἵνα χωρηθῇ ὁ ἀχώρητος, *Or.* 39.13).[59] The three divine persons work in one accord to bring us from darkness into the life of triune light.

In *Orations* 38–40, which formed the "Christmas-Epiphany trilogy," extending from December 25, AD 380 to January 6, 381,[60] Gregory retold and expounded festal events on the birth and baptism of Jesus to "enact their anamnesis in liturgical celebration."[61] In re-presenting the nativity and baptism of Jesus Christ at the celebration, Gregory invited "his hearers to share in" these "past saving events as present realities" in worship:[62]

> This is our feast, this is what we celebrate today: God's coming to the human race, so that we might make our way to him, or return

---

57. The Greek text is from Grégoire de Nazianze, *Discours* 27–31, ed. Paul Gallay, SC 250 (Paris: Les Éditions du Cerf, 2008).

58. A. N. Williams, *The Divine Sense: The Intellect in Patristic Theology* (Cambridge: Cambridge University Press, 2007), 109.

59. English translation is mine.

60. Daley, *Gregory of Nazianzus*, 127.

61. Nonna Verna Harrison explains, "Anamnesis means re-presentation of God's saving works so that the worshipers can participate in these events as present realities and thereby receive the eschatological salvation, new life and sanctification divinely accomplished through them" (Saint Gregory of Nazianzus, *Festal Orations*, trans. Nonna Verna Harrison [Crestwood, NY: St. Vladimir's Seminary Press, 2008], 24–25).

62. Nazianzus, *Festal Orations*, 24–28.

> to him (to put it more precisely), so that we might put off the old humanity and put on the new, and that as we have died in Adam so we might live in Christ, being born with Christ and crucified with him and buried with him and raised with him. ... Let us celebrate, then: not like a public festival, but in a divine way; not like the world, but above the world; not celebrating what is ours, but what belongs to the One who is ours—to our Lord; not celebrating weakness, but healing; not celebrating this creation, but our re-creation. (*Or.* 38.4)
>
> And in the end, be crucified with him, die with him, be buried eagerly with him, so that you may also rise with him and be glorified with him and reign with him, seeing God, as far as that is attainable, and being seen by him: the one who is worshipped and glorified in a Trinity, who we pray might be revealed to us even now, as far as that is attainable in the bonds of flesh, in Christ Jesus our Lord, to whom be glory and power for the ages of ages. Amen. (*Or.* 38.18)
>
> Christ is full of light: let us shine with him! Christ is baptized: let us go down with him, that we may rise up with him! (*Or.* 39.14)

On December 25, 380, Gregory began *Oration* 38 with the celebration of Jesus' nativity, of God shining his light into the world baptized in darkness through Adam (*Or.* 38.2–4, 12; cf. 39.2). God created the first Adam and set him on the path "to see and experience the brilliance of God" (*Or.* 38.11), but the devil deceived Eve along with Adam to eat from the tree of knowledge before they were ready (*Or.* 38.12).[63] So Jesus Christ, the second Adam, came to perfect and return us to the state like "the first Adam" (*Or.* 38.16), but far better because Jesus inaugurated "a second communication, far more amazing than the first" between us and God (*Or.* 38.13).

Then, "probably during the night-vigil preceding January 6, AD 381," Gregory delivered *Oration* 39 to celebrate the "holy Day of Lights."[64] This celebration took its origin "from the baptism of Christ, the true lights,

63. Similar to Gregory of Nyssa, Gregory of Nazianzus understood that God intentionally placed the tree of knowledge in the garden of Eden to be enjoyed at the proper time. See A. N. Williams, *Divine Sense: The Intellect in Patristic Theology* (Cambridge: Cambridge University Press, 2007), 123.

64. Daley, *Gregory of Nazianzus*, 127.

which illumines every human being coming into the world, effects my purification, and strengthens the light we received from him from the beginning, which we darkened and blotted out through sin" (*Or.* 39.1; cf. 38.16). The Day of Lights celebrated how Jesus buried the "whole of the old Adam in the water" of baptism to open heaven (*Or.* 39.15),[65] "which Adam caused to be closed for himself and those who came after him" (*Or.* 39.16; cf. 38.16) by raising us with him, the last Adam, to the light of the Trinity (*Or.* 39.20).

On January 6, 381, Gregory concluded the festal celebration in *Oration* 40 with believers' baptism. He referred to our baptism as illumination (cf. John 3:3),[66] our "second" or "middle" birth (*Or.* 18.12–13; 40.3):[67]

> About two of the births, I mean the first and the last, I will not reflect at the present time; about the middle one indeed we must now reflect, since it gives its name to the Day of Lights. This illumination is radiance of souls, transformation of life, engagement of the conscience toward God. Illumination is help for our weakness, illumination is renunciation of the flesh, following of the Spirit, communion in the Word, setting right of the creature, a flood overwhelming sin, participation in light [φωτὸς μετουσία], dissolution of darkness. ... Illumination—what more need I add?—is the most beautiful and most magnificent of the gifts of God. As one speaks of the Holy of Holies and the Song of Songs, since they are more comprehensive and most excellent than others, so also this is more holy that [*sic.*] all other illumination that we possess. (*Or.* 40.3)[68]

---

65. Jesus' baptism begins his ministry, in order to "put an end to the condemnation of the flesh; death, in that flesh, was put to death" (*Or.* 39.13).

66. Cf. *Or.* 38.2: "Let 'the people who sit in the darkness' of ignorance see 'the great light' of divine knowledge. 'Old things have passed away; behold, all things have become new."

67. Cf.: "The word of Scripture recognizes three births for us: one from the body, one from baptism, and one from resurrection. The first takes place at night and in slavery and in passions. The second takes place in the day and in freedom and releases from passions, cutting away all the veil that has surrounded us since birth and leading us back toward the life on high. The third is more fearful and more swift, assembling in a moment all that has been created and presenting it to the Creator to give an account of its servitude and way of life here, as to whether one has followed only the flesh, or risen up with the Spirit and respected the grace of the re-creation" (*Or.* 40.2).

68. The Greek text is from Grégoire de Nazianze, *Discours 38–41*, ed. Paul Gallay, SC 358 (Paris: Les Éditions du Cerf, 1990).

Baptismal illumination is second birth because it purifies us to see Christ, the light of God, through the Spirit,[69] for life with God.[70] It is the means by which God brings us into contemplative union with God: it "is essentially God's contemplation and comprehension of himself, 'pouring himself out on what is external to him' as the Spirit enables one to know God in Jesus Christ; and it is at the same time the contemplation of the Father, Son, and Holy Spirit as a whole, 'whose riches is their unity of nature and the single outleaping of their brightness' (40.5)."[71] To put otherwise, the economy of illumination gives us God's own knowledge of himself, the self-knowledge between the Father and the Son in the Spirit. God, who is light, pours out his communicative light to us through his Son and in his Spirit to draw us into his life of light,[72] the life between the light of the Father and the Son in the Spirit.[73]

Contrary to Eunomius, who argues that the knowledge of the triune God is a reality that we can grasp, Gregory believes that it is one in which we participate and to which we must submit as God is "the Lord of one's life and of all creation."[74] Worship is the only proper response to knowing the one who is immeasurably more than what we can think and imagine (*Or.* 38.7), and "[i]llumination is a vehicle leading toward God [τὸ φώτισμα ὄχημα πρὸς Θεόν], departure with Christ, support of faith, perfection of mind, key to the kingdom of heaven, change of life, deliverance from slavery, release from bonds, [and] transformation of our composite nature" (*Or* 40.3). In sum, Gregory's account reinforces and developes three fundamental building blocks from the ante-Nicene fathers that will fund my dogmatic account in Part III: (1) the integral relationship between knowledge and transformation

69. In the same way that our "[s]ight cannot approach its objects without the medium of light and atmosphere," our mind's eye cannot see God without the light of Christ and the presence of the Spirit (*Or.* 28.12).

70. Cf. *Or.* 39.20: "'Be washed, make yourself pure.' ... It is so that 'you may become as lights to the world,' a living force for other men and women, so that as perfect lights you may stand with the great light, and in his presence be initiated into the Mystery of light, illuminated yet more purely and clearly by the Trinity, of which you have now received, in modest measure, this one ray of the one divinity, in Christ Jesus our Lord, to whom be glory for the ages of ages. Amen."

71. Beeley, *Gregory of Nazianzus*, 231.

72. Cf. *Or.* 40.5: "God is light ... he is in the world of thought, what the sun is in the world of sense, presenting himself to our minds in proportion as we are cleansed" (quoted in Ayres, *Nicaea*, 248; cf. also *Or.* 31.3).

73. In other words, to participate in light is to know and be known by God as the Father and the Son know and are known to each other in the Spirit (*Or.* 25.17).

74. Beeley, *Gregory of Nazianzus*, 229.

in the economy of illumination, (2) the correlation between the immanent Trinity and the economic Trinity in illumination, and (3) the source of our contemplative union with God.

GREGORY OF NYSSA (C. 335–395)

Gregory of Nyssa put an even greater emphasis than Gregory of Nazianzus on the incomprehensibility of God,[75] offering a notion of "illuminous darkness" for the process of being transformed and stretched forth from glory to glory in Christ (2 Cor 3:18). Gregory of Nyssa understands the "Christian's union with God through Christ as attaining 'a knowledge directed toward the infinite' (*gnōsis pros to achōriston*)."[76] God's infinity is his goodness, and union with God is a "conscious participation" in God's infinite goodness.[77] The economy of illumination is an aspect of union[78] because it provides the object and means to the knowledge of God's goodness: the "self-communication" of God's activities (ἐνεργείαι) in the Son (object) and the Spirit (means), mediated through Scripture and the sacraments of the church.[79] To be illumined is to be in luminous *darkness*, in awe and wonder of God's infinite goodness (Lam 3:22–23): the

75. Hans Urs von Balthasar writes, "Eunomius is like a child who would like to grab hold of a ray of the sun. He wants to understand rather than to adore," but for Gregory on the other hand, "[h]uman knowledge is therefore true only to the degree it renounces by a perpetual effort its own nature, which is to 'seize' its prey" (Hans Urs von Balthasar, *Presence and Thought: Essay on the Religious Philosophy of Gregory of Nyssa*, trans. Mark Sebanc [San Francisco: Ignatius Press, 1995], 92–93).

76. Anatolios, *Retrieving Nicaea*, 237. In other words, the knowledge of God is not something that we grasp, as it is a truth that we participate in through worship.

77. Anatolios, *Retrieving Nicaea*, 237.

78. Following the interpretive footsteps of Origen in the *Song of Songs* (*Comm. Cant.* 1.5), Gregory saw illumination as a means to participate in God through the light of Christ. "For the soul that has desired to touch the God with the tips of her lips and has laid hold on the Beautiful just to the extent that the strength of her prayer indicates (she prayed, one might say, to be made worthy of a kiss [φιλήματος] through the illumination of the Word [διὰ τῆς τοῦ λόγου ἐλλάμψεως]), this same soul, empowered by its success in slipping through to the interior of what thought cannot articulate, cries out her request that her running not be confined to the outer courts of the Good but that by the firstfruits of the Spirit (cf. Rom 8:23)—of which she was made worthy by the first gift of grace, that is, by a kiss [φιλήματος]—she may come to the inner shrine of paradise and search 'the depths of God' (1 Cor 2:10) and, like the great Paul, see (as he says) invisible things and hear unspeakable words (cf. 2 Cor 12:2–4)" (*Hom. Cant.* 1; the Greek text and English translation for *In Canticum canticorum* [*Hom. Cant.* 5] is from Gregory of Nyssa, *Homilies on the Song of Songs*, trans. Richard A. Norris Jr. [Atlanta: Society of Biblical Literature, 2012]). The "first gift of grace" or the "kiss" (φιλήματος) is to participate in the mind of God (or "depth of God") through illumination. The Spirit brings us into the "depths of God," a contemplative communion with God, which is unspeakable and inarticulable by human language.

79. Williams, *Divine Sense*, 109.

"human mind, when enlightened by faith, can journey endlessly within that plenitude [of God's goodness], which nevertheless remains always greater."[80]

While Gregory of Nazianzus and Gregory of Nyssa were conversant and shared many aspects of theology, the former centers his theology on light, while the latter on darkness.[81] In his reflection of Exodus 24:17, for example, Gregory of Nyssa details how we begin our contemplative journey to God by light, but progress more deeply through "luminous darkness" (τῷ λαμπρῷ γνόφῳ).[82]

> … as the mind progresses and, through an ever greater and more perfect diligence, comes to apprehend reality, as it approaches more nearly to contemplation, it sees more clearly what of the divine nature is uncontemplated.
>
> For leaving behind everything that is observed, not only what sense comprehends but also what the intelligence thinks it sees, it keeps on penetrating deeper until by the intelligence's yearning for understanding it gains access to the invisible and the incomprehensible, and there it sees God. This is the true knowledge of what is sought; this is the seeing that consists in not seeing, because that which is sought transcends all knowledge, being separated on all sides by incomprehensibility as by a kind of darkness [γνόφῳ]. Wherefore John the sublime, who penetrated into the luminous darkness [τῷ λαμπρῷ γνόφῳ], says, *No one has ever seen God*, thus asserting that knowledge of the divine essence is unattainable not only by men but also by every intelligent creature.
>
> When, therefore, Moses grew in knowledge, he declared that he had seen God in the darkness [τὸν Θεὸν ἐν γνόφῳ ἰδεῖν], that is, that he had then come to know that what is divine is beyond all knowledge and comprehension, for the text says, *Moses approached the dark cloud where God was* [Μωϋσῆς εἰς τὸν γνόφον, οὗ ἦν ὁ Θεός]. (*Vit. Moys.* 2.162–163; emphasis original)[83]

---

80. Anatolios, *Retrieving Nicaea*, 162.

81. See Williams, *Divine Sense*, 88.

82. Ronald E. Heine, *Gregory of Nyssa's Treatise on the Inscriptions of the Psalms* (Oxford: Clarendon Press, 1995), 50–71, details the five different stages to the beatific vision of God.

83. The English translation of *De vita Moysis* is from Gregory of Nyssa, *The Life of Moses*, trans. Abraham J. Malherbe and Everett Ferguson (New York: Paulist Press, 1978), and the Greek

To approach "luminous darkness" is to come into God's presence, where there is goodness forevermore. It is being illumined to what our minds cannot contain—being in awe, in wonder of how good God is through the Son in the presence of the Spirit.[84] It is coming to know and not know God at the same time. We know God is incomprehensible because we know that he is so much more: he is infinite.[85]

Gregory of Nyssa was one of the first to introduce God's infinity as it relates to God's perfection—his perfect goodness, that never ends.[86]

> The Divine One is himself the Good (in the primary and proper sense of the word), whose very nature is goodness. This he is and he is so named, and is known by this nature. Since, then, it has not been demonstrated that there is any limit to virtue except evil, and since the Divine does not admit of an opposite, we hold the divine nature to be unlimited and infinite. Certainly whoever pursues true virtue participates in nothing other than God, because he is himself absolute virtue.

---

text is from Grégoire de Nysse, *La Vie de Moïse*, ed. Jean Daniélou, SC 1 bis (Paris: Les Éditions du Cerf, 2007).

84. Knowledge of God is "union with God through Christ" (Anatolios, *Retrieving Nicaea*, 237) because it "is altogether inaccessible to reasoning and conjecture, nor has there been found any human faculty capable of perceiving the incomprehensible; for we cannot devise a means of understanding inconceivable things. ... the knowledge of the Divine Essence is inaccessible to thought" because it is "above knowledge" (*Beat.* 6; the English translation of *De beatitudinibus* [*Beat.*] is from Gregory of Nyssa, *The Lord's Prayer, the Beatitudes*, trans. Hilda C. Graef [New York: Newman Press, 1954]). Only "after a process of *aphairesis*, with all conceptual understanding abandoned," however, do we encounter God in a "union by means of faith" (Martin Laird, *Gregory of Nyssa and the Grasp of Faith: Union, Knowledge and Divine Presence* [Oxford: Oxford University Press, 2006], 53).

85. God's infinity cannot be grasped, so our knowledge of God through participation always "becomes a beginning of ascent towards the greater, and in Paul's words (*Phil* 3.13) never ceases to reach out to things before and to cast oblivion on things behind" (*C. Eun.* 3.6.74; the English translation of *Contra Eunomium* [*C. Eun.*] book 1 is from Gregory of Nyssa, *Against Eunomius*, trans. and eds. William Moore and Henry Austin Wilson, NPNF[2] 5 [1892; repr., Peabody, MA: Hendrickson, 2004]; and books 2 and 3 is from Gregory of Nyssa, *Contra Eunomium II*, trans. Stuart George Hall and ed. Lenka Karfíková, Scot Douglass, and Johannes Zachhuber [Leiden: Brill, 2007], and idem, *Contra Eunomium III*, trans. Stuart George Hall and ed. Johan Leemans and Matthieu Cassin [Leiden: Brill, 2010], respectively). Anatolios, *Retrieving Nicaea*, 160, argues, "At the heart of Gregory of Nyssa's anti-Eunomian apophaticism is his conception of the infinity of the divine essence. Because the divine essence is infinite, it is incomprehensible: it cannot be fully encompassed or circumscribed by thought or word."

86. According to Jonathan Hill, *The History of Christian Thought* (Downers Grove, IL: IVP Academic, 2003), 75, "for Origen, as for most Greeks, God is limited, because only limited things can be known; to be unlimited is to be imperfectly formed. But Gregory introduces the notion of God's infinity, a notion so commonplace today that it is hard for us to imagine that someone was once the first to defend it."

> Since, then, those who know what is good by nature desire participation in it, and since this good has no limit, the participant's desire itself necessarily has no stopping place but stretches out [συμπαρατείνουσα] with the limitless. (*Vit. Moys.* 1.7)

God's perfection is his goodness, which has neither variation nor end. The three divine *hypostaseis* are infinitely one in nature because they are one in perfection and perfect in goodness. To say that "there is one God is to designate one perfection, which can be conceived in diverse notions, such as infinite goodness, wisdom, power, and so on."[87]

The essential difference that separates God from the created realm is "between infinite perfection and participation in infinite perfection."[88] Again, God's perfection is his goodness. God does not participate in the good because God is simply good.[89] As a result of his goodness rather than necessity, God created us to participate in his perfect goodness through contemplation (*Or. cat.* 5). According to A. N. Williams, "The core of Nyssen's doctrine of contemplation has two foci: the activity in its more sheerly intellectual (and what we would call today theological) dimension and in its more spiritual one (which we would call prayer)."[90] To contemplate, in other words, is to reflect on and pray to God in God's presence, being aware that we are neither praying to the air nor doing theology in God's absence, but doing so in his presence. Contemplation is participation precisely because it is being illumined by God in his presence, "communion with the true light."[91] Contemplation also entails love. The beauty of God's goodness is "lovable" to all who contemplate it (*An. et res.* 81).[92] Love is "participation and union" with God, a bond between God, the lover, and us, his beloved.[93]

87. Anatolios, *Retrieving Nicaea*, 184; goes on to say, "Christian monotheism is first of all belief in a single divine perfection, which does not admit of variance or multiplicity *in itself*, such that there can never be more than one perfection, or greater and lesser perfection" (Anatolios, *Retrieving Nicaea*, 219).

88. Anatolios, *Retrieving Nicaea*, 216.

89. Anatolios, *Retrieving Nicaea*, 184.

90. Williams, *Divine Sense*, 136.

91. Jean Daniélou, *From Glory to Glory: Text from Gregory of Nyssa's Mystical Writings*, trans. and ed. Herbert Musurillo (New York: Scribner's Sons, 1961), 109.

92. See Daniélou, *From Glory to Glory*, 125.

93. Jean. Daniélou, *Platonisme et théologie mystique* (Paris: Aubier, 1944), 203, quoted by Giulio Maspero, "Love," in *The Brill Dictionary of Gregory of Nyssa*, eds. Lucas Francisco Mateo-Seco and

Gregory often described our participation in God's goodness with the term ἐπέκτασις ("stretching forward"),[94] in reference to Philippians 3:13, to highlight that our "ascension to God is an unlimited progress which will continue in heaven itself" because God's goodness never ends.[95] Our progress to God also involves change because we become what we contemplate in deifying light (*Hom. Cant.* 1–2; 5). So in "contemplative praise,"[96] our life always stretches forth

> in such a way that we ... constantly evolve towards what is better, being *transformed from glory to glory* (2 Cor. 3.18), and thus always improving and ever becoming more perfect by daily growth, and never arriving at any limit of perfection. For that perfection consist in our never stopping in our growth in good, never circumscribing our perfection by any limitation.[97]

The reason why this is possible is because God has made us capable not only to desire and love the beauty of God's goodness infinitely[98] but also to have God dwell in us.[99]

What God provides to access and sustain us in his goodness is his power (δύναμις), manifested objectively in the activities (ἐνεργεῖαι) of the Son's creative and salvific works (ἔργα) in the world,[100] but subjectively in us through

---

Giulio Maspero (Leiden: Brill, 2010), 459–61. The souls of those who are in God do not know God in a cold and detached manner, but their souls are "warmed by the Spirit and heated by the ray of the Word" (*Hom. Cant.* 5).

94. Anatolios, *Retrieving Nicaea*, 235–40.

95. Lucas Francisco Mateo-Seco, "Epektasis," in *The Brill Dictionary of Gregory of Nyssa*, eds. Lucas Francisco Mateo-Seco and Giulio Maspero (Leiden: Brill, 2010), 263.

96. Williams, *Divine Sense*, 136.

97. Daniélou, *From Glory to Glory*, 84, emphasis original.

98. Taking his cue from what Paul wrote in 1 Cor 13:8, "love never ends," Gregory of Nyssa asserted, "There is no limit to the operation of love, since the beautiful has no limit, so that love might cease with the limit of the beautiful" (*An. et res.* 81). The English translation here of *De anima et resurrectione* (*An. et res.*) is from Gregory of Nyssa, *On the Soul and the Resurrection*, trans. Catharine P. Roth (Crestwood, NY: St. Vladimir's Seminary Press, 1993), and it will be cited with the page number of this translation work as I have done here.

99. Gregory marveled at the self, in which the infinite God, who is neither bound by space nor time, dwells: "The whole heaven is contained in the span of God's hand; earth and sea are encompassed by his hand. But at the same time this One, being such as he is and so great as he is, grasping the whole creation in the palm of his hand, becomes limited for your sake and dwells in you and is not confined as he penetrates your nature" (*Hom. Cant.* 2).

100. Anatolios, *Retrieving Nicaea*, 217. For more discussion on the relationship between God's essence and power, see Michel René Barnes, "Divine Unity and the Divided Self," in *Re-Thinking*

the illumination of the Spirit.[101] "For he who is invisible in [his] nature (τῇ φύσει ἀόρατος) becomes visible in his activities (ἐνεργείας), inasmuch as he is contemplated in certain properties [which are] in connection with Him (ἔν τισι τοῖς περὶ αὐτὸν καθορώμενοις)' (*Beat*, GNO VII/2, 141, 25–27)."[102] The "power" (δύναμις) of God, i.e., the Son and the Spirit, is the object and means of knowledge and union with God.[103] It is the effect of the Father who himself is the cause.[104] Contrary to Eunomius, who viewed the relationship between the Father and the Son "simply in terms of the superiority of cause to effect" because he saw "the causal activity of the Father as extrinsic and posterior to the integrity of his essence,"[105] Gregory maintained that the Son is caused by the Father "in such a way that precludes differentiation in the nature (*kata physin*) but safeguards the distinction of *hypostaseis*," as Jesus said, '"the Father and I are one"' (John 10:30 NRSV).[106]

Gregory of Nyssa, ed. Sarah Coakley (Malden, MA: Blackwell, 2003), 48–52.

101. That is, the radiance of God's glory in the Son can only shine "'in souls by means of the Holy Spirit'" (*C. Eun.* 1.531 quoted by Anatolios, *Retrieving Nicaea*, 205).

102. Quoted in Giulio Maspero, "Energy (ἐνέργεια)," in *The Brill Dictionary of Gregory of Nyssa*, eds. Lucas Francisco Mateo-Seco and Giulio Maspero (Leiden: Brill, 2010), 259. For more discussion, see Hans Boersma, *Seeing God: The Beatific Vision in Christian Tradition* (Grand Rapids: Eerdmans, 2018), 78–82.

103. Both the Son and the Holy Spirit are referred to as the power and cause of God (Anatolios, *Retrieving Nicaea*, 189). The Son and the Spirit are the object and means of illumination because the Son is the image and the Spirit is the light that together enable us to know and commune with God.

104. Anatolios, *Retrieving Nicaea*, 188–91.

105. Anatolios, *Retrieving Nicaea*, 189. That is, the power of God's activities in the world through the Son is something *ad extra*, taking place outside of his essence.

106. Anatolios, *Retrieving Nicaea*, 189–90. Reflecting on speech, Gregory also discerned "some distinction of Persons in the unity" of God's nature (*Or. cat.* 1; the translation of *Oratio catechetica magna* [*Or. cat.*] is from Edward R. Hardy and Cyril C. Richardson, trans. and eds., *Christology of the Later Fathers* [Philadelphia: Westminster Press, 1954]. "In the moment," Gregory explained, "we give expression to a word our breath becomes an intelligible utterance which indicates what we have in mind" (*Or. cat.* 2). Likewise, the Father speaks with his breath, the Spirit (1 John 2:27; cf. John 14:26; 1 Cor 2:12), the Word that he has in mind (Heb 1:2; cf. Heb 12:24; John 7:16; 12:49). The components of speaker, word, and breath in speech illustrate how God is distinct in persons, but one in essence because the Word uttered by the Spirit (or breath) "comes from the mind [of God], and is neither entirely identical with it nor altogether different" (*Or. cat.* 1). However, divine speech is not exactly like our finite speech, in which neither word nor breath can subsist on its own but dissipates as soon as it is spoken. God's spoken *Word* has "subsistence" in himself, possessing his "own life, and does not participate in life" (*Or. cat.* 1). Likewise, God's *Spirit* is "a power really existing by itself and in its own special subsistence. It is not able to be separated from God in whom it exists, or from God's Word which it accompanies. It is not dissipated into non-existence; but like God's Word it has its own subsistence, is capable of willing, and is self-moved and active. It

In light of what Jesus said also in John 10:38, "'The Father is in me and I am in the Father,'" Gregory argued that "the cause indwells its perfect effect," so "there is no 'interval' (*diastēma*) or 'separation' in the movement of self-communication from Father to Son," who came to manifest God's power to us in the incarnation.[107] Like Gregory of Nazianzus, Gregory of Nyssa viewed the economy of illumination, the activities (ἐνεργεῖαι) of God's power in the world, as an outflow of God's being to draw us into his life[108]—into the "circle of mutual glorification" between the Father and the Son in the Spirit.[109] "Christian worship is thus a matter of being included within 'the circle' of the mutual glorification of Father, Son, and Spirit."[110] Worship ushers us into the mutual glorification of the Trinity because it is "permeated by wonder," which is integral to the "proper" knowledge of the Trinity.[111]

So, in conclusion, God enables us to participate in his circle of mutual glorification by illuminating us with his "self-presenting dynamism or power" in the Son and the Spirit through Scripture and the sacraments of the church.[112] Like his theological predecessors, Gregory viewed "the event of baptism as an entrance into divine 'life-giving power' (*hē zōopoios dynamis*)"[113] because we receive the Spirit who gives us what is in Christ (*or. Cat.* 40; *Hom. Cant.* 13).[114] The Spirit is the glory of God given to the Son in his humanity and now to

---

ever chooses the good; and to fulfill its every purpose it has the power that answers to its will" (*Or. cat.* 2). The Son and the Spirit subsist on their own because they are not "extrinsic and posterior to the integrity of [the Father's] essence" (Anatolios, *Retrieving Nicaea*, 189; cf. *C. Eun.* 1.39; 3.16–18). The Trinity is united in will and perfection, which lacks nothing and is bound by nothing, but is limitless and infinite (Anatolios, *Retrieving Nicaea*, 236; cf. *Vit. Moys*. prol. 7).

107. God's power is also manifested to us through the activities (ἐνεργεῖαι) of his Son and Spirit in the works (ἔργα) of creation and salvation (Anatolios, *Retrieving Nicaea*, 191, 217).

108. In other words, it is "a movement which corresponds to the nature or essence from which it comes" (Maspero, "Energy," 260).

109. Anatolios, *Retrieving Nicaea*, 209. The Father is glorified by the Son and the Spirit, and the Son and the Spirit have their glory from the Father.

110. Anatolios, *Retrieving Nicaea*, 191, 210.

111. Anatolios, *Retrieving Nicaea*, 164. Anatolios adds, our "knowing of God ... succeeds in being in touch with the reality of God only when it reacts to the divine self-manifestation in wonder and worship" (Anatolios, *Retrieving Nicaea*, 194).

112. Anatolios, *Retrieving Nicaea*, 194. Our contemplative praise and prayer in the *light* of Son takes place in the church because God has given his Spirt to work in and through the church.

113. Anatolios, *Retrieving Nicaea*, 187.

114. Hans Boersma, *Embodiment and Virtue in Gregory of Nyssa: An Analogical Approach* (Oxford: Oxford University Press, 2013), 182–86, and Anatolios, *Retrieving Nicaea*, 238.

us to be one with God (*Hom. Cant.* 15; John 17:22–23).[115] The Spirit empowers us to live a virtuous life in God (*Diem Lum.* 240.9–16) because he interprets, translates, and "communicates with us in our own terms" all that God has said concerning his Son in Scripture (*C. Eun.* 2.238; 1.280).[116] In the Eucharist, Jesus "'implants himself in all believers' and 'unites himself with [our] bodies'"[117] to "transform our lowly body to be like his glorious body" (Phil 3:21).[118] Our knowledge of God is a participation in God's goodness, so to participate in God is to be illumined to God. The economy of illumination is the inseparable operation of the Father shining forth the light of his Son into "our hearts by means of the Holy Spirit" through Scripture and the sacraments of his church,[119] to draw us into "the mutually self-glorifying being of the Trinity."[120] This process by which God brings us into this "circle of mutual glorification" offers another picture of our contemplative union with God.

CYRIL OF ALEXANDRIA (C. 375–444)

In On the Unity of Christ, Cyril employed 2 Cor 4:6 to demonstrate that the person of Christ cannot be divided. "Notice," he wrote, "how the radiance of the divine and ineffable glory of God the Father shines 'in the face of Jesus Christ.' The Only Begotten, even when he has become man, shows forth in himself the glory of the Father."[121] The sending of the only Begotten in the

115. Anatolios, *Retrieving Nicaea*, 211. Like Origen, Gregory believed that the glory the Father and the Son shared before the foundation of the world is the oneness, the communion, in which believers now partake in through the Spirit.

116. Anatolios, *Retrieving Nicaea*, 169–170. The Spirit enables Scripture to efficaciously reveal God to us and guide us into "'a union with the divine nature'" (*C. Eun.* 2.102 quoted by Anatolios, *Retrieving Nicaea*, 161).

117. Anatolios, *Retrieving Nicaea*, 237.

118. Boersma, *Embodiment*, 188, writes, "The Eucharist thus enables them to participate in the deifying effect of the incarnation." However, the "efficacy of the sacraments," in which we participate in God, "is dependent upon both faith and conduct" (Anatolios, *Retrieving Nicaea*, 237).

119. Anatolios, *Retrieving Nicaea*, 238.

120. For Gregory of Nyssa, Anatolios goes on to say, "Christian worship is thus a matter of being included within 'the circle' of the mutual glorification of Father, Son, and Spirit" (Anatolios, *Retrieving Nicaea*, 210). According to Anatolios, "Christians are continually invited to renew and deepen their participation in trinitarian life through eucharistic communion, whereby they are incorporated into the self-offering of the Incarnate Son to the Father in the Spirit and in the mutual glorification of the Father and the Son by the Spirit. Participation in the interrelations of Father, Son, and Spirit is simultaneously the goal and the means of Christian sacramental life" (Anatolios, *Retrieving Nicaea*, 285).

121. St. Cyril of Alexandria, *On the Unity of Christ*, trans. John Anthony McGuckin (Crestwood, NY: St. Vladimir's Seminary Press, 1995), 108.

economy of redemption and the receiving of him through the economy of illumination form the way the triune God deifies and restores us to the life with himself. In Cyril's reading of John 17:20–21, he underscored,

> It was impossible for us to be restored, once we had fallen because of the original transgression, back to our original beauty except by attaining an ineffable communion [κοινωνίας] and union [ἑνώσεως] with God. That is how the nature of those on earth was ordered in the beginning. No one could have union [ἕνωσις] with God except through participation [μετουσίας] in the Holy Spirit, who implants his own attribute of sanctification in us and refashions into his own life the nature that was subject to decay. (*In Jo.* 17.20–21 [Pusey, 2.730–731])[122]

God made our union possible through grace. Because of grace, the Holy Spirit is once again extended to us, so we may be one with God, "one in the Father and the Son and the Holy Spirit (one, I mean, by identical disposition …). We are also one by the form of godliness and by communion with the holy flesh of Christ and by communion with the one Holy Spirit" (*In Jo.* 17.20–21 [Pusey, 2.737]).[123] To appreciate how God has made union and communion with God possible again, we must understand what Cyril meant by *grace*.

GRACE AS GOD'S SELF-GIVING

According to Donald Fairbairn, one of the main issues surrounding the fourth century christological controversy was grace.[124] For Theodore of Mopsuestia and his pupil Nestorius, grace was the "power, aid, and co-operation" that God gives us to reach the second age of perfection.[125] Since grace is something

---

122. The translation of *In Joannem* (*In Jo.*; *Commentary on John*) comes from Cyril of Alexandria, *Commentary on John*, 2 vols., ed. and trans. David R. Maxwell and Joel C. Elowsky (IVP Academic, 2013 and 2015). The Greek text is from P. E. Pusey, *Sancti patris nostril Cyrilli Archiepiscopi Alexandrini in d. Joannis Evangelium*, 3 vols. (Oxford: Clarendon Press, 1872).

123. To be restored is to be baptized and partake in the oneness of holy Trinity: "those who rise to divine sonship through faith in Christ are baptized not into anything originate but into the holy Trinity itself through the Word who is the mediator" (*In Jo.* 1.13 [Pusey, 1.136]).

124. Donald Fairbairn, *Grace and Christology in the Early Church* (Oxford: Oxford University Press, 2003), 52, writes, "It was the idea of grace and the soteriological emphasis, rather than the more technical questions of whether one sufficiently explained that Christ was one person and whether one began with his unity or duality, that prompted the christological controversy."

125. Fairbairn, *Grace*, 28. Theodore and Nestorius maintain a "two-ages" concept of salvation, which saw salvation as an elevation from the first "age of mutability, corruption, and sin" to the second age of "immutability, incorruption, and perfection" (Fairbairn, *Grace*, 30; cf. 60). Cyril

that God bestows external to himself, "a direct personal presence of God in the world" is not necessary.[126] Jesus was only a "trailblazer" (ἀρχηγὸν),[127] for them, who opened and showed the way to perfection because he was the first man to cross into the second age through the "power" that the "Logos" had bestowed on him.[128] After he received the grace of the second age in the resurrection, Jesus became the mediator and giver of the grace from the Logos to us.

For Cyril, however, grace was primarily God's gift of *himself* in Jesus. Concerning the fullness of God's grace in "the Word [who] became flesh and dwelt in us" (ὁ λόγος σὰρξ ἐγένετο καὶ ἐσκήνωσεν ἐν ἡμῖν), Cyril wrote that John reveals a

> profound mystery to us when he affirms for our benefit that the Word "dwelt in us": We were all in Christ, and the shared properties of our human nature were taken up into his person. That is why he is called the last Adam. He gives all the riches of his tranquility and glory to our common nature, just as the first Adam gave corruption and shame. Therefore, the Word 'dwelt in' all people through the one man as that when the one man 'was designated Son of God in power according to the Spirit of holiness,' this honor might extend to all humanity. In this way, because of one of us, the words 'I said you are gods, and you are all sons of the Most High' might come to us as well. Therefore, the slave is truly freed in Christ and ascends into mystical unity [εἰς ἑνότητα τὴν μυστικήν] with the one who bore the form of a slave, while at the same time Christ is in us in the sense that we are like him because of our kindship with his flesh. Why, after all, does he 'take on not the nature of angels, but the seed of Abraham; therefore, he had to be like his brothers in every way' and truly become human? Is it not therefore perfectly clear to all that he came down into that which was in slavery, not to do anything for himself but to give himself to

---

viewed salvation as a "three-acts scheme" (Fairbairn, *Grace*, 17). The first act concerns creation, God creating us for fellowship by being present with us in the Holy Spirit. The second act consists of the fall, where Adam sinned and lost the Spirit for communion with God. So a third act is required, where God gives himself in Christ who is both God and man to restore us back to communion with God (Fairbairn, *Grace*, 68–69).

126. Fairbairn, *Grace*, 40–41. The concept of grace, Fairbairn notes, is also what allows them to distinguish "sharply between divine and human in Christ" (Fairbairn, *Grace*, 40).

127. Fairbairn, *Grace*, 45.

128. Fairbairn, *Grace*, 28; cf. 60–62.

> us [ἡμῖν ἑαυτὸν χαριζόμενος] 'that by his poverty, we might become rich' and that we might ascend by likeness with him to his own exceptional dignity and be shown to be gods and children of God through faith? He who is by nature Son and God 'dwelt in us.' Therefore, in his Spirit 'we cry Abba! Father!' The Word dwells in the one temple, taken from us and for us, as he dwells in all people, so that having everyone in himself he might reconcile everyone in one body with the Father, as Paul says. (*In Jo.* 1.14 [Pusey, 1.141–142])

It was necessary for Jesus to take on human nature,[129] without losing his own divine nature,[130] so he may "give himself to us" (ἡμῖν ἑαυτὸν χαριζόμενος), in order to allow us to participate in his divine nature and enjoy communion with God as children of God "by adoption and imitation" (*In. Jo.* 1.12 [Pusey, 1.134]; 4.2 [Pusey, 1.363]; 6.35 [Pusey, 1.473]).[131]

PARTICIPATION IN THE REDEEMED HUMANITY OF THE SON

In his incarnation, Jesus became the last Adam to recapitulate and restore what the first Adam lost, namely the Holy Spirit.[132] To restore us in communion with God, Jesus had to renew humanity *first* in himself by taking on

129. According to Daniel A. Keating, "Divinization in Cyril: The Appropriation of Divine Life," in *The Theology of St. Cyril of Alexandria*, ed. Thomas G. Weinandy and Daniel A. Keating (London: T & T Clark, 2003), 179: "For Cyril, Christ not only provides the link in himself between divinity and humanity; he also *remains*, as fully divine and fully human, the sole and irreplaceable locus of our dynamic participation in the divine life."

130. For instance, Cyril, *Unity of Christ*, 88, writes, "God the Word did not change even when he assumed flesh endowed with a *rational soul*. ... In this way he saved his own people, not as a man conjoined to God, but as God who has come in the likeness of those who were in danger, so that in him first of all the human race might be refashioned to what it was in the beginning" (emphasis mine). Elsewhere, he wrote, "While still being God, he became a human being without being separated from his divinity, and he is Son even with his flesh. The most perfect confession and knowledge of faith in him consists in these truths" (*In Jo.* 9.37 [Pusey, 1.201]).

131. To participate in the divine nature is to share in the incorruptible life and the communicative light of Father, Son, and Spirit, which God gives in the Son, the fullness of grace and truth (John 1:14). For Cyril, to participate in Christ's divine nature for communion with God presupposes the creature-Creator distinction because to participate means to receive and take part in what is not ours by nature. Our bond of union with God is also distinct from the bond between the Father and the Son: "the bond of love in us and the power of concord will not completely prevail to the point of being unchangeable, as the Father and the Son are, since they preserve their unity by the identity of their essence" (*In Jo.* 17.20–21 [Pusey, 1.731–732]).

132. Keating, "Divinization in Cyril," 152–60. Adam lost the Holy Spirt because of disobedience: "For in the beginning it was given to the first-fruits of our race, that is, to Adam. But he became careless about observing the commandment given to him, neglected what he had been

flesh.[133] He took on our corruptible nature in *himself* to make it incorruptible with his divine nature (*In Jo.* 1.14 [Pusey, 1.138–139]; cf. 6.40 [Pusey, 1.499]),[134] and he received the Spirit on our behalf as the last Adam in baptism (Matt 3:11; Luke 3:21–22; Mark 1:9–13; John 1:33),[135] so he may extend the Spirit to us for communion with God:[136]

> He is God and a human being in the same person so that by uniting in himself, as it were, things that are very different by nature and essentially distinct from each other he may make humanity share and participate in the divine nature. The communion and abiding presence of the Holy Spirit extended to us, beginning through Christ and in Christ first, when he became human like us and was anointed and sanctified—even though he is by nature God, in that he arose from the Father and sanctified his own temple by the Holy Spirit along with all

---

instructed to do and sank into sin, with the result that the Spirit found nowhere to rest among men" (*Comm. Is.* 2.4 [PG 70.313c]; the English translation here is from Norman Russell, *Cyril of Alexandria* [London: Routledge, 2000]).

133. See Keating, "Divinization in Cyril," 157. Cyril, *Unity of Christ*, 62–63, wrote concerning one of the purposes of the incarnation: "This was why he himself became the first one to be born of the Holy Spirit (I mean of course after the flesh) so that he could trace a path for grace to come to us. ... This is how he transmits the grace of sonship even to us so that we too can become children of the Spirit, insofar as human nature had first achieved this possibility in him."

134. See Cyril, *Unity of Christ*, 59. Jesus renews human nature in himself and then all those who participate in him, giving life and light to those who are in him by faith: "our Lord Jesus Christ hides life in us through his own flesh, and like a seed he places immortality in us, abolishing all the decay that is in us" (*In Jo.* 6.54 [Pusey, 1.533]). Earlier in his commentary, Cyril wrote: "The Son receives them and gives them life. By placing his own good attribute into those who by their own nature are corruptible, and by pouring the life-giving power of the Spirit into them like a spark of fire, he refashions them completely, making them immortal" (*In Jo.* 6.40 [1.499]).

135. Jesus did not receive the Spirit for himself, but for us and our restoration: "He [Jesus] did not receive anything for himself personally because he himself is the supplier of the Spirit. But the one who knew no sin received the Spirit as man in order to keep the Spirit in our nature and root in us once again the grace that had left us. ... The Spirit flew away from us because of sin, but the one who knew no sin became one of us so that the Spirit might become accustomed to remain in us, since the Spirit finds no reason in him for leaving or shrinking back" (*In Jo.* 1.32–33 [1.184]).

136. In other words, the redemption of humanity takes place first in Christ because he is the first man to receive again the Holy Spirit that Adam had lost through sin. Keating, "Divinization in Cyril," 157, writes, "Christ also carries out the work of redemption and re-creation upon himself, as representing in himself the new humanity." The incarnation was the refashioning of humanity first in the Logos and then all who participate in him by faith: "God the Word did not change even when he assumed flesh endowed with a rational soul. ... In this way he saved his own people, not as a man conjoined to God, but as God who has come in the likeness of those who were in danger, so that in him first of all the human race might be refashioned to what it was in the beginning. In him all things become new (cf. 2 Cor 5:17)" (Cyril, *Unity of Christ*, 88).

> creation, which came to be through him and to which sanctification applies. The mystery of Christ, then, has become a beginning and a way for us to attain participation in the Holy Spirit and union with God. We are all sanctified in him in the way that has already been explained. (*In Jo.* 17.20–21 [Pusey, 2.734–735])

In baptism, we receive the Spirit from Christ, and the Spirit in turn enables us to partake in Christ. We become partakers of the divine life in the "holy flesh [of Christ] ... through holy baptism" (*In Jo.* 9.6–7 [Pusey, 2.157])[137] because we receive the Spirit and his "spiritual ray, so to speak (I mean illumination by the Spirit)" (*In Jo.* 9.25 [Pusey, 2.179–180]).[138] The illumination of the Spirit allows us to partake of Jesus' flesh in the eucharist by faith (*In Jo.* 6.45 [Pusey, 1.509).[139] Without faith, we cannot receive and partake "in the mystical blessing [of the eucharist] by which we are joined to the living and lifegiving Word" (*In Jo.* 17.3 [Pusey, 2.669]; cf. 6.69 [Pusey, 1.576]).

The Spirit enables us to participate in Christ spiritually because the Spirit is himself "the mind of Christ ... know[ing] all that is in him" (*In Jo.* 14.25–26 [Pusey, 2.506]; cf. 16.12–13 [Pusey, 2.628]).[140] The Spirit illumines us to the mind of Christ through our contemplation of Scripture,[141] so we may be one with Christ

137. Daniel A. Keating, *The Appropriation of Divine Life in Cyril of Alexandria* (Oxford: Oxford University Press, 2004), 101–2, writes, "On the sacramental level, if the Eucharist is the summit to which baptism leads, baptism is distinctive by being the point of transfer, that initial indwelling of God that makes us in truth, for Cyril, new creations, 'children of God', and partakers of the divine nature."

138. Partaking in the holy flesh of Christ means to participate in the redeemed humanity of Christ who took on our corrupt nature to make it incorruptible with his own life as God.

139. The illumination of the Spirit enables us to see beyond the humanity of the person of Christ with our physical eyes to behold his divinity with the eyes of faith (*In Jo.* 9.38 [Pusey, 2.201]). Put it another way, the Spirit in baptism washes "away the defilement and impurity of the eyes of the mind" with faith to allow us to behold the "beauty" of Christ (*In Jo.* 9.6–7 [Pusey, 2.157–158]; cf. 6.46 [Pusey, 1.513]). The faith, which the Spirit illumines us to in Scripture, allows us to partake of the body of Christ, which gives us life and incorruption: "Faith then is the door and way to life, and the ascent from decay to incorruption. ... And since he [Jesus] himself is eternal life, he is promising to grant himself to those who believe, which is the meaning of the passage, 'that Christ may dwell in our hearts through faith' [Eph 3:17]" (*In Jo.* 6.46 [Pusey, 1.513]). So by receiving the elements of the Eucharist through faith, we partake in redeemed humanity in the person of the Logos. Cyril, however, did not explain how the elements of the Eucharist are transformed into the body and blood of Christ (Keating, *Cyril*, 68).

140. In fact, it was Jesus' "predetermined intention (προτεθέντα σκοπόν) of kindness toward us ... to illuminate (καταφωτίσαι) everyone by the torch of the Spirit," so we may partake of Jesus by faith and be restored to God (*In Jo.* 9.39 [Pusey, 2.204]).

141. According to Matthew R. Crawford, *Cyril of Alexandria's Trinitarian Theology of Scripture* (Oxford: Oxford University Press, 2014), 178, "being 'partakers of Christ' results from the process

in mind and disposition (*In Jo.* 17.20–21 [Pusey, 2.737]; 9.10 [Pusey, 2.160]).[142] In the same breath, however, Cyril referred to the Father and the Son as the ones who illumine and awaken faith for communion in our reading of Scripture.

> Father may be understood to implant the knowledge of his own offspring in us not with a voice booming from above and resounding through the earth like thunder but with divine illumination shining [φωταγωγίας ἀναλαμπούσης] in us from the understanding of the God-breathed Scripture. And you will find even in this case the work of the Son in us. It is written somewhere concerning the holy disciples, "Then he opened their eyes," namely, to understand the Holy Scriptures. (*In Jo.* 6.45 [Pusey, 1.510])

So, like the Cappadocians, Cyril viewed the operations of the Trinity as inseparable in the economy of illumination.[143] All three divine persons are involved in the process of illumination, which brings us into communion with their life of light (*In Jo.* 3.31 [Pusey, 1.240]; 6.38–39 [Pusey, 1.495]; 6.63 [Pusey, 1.554]; 7.16 [Pusey, 1.603]; 7.17 [Pusey, 1.606]).

The economy of illumination is a mode of communion with God. On the one hand, the Father illuminates us through the Spirit, so we may come and partake in the flesh of Christ (*In Jo.* 6.45 [Pusey, 1.507–510]). On the other hand, to partake in the flesh of Christ is to "behold the divine and holy light, that is, to receive knowledge of the holy and consubstantial Trinity (ἁγίας καὶ ὁμοουσίου Τριάδος)" because "it is the body of the one who is the true light by

---

of allowing the 'divine word' to operate within the mind and heart. In other words, participating in the living Word comes through contemplating of the written word." The Spirit's illumination enables those inside the church to contemplate the "mystery of Christ" in Scripture (Crawford, *Cyril*, 209; cf. 219).

142. Concerning our union and communion with God, Cyril wrote, "There is only one way union with God can take place, even in the case of Christ (insofar as he appeared as and bears the name of a human being). That way is this: the flesh is sanctified by union with the Spirit in an ineffable manner of concurrence and thus ascends to an unconfused union with God the Word and through him to a union with the Father—a union by disposition, that is, not by nature" (*In Jo.* 17.22–23 [Pusey, 3.2]).

143. Cyril, for example, wrote, "Understand, rather, that the Father is a coworker with the Son, and the Son in turn is a coworker with the Father, and our salvation and rising again from death to life is a work of the entire (so to speak) holy Trinity. ... Blessings come to us through the entire holy Trinity, and God the Father is found to be entirely all in all, through the Son in the Spirit" (*In Jo.* 6.40 [Pusey, 1.500]).

nature" (*In Jo.* 9.6–7 [Pusey, 2.157–158]).[144] Knowledge of God through illumination is "eternal life" with God (*In Jo.* 17.3 [2.667–670) because it is communion, which consists of knowing and being known by the triune God (*In Jo.* 10.14–15 [Pusey, 2.231–232]). To participate in Christ is to be illumined by the Spirit because it is to have the mind of Christ through the Spirit, which makes us one with Christ in "disposition of mind and heart" (*Comm. Hos.* 7.13–14).[145] In Cyril's account, we find support for my biblical sketch of the economy of illumination as a mode of participation in Christ, insights into the indispensable agency of the Spirit for the knowledge of God even in the garden of Eden, and a way to understand what Calvin will argue later that we receive all God's benefits in union with Christ because Christ *himself* is the gift of God, in which all other spiritual blessings flow.

GREGORY OF PALAMAS (C. 1296–1359)

In his defense of the holy hesychasts from the charge of Barlaam of Calabria, Gregory of Palamas employed Gregory of Nyssa's distinction between the energy and essence of God to show how the "transcendent God remains transcendent, as He also communicates Himself to humanity."[146] Barlaam alleged the monks had mistakenly seen physical and created light for God's uncreated light (*Triad* 3.1.5; 3.3.11–13)[147] because he did not believe that God communicates himself to us directly. Knowledge of God, for Barlaam, is possible only symbolically through the mediation of created things, our physical senses,

144. Crawford, *Cyril*, 196–97, notes that the trinitarian and christological content here is what separates general illumination from redemptive illumination in the Spirit. All humanity has general illumination, which makes them "intelligent" because all whom God created in his image participate in the Word who is "intelligence" by nature (*In Jo.* 1.9 [Pusey, 1.111]). Only those who have the Spirit have redemptive illumination, which gives spiritual insight into the oneness of the Trinity and the word of God in Scripture: "Scripture, as the book inspired by the Spirit for the church's well-being, is only intelligible for believers within the church who have the aid of the same Spirit" (Crawford, *Cyril*, 219).

145. English translation from St. Cyril of Alexandria, *Commentary on the Twelve Prophets*, vol. 1, trans. Robert C. Hill, FC 115(Washington: Catholic University of America Press, 2007). According to Cyril, "the Spirit transfers those in whom he comes and dwells into a new disposition and transforms them into newness of life" (*In Jo.* 16.7 [2.620]).

146. Gregory Palamas, *The Triads*, ed. John Meyendorff and trans. Nicholas Gendle (New York: Paulist, 1983), 20. Unless noted otherwise, the English translation of *Triads in Defense of the Holy Hesychasts* is also from this work, and the Greek text is from Grégoire Palamas, *Défense des saints hésychastes*, 2 vols., ed. Jean Meyendorff (Louvain: "Spicilegium Sacrum Lovaniense" Admistration, 1959).

147. Russell, *Deification*, 305.

and apophatic theology, "saying only what *God is not*, but not what *He is*."[148] So Barlaam was shocked to hear that the hesychasts claimed to have seen God's uncreated light, for this would imply that "human beings could participate in God," which in Barlaam's mind was impossible.[149] In response to Barlaam, Palamas argued that this light is the uncreated energy (ἐνέργειά),[150] which Gregory of Nyssa has taught[151] is distinct from God's essence (οὐσία)[152] but flows from it[153] because God's energy is God acting according to what he is.[154] So while we do not participate in God's essence, which is "imparticipable," we participate in God through his energy (*Triad* 2.3.66; 3.1.24; 3.2.13). Palamas referred to this energy as "enhypostatic light" (ὑποστατικοῦ φωτός, *Triad* 1.3.7, or φῶς ἐνυποστάτως, *Triad* 2.3.8). Unpacking the nature of enhypostatic light will

---

148. Palamas, *Triads*, 12–13.

149. Russell, *Deification*, 304.

150. John Meyendorff, *A Study of Gregory Palamas*, trans. George Lawrence (Leighton Buzzard: Faith Press, 1964), 223, puts it this way, "For him [Palamas], these uncreated and eternal energies are the thoughts of God, who is himself present in each of them."

151. Maspero, "Energy," 261, offers a concise summary of Gregory of Nyssa's energy (ἐνεργεία) as the "manifestation of the divine richness which is poured out in the Trinitarian *exitus*, and which can be followed back in the *reditus* which became accessible in Christ, uniting the divine immanence to the economy in dynamic of personal participation which is the basis of divinization itself." See Torstein Tollefsen, "Gregory of Palamas," in *The Brill Dictionary of Gregory of Nyssa*, eds. Lucas Francisco Mateo-Seco and Giulio Maspero (Leiden: Brill, 2010), 382, who shows how Palamas's understanding of energy "owes much to his reading of Gregory of Nyssa." For some of Palamas's reasons for why this light is uncreated, see *Triad* 3.1.112–14.

152. Meyendorff, *Palamas*, 225, writes, "The energies are inseparable from the essence, but not identical with it: 'In a certain sense,' Palamas writes, 'essence and energy are identical in God, but in another sense, they are different.'"

153. Gregory argued that as God's essence is uncreated, God's energy is uncreated (*Triad* 3.2.5) because God by nature must also have energy before the foundation of the world, in order to create the world in the first place: "For was it not needful for the work of providence to exist before Creation, so as to cause each of the created things to come to be in time, out of nonbeing? Was it not necessary for a divine knowledge to know before choosing, even outside time? But how does it follow that the divine prescience had a beginning? How could one conceive of a beginning of God's self-contemplation, and was there ever a moment when God began to be moved toward contemplation of Himself? Never! ... These works of God, then, are manifestly unoriginate and pretemporal: His foreknowledge, will, providence, contemplation of Himself, and whatever powers are akin to these. ... each of His works is a virtue" (*Triad* 3.2.6).

154. For example, Palamas wrote, "And according to St. Gregory of Nyssa and all the other Fathers, the natural energy [ἐνέργειά] is the power [δύναμις] which manifests every essence, and only nonbeing is deprived of this power; for the being which participates in an essence will also surely participate in the power which naturally manifests that essence" (*Triad* 3.2.7). Palamas, however, does not seem to differentiate God's power from his energy as Nyssen has done. For more discussion, see Tollefsen, "Palamas," 382.

lead us to a closer understanding of the way Gregory conceptualized his account of illumination as a mode of union with God.

ENHYPOSTATIC LIGHT

There are two things that Palamas has in mind when he refers to God's energy as enhypostatic light. First, this light is not symbolic, but really exists. He wrote, "[t]his hypostatic light [φῶς ἐνυποστάτως], seen spiritually by the saints, they know by experience to exist, as they tell us, and to exist not symbolically only, as do manifestations produced by fortuitous events, but it is an illumination immaterial and divine, a grace invisibly seen and ignorantly known. *What* it is, they do not pretend to know" (*Triad* 2.3.8). It is the light that Peter, James, and John encountered and beheld with their *eyes* on Mount Tabor from the transfiguration of Jesus Christ (Matt 17:1–8; Mark 9:2–8; Luke 9:28–36; 2 Pet 1:16–18). So if the light of Tabor was symbolic, "then Christ never really was, is or will be such as He appeared on Thabor" (*Triad* 3.1.14). Though this light does not bypass our senses and intellect, it transcends them[155] because it is a "spiritual and divine" light that shines from glory to glory (*Triad* 3.2.14–15; cf. 2 Cor 3:18). It is the light that "existed from the beginning" (*Triad* 3.1.15) and "will continually and endlessly dazzle us 'with its most brilliant rays' in the Age to come, when we will be 'always with the Lord', according to His promise" (*Triad* 2.3.20; cf. 3.1.10, 14; Rev 22:5).

Second, the word "enhypostatic" has a sense of "personalized existence,"[156] not in the way of constituting a fourth hypostasis in the Trinity as some have accused Palamas of doing, but in a sense of "personal attributes," which "must have a personal (or hypostatic) *locus*" in the divine hypostases.[157] So, even though divine light always exists, it never exists independently or outside of the hypostases of God.[158] Palamas explained,

155. Cf.: "The light, then, became accessible to their [i.e., the first disciples'] eyes, but to eyes which saw in a way superior to that of natural sight, and had acquired the spiritual power of the spiritual light. This mysterious light, inaccessible, immaterial, uncreated, deifying, eternal, this radiance of the Divine Nature, this glory of the divinity, this beauty of the heavenly kingdom, is at once accessible to sense perception and yet transcends it" (*Triad* 3.1.22).

156. Meyendorff, *Palamas*, 217.

157. Palamas, *Triads*, 140.

158. Cf.: "Nonetheless, there is only one unoriginated essence, the essence of God; none of the powers that inhere in it is an essence, so that all necessarily and always are *in* the divine essence" (*Triad* 3.2.5).

> It is "enhypostatic", not because it possesses a hypostasis of its own, but because the Spirit 'sends it out into the hypostasis of another', in which it is indeed contemplated. It is then properly called 'enhypostatic', in that it is not contemplated by itself, nor in essence, but in hypostasis. ... But the Holy Spirit transcends the deifying life which is in Him and proceeds from Him, for it is its own natural energy, which is akin to Him, even if not exactly so. For it is said, "We do not see any deification nor any life exactly similar to the Cause which goes beyond all things in its sublime transcendence." (*Triad* 3.1.9; cf. 3.1.18)

The other point that Palamas was trying to make here is that enhypostatic light is like God and comes only from God, but it is not the same as God who is infinitely more. However, this "light may be said to be God when we are speaking of God as self-communicating or participable."[159] It is God manifesting himself in his glory, splendor, and power.

Putting these two meanings together, divine light is enhypostatic because it is neither fleeting nor independent of God, but eternal and inheres in God by nature, but in us by grace (*Triad* 3.1.9, 18), for "God, while remaining entirely in Himself, dwells entirely in us by His superessential power; and communicates to us not His nature, but His proper glory and splendour" (*Triad* 1.3.23; 2.3.66).

UNION WITH GOD: CONTEMPLATING ENHYPOSTATIC LIGHT

We participate in communion with God through contemplating his enhypostatic light because the "contemplation [θεωρία] of this light is a union [ἕνωσις]" (*Triad* 2.3.36; cf. 1.2.9). "Now," Palamas asked, "this union with the illuminations—what is it, if not a vision [ὅρασις]" (*Triad* 3.2.14)? This union is a vision because it is the "contact" (ἐπαφῆς, *Triad* 3.2.14), which I have described as a oneness between the beholder and the beheld.[160] Contemplation is the "activity" of the "intellectual sensation" or "spiritual sense" within our "heart" (*Triad* 1.3.20; 1.2.4),[161] which sees "neither by the intellect or by the body, but

159. A. N. Williams, *The Ground of Union: Deification in Aquinas and Palamas* (New York: Oxford University Press, 1999), 117.

160. It is a union with God in his glory and splendor (*Triad* 1.3.23).

161. Contemplation is described as "mystical and ineffable" because what takes place in Christ and what we see through the Spirit is "untraceable" (*Triad* 1.3.21).

by the Spirit ... a light which surpasses light" (*Triad* 1.3.21).[162] The heart is the center of our being—our innermost; it is the "throne of grace," where we encounter God (*Triad* 1.2.3).[163] Contemplation, in other words, is sensing the presence of God within the core of our being, as God dwells there, communicating the light of his glory and splendor in the Son through the illumination of the Spirit:[164] "The perfect illumination of the Spirit is not only like the revelation of thought, but an enhypostatic light in the soul, steadfast and continuous illumination. For the one who said, 'Let light shine out of darkness,' has shone in our heart" (*Triad* 1.3.7; 1.2.2; 2 Cor 4:6).[165] Although contemplation is a supernatural gift from God (*Triad* 1.3.17, 19),[166] we are responsible to purify our hearts, so that the "light of the Holy Trinity [may] shine forth [into our heart] at the time of prayer" (*Triad* 1.3.21; 2.3.11).

This light is not only the object of our vision, but also the power and means to see.[167] In the light of the Father, Son, and Spirit, we not only see, but also become the light that we contemplate[168] because it is a "deifying

162. Palamas gave an example of Paul in Scripture who said, "'I know not whether I saw out of the body or in the body.' In other words, he did not know whether it was his intellect or his body which saw" (*Triad* 1.3.21; 2 Cor 12:2). It is being "ravished beyond all objects and all objective thought, and even beyond" oneself (*Triad* 1.3.21). It is seeing Christ, the enhypostatic light, in the "power" (*Triad* 1.3.17) and "divinising communion of the Spirit" within our heart (*Triad* 1.3.5).

163. "And the great Macarius says also, 'The heart directs the entire organism, and when grace gains possession of the heart, it reigns over all the thoughts and all the members; for it is there, in the heart, that the mind and all the thoughts of the soul have their seat'" (*Triad* 1.2.3).

164. Williams, *Union*, 113, defines contemplation as a "union and divinization that occurs mystically and ineffably by the grace of God (1.3.17)."

165. My English translation of "Ἡ *τελεία τοῦ Πνεύματος ἔλλαμψις οὐχ οἷον νοημάτων μόνον ἀποκάλυψίς ἐστιν, ἀλλ' ὑποστατικοῦ φωτὸς ἐν ταῖς ψυχαῖς βεβαία καὶ διηνεκὴς ἔλλαμψις · το γάρ, ὁ εἰπὼν ἐκ σκότους φῶς λάμψαι ὃς ἔλαμψεν ἐν ταῖς καρδίαις ἡμῶν.*" Cf.: "God who while remaining imparticipable, invisible and impalpable, becomes participable by His superessential power, and communicates Himself and shines forth and becomes in contemplation 'One Spirit' with those who meet Him with a pure heart, according to the most mystical and mysterious prayer which our common father addressed to His own Father? 'Grant them,' He says, 'that as I am in you, Father, and you in me, so they too may be one in us', in truth" (*Triad* 2.3.66).

166. For if God did not give us light, then would there be anything to see (Williams, *Union*, 113; cf. *Triad* 2.3.23)?

167. Cf.: "This spiritual light is thus not only the object of vision, but it is also the power by which we see; it is neither a sensation nor an intellection, but is a spiritual power, distinct from all created cognitive faculties in its transcendence, and made present by grace in rational natures which have been purified" (*Triad* 3.2.14).

168. Palamas pointed to Moses, Stephen, and Arsenius as examples of the transformation that takes place in light (*Triad* 2.3.9).

light" that transforms us as we see God as he is (*Triad* 1.3.5, 23; 3.1.15–17; cf. 2 Cor 3:18; 1 John 3:2).

> For it is in light that the light is seen, and that which see operates in a similar light, since this faculty has no other way in which to work. Having separated itself from all other beings, it becomes itself all light and is assimilated to what it sees, or rather, it is united to it without mingling, being itself light and seeing light through light. If it sees itself, it sees light; if it beholds the object of its vision, that too is light; and if it looks at the means by which it sees, again it is light. For such is the character of the union, that all is one, so that he who sees can distinguish neither the means nor the object nor its nature, but simply has the awareness of being light and of seeing a light distinct from every creature. (*Triad* 2.3.36).

To see light is to be in light and to reflect and become light.

Gregory tendered an Orthodox view of how contemplation through illumination in 2 Cor 3:18 and 4:6 is a transformative union because it is to see and be "assimilated" to the light of the Son through the presence of the Spirit to be with God who dwells in our heart. "Contemplation," Palamas wrote, "is a union and a divinisation which occurs mystically and ineffably by the grace of God, after the stripping away of everything from here below which imprints itself on the mind" (*Triad* 1.3.17). The Orthodox Church has employed the Jesus Prayer, "Lord Jesus Christ, Son of God, have mercy on me, a sinner," to return the divided mind, scattered by the bodily senses, to the heart to desire God singularly by stripping away all desires below that hold us captive from contemplating God above, ravished and enthralled by the beauty of his light, no longer loving, desiring, or seeing anything else, but God, in whom we in turn see and love everything more purely and properly (*Triad* 1.2.2–9). Palamas's concept of enhypostatic light describes another aspect of the uncreated energy of God, by which we participate in God. And he beautifully paints a picture of the way our contemplation of light in light transforms us into light.

DUMITRU STANILOAE (1903–1993)

The works of Dumitru Staniloae offer an apropos ending to our chapter because they present a "neo-patristic synthesis," that retrieves from all the theologians we have covered in this chapter to engage modern questions of faith, such as what it means to know God in the modern world.[169] For the Orthodox Church, Staniloae argues, knowledge of God is union, as ignorance is separation from God. Our ascent in the knowledge of God then is an ever-increasing union with God.[170] Staniloae's retrieval work is an integration of the past with the present. For example, he employs Martin Buber's *I and Thou* to make sense of how and why the fathers saw knowledge of God as union and the Spirit as the bond of union between God and us in illumination.[171]

KNOWLEDGE OF GOD AS UNION WITH GOD

Following St. Symeon, the New Theologian, Dumitru Staniloae perceives "knowledge of God as a kind of 'seeing.'"[172] As we will see, this idea of seeing offers another way for us to understand why knowledge of God is union because it is a seeing of oneself in God and God in oneself. Staniloae also describes the knowledge of God as "a contact or a 'feeling' of the mind" because the "reality of God radiates a spiritual 'light' that penetrates the human mind, just as created things radiate a material light."[173] In Staniloae's later work, he maintains that to know God is to live in the "light of communion with God" or the reality of the presence of the Father in the Son through the Spirit.[174] Staniloae understands knowledge as

---

169. Radu Bordeianu, *Dumitru Staniloae: An Ecumenical Ecclesiology* (London: Bloomsbury, 2011), 5, 13. Cf. Dumitru Staniloae, *Revelation and Knowledge of the Triune God*, vol. 1 of *The Experience of God: Orthodox Dogmatic Theology*, trans. and ed. Ioan Ionita and Robert Barringer (Brookline, MA: Holy Cross Orthodox, 1998), xvi.

170. Cf.: "The Eastern Fathers in general declare that full knowledge is the union between the one who knows and the one who is known, just as ignorance causes separation or is the effect of separation. ... Therefore by knowing God perfectly in the life to come we will also be united permanently with him. ... This conception of knowledge through union, and of our progress in knowledge as a progress in union, stands in solidarity with the understanding of time as a path towards eternity and towards union with God in love. Progress in the love of God is progress in the union with him, and this in turn is progress in the knowledge of God and of creatures until they are fully known within the full union and love that are identical with 'eternal life' (Jn 3.16)" (Staniloae, *Triune God*, 201–202).

171. Emil Bartos, *Deification in Eastern Orthodox Theology: An Evaluation and Critique of the Theology of Dumitru Staniloae* (Carlisle: Paternoster Press, 1999), 271–272.

172. Dumitru Staniloae, *The World: Creation and Deification*, vol. 2 of *The Experience of God: Orthodox Dogmatic Theology*, trans. and ed. Ioan Ionita and Robert Barringer (Brookline, MA: Holy Cross Orthodox, 2000), 75.

173. Staniloae, *World*, 75.

174. Dumitru Staniloae, *The Fulfillment of Creation*, vol. 6 of *The Experience of God: Orthodox Dogmatic Theology*, trans. and ed. Ioan Ionita (Brookline, MA: Holy Cross Orthodox, 2013), 154.

union in both language and Scripture. He sees, for instance, in the Latin etymology, *cognosco* (*cum* + *gnosco*), and the Romanian word, *con-stiinta* ("consciousness"), the ancients' awareness of the "interpersonal character of knowledge."[175] Knowledge takes place in communion. In sharing and exchanging with others what is interior, we become more cognizant and conscious not only of others, but also of ourselves. It is in opening ourselves and embracing others that we perceive the meaning of our existence. From Scripture, Staniloae reads the substance of union and eternal life as the knowledge of God (cf. John 17:3) because God knows and is known by his children who share his life, but he "does not know those who do not do his will, those who are not his own" (cf. Ps 1:6; 33:15; 44:22, 24; Matt 7:23; Luke 13:25–27; 1 Cor 8:3; 2 Tim 2:19).[176]

Knowledge of God is union with God because it involves *love*.[177] Like Buber, Staniloae argues that our knowledge of God does not consist of an *Ich-Es* (I-It) relation because God is not a "thing," which has "no free dimension of depth, distinct from [its] surface dimension, something which [it] could voluntarily keep hidden."[178] A thing neither hides nor reveals what it thinks or feels, so a reciprocal relation is not necessary. "In the case of a person, however, one person must be united in love with another in order to know that person from within in the same way as he is known by himself, and in order for both of them to be enriched through this knowledge."[179] Love unites us to God and each other because it frees us from the self-confinement of our sin to go outside of ourselves to the interior of another person, since love allows for transparency. Love allows us to give ourselves to the other person and to receive the other person into ourselves.

Love joins the knowing subjects in a reciprocal relationship that enriches their knowledge of self and the other because self-understanding

175. Staniloae, *Triune God*, 204.

176. Staniloae, *Triune God*, 206. For example, the psalmist highlighted that the basis for the divergent terminus between the righteous and the wicked is because the "Lord knows [MT: יוֹדֵעַ or LXX: γινώσκει] the way of the righteous, but the way of the wicked will perish" (Ps 1:6 ESV). In Scripture, knowledge is relational and covenantal.

177. Staniloae, *Triune God*, 205

178. Staniloae, *Triune God*, 202.

179. Knowledge is union because it "is the loving reference of one subject to another subject. ... it is only through this reference that he knows himself and actualizes himself as subject" (Staniloae, *Triune God*, 202–3).

and the understanding of another person arises from seeing oneself in another and the other in oneself. This knowledge, which stems from the "loving reference" of oneself as another and vice versa, is found perfectly within the Trinity.[180] Staniloae referred to it as an "infinite spiritual *perichôrêsis* of conscious love"[181] because the three divine hypostases are wholly "interior to each other,"[182] the Father seeing himself in the Son and the Son in himself through love.[183] The Spirit is the "love" between the Father and the Son "extending itself to subjects outside themselves."[184] Love is why God has come to us[185] and why we have returned to him in Christ.[186] At Pentecost, God's love, the Spirit of Christ, came to establish the communion of saints in the communion of God.[187] Through the indwelling of the Spirit, "Christ descends now for the first time within human hearts."[188] The *love* between Father and Son in the Spirit is God's "movement towards" us, an "eternal

---

180. Staniloae, *Triune God*, 202. In Staniloae's own words, "This kind of pole of perfect reference is possessed by God within himself. He refers to himself as to other persons and these persons refer one to the other reciprocally and perfectly. In his continuous movement towards the Son who is in him, and in the continuous movement of the Son towards the Father, the Father knows himself in his reference to the Son, knowing the Son and knowing himself in the Son" (Staniloae, *Triune God*, 203). Elsewhere, he wrote similarly that each divine hypostasis "sees himself only in relation to the other, or regards only the other, or sees himself only in the other. The Father sees himself only as subject of the love for the Son" (Staniloae, *Triune God*, 264; cf. 259).

181. Staniloae, *Triune God*, 203; cf. 255.

182. Staniloae, *Triune God*, 172.

183. As Dumitru Staniloae, *Theology and the Church*, trans. Robert Barringer (Crestwood, NY: St. Vladimir's Seminary Press), 97, writes, "Love, as the Spirit of Truth, forges the link between one who knows the Truth and the Truth itself, which means, in this case, between the Father and his Image which he thinks from all eternity."

184. Staniloae, *Triune God*, 267, added: "Only through the Holy Spirit, therefore, does the divine love radiate to the outside." Bartos, *Deification*, 271–72, writes, "The Holy Spirit assures the living relation because 'He is the person between the two.' Thus in the Spirit we find 'a position between ourselves and the others,' for He is 'the mid-point between us, the milieu in which we really transcend both the one and the other.'" The Spirit offers the ground of communion for oneself and the divine or human other.

185. In other words, the purpose for the incarnation is to give us the Spirit (Staniloae, *Triune God*, 30–33).

186. Cf.: "The unifying force of good, or of love, or of *erôs* lies in the face that the divine yearning (*erôs*) 'brings ecstasy so that the lover belongs not to self but to the beloved.' This tendency, whether it is called *good* or *agapê* or *erôs*, does not merely urge the creature towards God, but also God towards the creature" (Staniloae, *Triune God*, 239).

187. Dumitru Staniloae, *The Church: Communion in the Holy Spirit*, vol. 4 of *The Experience of God: Orthodox Dogmatic Theology*, trans. and ed. Ioan Ionita (Brookline, MA: Holy Cross Orthodox, 2012), 1–11.

188. Staniloae, *Church*, 7.

movement" that stems from his own being.[189] To know and commune with God, in other words, is to partake in the movement of love between the Father and the Son in the Holy Spirit from eternity to eternity.

THE LIGHT OF THE WORLD

We participate in this communion between the Father and Son in the Spirit by receiving and offering up all that God has given us in the world. In the beginning, God has made us and set us in the world to progress in communion with God.[190] The world is a light that points us to God[191] because it is where God gives his "natural revelation."[192] The world is God's gift and word that communicates God's love, God as giver, and the meaning of existence as communion with God.[193] The world is also where we communicate our love to God, as we offer everything we have received from God to God in love. In this dialogical exchange of giving and receiving, the world becomes the means and place of dialogue and communion with God.

THE LIGHT OF THE SON

Our union with God through the world, however, is not complete without the gift and light of the Son,[194] who "is the 'Teacher' and the 'teaching' in person if He is the 'light' in person. He is the one who preaches and the one who

189. Staniloae, *Triune God*, 240.

190. Since the world was made by the Word of God, the world reflects the Word as a light, continuously communicating and directing us back to the Word, and it is only in the Word that the world is properly understood. Staniloae, for example, quotes Heinrich Schlier saying, "'By being brought into existence through the Word who enlightens life, they [things in the world] are in themselves indications, directions back to the Word and in the Word,'" and Wolfgang Beinert saying, "'The Cosmos can and must be interpreted from the Word'" (Staniloae, *World*, 21).

191. Staniloae, *World*, 22, 29–30.

192. Staniloae, *Triune God*, 1–13.

193. Staniloae, *World*, 21–63. For example, Staniloae wrote, "Through the gift of the world, God wishes to make himself known to the human person in his love. ... As a sign of one person's love for another, the gift has imprinted upon it the destination that the one who receives it must go beyond. In a way, the gift is what the person who offers it renounces for love of the person to whom it is offered" (Staniloae, *World*, 24).

194. "Thus, supernatural revelation," Staniloae, *Triune God*, 16, wrote, "represents a bringing back of human nature to its own true state, while giving human nature, at the same time, power to reach the final goal towards which it naturally aspires. In this way, supernatural revelation confirms and restores natural faith or nature itself as natural revelation. Only through supernatural revelation do we fully know what nature, and the revelation it

preaches about Himself. In Him the subject of the teaching is identified with its 'object.'"[195] To put it another way, the Son is the "climax of supernatural revelation," which restores and perfects natural revelation.[196] After the fall, human beings are in a state of death,[197] enmity, and separation from God.[198] So although God has given them a sign of his love through the world and the freedom to respond back to God in love, they have become blind to God and his love because they have refused to grow in their "freedom" and have "fallen into the slavery of the easy pleasure afforded by the senses."[199] They are blinded to God by the very gifts that were supposed to point them to God because they are enslaved by the desire of the flesh, which confines them from seeing that the "giver is greater than the gift."[200] Because of the state of sin, which is a "self-confinement within,"[201] God "makes himself transparent to us through the cross against our will" to live for ourselves and the world as an end without reference to God, from whom all blessings flow.[202] The cross of Jesus Christ reestablishes our communion with God by restoring dialogue between God and us for, in receiving the cross as a gift, we receive the Giver himself because the cross is God's gift of himself, which compels us in turn to offer ourselves to God as a gift in Christ.[203]

---

represents, are. Natural revelation appears to us in its full meaning only through supernatural revelation."

195. Dumitru Staniloae, *The Person of Jesus Christ as God and Savior*, vol. 3 of *The Experience of God: Orthodox Dogmatic Theology*, trans. and ed. Ioan Ionita (Brookline, MA: Holy Cross Orthodox, 2011), 91.

196. Cf.: "Christ represents the climax of supernatural revelation and the full confirmation and clarification of the meaning of our existence through the fulfillment of this existence within himself, the one in whom our ultimate union with God, and thus our perfection also, is achieved" (Staniloae, *Triune God*, 28, cf. 16, 22–23).

197. Because of "sin and death," human "nature now finds itself in an unnatural state" (Staniloae, *Triune God*, 16, cf. 20), but the supernatural revelation of God in Christ raises "our human nature enslaved to death ... spiritually to be able to pass over to the plane of communion with him—a plane not subject to death—and to understand this passing over" (Staniloae, *Triune God*, 24).

198. Staniloae, *Jesus Christ*, 105, argued, "God could not love man's state of sin, which is his state of enmity toward God." Only the cross can remove our "egoism" and enmity against God, so we may enjoy and respond to God's love in offering ourselves back to God (Staniloae, *Jesus Christ*, 114).

199. Staniloae, *World*, 166.

200. Staniloae, *World*, 24.

201. Staniloae, *World*, 166.

202. Staniloae, *World*, 166.

203. So Staniloae writes, "For He enters to the Father as a pure sacrifice, or He restores His communion with the Father in order to introduce us, too, into the communion with the Father. By this we also enter into communion with Christ as God, because we enter into communion

Restored dialogue between God and humanity takes place in the church, in the ones *baptized*[204] and so illumined by the Spirit to see and receive Christ through Scripture and tradition.[205] "The Church," Staniloae writes, "is the dialogue of God with the faithful through Christ in the Holy Spirit. ... The Church is Christ united in the Holy Spirit those who believe and over whom has been spread and through whom is spreading Christ's own act of drawing the faithful—by means of dialogue with them—in the process of growing into his likeness."[206] The church is an icon of Christ, pointing the world to the light of Christ with the likeness and presence of Christ in her as his body and bride.[207] Scripture is the written expression of the light of Christ, and through Scripture, "Christ continues to speak" and "continues to be at work in us through the Holy Spirit: 'I am with you always, to the close of the age' (Mt 28.20)."[208] The apostolic tradition "gives a permanent reality to the dialogue with the Church with Christ" in God[209] because it is the "authentic and apostolic way of making the content of Scripture explicit on the basis of its sacramental and spiritual application in the lives of the faithful."[210] The Spirit is the divine agent who unites the church to Christ[211] because the Spirit "is active in the Church where tradition is put into practice"[212] by illuminating her "to understand and to appropriate, in an authentic and practical way, the content of Scripture, that is, Christ in the fullness of his gifts."[213] The Spirit

---

with His Father, who thus becomes our Father. The sacrifice is necessary for communion. The sacrifice is animated by the tendency toward communion; it is self-denial for the sake of the other; it is self-forgetfulness out of love for the other. Thus communion is the result of sacrifice" (Staniloae, *Jesus Christ*, 110).

204. In step with the patristics' idea of baptism as illumination, Staniloae wrote, "*The Fathers gave baptism the name 'illumination.'*" (Dumitru Staniloae, *The Sanctifying Mysteries*, vol. 5 of *The Experience of God: Orthodox Dogmatic Theology*, trans. and ed. Ioan Ionita and Robert Barringer [Brookline, MA: Holy Cross Orthodox, 2012, 45–46 [emphasis original]).

205. Staniloae was following the stance of his theological predecessors (cf. Anatolios, *Retrieving Nicaea*, 237).

206. Staniloae, *Triune God*, 38.

207. Bordeianu, *Dumitru Staniloae*, 43–46.

208. Staniloae, *Triune God*, 40.

209. Staniloae, *Triune God*, 45.

210. Staniloae, *Triune God*, 53.

211. Staniloae, *Triune God*, 29–30; cf. 41.

212. Staniloae, *Triune God*, 55.

213. Staniloae, *Triune God*, 58.

illumines and causes the love of God in his Son to dwell in the church, so the church may once again offer herself to God who gave himself to her in love.

Staniloae helps us see why communion with God consists in knowledge and love because it is a loving knowledge of seeing ourselves in God and God in ourselves. He also draws out what I have touched on in chapter 2 concerning the whole Trinity dwelling in our hearts through the presence of the Spirit, an eternal movement that draws us into God's life of light and love.

CONCLUSION

Although our theologians from the East do not use the term, "the economy of illumination," the notion of it runs through their works—the Father shining into our hearts the light of the Son through the Spirit to bring us into light. For the Orthodox tradition, this light of knowledge flows from the essence (οὐσία) of God as the uncreated energy (ἐνέργεια) of God because the "reality of God radiates a spiritual 'light' that penetrates the human mind."[214] We participate, in other words, in God's energy rather than his essence because God's essence is unapproachable and imparticipable. Following Athanasius and Gregory of Nyssa, Gregory of Palamas writes, "God, while remaining entirely in Himself, dwells entirely in us by His superessential power; and communicates to us not His nature, but His proper glory and splendour" (*Triads* I, 3, 23). As we participate in the light of the sun through its rays rather the sun itself, we participate in the energies of God, which flow from the essence of God, but not in the essence of God itself.

The theological configuration of the Orthodox tradition offers ways to refine my sketch of the economy of illumination and contemplative union in chapter 2. This tradition configures the economy of illumination as the outflow of God's being, the inseparable operations of the light of splendor from the Father, Son, and Holy Spirit in our hearts. It is "a flash of ... light which is both one and three" (*Or.* 39.11), three distinct operations working as one to bring us into contemplative union with the Trinity, "the contemplation of the Father, Son, and Holy Spirit as a whole."[215] As image and light are inseparable in sight, the Son and the Spirit are inseparable in our sight of God in contemplative union. Knowledge of God through illumination is

214. Staniloae, *World*, 75.

215. Beeley, *Gregory of Nazianzus*, 231.

a contemplative union with the triune God because it is a "vision" (ὅρασις) of God, a "contact" (ἐπαφῆς) between God and us (*Triad* 3.2.14), and a "rational" or "conscious participation" in God.[216] Contemplative union is not only a union between a beholder and the object beheld through beholding, but also a union between a lover and the object loved through love. It is sharing in the self-love and knowledge of God poured out in Christ through the Spirit that brings us into the "circle of mutual glorification" between the Father and Son in the Spirit that results in praise (Gregory of Nyssa). It is, in other words, not a knowledge of things but of divine persons that requires us to open ourselves to God and to receive God into ourselves.

We come into this knowledge of God through a "second communication, far more amazing than the first," established in the Son (*Or.* 38.13). Communication with God after the fall in the Son is far greater than it was before the fall in Adam because the Son has received the Spirit permanently in himself as a man, so he can give us the Spirit permanently as God. Where the Spirit of the Lord is, there is freedom for communication with God (2 Cor 3:17). Redemption, we can say, takes place in the humanity of Christ, and then in us, when we participate in him. In chapter 7, I will build on this and explain further how Jesus Christ became the substance of our participation and how the economy of illumination became a means by which God applies what the Son has accomplished to us, allowing us to enter the second covenant (of grace) in the Son through the presence of Spirit for communion with God.

The reading of 2 Cor 3:18 and 4:6 from the Orthodox tradition puts the emphasis on the transformative process of illumination, in which the Father shines the deifying light of the Son into our hearts through the presence of the Spirit at baptism because it is "regeneration" (παλιγγενεσίας, *Spir.* 10.26) or "second birth" in God's deifying light (*Or.* 18.12–13; 40.3). I will rephrase this deifying process in my constructive moment as the "cardiac process" from the light of new creation. This transformative process not only begins our ascent but draws us *eternally* into the glory and goodness of God because God is infinite, so his goodness never ends. In God's light, we not only see light but become and reflect light to fill the world with the knowledge of God as the water fills the sea (Hab 2:14).

216. Anatolios, "Christ's Humanity," 275; idem., *Retrieving Nicaea*, 237.

5

ECONOMY OF ILLUMINATION IN ROMAN CATHOLIC TRADITION

"And do not be called teachers; for One is your Teacher, the Christ."

—Matt 23:10 NKJV

Turning to the account of divine illumination from the Roman Catholic tradition, we will notice a common Augustinian thread that consists of Irenaeus's and Clement's concept of Christ as divine teacher, Origen's view on the mind's participation in Christ, the Word eternally proceeding from the Father's Mind, and Tertullian's concept of the "psychological image of the divine Trinity."[1] The economy of illumination, for the Catholic tradition, is a movement of the mind into God, the object of its remembering, understanding, and loving, in the Son, the Wisdom and light of God, through the Spirit, the love of God. The Catholic tradition diverges from the Orthodox tradition on the nature of the life, light, and love of God in the economy of illumination. According to Vladimir Lossky,

> When we say that God is Wisdom, Life, Truth, Love—we understand the energies, which are subsequent to the essence and are its natural manifestations, but are external to the very being of the Trinity. That is why, in contrast to western theology, the tradition of the Eastern Church never designates that relation between the Persons of the Trinity by the name of attributes. We never say, for example, that the Son proceeds by the mode of the intelligence and the Holy

1. A. N. Williams, *Divine Sense: The Intellect in Patristic Theology* (Cambridge: Cambridge University Press, 2007), 39.

> Spirit by the mode of the will. The Spirit can never be assimilated to the mutual love of the Father and the Son.[2]

By virtue of its view on divine simplicity, the Catholic tradition does not perceive God's perfections as his energies, but as God in himself because he *is* his life, light, and love. So, with regard to our participation in God, the Catholic tradition does not describe it as a participation in the uncreated energies of God, but a participation through the divine missions, "the eternal procession" of God, which has "temporal effect" on us (*ST* I, q.43, a. 2, ad. 3).

The economy of illumination, for the Catholic tradition, is God's concerted action in the invisible missions to enable us to know and participate in God himself who *is* light and love by grace until we come to the beatific vision of God's essence in glory. To present a Roman Catholic configuration of the economy of illumination, I begin with the reading of 2 Cor 3:18 and 4:6 from Augustine, the theory's fountainhead, and then trace the trajectory of his theory of illumination in the works of Bonaventure, Aquinas, and Balthasar, before wrapping up the chapter with a comparison between the Orthodox and Catholic traditions.

AUGUSTINE (354–430)

Building on Carol Harrison's revision of Peter Brown's early and late Augustine theory,[3] Lydia Schumacher argues that Augustine's theory of illumination should be read in a theological framework rather than a philosophical one. Augustine, Schumacher reasons, was first and foremost a Christian theologian,

---

2. Vladimir Lossky, *The Mystical Theology of the Eastern Church* (Crestwood, NY: St. Vladimir's Seminary Press, 1976), 80–81.

3. Peter Brown's 1967 publication, *Augustine of Hippo: A Biography*, has shaped the way readers have read Augustine's account of divine illumination. In Brown's biography, he proposes a theory of an early and later Augustine. The early Augustine of 386 was a convert to Christianity, whose writings at that point were more philosophically inclined, but a paradigm shift occurred in his later writings, when he became the bishop of Hippo in 396 and wrote theologically to edify the church. As a result, readers of Augustine have generally read his theory of illumination in a philosophical context. They begin with his early philosophical works, *Soliloquia* and *De magistro*, to find his detailed discussion on the theory, and then move to his later and more dogmatic works, such as *De Trinitate*, *Confessiones*, and *De Genesi ad litteram*, for "additional references to the divine light rather than the theological context." Lydia Schumacher, *Divine Illumination: The History and Future of Augustine's Theory of Knowledge* (Oxford: Blackwell, 2011], 25). Carol Harrison, *Rethinking Augustine's Early Theology: An Argument of Continuity* (Oxford: Oxford University Press, 2006), however, challenges the "two Augustines" theory and argues that there is continuity between his early and later works because the real turning point in Augustine's thought took place in 386 rather than 396.

so to read him otherwise would impose categories foreign to his theory.[4] I follow Schumacher's advice and read Augustine in the context of creation, fall, and the incarnation of the Son. In Augustine's theory of illumination, I find a development of Irenaeus and Clement's concept of the movement of the mind from faith to contemplation in the light of Jesus Christ, our "inner Teacher" who dwells in our innermost and with whom we enjoy dialogical union. This movement from beholding Christ by faith to sight illustrates the way Augustine understood the transformation of our *imago Dei* from glory to glory in 2 Cor 3:18. Augustine's idea of the actualizing of the *imago Dei* within us through the light of Christ will become an essential building block in my construction of the cardiac and cognitive processes in the economy of illumination for Part III of my study.

THE CREATION AND FALL OF THE IMAGO DEI

Like the Greek fathers, Augustine thought that God has made our minds in his image, so we may know and share in his life of light (*Trin.* 15.27.49).[5] Augustine viewed the *imago Dei* in us as our mental activities,[6] which is "both given and yet to come."[7] Our *imago Dei* is only actualized when God becomes

4. Schumacher, *Illumination*, 16. Schumacher suggests that a "theologically contextualized investigation of illumination theory will reveal that ... Augustine conceived the light as the source of an intrinsic cognitive capacity that the mind gradually recovers as it forms a habit of operating by faith in God—that illumination is not, therefore, some form of extrinsic intellectual conditioning" (Schumacher, *Illumination*, 18–19). Illumination is the source that aligns our intrinsic cognitive capacity to see "the way God has made things to be: good," seeing them as *signa* to the *res*, the reality of God's goodness everywhere we turn. (Schumacher, *Illumination*, 63). The mind aligns itself to this reality and recovers its capacity "by following the example [Jesus] set through engagement in the process of cognition that is analogous to His and that results in a growing understanding of and certainty about the Being of God that He always knows in full" (Schumacher, *Illumination*, 65).

5. Or as Williams, *Divine Sense*, 146, puts it, "God is both Mind and the creator of minds." God is Mind because he knows himself and makes himself known, and he has made us like him to know him and make him known.

6. In Augustine's words: "This trinity of the mind is not really the image of God because the mind remembers and understands and loves itself, but because it is also able to remember and understand and love him by whom it was made. And when it does this it becomes wise. If it does not do it, then even though it remembers and understands and loves itself, it is foolish. Let it then remember its God to whose image it was made and understand and love him. To put in a word, let it worship the uncreated God, by whom it was created with a capacity for him and able to share in him. In this way it will be wise not with its own light but by sharing in that supreme light, and it will reign in happiness where it reigns eternal" (*Trin.* 14.12.15). English translation of *De Trinitate* is from Augustine, *The Trinity*, trans. Edmund Hill (Hyde Park, NY: New City Press, 1991).

7. See A. N. Williams, "Contemplation," in *Knowing the Triune God: The Work of the Spirit in the Practice of the Church*, ed. James J. Buckley and David S. Yeago (Grand Rapids: Eerdmans,

the object of its remembering, understanding, and love,[8] and "the image of God will achieve its full likeness of him when it attains to the full vision of him," the beatific vision of God (*Trin.* 14.18.24; cf. 1 John 3:2).[9] So, Augustine understood our beholding of God from glory to glory in 2 Cor 3:18 as the process by which our image of God achieves its fullness (*Trin.* 14.5.23–24). He read κατοπτριζόμενοι (beholding) in the Latin as *speculantes* and interprets it as the "seeing in a *speculum* (mirror), not looking out from a *specula* (a lookout point)" (*Trin.* 15.3.14). Our mind, which is made in God's image, is this *speculum* (mirror), by which we see God because what we see "in a mirror is an image" (*Trin.* 15.3.14). Like a "mirror" that reflects the object in front of it, our mind images and reflects God as God increasingly becomes the object of its mental activities.[10] In contemplating God, our mind is transformed "from the glory of faith to the glory of sight; from the glory by which we are sons of God to the glory by which we shall be like him, because we shall see him as he is" (*Trin.* 15.3.14).

God is the proper object of the activities of the mind because he has made us with himself as our *summum bonum*, or highest good (*Conf.* 7.5.7), so our mind is restless until it rests in him (*Conf.*1.1.1). To have anything else in God's place is to deviate from our *telos*, to fall short of God's glory and become less of who we are (Rom 3:23). This is what took place in the fall, when Adam sinned, "forfeiting the knowledge of God as Highest Good."[11] Because of the fall, all humanity in Adam instinctually perceives "tangible things and temporal circumstances as the ultimate realities that only God is."[12] We fail "to see the signs of God's good-

---

2001), 128; 121–46.

8. Rowan Williams, *On Augustine* (New York: Bloomsbury, 2016), 173.

9. The *imago Dei* in us is our mental activities, so it is only realized when God is the proper object of its activities. So when "the image of God in human beings is realized; we come to share in God's relation to God. Our unlimited, dependent openness to God is a finite sharing in God's eternal openness to God, the divine life aware of itself and understanding itself and loving itself" (Williams, *Augustine*, 139).

10. The mind is activated only when it has an object before its gaze. That is because our "mind is simply not there except as acting in relation to something. If we want to find where the image of God really is, we have to think of the mind thinking of itself in relation to the supreme, unique immaterial reality, God. ... the image of God in us is ... the mind completely caught up in contemplating God—aware of itself before God, opening its intelligence to God (though God can never be captured in a concept), directed in love towards God—held by this infinite 'object' which is endless awareness, intelligence and love" (Williams, *Augustine*, 136).

11. Schumacher, *Illumination*, 39.

12. Schumacher, *Illumination*, 39.

ness everywhere" we turn[13] because we have turned with Adam from God, our "Intelligible Light, in, by and through whom all intelligible things are illumined" (*Solil.* 1.1.3). To see God and his goodness everywhere in creation, we need divine illumination, which is the process of conforming and aligning our minds to God by following and thinking "in the way the Incarnate Son Himself exemplified: in the Spirit that glorifies God the Father."[14] To see light we need to follow and be *in* light (Ps 36:9): "a man who is not in light should not see light, that is not see God, because he is in darkness" (*Trin.* 8.8.12).

THE WAY TO WISDOM

Jesus who "bestowed 'the light of the mind by His enlightening act' at creation" is also the one who reminds us "that the light was dwelling within at His Incarnation."[15] He is the true light, which gives light to everyone, coming into the world (John 1:9). Our mind recovers its light, cognitive capacity to remember, understand, and love God, by following the light of Christ from knowledge (*scientia*) to wisdom (*sapientia*), a contemplation of God in God, our eternal rest.[16] The economy of illumination is the process by which God moves us from knowledge to wisdom, following Christ by faith to contemplate God in truth.[17]

The incarnation of the Word is the bridge to move us from knowledge by faith to the wisdom of God in truth (*Trin.* 4.18.24). Knowledge concerns the content of faith, what Jesus "did and suffered for us in time and space" (*Trin.* 13.19.24), but wisdom refers to the contemplation of the truth of Jesus as eternal Son, "without time and without space, coeternal with the Father and wholly present everywhere" (*Trin.* 13.19.24; cf. 12.22).[18] To become wise is to move from knowledge to wisdom in Jesus, "in whom are hidden all the treasures of wisdom and knowledge" (Col 2:3; *Trin.* 1.12.27, cf. 4.2.4; 15.27.49), by growing in the virtues of faith,

---

13. Schumacher, *Illumination*, 63.

14. Schumacher, *Illumination*, 63.

15. Schumacher, *Illumination*, 59.

16. "*Sapientia*," Williams, *Augustine*, 149, argues, "is indeed and ultimately the contemplation of God by God, but it is also that which prompts and makes possible the presence of God in what is not God."

17. Faith, grace, and knowledge refer to understanding the visible salvific work of the incarnated Word. Contemplation, truth, and wisdom refer to the beholding of the invisible, unchanging, and eternity of God. The transformation is a movement from the later to the former.

18. Williams, *Augustine*, 135.

hope, and love (1 Cor 13:13).[19] "And what is the worship of him," Augustine asks, "but the love of him by which we now desire to see him, and believe and hope that we will see him?" (*Trin.* 12.13.22). Jesus appeared to our physical eyes in time and space (*Trin.* 13.20.25), so our mind, "the interior eye of the heart" (*Serm.* 67.15),[20] may be healed by faith[21] and assured by hope to look and see God with love,[22] in a mirror dimly until face to face (*Trin.* 12.13.22; 13.20.25; 14.17.23; cf. 1 Cor 13:12; 2 Cor 3:18).[23] Since we cannot come to God, his Son, light from light, came to us to allure us with the light of his beauty and raise us up with him to God through the "weight" of love (*Conf.* 13.9.10), affected by the Spirit (*Enchir.* 117).[24] To see the Wisdom of God in Christ is to be taught by God "through the grace of the Spirit

19. Augustine writes, "There are three stages in the soul's progress [to contemplate God]: healing, looking, seeing. Likewise there are three virtues: faith, hope, love. For healing and looking, faith and hope are always necessary. For seeing, all three are necessary in this life, but in the life to come love only" (*Solil.* 1.7.14).

20. English translation of *Sermones* (*Serm.*) is from St. Augustine, *Sermons on Selected Lessons of the New Testament*, trans. and ed. R. G. MacMullen and Philip Schaff, NPNF[1] 6 (1888; repr., Peabody, MA: Hendrickson, 2004).

21. Cf.: "the Son of God came in order to become Son of man and to capture our faith and draw it to himself, and by means of it to lead us on to his truth" (*Trin.* 4.18.24). In order for us to contemplate the truth of Christ, "some of our rational attention . . . has to be directed to the utilization of changeable and bodily things without which this life cannot be lived . . . in order to do whatever we do in the reasonable use of temporal things with an eye to the acquisition of eternal things, passing the former on the way, setting our hearts on the latter to the end" (*Trin.* 12.13.21).

22. Faith in Christ reminds our mind that we were made in God's image to know God and his goodness (*Gen. litt.* 3.20.32). Hope strengthens our faith to look forward to our reward, the contemplation of God in full: "Contemplation in fact is the reward of faith, a reward for which hearts are cleansed through faith, as it is written, *cleansing their hearts through faith* (Acts 15:9)" (*Trin.* 1.17). Faith and hope transfer our *love* for temporal things to eternal things, so we could look heavenward: "So then the man who is being renewed in the recognition of God and in justice and holiness of truth by making progress day by day, is transferring his love from temporal things to eternal things, from visible things to intelligible things, from carnal things to spiritual things; he is industriously applying himself to checking and lessening his greed for the one thing and binding himself with charity to the other" (*Trin.* 14.17.23).

23. The reason why Augustine associated seeing God with loving God is because he saw the knowledge of God as union with God: "This truly is perfect virtue [i.e., love], reason achieving its end, which is the happy life. This vision is knowledge compounded of the knower and that which is known; just as vision in the ordinary sense is compounded of the sense of sight and the sensible object, of which if either is lacking there is no seeing" (*Solil.* 1.7.14). So we "love God now by faith, then we shall love Him through sight" (*Enchir.* 121). English translation of *Enchiridion de fide, spe, et caritate* is from St. Augustine, *Enchiridion on Faith, Hope, and Love*, trans. Thomas S. Hibbs (Washington, D.C.: Regnery, 1996).

24. Unless noted otherwise, the English translation of *Confessiones* is from Augustine, *Confessions*, trans. Henry Chadwick (Oxford: Oxford University Press, 1991). For more discussion of love as the weight, see Jean-Luc Marion, *In the Self's Place: The Approach of Saint Augustine*, trans. Jeffrey L. Kosky (Stanford: Stanford University Press, 2012), 269.

rather than the letter of the law," and the result of this divine teaching "is not simply that a person is aware of what he has learned by knowing but also that he seeks it by willing and accomplishes it by acting" (*Grat. Chr.* 14.15).

So, to be illumined is not simply to know God cognitively, but to will and act out the Word of God with the "word" of our heart. Augustine writes,

> the reason why it was not God the Father, not the Holy Spirit, not the trinity itself, but only the Son who is the Word of God that became flesh (although it was the trinity that accomplished this), is that we might live rightly by our word following and imitating his example: that is, by our having no falsehood either in the contemplation or in the operation of our word. However, this is a perfection of the image that lies some time in the future. To achieve it we are instructed by the good master in Christian faith and godly doctrine, in order that *with face unveiled* from the veil of the law *which is the shadow of things to come* (Heb 10:1; Col 2:17), *looking at the glory of the Lord through a mirror, we might be transformed into the same image from glory to glory, as by the Spirit of the Lord.* ... (*Trin.* 15.11.20; emphasis original; 2 Cor 3:18)

Jesus illumines our minds to reflect the image of God in him by nature through setting an example as the Word incarnate for our "word" to follow.[25] This "word" of ours is not a written or spoken word, which belongs to "language" (*Trin.* 15.10.19), but an "inward utterance" of our heart (*Trin.* 15.10.18), a "kind of sight of the consciousness" (*Trin.* 15.9.16), which the Lord sees (cf. Matt 15:18–19; Mark 7:21). This word is our conscious experience, inner life and thought, analogous to the Word, the only begotten from the Father. As the Word became flesh without being changed into flesh, "our word becomes sound without being changed into sound"; and just as God created all things by his Word, "we cannot have a work which is not preceded by a word" (*Trin.* 15.11.20). As our spoken and written words give form to our thought, the mind and thought of God is embodied and

25. Concerning the process of illumination, Schumacher, *Illumination*, 65, writes, "This is not because Christ the illuminator directly instigates or interferes with the cognitive process or imposes ideas and certainty about them, but because human mind can only recover its capacity by following the example He sets through engagement in a process of cognition that is analogous to His and that results in a growing understanding of and certainty about the Being of God that He always knows in full."

expressed in the person and work of Jesus Christ, whose blood speaks a better word (Heb 12:24).[26] That is why, if we come to see Christ as the knowledge and wisdom of God, then we have heard and been taught by God (John 6:45). When our word follows the Word, the light of God, we become conscious of God. God, in other words, becomes the object of our remembering, understanding, and loving in the light of Christ.

There is a quandary, however, to illumination. We can only be illumined *in* Christ, but we are unfit to be *in* him due to sin.[27] This quandary is resolved on the cross, says Augustine:

> Our enlightenment is to participate in the Word, that is, in that *life which is the light of men* (Jn 1:4). Yet we were absolutely incapable of such participation and quite unfit for it, so unclean were we through sin, so we had to be cleansed. Furthermore, the only thing to cleanse the wicked and the proud is the blood of the just man [*sanguis iusti*] and the humility of God [*et humilitas dei*]; to contemplate God, which by nature we are not, we would have to be cleansed by him who became what by nature we are and what by sin we are not. By nature we are not God; by nature we are men; by sin we are not just. So God became a just man to intercede with God for sinful man. The sinner did not match the just, but man did match man. So he applied to us the similarity of his humanity to take away the dissimilarity of our iniquity, and becoming a partaker of our mortality he made us partakers of his divinity. It was surely right that the death of the sinner issuing from the stern necessity of condemnation should be undone by the death of the just man issuing from the voluntary freedom of mercy, his single matching our double. (*Trin.* 4.2.4)[28]

26. Williams, *Augustine*, 44, illustrates, "the mind of God is embodied in Christ as our thoughts are in our words, and by this means God can be truly enjoyed by us, perceived, contemplated and loved in his self-sufficient being."

27. To be clear, it is sin rather than our nature that makes it impossible for us to participate in Christ because, although our mind "has lost its participation in him it still remains the image of God, even though worn out and distorted. It is his image insofar as it is capable of him and can participate in him" (*Trin.* 14.8.11). So following Irenaeus (*Haer.* 5.6.1; 5.11.2; 5.16.2; *Epid.* 11), Augustine also believed we are not *free* to come to God (*Conf.* 8.5.10).

28. The Latin text is from Sancti Avrelii Avgvstini, *De Trinitate, Libri XV*, CCSL 50, ed. W. K. Mountain (Turnholti: Brepols, 1968).

On the cross, the justice of man and the humility of God meet to open the way for sinful man to be in the light of the Son to see the Father of light.[29] Jesus made a way for us to participate in him again by his great exchange, the death of the just for the unjust and the humility of God to become man in the place of the pride of man to become god (Phil 2:8).[30] By taking on flesh, Jesus "paid" the death he did not owe, so that the "death we do owe might do us no harm" (*Trin.* 4.13.17).[31] Jesus makes us one with him in death, so we may be one with him in God:[32] "And this one true Mediator, in reconciling us to God by his sacrifice of peace, would remain one with him to whom he offered it, and make one in himself those for whom he offered it, and be himself who offered it one and the same as what he offered" (*Trin.* 4.14.19).

And by humbling himself to come down to die in our place,[33] Jesus raised us up in his humility as the Wisdom of God to contemplate God.[34] We participate in the heart of divine self-knowledge and love by following Jesus's example of

29. The mission of the incarnation of the Word and Wisdom of God was to become the "*mediator of God and men* (1 Tm 2:5)," in order to bring "believers to a direct contemplation of God and the Father" by his death (*Trin.* 1.16).

30. Following J.-M. Le Blond, *Les conversions de s. Augustin* (Paris: Aubier, 1950), 145, Williams, *Augustine*, 141, argues that the "organizing principle in Augustine's theology" is the incarnation of Jesus as the "path to and the form of transfiguring and participatory knowledge of the transcendent God."

31. In so doing, he also heals us and removes the barrier that separates us from God by purging, abolishing, and destroying "whatever there was of guilt" (*Trin.* 4.13.17; 15.27.50). "So then," Augustine explains, "into the place where the mediator of death transported us without accompanying us there himself, that is into the death of the flesh, there the Lord our God by the hidden and wholly mysterious decree of his high divine justice introduced the healing means of our amendment, which he did not himself deserve" (*Trin.* 4.12.15). In other words, Jesus's obedience heals and restores us back to life by dying our death, "so while our death is the punishment of sin, his death became a sacrifice for sin" (*Trin.* 4.12.15).

32. Williams offers us this insight on Augustine: "We are unfit for the contemplation of God because of our sin. Wicked and proud as we are, we can be made capable of participating in the divine Word, being illuminated, only by means of *sanguis iusti et humilitas dei*. God stoops to become a righteous human being so that, as human but not sinful, he may intercede for us so that created though we are, we may still contemplate God. God is what we are not by nature; but by the Word's participation in humanity, we may share the Word's divinity in being enlightened with his light (and thus, by implication, sharing his contemplative relation to the Father)" (Williams, *Augustine*, 144).

33. Cf.: "Just as the devil in his pride brought proud-thinking man down to death, so Christ in his humility brought obedient man back to life" (*Trin.* 4.10.13).

34. According to Rowan Williams, *Augustine*, 149, "The *persona* [of Jesus] is Wisdom-in-action, Wisdom engaging with what is not by nature God (cf. *trin.* I.V.ii.4) so as to incorporate it into the divine life and make it capable of seeing what Wisdom sees, knowing what it knows, contemplating the absolute otherness of the creator as if it were located where eternal Wisdom is located, in the heart of the divine self-knowledge and self-love." Jesus is the Wisdom of God

humility (*Trin.* 15.5.7). Humility sets us free to contemplate God in God because it is "a medicine to heal the tumor of our pride and a high sacrament to break the chain of sin" (*Trin.* 8.4.7). Humility aligns our minds to the mind of Christ, who humbled himself (Phil 2:5–8),[35] to set us free from our pride to see it was impossible for us to come to God, so God came to us in Christ.[36] Therefore, we come into light and see light because the Son who is light came to us and illumines our darkness with his light in the incarnation to see light, the wisdom and truth of God.

DIALOGICAL UNION WITH DIVINE LIGHT

Humility enables us to participate in a dialogical union with Jesus[37] because Jesus dwells in the heart of the humble (*"humiles corde sunt domus tua," Conf.* 11.31.41).[38] Illumination is activated in dialogical union with Jesus, our inner teacher, where our mind touches his as we share our thoughts with him and think his thoughts after him. Dialogical union with Christ was a

---

because he is the "substance" of God and "the light in which things are seen that cannot be seen with the eyes of the flesh" (*Trin.* 15.3.14).

35. As we align our mind with the mind of Christ, our mind becomes light, reflecting the light of Christ in a similar fashion to the moon reflecting the sun: "For we too are the image of God, . . . made by the Father through the Son, . . . because we are illuminated with light; that one is so because it is the light that illuminates, and therefore it provides a model for us without having a model itself . . . we by pressing on imitate him who abides motionless; we follow him who stands still, and by walking in him we move toward him, because for us he became a road or way in time by his humility, while being for us an eternal abode by his divinity" (*Trin.* 7.5).

36. According to Williams, Augustine came to Christianity when he was illumined to his fallen state and God's grace in Christ: "Instead of climbing up to Heaven to find the eternal Word, you have to grasp that the eternal Word has come down from Heaven to find you. And this happens when you see yourself not as a boldly questing intellectual mystic, but as a sick person in desperate need of healing, someone whose reality cannot be completed by their own work and attainments but only by a relationship offered completely from outside. ... When you see God in Jesus, it is as if you see him at your feet, the suffering or dead body laid out before you; throw yourself down on to that level, 'and when he rises, you will rise'" (Williams, *Augustine*, 131–132).

37. Jesus didn't come only to set an example for us, but to dwell in us: "the word of God became flesh in order to live in us but was unchanged" (*De doctr. chr.* 1.26). English translation from Augustine, *On Christian Teaching*, trans. R. P. H. Green (Oxford: Oxford University Press, 1991). So we can enjoy a dialogical union with him, "since in the interior life [we] have Christ, present in [our] heart by faith," "hope and charity, which are diffused through the hearts of the faithful by the Holy Spirit" (*ep.* 92). The English translation of the *Epistula* (*ep.*) is from Saint Augustine, *Letters*, vol. 2 (83–130), trans. Sister Wilfrid Parsons, FC 46 (Washington: Catholic University of America Press, 1953).

38. Williams, *Augustine*, 152.

habit in Augustine's life, as he shares and consults with Christ, his light, in every matter of life:

> Is there any place, O Truth, where you have not walked beside me, teaching me what to eschew and what to pursue, when I used to refer to you such meager insights as I was capable of, and when I used to ask your guidance? ... you are everlasting Light, and I asked your guidance on everything—what existed, what things were, what they were worth: and I listened as you taught me and laid commands upon me. I often do this, for it brings me pleasure, and whenever I have time to myself, I abandon matters of business and have recourse to that pleasure. I consult you on every matter in which I busy myself, and I find that there is no safe place for my soul except in you; you bind my shattered self together, and no part of me can fall away from you" (*Conf*. 10.40.65; cf. *Mag*. 11.38).[39]

Dialogical union with Christ is the fruit of listening and speaking to Christ through the words of Scripture (*civ. Dei*. 11.3).[40] We find dialogical union with Christ throughout Augustine's corpus.[41] In the *Confessiones*, for example, all thirteen books open and close with prayer and praise immersed in Scripture to begin and end Augustine's theological reflection of the God of his life. Augustine believed that we cannot understand and speak well of the God of Scripture without listening and speaking to God through Scripture. The words of Scripture allowed him to hear God, taught him how to speak to God, and gave him words to pray to God.[42] Humility in

39. The English translation of the *Confessiones* here is from Augustine, *Confessions*, vol. 2: Books 9–13, trans. Carolyn J.-B. Hammond, LCL 27 (Cambridge, MA: Harvard University Press, 2016).

40. "For Augustine," Williams, *Divine Sense*, 145, tells us, "the Bible is certainly the sine qua non of our knowledge of God." As a child learns how to speak by listening to his parent, Augustine learns how to speak to God by listening to God speak to him in Scripture.

41. In many of Augustine writings (e.g., *Mag*., *Solil*., *Conf*., *Trin*., *civ. Dei*., etc.), we find Augustine praying and talking to God as he talked about God and everything else in relation to God's goodness. For example, J. H. S. Burleigh, writes that the whole of the *Soliloquies* "is conceived in a framework of prayer" (Augustine, *Earlier Writings*, ed. and trans. J. H. S. Burleigh [Louisville, KY: Westminster John Knox, 2006], 19).

42. In the *Confessiones*, Augustine recounted how the Platonist writings gave him a "glimpse" of divine light, but were unable to provide the *way* to sustain his contemplation of God (*Conf*. 7.9.13; 7.10.16; 7.20.26; 8.2.3). Scripture instead provided Augustine the way to contemplate God in Christ through the Spirit because it bears witness to Christ (*Conf*. 6.5.8; 8.5.10; 8.12.29). As the

turn gave Augustine the proper posture in listening to Christ, our inner teacher, speak to us through the sign of Scripture the truth and love of God that transcend all understanding (Eph 1:19; 3:18–19; Phil 4:7). "Our real Teacher is he who is so listened to, who is said to dwell in the inner man, namely Christ, that is, the unchangeable power and eternal wisdom of God" (*Mag.* 11.38).[43] It is by listening to him that we see light, God, and become light, wise like God.[44]

Augustine offers a picture of what it means to be transformed into the image of Christ through the Spirit, as referred to in 2 Cor 3:18. The object of truth and wisdom, to which the *imago Dei* in us is made to reflect as in a mirror through remembering, understanding, and loving, is the Son. To be illumined in Christ has both a passive and active side—passive because Christ brings us into his light by coming to die and set an example, but active because we are to follow and dialogue with Christ, the light of our heart. Christ is light because he is the beauty, wisdom, and truth of God in person, so what he does, thinks, and is—is light. The economy of illumination, for Augustine, concerns the light of Christ, our inner teacher, enlightening and affecting our minds through the Spirit, the *gravitas* of love that lifts and carries us to contemplate the Father.[45]

BONAVENTURE (1221-1274)

Following Augustine, Bonaventure maintained that we have only "one fontal principle of cognitive illumination; namely Christ" (*C. Mag.* 1; cf. Matt 2:10; Heb 1:3; Sir 1:1).[46] The primary metaphor of illumination,

---

thought from one person's mind reaches another person's mind through language, the thought of God in his Word reaches us through the sign of Scripture that bears witness to his Word in human language.

43. English translation from Augustine, *Earlier Writings*, ed. and trans. J. H. S. Burleigh (Louisville, KY: Westminster John Knox, 2006).

44. The *telos* of being human is to follow God and become wise, but because of the fall, we cannot see God to follow him, so the Word made himself visible by becoming flesh: "Man ought to follow no one but God in his search for bliss, and yet he was unable to perceive God; so by following God made man he would at one and the same time follow one he could perceive and the one he ought to follow" (*Trin.* 7.5).

45. Cf.: "The weight's movement is not necessarily downwards, but to its appropriate position: fire tends to move upwards, a stone downwards. ... My weight is my love. Wherever I am carried, my love is carrying me. By your gift [the Spirit] we are set on fire and carried upwards: we grow red hot and ascend" (*Conf.* 13.9.10).

46. Cf.: "At one and the same time He was perfectly a man in history and yet in possession of the goal. Therefore He alone is the principal teacher" (*C. Mag.* 19). The English translation of

for Bonaventure, is not light, but Jesus, the divine teacher who enlightens. Jesus is the one teacher of all our modes of understanding, the teacher of truth for both scientific and sapiential knowledge.[47] Readers of Bonaventure have often viewed his theory of illumination as his attempt to solve the problem of certitude, combining Aristotle's concept of abstraction with Plato's theory of universals to demonstrate how certitude comes through the illumination of Christ, our divine teacher (*C. Mag.* 18).[48] But Bonaventure's primary concern, I argue, lies in the way the illumination of Christ enables our mind to journey into God from faith to sight. "Since there are three modes of knowledge, namely, that of faith, that of rational discourse, and that of contemplation," Bonaventure said, "Christ is the principle and the cause of all of these. He is the principle of the first in as far as He is the Way; of the second in as far as He is the Truth, and of the third in as far as He is the Life" (*C. Mag.* 1). These three modes of knowledge offer a Franciscan take on the transformation from glory to glory in 2 Cor 3:18 because they are the order of progression from knowledge to wisdom, beholding God in the mirror dimly by faith until sight (1 Cor 13:12).[49] Our knowledge by faith and reason is not complete until it leads us to contemplation of God (*C. Mag.* 16).[50]

Christus unus omnium Magister is from Bonaventure, "Christ, the One Teacher of All," in *What Manner of Man? Sermons on Christ by St. Bonaventure*, trans. Zachary Hayes (Chicago: Franciscan Herald Press, 1974).

47. This does not mean that Jesus is the only source and the "total ground" of knowledge (*C. Mag.* 18), but rather Jesus provides the normative truth and paradigm to understand and judge all things (*s. C. qu.* 4).

48. According to Etienne Gilson, *The Philosophy of St. Bonaventure*, trans. Dom Illtyd Trethowan and F. J. Sheed (London: Sheed & Ward, 1940), 402–03, Bonaventure's "description of illumination by the eternal principles contains ... the only complete reply that philosophy can give to the problem of the basis of certitude." Also see M. Hurley, "Illumination according to S. Bonaventure," *Gregorianum* 32.3 (1951): 390–95; Ignatius Brady, "St. Bonaventure's Doctrine of Illumination: Reactions Medieval and Modern Author(s)," *The Southwestern Journal of Philosophy* 5.2 (1974): 30–31; Patrick James Doyle, "The Disintegration of Divine Illumination Theory in the Franciscan School, 1285–1300: Peter of Trabes, Richard of Middleton, William of Ware" (PhD diss., Marquette University, 1984), 50–53; and Christopher M. Cullen, *Bonaventure* (Oxford: Oxford University Press, 2006),

49. For example, Bonaventure wrote, "we begin with the firmness of faith and proceed through the serenity of reason so as to arrive at the sweetness of contemplation" (*C. Mag.* 15).

50. This is the premise of Bonaventures' *Itinerarium mentis in Deum* (*The Journey of the Mind to God*).

ASCENDING TO GOD IN BODY AND MIND

Bonaventure followed Augustine and understood that we were made in God's image[51] to relate "to God as to [an] object," because God is our "moving cause" or "motivating principle" (*s. C. qu.* 4).[52] In other words, God is the object to which our "memory, understanding, and will" are directed because he is our highest good (*Brev.* 2.12.3;[53] *Itin.* 3.1–7; *C. Mag.* 16). The reason why God created us in God's image, "capable of union with God through memory, understanding, and will" (*Brev.* 2.9.3), is so we may become like God and embody the truth of God. This process occurs as God becomes more and more the proper object of our mental activities and the "norm" of the way we live (*Coll.* 4.3) because we are made not only with a soul, but also with a body—"to body forth some idea which existed in the mind of God."[54]

As God has endowed us with two senses, "one in the mind and the other in the flesh" (*Brev.* 2.11.1; cf. 2.10.2–4), so he moves us to himself by providing a "two-fold good, 'one visible; the other invisible'" (*Brev.* 2.11.4) because "to every motion and sense there is a corresponding appetite toward some good" (*Brev.* 2.11.4). Unlike the beasts of the field and the angelic beings who have only an outer or inner sense respectively, we are made with both senses to

---

51. Doyle, "Divine Illumination," 51, writes, "It is because man is made in the image of God that illumination is possible."

52. The English translation of *Quaestiones disputatae de scientia Christi* is from Bonaventure, *Disputed Questions on the Knowledge of Christ*, vol. 4 of *Works of St. Bonaventure* (St. Bonaventure, NY: Franciscan Institute Publications, 2005).

53. The English translation of *Breviloquium* is from Bonaventure, *Breviloquium*, vol. 9 of *Works of St. Bonaventure* (St. Bonaventure, NY: Franciscan Institute Publications, 2005).

54. Hurley, "Illumination," 389. God has made us for himself and a world to lead us to himself because all creation is a road and sign leading us to God, "the origin, exemplar, and goal of all creation" (*Itin.* 2.12). Cullen, *Bonaventure*, 76–77, offers a succinct summary of Bonaventure's exemplarism to explain how he saw all knowledge and wisdom as taking place in God and a journey to God: "According to Bonaventure's exemplarism, reality reflects the divine ideas that are exemplars in the divine mind. ... Bonaventure thinks that knowing truth involves attaining or 'glimpsing' these eternal reasons, though in an opaque manner. Therefore, while Bonaventure maintains with Aristotle that cognition is a mode of being and thus a way of union, the union is never just between the object and the knower, for the object is also a sign that points to a transcendent order, which is found in the mind that knows all forms. Reality is the expression of the Mind that knows it; hence, our knowing is always a journey of the mind to God. Bonaventure develops what may be called a semiotic metaphysics. All things or substances are signs, intentionally expressed by a sign-giver. Indeed, so thoroughly is the divine mind and its own interior word expressed in the universe that the world is truly a book—an intelligible, coherent, structured monograph expressing the Great Mind of all the ages." For more discussion, see J. M. Bissen, *L'Éxemplarisme Divin selon saint Bonaventure* (Paris: J. Vrin, 1929).

know God in the two books he composed: "one written within, which is the Eternal Art and Wisdom of God; the other written without, which is the perceptible world" (*Brev.* 2.11.2). The external book of the world raises a three-step ladder (*scala*) of vestige, image, and likeness to God.[55] By ascending these steps from below, within, and above our mind, we journey into God.[56]

After the fall, however, the ladder fell into disrepair because "this book, the world, became as dead and deleted" (*Coll.* 13.12).[57] So another book is required to be as a light to illumine the signs and the symbol of the book of the world to God. "Such a book," Bonaventure claimed, "is Scripture which establishes the likenesses, the properties, and the symbolism of the things written down in the book of the world. And so, Scripture has the power to restore the whole world toward the knowledge, praise, and love of God" because Scripture bears witness to Jesus Christ (*Coll.* 13.12).[58] Jesus is the one

---

55. Bonaventure writes, "the created world is a kind of book reflecting, representing, and describing its Maker, the Trinity, at three different levels of expression: as a vestige, as an image, and as a likeness. The aspect of vestige ('footprint') is found in every creature; the aspect of image, only in intelligent creatures or rational spirits; the aspect of likeness, only in those spirits that are God-conformed. Through these successive levels, comparable to steps, the human intellect is designed to ascend gradually to the supreme Principle, which is God" (*Brev.* 2.12.1). Elsewhere he adds, "For it is in harmony with our created condition that the universe itself might serve as a ladder [*scala*] by which we can ascend into God. ... In order to arrive at that First Principle which is most spiritual and eternal, and above us, it is necessary that we move through the vestiges which are bodily and temporal and outside us" (*Itin.* 1.2). We see God through the created things in the world because God's "supreme power, wisdom, and benevolence ... shines forth in created things as the bodily senses make this known to the interior senses" (*Itin.* 1.10). The English translation and Latin text of *Itinerarium mentis in Deum* (*The Journey of the Mind into God*) are from Bonaventure, *Itinerarium Mentis in Deum*, vol. 2 of *Works of St. Bonaventure* (St. Bonaventure, NY: Franciscan Institute Publications, 2002).

56. To ascend to God in contemplation is, for Bonaventure, to do theology (*Itin.* 1.7; *Brev.* Prol. 3.2). Bonaventure differentiated philosophy and theology in this way: "Philosophical knowledge is nothing other than the certain knowledge of truth in as far as it can be investigated. Theological knowledge is the pious knowledge of truth as believable" (*De don. Spir.* 4.5). The English translation of *Collationes de septem donis Spiritus sancti* (*De don. Spir.*) is from Bonaventure, *Collations of the Seven Gifts of the Holy Spirit*, vol. 14 of *Works of St. Bonaventure* (St. Bonaventure, NY: Franciscan Institute Publications, 2008).

57. The English translation of *Collationes in Hexaemeron* is from Bonaventure, *Collations on the Six Days*, trans. José de Vinck (Paterson, NJ: St. Anthony Guild Press, 1970). The world is meant to be a sign and symbol to point us to God, but after the fall, we no longer see it as a sign, but something that we desire and exploit. Our desire has been altered and inverted, from desiring the highest and immutable good to created and mutable good (*Brev.* 3.3.4; 3.5.4–5; 3.6.3; 3.8.2).

58. Ilia Delio, "Theology, Spirituality and Christ the Center," in *A Companion to Bonaventure*, ed. Jay H. Hammond, J. A. Wayne Hellmann, and Jared Goff (Leiden: Brill, 2014), 381, writes, "the self-communicative nature of God is the total communication of God, which is the meaning of revelation in the Person of Jesus Christ, in whom the Trinity is revealed."

who repairs the ladder in himself (*Itin.* 4.2)[59] because (1) he became man "'to beatify the whole man in Himself'" (*C. Mag.* 14) and (2) "in Christ eternal Wisdom and its work coincide in the same person ... for the restoration of the world" (*Brev.* 2.11.2).[60] Jesus offers us in himself the way, the truth, and the life to contemplative union with God (*red. art.* 18; *C. Mag.* 15; *Itin.* 1.3; cf. John 14:6).

JESUS, THE WAY, TRUTH, AND LIFE

To begin, Jesus is the way to the knowledge of faith (*Hex.* 9.2) because he "is the principle of all revelation by His coming into the mind, and the foundation of all authority by His coming into the flesh" (*C. Mag.* 2; cf. *Coll.* 4.3). Like the light of dawn, the coming of Jesus awakens our mind from its spiritual slumber "as the revelatory light of all prophetic vision" because he is the key to unlock all the "mysteries of faith" (*C. Mag.* 3). The coming of Jesus into the flesh, on the other hand, fulfills all revelation of the prophets because all God's promises find their *yes* in him (2 Cor 1:20). Thus, Jesus is the one, to whom all the revelation of Scriptures bear witness and in whom our "entire Christian faith" stands (*C. Mag.* 4–5; 1 Cor 3:10–11).

Second, Jesus is the *truth*, leading to rational or scientific knowledge[61] because he offers the light of reason to understand the rules, laws, and forms of the world in himself (*C. Mag.* 6–8; *Coll.* 5.1; *s. C. qu.* 4). Bonaventure explains,

> Scientific knowledge necessarily requires immutable truth on the part of the thing known and infallible certitude on the part of the

59. "So it is that," Bonaventure goes on to explain, "no matter how enlightened one might be with the light of natural and acquired knowledge, one cannot enter into oneself to *delight in the Lord* except by means of the mediation of Christ" (*Itin.* 4.2). Bonaventure employed Jacob's dream in Gen 28:12 to illustrate how Jesus illuminates our inner and outer senses to contemplate God: the ladder symbolizes Jesus, and the ascension and descension of the angels "symbolizes the illumination of contemplative men ascending and descending, thus indicating the two modes of contemplation carried out by the interior and exterior reading of the book written within and without" (*C. Mag.* 14).

60. Cf. "when 'the fulness of time came,' He was united as never before to a mind and to flesh and assumed a human form. Through Him all our minds are led back to God when, through faith, we receive the Similitude of the Father into our hearts [*similitudinem Patris per fidem in corde suscipiunt*]" (*red. art.* 8). The English translation and Latin of *De reductione artium ad theologiam* are from Bonaventure, *On the Reduction of the Arts to Theology*, vol. 1 of *Works of St. Bonaventure* (St. Bonaventure, NY: Franciscan Institute Publications, 1996).

61. Bonaventure argued that all the disciplines in the liberal arts are to bring us to God in Jesus Christ: "Through Him all our minds are led back to God, when, through faith, we receive the Similitude of the Father in our hearts" (*red. art.* 8).

> knower. Whatever is known, indeed, is necessary in itself and certain to the knower. For we know [Arist. *I. Poster. C.2.*], "when we judge the reason why a thing is, and we know that it is impossible for it to be otherwise." (*C. Mag.* 6; cf. *s. C. qu.* 4; *Ps* 102:26–28; 119:89).

We know with certainty, for example, that a circle is always round and never square. But how are we certain of this, if we ourselves are fallible as knowers and the form of the circle that we observe in the concrete objects of the world is mutable? Our soul, Bonaventure argued, must somehow attain these truths "as they exist in the eternal art" or in Christ[62] because "this is the Being that sustains the form in all things and the rule that directs all things. And it is through this that our mind comes to judge about all those things which enter into it through the senses" (*s. C. qu.* 4; Heb 1:2–3).[63] The world, in which we dwell, is God's ideas, arranged and put into creative form by the power of his Word (*Itin.* 1.7–8; 11; 13–14; *red. art.* 12). The world, therefore, serves "as a footprint and a mirror to lead humankind to love and praise God, its Maker" (*Brev.* 2.11.2; cf. 2.12.1),[64] and God has also made our mind in such way that we can discern his truths in creation by subjecting ourselves "'to intelligible realities according to the arrangement'" of God in Christ (*C. Mag.* 10; *red. art.* 12).[65] As our eyes are made to see the world

62. Similarly, how does an unrighteous person, or society for that matter, know what is righteous? The "rules" of what is righteous are "unchangeable," but the mind, by which a person sees these rules, is mutable (*C. Mag.* 8). So the person knows righteousness not because he possesses it in himself, but because Jesus illumines his mind with his own righteousness, by which all righteousness is judged (*C. Mag.* 8–9; *s. C. qu.* 4; cf. *Wis.* 7:17–18, 22–26; 8:1).

63. The things that we know exist in the world, in our mind, and in Christ: "While things have existence in matter, they have existence also in the soul through acquired knowledge, through grace, and through glory; and they have existence in the Eternal Art" (*Brev.* Prol. 3.2). But their existence in the mind and in matter is insufficient because they are mutable (*s. C. qu.* 4). Only in Christ are these things (ideas or species) immutable: "While things have being in themselves, they also have being in the mind and in the eternal reason as well. They are not entirely immutable in the first and second modes of being, but only in the third; namely, in as far as they are in the eternal Word. It follows, therefore, that nothing can render things perfectly knowable unless Christ is present, the Son of God and the Teacher" (*C. Mag.* 7).

64. The things in the world are signs pointing to the things in the mind of God: "For the created beings of this sensible world signify the invisible things of God partly because God is the origin, exemplar, and goal of all creation, and every effect is a sign of its cause; every copy is a sign of its exemplar; and the road is a sign of the goal to which it leads" (*Itin.* 2.12).

65. Put otherwise, we perceive and judge things in the created order by eternal rules and laws, "existing eternally in the eternal Art from which, and through which, and in accordance with which all beautiful things are formed" (*Itin.* 2.9). The laws and rules set and arranged in the world form our mind by impressing our sense, memory, and experience: "knowledge is

in light, our mind is created likewise to understand and judge all things in Jesus Christ, the Wisdom of God.[66]

Finally, Jesus is *food* for contemplating God because he provides nourishment for both our senses to contemplate God, "the inner nourishment in the Godhead, and the external nourishment in the humanity" (*C. Mag.* 11). So, whether we contemplate God in the book of the world or the book of Wisdom with our outer or inner sense, we find food for contemplation in Christ. As the Wisdom of God, Jesus enables us to contemplate God's paternal light in his light because to see him is to see the Father (*C. Mag.* 12; John 14:9).[67] As the incarnate Word, Jesus gives us food for contemplation in his flesh sacramentally through faith.[68] By partaking in his flesh through the eucharist, "we are incorporated into Christ" and "preserved by him through eating" (*Comm. Jn.* 6.90) because we partake in the life that he has "from the Father and abides in the Father" through him (*Comm. Jn.* 6.93).[69] The purpose of the two modes of contemplation is so our whole being, both body and soul,

generated in us by way of sense, memory, and experience, from which the universal is formed in us. And the universal is the principle of art and science" (*C. Mag.* 18).

66. Cullen, *Bonaventure*, 81, explains, "Everything that we judge with certitude, we judge by a standard (*regula*) that is immutable and beyond limits in time or space. 'But nothing is absolutely immutable and unlimited in time and space unless it is eternal, and everything that is eternal is either God or in God.' Consequently, Bonaventure concludes that we judge by a higher light than just our intellect." Put otherwise, Christ, the truth of God, for Bonaventure, is the "light of the soul" (*Coll.* 4.1), by which we perceive and judge all things fittingly (*C. Mag.* 10) because God has made all things according to his truth and purpose in Christ, so the existence, truth, and purpose of all things come from and are brought to light in Christ: "*For from Him and through Him and unto Him are all things*. Hence truth indicates that our mind is carried by a natural inclination to the supreme Truth in that it is the cause of being, the reason of understanding and the norm of life. From the cause of being comes forth the truth of things; from the reason of understanding, the truth of words; from the norm of life, the truth of moral behavior" (*Coll.* 4.3; cf. Rom 11:36; 1 Cor 8:6; Col 1:16; Heb 2:10).

67. Christ is also the life of the mind because it is in him that our mind is nourished to become what it is intended to be in God. Bonaventure compared the "potency" of our mind to a child because, like a child who can only reach her potential through the guidance and nourishment of an adult, our mind can only actualize its potential in knowledge and wisdom through "someone who has an actual knowledge of all things" (*s. C. qu.* 4).

68. In his incarnation and death on the cross, Jesus formed the "holy Mother Church ... from His side as Eve was formed from the side of the man. Therefore through that flesh the entire ecclesiastical hierarchy is purged, illuminated, and perfected. So it is to be looked upon as the life-giving nourishment of the entire Church" (*C. Mag.* 13).

69. The English translation of *Commentarius in Evangelium Ioannis* is from Bonaventure, *Commentary on the Gospel of John*, vol. 11 of *Works of St. Bonaventure* (St. Bonaventure, NY: Franciscan Institute Publications, 2007).

may become the *likeness* of God, as we see Jesus as he is (*C. Mag.* 25; *Coll.* 5.1–2; *Brev.* 2.11.3; 1 John 3:2).[70]

While Jesus Christ seems to be the sole agent of illumination, the agencies of the Father and the Spirit are assumed, as the three persons are inseparable in their distribution of light. "Years later," Ignatius Brady tells us, "Bonaventure returned to the theme of illumination in the Lenten Conferences of 1268, on the gifts of the Holy Spirit, without perhaps adding any new facet of doctrine, except to attack three errors current in the Arts faculty at Paris."[71] While Bonaventure did not add anything new to his doctrine of illumination, he made the inseparable operations of the Father, Son, and Spirit explicit in his later work on the Spirit. Bonaventure wrote, for example,

> Therefore, whatever the Father does or the Son suffers is nothing without the Holy Spirit. The Spirit unites us to the Father and the Son. This is why the Apostle states in 2 Cor 13:13: 'The grace of the our Lord Jesus Christ'—in relation to the second person—'the love of God'—in relation to the first person—'and the fellowship of the Holy Spirit'—in relation to the third person—'be with you all. Amen.' (*De don. Spir.* 1.7).

There is no life of light with the Father and Son without the Spirit. The three are indivisible in all their works and ways they relate to us.

In his work on the Spirit, Bonaventure also offered a reading of 2 Cor 3:18 and 4:6 within the framework of his theory of illumination (*De don. Spir.* 4.1–3). Bonaventure contrasts the light of glory from darkness in 2 Cor 3:18 thus: glory or "radiance of the soul is knowledge," and so "the darkness of the soul is ignorance" (*De don. Spir.* 4.2). With a view that "the soul possesses a multiform radiance," Bonaventure interpreted our transformation from glory to glory as going from "a radiance of philosophical knowledge, of theological knowledge, of the knowledge of grace" to "the radiance of the

---

70. Contemplation and morality are inseparable (Christopher M. Cullen, "Bonaventure's Philosophical Method," in *A Companion to Bonaventure*, eds. Jay H. Hammond, J. A. Wayne Hellmann, and Jared Goff [Leiden: Brill, 2014], 158). In order to contemplate God, we need to do God's will on earth as we will in heaven: "Christ teaches us not only in word, but also in example. Therefore, he who hears does not hear perfectly unless he brings understanding to the words and obedience to the deeds" (*C. Mag.* 21). To journey deeper into union with God, our mind needs to lead our body to live by God's truth and norm (*red. art.* 9–10) by considering and following Jesus, the way, truth, and life in contemplative union with God (*Trip. via* 3.8).

71. Brady, "St. Bonaventure's," 30.

knowledge of glory" that perfects our soul as a "reward" in heaven (*De don. Spir.* 4.3–4). Bonaventure read 2 Cor 4:6 from the Latin Vulgate, which renders the knowledge of God's glory as the result of divine illumination: God "has shone in our hearts to give enlightenment [*inluminationem*] concerning the knowledge of the splendor of God's shining on the face of Christ Jesus" (*De don. Spir.* 4.1). Bonaventure observed that there are "two things" that come before and "two things" that come after the gift of the knowledge of glory (*De don. Spir.* 4.2). The two things that come before are the "innate light … of natural judgment and reason" and the "infused light" of faith (*De don. Spir.* 4.2). The two things that come after are "clear knowledge of the Creator and the revealed knowledge of the Savior" (*De don. Spir.* 4.2). God gives us light, so we may be in light, illumined to the knowledge of God revealed in Christ, our innermost Teacher.

AQUINAS (1225–1274)

Thomas Aquinas, Bonaventure's Dominican counterpart, developed the bishop of Hippo's theory of illumination with his concept of the invisible missions of the Son and the Spirit that make God the object of our knowledge and love. The economy of illumination, for Aquinas, is a movement of light that brings us into light. I begin this section with Aquinas's commentary on 2 Cor 3:18 and 4:6 and then build on his concept of the economy of illumination here with his other works.

AQUINAS ON 2 COR 3:18 AND 4:6

Aquinas interpreted 2 Cor 4:6 as Paul's conversion experience of coming out of darkness to light (*In 2 Cor.* 4:3–6 §129). The experience of God's illumination refers to being filled with "the knowledge … of the glory of God, i.e., the clear vision of God" "in our minds, previously darkened by the absence of the light of grace and by the obscurity of sin" (*In 2 Cor.* 4:3–6 §130).[72] The "face of Jesus" (*facie Iesu Christi*) is the light of the knowledge of God's glory because he "is the face of the Father" (*est facies Patris, In 2 Cor.* 4:3–6 §130). In 2 Cor 3:18, Aquinas understood the Spirit's unveiling of the face to the glory

72. The Latin and English translation is from Thomas Aquinas, *Commentary on the Letters of Saint Paul to the Corinthians*, trans. Fabian R. Larcher, Beth Mortensen, and Daniel Keating, and ed. J. Mortensen and E. Alarcón (Lander, WY: Aquinas Institute for the Study of Sacred Doctrine, 2012).

of God as the opening of "the heart or the mind, because just as a person sees bodily with the face, so spiritually with the mind" (*In 2 Cor.* 3:12–18 §113) and beholding God in a mirror as "knowing the glorious God himself by the mirror of reason, in which there is an image of God" (*In 2 Cor.* 3:12–18 §114). In beholding, our *imago Dei* is transformed because

> all the knower's being assimilates to the thing known, it is necessary that those who see be in some way transformed into God. If they see perfectly, they are perfectly transformed, as the blessed in heaven by the union of enjoyment: *when he appears we shall be like him* (1 John 3:2); but if we see imperfectly, then we are transformed imperfectly, as here by faith: *now we see in a mirror dimly* (1 Cor 13:12). (*In 2 Cor.* 3:12–18 §114; emphasis original)

Being "*transformed from clarity to clarity*" represents "a triple degree of knowledge in Christ's disciples," first from "natural knowledge" to "knowledge of faith," second from "knowledge of the Old Testament" to "the knowledge of the grace of the New Testament," and finally from the two previous degrees of knowledge "to the clarity of eternal vision," the beatific vision of God (*In 2 Cor.* 3:12–18 §115; emphasis original). The *imago Dei* within us is being transformed from one degree of glory to another into the image of Christ. I turn to Aquinas's other works to elaborate the transformation that we undergo in the economy of illumination.

THE LIGHT OF NATURE, GRACE, AND GLORY

In *Summa Theologiae Prima Pars*, Thomas followed Augustine and argued that the *imago Dei* is found in the activities of our mind and will (*ST* I, q.93, a.7, *resp.*). The image of God is not so much what we are as what we will be as God becomes the proper object of our mind and will (*ST* I, q.93, a.8, *resp.*; cf. I, q.12, a.1, *resp.*).[73] God made us to know and love him as he knows and loves

73. In other words, the "*imago Dei* is no static endowment, a given to be taken for granted, but principally, what we become in virtue of the acquisition and exercise of habits, and secondarily, the natural precondition of the development and exercise of those habits" (A. N. Williams, *The Ground of Union: Deification in Aquinas and Palamas* [New York: Oxford University Press, 1999], 71). God has made us in proportion to him, in that we are related to God "as effects to cause and as the partially realized to the absolutely real," so we may grow in our knowledge of him and become as he is (*ST* I, q.12, a.1, ad.4). That is why the human being's proclivity is to search and understand the "cause of things" and ultimately the "first cause of things" (*ST* I, q.12, a.1, *resp.*).

himself. So, the divine image in us is fully realized, when we perfectly imitate "God's understanding and loving of *himself*" (*ST* I, q.93, a.4, *resp.* [emphasis original]).[74] So, in beholding God, we become like God in his self-knowledge.

Aquinas described the "triple degree of knowledge" in 2 Cor 3:18 as three stages:

> the first stage is man's natural aptitude for understanding and loving God, an aptitude which consists in the very nature of the mind, which is common to all men. The next stage is where a man is actually or dispositively knowing and loving God, but still imperfectly; and here we have the image by conforming of grace. The third stage is where a man is actually knowing and loving God perfectly; and this is the image of likeness of glory. Thus on the text of *Psalm, The light of thy countenance O Lord is sealed upon us, the Gloss* distinguishes a threefold image, namely the image of *creation, of re-creation, and of likeness.* The first stage of image then is found in all men, the second only in the just, and the third only in the blessed. (*ST* I, q.93, a.4, *resp.*)

Our progress through these three stages comes through our participation in the "light of nature, grace, and glory" (*lumen naturae, vel gratiae, vel gloriae, ST* I, q.106, a.2, ad.2).[75] These three variants of light describe the degree of our participation in God who is light, from reason to faith and from faith to sight (*In II Cor.* 3:3 §115; cf. *In I Cor.* 13.4 §800–803). We participate in God in illumination because we receive from one degree to another the light in God by nature, given and manifested to us by grace for glory.[76]

At creation, God graciously conferred the light of nature to all human beings, setting them apart from the beast of the earth (*In Ioan.* 1.3 §101; Job 35:11). While all created things partake in God by his power, presence, and

---

The Latin text and English translation of *ST* I, q.12 are from Thomas Aquinas, *Summa Theologiae*, vol.3, ed. and trans. Herbert McCabe (London: Blackfriars, 1964).

74. The Latin text and English translation of *ST* I, q. 93 are from Thomas Aquinas, *Summa Theologiae*, vol.13, ed. and trans. Edmund Hill (London: Blackfriars, 1964).

75. The Latin text and English translation of *ST* I, q. 106 are from Thomas Aquinas, *Summa Theologiae*, vol.14, ed. and trans. T. C. O'Brien (London: Blackfriars, 1975).

76. David L. Whidden III, *Christ the Light: The Theology of Light and Illumination in Thomas Aquinas* (Minneapolis: Fortress, 2014), 100. God is light because he is intelligible in himself, but we are light insofar as we receive the manifestation of the light of God's knowledge of himself.

essence (*ST* I, q.8, a.3, *resp.*), rational beings are unique in that they also share in his light.[77] The light of nature is our ability to reason (*ST* II-II, q.8, a.1, ad. 2) and to abstract from concrete forms and events the truth of God (*ST* I, q.12, a.4), such as, he exists, he is the first cause of all things, and he is one (*In II Cor.* 2.3 §73; *ST* I, q.12, a.12), but not the mystery of faith, such as the incarnation and the triunity of God as Father, Son, and Spirit (*ST* I, q.32, a.1). After the fall, however, we can still know God through natural light, but often in a cold, distant, and even subversive way because, although we can know the truth of God in creation, we can still suppress his truth in unrighteousness and fail to glorify God as God (*ST* I, q.32, a.1, ad.1; cf. Rom 1:21).[78]

So with natural light alone, we can never reach our full actualization as the image of God, which takes place in the beatific vision of God, when we see God's essence (*ST* I-II, q.3, a.8) and enjoy an "intellectual union" with God consisting of the perfect[79] knowledge and love of God:[80] "the contemplation and crown of beatitude is the delight experienced in the enjoyment of God and this is caused by charity" (*In Ioan.* 17.1 §2186).[81] To see God's essence is to have God present in our intellectual sight. "In order to see, whether with the senses or the mind," Aquinas writes, "two things are needed; there must be a power of sight and the thing to be seen must come into sight" (*ST* I, q.12, a.2, *resp.*). In the case of God, he is "both the thing seen and the source of power of sight" (*ST* I, q.12, a.2, *resp.*), so we must receive both from God, who gives himself to us in an intellectual union, where his "divine essence is united to a created mind so as to be what is actually understood and through its very self

77. Cf.: "We see everything in God and judge everything by him in the sense that it is by sharing in his light that we are able to see and judge, for the natural light of reason is a sort of sharing in the divine light" (*ST* I, q.12, a.11, ad.3; cf. I, q.12, a.2, *resp.*).

78. Cf. Whidden, *Christ the Light*, 25.

79. To know and love God perfectly do not mean that we know and love God to the degree that God knows and loves himself because God knows and loves himself infinitely, but we love and know God perfectly in the sense of knowing and loving God as completely as finite creatures can through the light of God's glory (*ST* I, q.12, a.7, *resp.*).

80. Williams, *Ground of Union*, 44–46. For rational beings, to live is to act, and the highest act for us is to know God, the first cause of all things. To know God is eternal life, participating in our perfection, the highest good and beatific vision of God (*In Ioan.* 17.1 §2186): "The ultimate happiness of man consists in his highest activity, which is the exercise of his mind" in knowing and loving God (*ST* I, q.12, a.1, *resp.*).

81. The Latin text and English translation are from Thomas Aquinas, *Commentary on the Gospel of John*, trans. Fabian R. Larcher and ed. Aquinas Institute (Lander, WY: Aquinas Institute for the Study of Sacred Doctrine, 2013).

making the mind actually understanding" (*ST* I, q.12, a.2, ad.3). This union is to see God face to face in the light of his glory, for to see "God's essence some likeness is required on the part of the power of sight, namely the light of divine glory strengthening the mind, of which the *Psalm* speaks, *In thy light shall we see light*" (*ST* I, q.12, a.2, *resp.*; Ps 36:9). To see God in the light of glory is only for the blessed in heaven because it is becoming like God as one sees God as he is (1 John 3:2; 1 Cor 13:12).

Since the light of nature is necessary, but "not sufficient to see the essence of God," the light of grace is needed to strengthen and instill in our mind a "disposition ... to the understanding beyond its own nature so that it can be raised to such sublimity" (*ST* I, q.12, a.5, *resp.*; I-II, q. 109, a. 1, *resp.*).[82] What the light of grace strengthens us to understand is the object of faith, the "First truth" (*veritas prima*)—the Trinity (*ST* II-II, q.1, a.1, *sed contra*; cf. II-II, q.8, a.2).[83] The act of faith is an intellectual "assent" to God, its object (*ST* II-II, q.1, a.4, *resp.*; *In Heb.* 6.1 §281), because faith will not stop seeking understanding until it reaches sight (*ST* II-II, q.2, a.1). The light of grace raises our mind to know God not only by faith (*ST* II-II, q.1, a.2, *resp.*; cf. II-II, q.2, a.3, ad.2; I, q.12, a.5, ad.2), but also by increasing our love for God (*ST* I-II, q.89, a.1, ad.3) because "a greater charity implies a greater desire, and this itself in some way predisposes a man and fits him to receive what he desires" (*ST* I, q.12, a.6, *resp.*). Love moves us to God, the object of love (*ST* I, q.36, a.1).

THE INVISIBLE AND INDIVISIBLE MISSIONS OF THE SON AND THE SPIRIT

To be illumined by the light of grace is the formal and material effect of the invisible missions of the Son and the Spirit from the Father: "God comes to us by enlightening us; and we go to him by thinking of him: *come to him and be enlightened* (Ps 33:6)" (*In Ioan.* 14.6 §1945). The formal and material effects refer to the effects that the divine missions leave upon our heart and mind because a heart and mind illumined loves and knows God like the Son

82. Cf.: "Hence since the created mind has the capacity by nature to see the concrete form or concrete act of existence in abstraction by analysis, it can by grace be raised so that it may know unmixed subsistent being and unmixed subsistent existence" (*ST* I, q.12, a.4, ad.3).

83. Aquinas referred to this "increase in the power of understanding" (augmentum *virtutis intellectivæ*) as the "'illumination' of the mind" (*ST* I, q.12, a.5, *resp.*; II-II, q.8, a.1).

through the Spirit (formal effect) with the wisdom and love of the Son and Spirit (material effect).[84] God's coming to us is our renewal and return to God (*ST* I, q.43, a.2, ad.2; I, q. 105, a.3, *resp.*; I-II, q.109, a.7):

> God is said to come to us not because he moves to us, but because we move to him. Something comes into a place in which it previously was not: but this does not apply to God since he is everywhere: *do I not fill heaven and earth?* (Jer 23:24). Rather, God is said to come to someone because he is there in a new way, in a way he had not been there before, that is, by the effect of his grace. It is by this effect of grace that he makes us approach him. (*In Ioan.* 14.6 §1944)

Although Aquinas did not explicitly say that the invisible missions of the Son and the Spirit constitute the light of grace, it is implied because the invisible missions affect the "sort of enlightening that bursts forth into love" (*ST* I, q.43, a.5, ad 2).[85] While the missions of the Son and the Spirit are distinct, they are one in grace: "the two missions have grace as their common root, but they are distinct as to the effects grace has, i.e. the enlightenment of the mind and the enkindling of the affection [*illuminatio intellectus et inflammatio affectus*]" (*ST* I, q.43, a.5, ad.3).[86] The missions of the Son and

84. The formal effect refers to the shape of our love and knowledge that resembles the Son and the Spirit, and the material effect is the content of our knowledge and love that comes from the Son, the wisdom of God, and the Spirit, the love of God poured into our hearts.

85. In *ST* I-II, q.110, a.3, *resp.*, Aquinas states that the virtues of faith and love are derived from the "light of grace," so it follows that the invisible and inseparable missions of the Son and Spirit constitute this light of grace because the divine missions are the efficient, formal, and material causes of our union with God through our love and knowledge of God (*ST* I, q.43, a.3, *resp.*; cf. I, q.43, a.3, ad.2; *In Ioan.* 1.5 §125; 14.4 §1909). Matthew Levering, *Scripture and Metaphysics: Aquinas and the Renewal of Trinitarian Theology* (Oxford: Blackwell, 2004), 140, points out that the knowledge of God is participation in the Word by faith through the sanctifying grace of the Spirit. The experience of this grace "is an effect of God's eternal love in us. God's love makes us worthy of union with him by freeing us from the guilt of sin and enabling us to cleave to God" (Matthew Levering, *Paul in the Summa Theologiae* [Washington: Catholic University of America Press, 2014], 158; cf. *ST* I-II, q.109, a.7. *resp.*). To clarify, moreover, the love of God poured out in our hearts through the Spirit is not "the act of loving but the 'affection' that is found in the human will at the beginning of the act of loving, that is, what 'moves and impels the will of the lover towards the beloved' (I.36.1*corp*)" (Gilles Emery, "Holy Spirit," in *Cambridge Companion to the Summa Theologiae*, ed. Philip McCosker and Denys Turner [New York: Cambridge University Press, 2016], 131). By the grace of the Spirit, we are able to love God, whom we know through the light of the Word.

86. Aquinas emphasizes, "Plainly, then, one effect cannot take place without the other, since neither occurs without sanctifying grace nor can one person be present without the other" (*ST*

the Spirit are the "sanctifying grace" (*ST* I, q.43, a.3, *resp.*) that unites us to God (*ST* I-II, q.111, a.1, *resp.*).[87]

Sanctifying grace affects union with God because it disposes us to receive the divine persons.[88] To receive the Son and the Spirit is to know and love God because we "participate in the Son's and the Spirit's distinct relations to the Father as we return to him via assimilation to the Son's eternal property (in wisdom) and to the Spirit's eternal property (in love [*I Sent.*, d.15, q.4, a.1c, 350])."[89] In knowing and loving God in the Son, the Wisdom of God, and the Spirit, the Love of God, through sanctifying grace, God is present with us in our innermost:

> Over and above this [i.e., divine omnipresence] there is a special presence consonant with the nature of an intelligent being, in whom God is said to be present as the known in the knower and the loved in the lover. And because by these acts of knowing and loving the intelligent being touches God himself, by reason of this special way of being present we have the teaching that God is not merely in the intelligent creature, but dwells there as in his temple. No other effect but sanctifying grace, then, is the explanation of a divine person's being present to the intelligent being in this new way. The conclusion is that there is no mission or temporal procession of a divine person except by reason of grace. (*ST* I, q. 43, a.3, *resp.*)

I, q.43, a.5, ad.3). The Latin text and English translation of *ST* I, q.43 is from Thomas Aquinas, *Summa Theologiae*, vol.7, trans. T. C. O'Brien (London: Blackfriars, 1976).

87. In fact, Aquinas maintains: "The entire Trinity abides in the soul by reason of sanctifying grace" (*ST* I, q.43, a.5, *resp.*). Sanctifying grace also orders our mind to God (*ST* I, q.100, a.1, ad.2).

88. Bernard Blankenhorn, *The Mystery of Union with God: Dionysian Mysticism in Albert the Great and Thomas Aquinas* (Washington: Catholic University of America Press, 2015), 253, points out, "As 'formal effects' of habitual sanctifying grace, the gifts of grace (wisdom and charity) are the created principles that account for the persons' *missions*" (cf. *I Sent.* d.15, q.4, a.1c, 350). Williams, *Ground of Union*, 62–63, also observes the way Aquinas connects sanctification in this life to perfection in the next: "The gift of sanctifying grace is said to perfect the rational creature in such a way that she can both use the created gift and even enjoy the divine person himself. Here Aquinas allies the gift of grace with perfection, implying precisely that kind of seamlessness between sanctification in this life and consummation in the next that is characteristic of a doctrine of theosis."

89. Blankenhorn, *Mystery of Union*, 252.

In the invisible missions of the Son and the Spirit, God makes himself present to us as the *object* of our love and knowledge.[90] So, we are united as knowers and lovers to God, the object of our love and knowledge, by our act of knowing and loving God. If the invisible missions of the Son and Spirit are the material and formal causes of our return to God, then being illumined by the "Word breathing Love" is the effect of our union with God (*ST* I, q.43, a.5, *resp.*) because we return into God by assimilating the property of the Son as wisdom of God and the property of the Spirit as the love of God (*I Sent.* d.15, q.4, a.1c, 350).[91] If like attracts like, then becoming like God through grace in the knowledge and love of the Son and Spirit returns us to God.

Orthodox theologians have argued that God is knowable and participable in his energy rather than his essence to safeguard the creature-Creator distinction. But Aquinas claimed that we will see God's essence. What was Aquinas trying to do? For one, he was not trying to cross the creature-Creator distinction. Aquinas was trying to show that the invisible missions of God consist of God's "eternal procession, with the addition of a temporal effect" (*ST* I, q.43, a. 2, ad. 3).[92] God himself came to bring us to himself from the light of grace to the light of glory. So, our vision of God always depends on God because we do not have the object and power of sight in ourselves, but only as ones who participate in God who has the object and power of sight in himself and comes to us by grace to proceed to us. There is no crossing the creature-Creator distinction.

HANS URS VON BALTHASAR (1905–1988)

Like Thomas, Hans Urs von Balthasar viewed the economy of illumination as a movement between God and human beings in his theological aesthetics:

---

90. See Gilles Emery, *The Trinitarian Theology of Saint Thomas Aquinas*, trans. Francesca A. Murphy (Oxford: Oxford University Press, 2007), 379–87.

91. Cf.: "Another interpretation: *and you in me, and I in you*, that is, by our mutual love, for we read: *God is love, and he who abides in love abides in God, and God abides in him* (1 John 4:16)" (*In Ioan.* 14.4 §1930). Williams, *Ground of Union*, 61, writes, "As the Three are present to one another in knowledge and love, so the Trinity's mission is present in creation's end." Blankenhorn, *Mystery of Union*, 252, similarly adds, "We return to God through the habitual possession and actualization of charity and faith. These virtues are created reflections of the Spirit's procession as Love and the Son's procession as the Word, respectively."

92. For discussion on the eternal procession of the Son and his temporal effect in the divine mission, see Dominic Legge, *Trinitarian Christology of St. Thomas Aquinas* (Oxford: Oxford University Press, 2017).

> For the object with which we are concerned is man's participation in God which, from God's perspective, is actualized as "revelation" (culminating in Christ's Godmanhood) and which, from man's perspective, is actualized as 'faith' (culminating in participation in Christ's Godmanhood). This double and reciprocal *ekstasis*—God's 'venturing forth' to man and man's to God—constitutes the very content of dogmatics, which may thus rightly be presented as a theory of rapture: the *admirabile commercium et connubium* between God and man in Christ as Head and Body.[93]

Balthasar finds this movement of beholding the vision of the beauty of Christ and being raptured by it in 2 Cor 3:18–4:6.

> The "image," the "splendour" to which "we look in order to be transformed into the same image, from splendour to splendour," radiates from the Incarnate Lord. He is the Spirit, he is the access to the Father and his "precise image," and even the most intimate subjective "illumination" of God "in our hearts" occurs only in virtue of the fact that "the knowledge of the glory of God shines forth from the face of Christ," or what amounts to the same thing, in virtue of the fact that the "radiance of the Gospel" is seen and understood "because of the glory of Christ." (2 Cor 3.18–4.6)[94]

Balthasar interpreted the image as the beauty of God in Christ and the transformation of the beholder into the same image as the rapture in the beauty of Christ. To behold beauty is to be raptured into the reality that it illumines because the beauty of Christ captivates and brings us into his light. In what follows, I want to draw out the role of the beauty of Christ in the economy of illumination and the particular form that our transformation takes in beholding the beauty of Christ. To be transformed from glory to glory into the image of Christ is to become more and more beautiful because Christ is the beauty of God. But as we will see, the form of beauty that Christ puts on is scandalous.

93. Hans Urs von Balthasar, *Seeing the Form*, vol. 1 of *The Glory of the Lord: A Theological Aesthetics*, trans. Erasmo Leiva-Merikakis (San Francisco: Ignatius Press, 1982), 125–26.

94. Balthasar, *Seeing*, 437.

BALTHASAR ON 2 COR 3:18–4:6

In 2 Cor 3:18, Balthasar saw the "two phrases" of theological aesthetics, namely the "theory of vision" and "theory of rapture."[95] He wrote, for instance, "Paul, in the *locus classicus* of his theological aesthetics, nevertheless speaks of a 'vision of the Lord's splendour with unveiled face,' through which 'we are transformed into the same image' (2 Cor 3.18). Paul thus unites vision and rapture as a single process."[96] The vision is the "form of God's self-revelation," and the rapture concerns "the incarnation of God's glory and the consequent elevation of man to participate in that glory."[97] The former is the objective side of theological aesthetics because it has to do with what God has revealed objectively in the coming of his Son. The latter is the subjective side of theological aesthetics because it concerns our faith and participation in what God has revealed. These two aspects are inseparable on "a road which the human spirit takes as it seeks for the Christian truth (*intellectus quaerens fidem*)," and "this road itself already stands in the rays of the divine light, a light which, in an objective sense, makes the form visible and which, in a subjective sense, clarifies and illumines the searching spirit, thus training it in an act and a *habitus* which will become perfect faith once the vision has itself been perfected."[98]

What God shines objectively on the road of truth is not merely the content, but the *beauty* of his truth in the vision or image of Christ. Following Aquinas, Balthasar argues, "[t]he beautiful is above all a *form*, and the light does not fall on this form from above and from outside, rather it breaks forth from the form's interior."[99] The form of divine light is not left behind, once we have the content of its truth because the "content (*Gehalt*) does not lie behind the form (*Gestalt*), but within it. Whoever is not capable of seeing and 'reading' the form will, by the same token, fail to perceive the content. Whoever is not illumined by the form will see no light in the content either."[100]

95. Balthasar, *Seeing*, 125.

96. Balthasar, *Seeing*, 126–27; emphasis original.

97. Balthasar, *Seeing*, 125.

98. Balthasar, *Seeing*, 126.

99. Balthasar, *Seeing*, 151; cf. 118. For more discussion, see Stephen M. Garrett, *God's Beauty-in-Act: Participating in God's suffering Glory* (Eugene, OR: Wipf & Stock, 2013), 68–69.

100. Balthasar, *Seeing*, 151.

In other words, "[*s*]*pecie* and *lumen* in beauty are one."[101] Jesus is the beauty of God because he wraps the *light* of God's glory and truth in the *form* of the Servant, "a beauty crowned with thorns and crucified."[102] Jesus wraps the beauty, the radiance of God's splendor, by taking on flesh and ultimately by dying on the cross: "God's light, which 'shines in our hearts' (2 Cor 4.6), shines so that we may know the Son; but it also shines through him who makes the radiance of this light possible by dying in the world God's death of love and by purging through his atonement the darkness in our hearts."[103] The light of beauty, breaking forth in Christ, is "God's *amor invisibilis*," invisible love.[104] To see the beauty of Christ is to participate in the love of God, for the beauty of Christ enraptures us into the love of God through the Spirit.[105]

The Spirit makes what is objective and exterior in the form of Jesus Christ *subjective* and *interior* to us. The Spirit is "divine subjectivity," so he is "able to adopt created subjectivity, refashioning, inhabiting and irradiating it until, in the medium of the Spirit of God, it blossoms forth in a mode of being and produces acts and states which were not even present in germ in the creature as such."[106] The Spirit can illumine us subjectively and transform us objectively to the beauty of Christ as the church of Christ because the Spirit dwells in Christ, the form of beauty, and shines forth with Christ the splendor of the Father's love for us.

> The Holy Spirit is, in identity, *both* the Spirit of God's objective revelation in Christ and of the objectivation of the existential Christ-form in the form of the Church—her offices, charisms and sacraments—*and* the Spirit of Christian subjectivity as faith, hope,

---

101. Balthasar, *Seeing*, 151.

102. Balthasar, *Seeing*, 33.

103. Balthasar, *Seeing*, 156–57.

104. Balthasar, *Seeing*, 121.

105. Balthasar, *Seeing*, 197. It is the beauty of God's love in Christ that awakens the knowledge of God's love in us through the Spirit. As the mother manifests her love, the child comes to know her love. "God interprets himself to man as love in the same way: he radiates love, which kindles the light of love in the heart of man, and it is precisely this light that allows man to perceive this, the absolute love ... just as no child can be awakened to love without being loved, so too no human heart can come to an understanding of God without the free gift of his grace—in the image of his Son" [Hans Urs von Balthasar, *Love Alone Is Credible*, trans. D. C. Schindler (San Francisco: Ignatius Press, 1963], 76).

106. Hans Urs von Balthasar, *Prayer*, trans. Graham Harrison (San Francisco: Ignatius Press, 1986), 75.

> and love, and it is in this Spirit alone [t]hat we can say "*Kyrios Jesus*" (1 Cor 12.13). This identity—not the immediate identity of the believer with Christ, since faith makes just the opposite obvious—the identity of the Spirit dwelling in Christ and shining forth from him with the Spirit who opens up the recalcitrant sinner so as to unite him, against his sinful will and beyond it, with Christ and, in Christ, with the Father: this identity of God's Spirit, uniting subject and object (whether it is understood more as the work of the person of the Spirit or of the whole trinitarian spiritual God), is the very foundational possibility which cannot be absent from any conscious and psychological act of faith and which cannot be excluded from the consciousness of the act of faith as being unimportant or irrelevant. "In your light we see light." (emphasis original)[107]

It is in the light of the Spirit that we come to see the light of God's beauty in Christ. The way the Spirit leads us to the beauty of God's love is then "quite different from the imparting of information; rather, he leads us from inner participation into inner participation."[108] The Spirit draws us into the beauty of Christ to be transformed by it. "Constant contemplation of the whole Christ, through the Holy Spirit," Balthasar wrote, "transforms the beholder as a whole into the image of Christ (2 Cor 3:18)."[109] The Spirit enables the image of Christ to take us up and transforms us for the life, which it allows us to behold: the life of the Trinity.

So, to be illumined *subjectively* through the Spirit to behold the beauty of the Father's love, *objectively* revealed in the life, death, and resurrection of the Son, is to be drawn into the love that the Father and the Son share in the Spirit from all eternity.[110] We are drawn into God's life of light through

---

107. Balthasar, *Seeing*, 195–96; cf. idem, *Prayer*, 71.

108. Hans Urs von Balthasar, *The Spirit of Truth*, vol. 3 of *Theo-Logic*, trans. Graham Harrison (San Francisco: Ignatius Press, 1987), 74. In this way, the Spirit opens up a new and living way for us "to participate in the divine realm of the Father-Son relationship (thus this initiation can be called a 'divinization')" (Balthasar, *Spirit*, 75).

109. Balthasar, *Seeing*, 242.

110. Jesus is the splendor of "God's *amor invisibilis*," which draws us to himself by the Holy Spirit who "en-thuses and in-spires" us to take part in the "movement" away from our self toward God because the beauty of the light of his love allures us (Balthasar, *Seeing*, 121–22). Concerning the revelation of God's love in Jesus, see Aidan Nichols, "The Theo-logic," in *Cambridge Companion to Hans Urs von Balthasar*, ed. Edward T. Oakes and David Moss (Cambridge: Cambridge University Press, 2004), 167–68.

contemplation. In contemplation, God "gives us a concrete vision of triune life by involving us in it through grace and our serious discipleship of Christ. This vision is simply the inner illumination of the obedience of faith rendered to the Father, together with Christ, in the Spirit."[111]

Balthasar brought to light another component in 2 Cor 3:18–4:6: namely, the beholder cannot abstract himself from the beauty beheld because the form and the light that illumines her to the beauty of God are one as the Son and the Sprit are one with the Father who shines the light of his splendor. The one who beholds beauty can abstract neither the content from its form nor herself from what she beholds because she is raptured and transported into the vision "from inner participation into inner participation."[112] The more we contemplate the beauty of Christ, the more we participate and are transformed by his beauty.

> All this "bearing death in the body" is the result of a contemplation of the resurrection in which we are assimilated more and more efficaciously to the glory of the Son, who transforms the beholder into himself: "We all, with unveiled face, beholding the glory of the Lord, are being changed into his likeness from one degree of glory to another; for this *comes from the Lord who is the Spirit*" (2 Cor 3:18).[113]

The more Christ becomes beautiful to us, the more beautiful we become in Christ because the beauty of Christ draws us and transforms us into the light of Christ.

CONCLUSION

Let me now draw out some key distinctions from the Roman Catholic account of the economy of illumination by way of comparison. Like the Orthodox tradition, the Roman Catholic tradition holds that we participate in God through the economy of illumination, but it departs from the Orthodox tradition on the nature of our participation in God. For the Orthodox tradition, we participate in God's uncreated energies rather than his essence, but for the Catholic tradition, we participate and see God in himself in the Son, the light

111. Balthasar, *Prayer*, 193.

112. Balthasar, *Spirit of Truth*, 74.

113. Balthasar, *Prayer*, 297.

of God, through the Spirit, the love of God, from faith to sight in the beatific vision of God's essence.[114]

The reason why the two traditions part ways on the nature of participation is due to their understanding of divine perfection. The Orthodox tradition understands God's perfection as the manifestation and outflow of God's essence and so external to God's essence, whereas the Catholic tradition believes that God *is* his perfection as light and love by virtue of divine simplicity. Augustine, for example, writes, "the Father is light, the Son is light, the Holy Spirit is light; but together they are not three lights but one light. And so the Father is wisdom, the Son is wisdom, the Holy Spirit is wisdom; and together they are not three wisdoms but one wisdom; and because in their case to be is the same as to be wise, Father and Son and Holy Spirit are one being" (*Trin.* 7.3.6). God who is light and love shines his light and fills us with his love in the persons of the Son and the Spirit, so we can be in his light and love, that is, one with God himself. Aquinas described the economy of illumination as the invisible missions of the Son, the light of God, and the Spirit, the love of God, which draw us into God who is light and love from one degree of glory to another, a "sort of enlightening that bursts forth into love" (*ST* I, q.43, a.5, ad 2). The invisible mission is God himself affecting our hearts because "it includes the eternal procession, with the addition of a temporal effect" (*ST* I, q.43, a. 2, ad. 3). The Orthodox tradition, on the other hand, understands the light of God's knowledge as enhypostatic light (φῶς ἐνυποστάτως, *Triad* 1.3.23; 2.3.66) because this uncreated light comes from the person of God, but is distinct and outside of God. As the sun becomes present to us by its rays rather than its essence, God makes himself present to us by the rays of his energies rather than his essence.

While the Orthodox tradition believes that this ray, which we can see on earth as the disciples have beheld at Jesus's transfiguration, "will continually and endlessly dazzle us 'with its most brilliant rays' in the Age to come, when we will be 'always with the Lord', according to His promise" (*Triad* 2.3.20; cf. 3.1.10, 14; Rev 22:5), the Roman Catholic tradition teaches that we participate and see God through various stages of light (e.g., the light of nature, grace, and glory, *ST* I, q.106, a.2, ad.2; or from knowledge and faith to Wisdom and contemplation in Christ, our divine light and inner teacher,

114. In fact, Aquinas believed that all things participate in God's essence (*ST* I, q.8, a.3, *resp*).

Trin. 4.18.24; 13.19.24; *C. Mag.* 15). Each stage of light leads us to the next until we see God face to face. So, unlike the Orthodox tradition, which interprets the light of glory as continuous and ever-increasing from now to all eternity, there is continuity and discontinuity from one stage of light to another in the Catholic understanding. For example, though the light of grace leads us to behold God in the light of glory, to see God in the light of grace is distinct from beholding God in the light of glory because, while we see God in the light of grace in the present, we can only see God face to face in the light of glory in the new heaven and earth.

Let me now end this chapter with some of the ways the Catholic tradition has thickened our understanding of the reciprocal nature between knowledge and transformation in the economy of illumination from 2 Cor 3:18: "all of us, with unveiled faces, seeing the glory of the Lord as though reflected in a mirror, are being transformed into the same image from one degree of glory to another; for this comes from the Lord, the Spirit" (NRSV). The image we behold, for Balthasar, is the beauty of Christ, and the transformation we undergo is the process of being raptured in his beauty. We cannot abstract the light from the form of beauty, so to see the beauty of Christ is to be raptured and transformed into the beauty that Christ reveals. The Catholic tradition also helps us understand the *imago Dei* as our mental powers, so our *imago Dei* is actualized to God's likeness as God becomes the object of its remembering, knowing, and loving. As God becomes more and more the object of our knowledge and love, we become more and more like God, growing in knowing and loving God in the likeness of the way God knows and loves himself from eternity. This knowledge and love of God are in reciprocal relationship because to love God we must know God and to know God is to love God more, for God is true beauty, goodness, and truth.

6

—

ECONOMY OF ILLUMINATION IN THE REFORMED TRADITION

Augustine's theory of illumination also left its mark on the Reformed tradition. Like the Orthodox and Roman Catholic traditions, the Reformed tradition focuses on the economy of illumination as a means of participation in God, but the Reformed tradition focuses on the function of illumination that enables the person to hear and respond to the word of the gospel in union with Christ through the Spirit to the glory of God. This focus is exemplified in the five *solas* (*sola fide, sola gratia, sola Scriptura, solus Christus, soli Deo gloria*). From the Orthodox and Catholic traditions, we have received the inseparable components of "object" and "light" to contemplate God in the economy of illumination. The Reformed tradition offers implications for a third component in the economy of illumination: namely, the very sight we have of God is God's sight of himself because we see the Son from the Father's perspective (John 6:44–45). These three components (object, light, and sight) provide the building blocks for my dogmatic account of the economy of illumination that comprises beholding God in the object of the Son through the luminous power of the Spirit from the sight of the Father. The centrality of Scripture in the Reformed tradition will also be instrumental for my exposition on our participatory actions in the economy of illumination, which we will turn to in chapter 9. Through the spectacle of Scripture, the Spirit enables us to see, receive, and perform the good works that God has prepared for us beforehand in Christ (Eph 2:10).

JOHN CALVIN (1509–1564)

"While Augustine was a profound influence on pre-Enlightenment Protestantism with respect to grace," Carl Trueman argues, "this was not so marked with respect to illumination"—pre-Enlightenment theologians, such as John Calvin, identified illumination with "the internal testimony of the Holy Spirit" rather than with Christ, our inner teacher.[1] But what do we do with the places where Calvin ascribed to Christ the office of illumination? For example, Calvin writes, "Christ, when he illumines us into faith by the power of his Spirit, at the same time so engrafts us into his body that we become partakers of every good,"[2] or, "[the apostle John] justly ascribes to Christ this office of illuminating our minds as to the knowledge of God."[3] To reduce Calvin's theory of illumination to the Spirit's work is to miss how he developed Augustine's theory of illumination.

Calvin did not shift from the bishop's theory but advanced it with his concept of union with Christ through the Spirit and Scripture.[4] The similarities

1. Carl R. Trueman, "Illumination," in *Dictionary for Theological Interpretation of the Bible*, ed. Kevin J. Vanhoozer (Grand Rapids: Baker Academic, 2005), 317. A consensus among Calvin scholars is that the third person of the Trinity is the agent of illumination in Calvin's theology. See John Calvin, *Calvin's First Catechism: A Commentary*, ed. I. John Hesselink (Louisville: Westminster John Knox, 1997), 179–82; Barbara Pitkin, *What Pure Eyes Could See: Calvin's Doctrine of Faith in Its Exegetical Context* (New York: Oxford University Press, 1999), 56–59; Randall C. Zachman, *Image and Word in the Theology of John Calvin* (Notre Dame: University of Notre Dame Press, 2007), 79–80; and David L. Puckett, *John Calvin's Exegesis of the Old Testament*, Columbia Series in Reformed Theology (Louisville, KY: Westminster John Knox, 1995), 142–43. B. B. Warfield and Kenneth Kantzer offered perhaps the most comprehensive English accounts of Calvin's doctrine of illumination. While they agreed that Calvin's illumination is concerned with the internal testimony of the Spirit, they differed on the nature of the Spirit's testimony. In "Calvin's Doctrine of the Knowledge of God," for example, Warfield argues that for Calvin, the inner testimony of the Holy Spirit can only illuminate us through *indicia* of Scripture. The Spirit, in other words, convicts us of the revelation of Scripture and the nature of Scripture as God's word. Kenneth S. Kantzer, "John Calvin's Theory of the Knowledge of God and the Word of God" (PhD diss., Harvard University, 1950), however, argues that believers' conviction comes *solely* from the illumination of the Spirit, rather than *both* the inner testimony of the Spirit and the *indicia* of Scripture. What Kantzer wanted to highlight was that "the Spirit produces a grounded conviction. This is far from saying, however, that the witness of the Spirit properly considered merely illuminates us to see the evidences" (Kantzer, "Calvin's Theory," 430–31). I believe Warfield's account of illumination captures more of what Calvin wanted to communicate. For example, Calvin said, "the Word is the instrument by which the Lord dispenses the illumination of his Spirit to believers. For they know no other Spirit than him who dwelt and spoke in the apostles, and by whose oracles they are continually recalled to the hearing of the Word" (*Inst.* 1.9.3).

2. John Calvin, *Institutes of the Christian Religion*, vol. 1, ed. J. McNeill; trans. F. Battles (Louisville, KY: Westminster John Knox, 1960), 583; hereafter cited as *Inst.* 3.2.35.

3. John Calvin, *Commentaries on the Catholic Epistles*, trans. John Owen; The Calvin Translation Society, 1849–1850; (repr., Grand Rapids: Baker Books, 1999); hereafter cited as Comm. 1 John 5:20.

4. It is possible that Calvin had picked up the concept of Christ as divine Teacher from Clement of Alexandria's *Paedagogus*, but it is more likely that he encountered the concept in the writings of Augustine. Augustine's theory is found in Augustine's *The City of God*, books 8.1–12 and 11.26–27; *On the Trinity*, books 8 and 10, *Soliloquies*, books 1–2, and *Confessions*, book 10. Calvin either has quoted from or alluded to all these books in the *Institutes*. For discussion on

between the two suggest that Augustine had left an imprint on Calvin's understanding. The differences allow us to see how Calvin advanced the bishop's theory further with his concept of union with Christ. Calvin's doctrine of union helps us see how the light of Christ, the light of the Spirit, and the light of the gospel work together to unveil us to the light of the knowledge of the glory of God. In his commentary to 2 Cor 4:6, for instance, John Calvin spoke of the gospel and the work of the Spirit as a "twofold illumination" in Christ:

> the one is that of the gospel, the other is secret, taking place in our hearts. For as God, the Creator of the world, pours forth upon us the brightness of the sun, and gives us eyes to receive it, so, as the Redeemer, in the person of his Son, He shines forth, indeed, upon us by His gospel, but, as we are blind, that would be in vain, if He did not at the same time enlighten our understandings by His Spirit. His meaning, therefore, is, that God has, by His Spirit, opened the eyes of our understandings, so as to make them capable of receiving the light of the gospel. (Comm. 2 Cor. 4:6)[5]

The light of Christ comes through the gospel and comes into our hearts through the Holy Spirit. The transformation "*from glory to glory ... by the Spirit of the Lord*" concerns the restoration of the image of God in us, and the "Gospel" is the instrument that God uses to administer his light through the Spirit until his Son appears and perfects us into his likeness (Comm. 2 Cor. 3:18). To elaborate more, I turn to Calvin's other works.

THE SPECTRUM OF DIVINE LIGHT

The knowledge of God, Calvin believed, is innate in all human beings because God has made us with a *sensus divinitatis*, sense of divinity (*Inst.* 1.3.1). Calvin follows Augustine and views pride as the sin that blinds our mind from the knowledge of God in Christ,[6] and refers to Christ as "divine light" (Comm.

Augustine's influence on Calvin, see Todd Billings, *Calvin, Participation, and the Gift: The Activity of Believers in Union with Christ* (Oxford: Oxford University Press, 2007), 39–41.

5. John Calvin, *The Commentaries of John Calvin on the Second Epistle of Paul the Apostle to the Corinthians*, The Calvin Translation Society, 1849–1850; trans. John Pringle (repr., Grand Rapids: Baker Books, 1999); hereafter cited as Comm. 2 Cor. 4:6.

6. Cf.: "Hence, where we see a false estimate of one's own excellence, where we see arrogance, where we see pride, *there* let us be assured that Christ is not known. On the other hand, so soon as Christ shines forth all those things that formerly dazzled our eyes with a false splendor

John 9:39; 12:46),[7] "heavenly Teacher,"[8] "inner Schoolmaster,"[9] and the one who illumines our mind to see God and his goodness everywhere we turn (*Inst.* 3.2.7).[10] While Calvin shared Augustine's view that the "light of understanding," which Christ bestowed on us at creation, separates us from other creatures,[11] he was more keen on the "spiritual light" of Christ,[12] which vanquishes the darkness of sin with "the doctrine of his word" (Comm. Isa. 9.2).[13] This becomes evident as we explore Calvin's works. However, it is difficult to pinpoint exactly what Calvin meant by the metaphor of light because Calvin at times referred to Christ, the Spirit, and Scripture simultaneously as light.[14]

instantly vanish, or at least are disesteemed" (John Calvin, *Commentary on the Epistle of Paul the Apostle to the Philippians, Colossians, and Thessalonians*, The Calvin Translation Society, 1849–1850; trans. John Pringle [repr., Grand Rapids: Baker Books, 1999]; hereafter cited as Comm. Phil. 3:7). Elsewhere, Calvin stated that our blindness is remedied by the illumination of the Spirit; see John Calvin, *Commentary on the Book of Psalms*, The Calvin Translation Society, 1849–1850; trans. James Anderson (repr., Grand Rapids: Baker Books, 1999); hereafter cited as Comm. Psa. 119:73.

7. Similar to Augustine, Calvin argues that this divine light "forms us to the image of God" (Comm. John 12:40).

8. John Calvin, *Commentary on the Epistle of Paul the Apostle to the Romans*, The Calvin Translation Society, 1849–1850; trans. John Owen (repr., Grand Rapids: Baker Books, 1999); hereafter cited as Comm. Rom. 8:15–18. Cf. John Calvin, *Commentary on a Harmony of the Evangelists*, The Calvin Translation Society, 1849–1850; trans. William Pringle (repr., Grand Rapids: Baker Books, 1999); hereafter cited as Comm. Matt. 7:13.

9. For example, Calvin writes, "Paul so highly commends the 'ministry of the Spirit' [II Cor. 3:6] for the reason that teachers would shout to no effect if Christ himself, inner Schoolmaster, did not by his Spirit draw to himself those given to him by the Father [cf. John 6:44; 12:32; 17:6]" (*Inst.* 3.1.4.; cf. 3.2.1; John Calvin, *Commentary on the Gospel According to John*, The Calvin Translation Society, 1849–1850; trans. William Pringle [repr., Grand Rapids: Baker Books, 1999]; hereafter cited as Comm. John 15:20).

10. Cf. John Calvin, *Commentaries on the Catholic Epistles*, The Calvin Translation Society, 1849–1850; trans. John Owen (repr., Grand Rapids: Baker Books, 1999); hereafter cited as Comm. 1 John 5:20; and John Calvin, *Commentary on the Book of the Prophet Isaiah*, The Calvin Translation Society, 1849–1850; trans. William Pringle (repr., Grand Rapids: Baker Books, 1999); hereafter cited as Comm. Isa. 42:6.

11. In Comm. John 1:4, Calvin wrote that John "speaks here, in my opinion, of that part of *life* in which men excel other animals; and informs us that *the life* which was bestowed on *men* was not of an ordinary description, but was united to *the light* of understanding. He separates man from the rank of other creatures; because we perceive more readily the power of God by feeling it in us than by beholding it at a distance."

12. John Calvin, *Commentaries on the Twelve Minor Prophets*, vol. 5, The Calvin Translation Society, 1849–1850; trans. John Owen (repr., Grand Rapids: Baker Books, 1999); hereafter cited as Comm. Mal. 4:2.

13. John Calvin, *Commentary upon the Acts of the Apostles*, The Calvin Translation Society, 1849–1850; trans. Henry Beveridge (repr., Grand Rapids: Baker Books, 1999); hereafter cited as Comm. Acts 13:47.

14. In the passage below, for example, Calvin spoke of the illumination of Christ, the Spirit, and Scripture in the same breath: "But we must notice in passing the names by which he

Scripture, for Calvin, is light because it presents the "Gospel" (Comm. Isa. 49:6)[15] and lights up our path to salvation,[16] pointing us to our deficiency and Christ's sufficiency,[17] and offering us Christ, his righteousness, holiness, and salvation (Comm. Rom. 1:16; cf. Comm. 1 Cor. 1:30). Scripture is light in the sense that it leads us to the light of the glory of the knowledge of God in Jesus Christ (Comm. 2 Cor 4:4–6). But the light of Scripture is ineffective without the Spirit. While "Scripture exhibits fully as clear evidence of its own truth as white and black things do of their color, or sweet and bitter things do of their tastes," the darkened mind of man cannot sense the evidence of divine truth in Scripture (*Inst.* 1.7.2). Faith is required for understanding, and faith comes from the light of the Spirit.[18]

The Spirit is the "inward light," which enters, opens, and affects the heart and mind of believers with God's word to unite them to Christ (Comm. Luke 24:44)[19] and enable them to receive Christ and "all his benefits" (*Inst.* 3.1.1). Put otherwise, the external call of the gospel in Scripture is made effective by the inward testimony of the Spirit.[20] The person with his mind

---

signalizes the knowledge of the Gospel. He calls it *illumination;* it hence follows that men are blind, until Christ, the light of the world, enlightens them. ... He calls it the *participation* of the Spirit; for he it is who distributes to every one, as he wills, all the light and knowledge which he can have; for without him no one can say that Jesus is the Lord [1 Corinthians 12:3]; he opens for us the eyes of our minds, and reveals to us the secret things of God. ... Let us then know, that the Gospel cannot be otherwise rightly known than by the illumination of the Spirit, and that being thus drawn away from the world, we are raised up to heaven, and that knowing the goodness of God we rely on his word" (John Calvin, *Commentary on the Epistle of Paul the Apostle to the Hebrews*, The Calvin Translation Society, 1849–1850; trans. John Owen [repr., Grand Rapids: Baker Books, 1999]; hereafter cited as Comm. Heb. 6:4).

15. John Calvin, *Commentary on the Book of the Prophet Isaiah*, The Calvin Translation Society, 1849–1850; trans. William Pringle (repr., Grand Rapids: Baker Books, 1999); hereafter cited as Comm. 49:6.

16. In Calvin's prayer for illumination, he writes, "Grant, Almighty God, that as thou shinest on us by thy word, and showest to us the way of salvation" (Comm. Zech 4:1–6).

17. John Calvin, *Commentaries on the Twelve Minor Prophets*, vol. 4, The Calvin Translation Society, 1849–1850; trans. John Owen (repr., Grand Rapids: Baker Books, 1999); hereafter cited as Comm. Hab. 2:4.

18. Cf.: "Yea, seeing that the true knowledge of God is a singular gift of his, and faith [by which alone he is rightly known] cometh only from the illumination of the Spirit" (John Calvin, *Commentary upon the Acts of the Apostles*, The Calvin Translation Society, 1849–1850; trans. Henry Beveridge [repr., Grand Rapids: Baker Books, 1999]; hereafter cited as Comm. Acts 17:27; 5:32). Cf. Comm. John 7:17; *Inst.* 3.2.33–35.

19. Cf. John Dillenberger, ed., *John Calvin: Selections from His Writings* (Missoula, MT: Scholars Press, 1975), 91.

20. Cf.: "Moreover, it is said that the door of faith was set open to the Gentiles, not only because the gospel was preached to them with the external voice, but because, being illuminated

and heart affected by the Spirit is renewed with God's mind to hear God's voice in Scripture (*Inst.* 1.7.4). Scripture without the Spirit "can do nothing" (*Inst.* 3.2.33), but the Spirit without the Scripture has nothing to illumine (*Inst.* 1.9.3).[21] The Spirit leaves the elect without a doubt to the truthfulness of Scripture (Comm. Zech. 4:1–6; *Inst.* 3.24.17)[22] because he enables the elect to taste in Scripture "those things which belong to the Kingdom of God" (*Inst.* 3.2.34; cf. 3.1.2).[23]

Calvin also referred to the coming of Christ as light because it reveals what was hidden in the Old Testament (Comm. Isa. 49:6). Like the sun that illumines our eyes to the things of the world, the light of Christ opens our mind's eye to the things of God, particularly the glory and the salvation of God on the cross,[24] through the Spirit and Scripture.[25] The *telos* of illumination is to see Christ.[26] To see him is to behold God because he is the

by the Spirit of God, they were called effectually unto the faith" (Comm. Acts 14:27). In other words, the Spirit causes the proclamation of God's word to be efficacious to hearers (John Calvin, *Commentary on the Epistles of Paul the Apostle to the Galatians and Ephesians*, The Calvin Translation Society, 1849–1850; trans. William Pringle (repr., Grand Rapids: Baker Books, 1999); hereafter cited as Comm. Eph. 1:13; cf. Comm. Heb. 6:4; Comm. John 10:26).

21. What the Spirit illumines is the word of God, so believers "acknowledge nothing but what God says in his word" (Comm. 2 Pet. 1:20). Put otherwise, the Spirit illumines the elect "chiefly by doctrine" of Scripture (Comm. 1 Thess. 5:19–20). The inner light of the Spirit leads the person to the light of the gospel (Comm. Zech. 4:1–6). That is, the Spirit opens the mind's eyes to understand and be affected by the truth of the gospel—Jesus Christ and his salvation.

22. According to Calvin, there are "two different things he intends to teach here: *first*, that the doctrine of the Gospel cannot be understood otherwise than by the testimony of the Holy Spirit; and *secondly*, that those who have a testimony of this nature from the Holy Spirit, have an assurance as firm and solid, as if they felt with their hands what they believe, for the Spirit is a faithful and indubitable witness" (John Calvin, The *Commentaries of John Calvin on the First Epistle of Paul the Apostle to the Corinthians*, The Calvin Translation Society, 1849–1850; trans. John Pringle (repr., Grand Rapids: Baker Books, 1999); hereafter cited as Comm. 1 Cor. 2:11).

23. Similarly, B. B. Warfield, *Calvin and Augustine* (Philadelphia: Presbyterian & Reformed Publishing Company, 1956), 78, argues that the elect, illumined by the Spirit to the revelation of Scripture, knows God in a supra rational way. She is persuaded and convinced that what God said about himself in Scripture is true and is from God. "It is a persuasion which does not require reasons—that is to say, it is a state of conviction not induced by arguments, but by direct perception" (Warfield, *Calvin and Augustine*, 79).

24. According to Calvin, "a person, ignorant and uneducated, and whose mind was altogether corrupted, should all at once, on receiving his earliest instructions, perceive salvation and heavenly glory in the accursed cross, was truly astonishing" (Comm. Luke 23:42).

25. Cf.: "Christ performs towards us the office of a sun, not to guide our feet and hands as to what is earthly, but that he brings light to us, to show the way to heaven, and that by its means we may come to the enjoyment of a blessed and eternal life" (Comm. Mal 4:2).

26. In Comm. 1 John 2:27, Calvin wrote that John shows that "the children of God are for no other end illuminated by the Spirit, but that they may know Christ."

image of the invisible God (Comm. 2 Cor. 2:4, 6; Comm. Col. 1:15).[27] Jesus is simply light because he is the substance of God (who *is* light) and the reality of what salvation is because he is the way, the truth, and the life.[28] "For Christ proves that he is *the life*, because God, *with whom is the fountain of life*, [Psalm 36:9] cannot be enjoyed in any other way than in Christ" (Comm. John 14:6).[29] This life is the light of man. This light, which God bestowed on man before the fall, is what Christ came to restore,[30] and once this light is kindled within the elect, it is "never extinguished" again (Comm. 1 John 5:20). It is the light of new birth because "when Christ enlightens us, we rise from death to life" (Comm. Eph. 5:14; cf. Comm. Isa 35:5) and see all things new (*Inst.* 2.5.5; cf. 2 Cor 5:16–17).[31]

DIVINE ILLUMINATION AND UNION WITH CHRIST

What is the relationship between the light of Christ, the light of the Spirit, and the light of Scripture in illumination? Calvin's concept of union with Christ allows us to see their relationship in illumination because illumination occurs in tandem with union with Christ. "Christ, when he illumines us into faith by the power of his Spirit, at the same time so engrafts us into his body that we become partakers of every good" (*Inst.* 3.2.35). Illumination is a means and fruit of our union with Christ because believers can neither participate in Christ without

---

27. For example, Calvin wrote: "And Christ is said to have *given us an understanding*, not only because he shews us in the gospel what sort of being is the true God, and also illuminates us by his Spirit; but because in Christ himself we have God manifested in the flesh, as Paul says, since in him dwells all the fullness of the Deity, and are hid all the treasures of knowledge and wisdom" (Comm. 1 John 5:20; cf. Comm. John 1:18).

28. Elsewhere, Calvin writes, "Therefore the whole substance of our salvation is in Christ's person" (Comm. Acts 13.47).

29. Cf.: "In the same manner as Christ is called 'the way, the truth, and the life' (John 14:6), because through the knowledge of the truth we obtain life, so in this passage he is called the "light" and salvation of the gentiles, because he enlightens our minds by the doctrine of the Gospel, in order that he may lead us to salvation. Two things, therefore, ought to be remarked; first, that our eyes are opened by the doctrine of Christ; and secondly, that we who had perished are restored to life, or rather life is restored to us" (Comm. Isa 49:6).

30. Cf.: "As it is not in vain that God imparts his light to their minds, it follows that the purpose for which they were created was, that they might acknowledge Him who is the Author of so excellent a blessing" (Comm. John 1:4). For discussion on the renewal of the image of God or the "light of the mind" in the elect, see *Inst.* 1.15.4.

31. To read more on how illumination renews the heart and mind of the elect, so that she is able to know God, see Comm. Col. 3:10; John Calvin, *Commentaries on the Book of the Prophet Jeremiah and the Lamentations*, The Calvin Translation Society, 1849–1850; trans. John Owen (repr., Grand Rapids: Baker Books, 1999); hereafter cited as Comm. Jer. 31:19.

faith from illumination[32] nor be illumined by the Spirit through Scripture apart from union with Christ (*Inst.* 3.1.4; cf. 2 Cor 3:14).[33] To understand participation in union with Christ is at the same time to see the operation of illumination.

The reality of this union is "incomprehensible by nature" (*Inst.* 4.17.1)[34] because it concerns a union with the second person of the Godhead (*Inst.* 3.2.24). But the process by which we participate in this union is clear. We are engrafted in Christ by faith and through the bond of the Spirit (*Inst.* 3.1.1),[35] which allow us to apprehend and receive what is in Christ (*Inst.* 3.2.35): "as long as Christ remains outside of us, and we are separated from him, all that he has suffered and done for the salvation of the human race remains useless and of no value for us" (*Inst.* 3.1.1). The death and resurrection of Christ would not be able to renew us without the "'testimony of the Spirit,'" which "seals the cleansing and sacrifice of Christ" in our heart (*Inst.* 3.1.1). But the testimony of the Spirit cannot seal our heart with the benefits of Christ without the light of the gospel because "spiritual gifts cannot be given for salvation, until, being illuminated by the doctrine of the gospel, we are led to know God" (Comm. 2 Pet. 1:3).

Like the Lord's Supper where the elements and the Spirit enable believers to feed on Christ who is in heaven through faith in union with Christ,[36]

---

32. According to Richard A. Muller, *Calvin and the Reformed Tradition: On the Work of Christ and the Order of Salvation* (Grand Rapids: Baker Academic, 2012), 210, "faith, bestowed by the Spirit, is the instrument of union."

33. In his commentary on Isaiah, for example, Calvin said that union with Christ affects illumination: "By the *tongue* and *ears* and *feet* [Isaiah] means all the faculties of our soul, which in themselves are so corrupt that nothing that is good can be obtained from them till they are restored by the kindness of Christ. The eyes cannot see what is right, and the ears cannot hear, and the feet cannot guide us in the right way, till we are united to Christ. ... therefore every part of us must be created anew by the power of Christ, that it may begin to understand aright, to feel, to speak, and to perform its offices" (Comm. Isa. 35:5).

34. English translation is from John Calvin, *Institutes of the Christian Religion*, vol. 2, ed. J. McNeill; trans. F. Battles (Louisville, KY: Westminster John Knox, 1960).

35. The bond of union is the Spirit because "Christ cannot be separated from his Spirit," so those who have the indwelling Spirit have Christ indwelling in them (Comm. 1 Cor. 11:27). In *Inst.* 3.1.3, Calvin added, "until our minds become intent upon the Spirit, Christ, so to speak, lies idle because we coldly contemplate him as outside ourselves—indeed, far from us."

36. Calvin writes, "first, the Lord teaches and instructs us by his Word. Secondly, he confirms it by the sacraments. Finally, he illumines our minds by the light of his Holy Spirit and opens our hearts for the Word and sacraments to enter in, which would otherwise only strike our ears and appear before our eyes, but not at all affect us within" (*Inst.* 4.14.9). See Mark A. Garcia, *Life in Christ: Union with Christ and Twofold Grace in Calvin's Theology*, Studies in Christian History and Thought (Colorado Springs: Paternoster, 2008), 162–63, 171, 188–90, who shows the way Calvin combined Chalcedonian Christology with the Augustinian *signa-res* relationship to

"Christ . . . daily illuminates [those in him from heaven] by his doctrine [in Scripture] and his Spirit" (Comm. Mal. 4:2):

> It must also be observed, that the power and office of illuminating is not confined to the personal *presence* of Christ; for though he is far removed from us with respect to his body, yet he daily sheds his light upon us, by the doctrine of the Gospel, and by the secret power of his Spirit. Yet we have not a full definition of this light, unless we learn that we are illuminated by the Gospel and by the Spirit of Christ, that we may know that the fountain of all knowledge and wisdom is hidden in him. (Comm. John 8:12, emphasis mine)

In union with Christ, the mind's eyes are opened, spiritual senses are restored to enable the elect to see and hear Christ daily in Scripture through the Spirit (Comm. Isa. 35.5). Like Calvin's *duplex gratia* of justification and sanctification, the subjective and objective testimonies of the Spirit and Scripture are inseparable but distinct in the illumination of Christ. Scripture and the *testimonium Spiritus Sancti*, in other words, form the "twofold illumination" that unveils believers to Jesus Christ, the light of the glory of the knowledge of God (Comm. 2 Cor. 4:6). They form the objective and subjective light to remedy human blindness.[37] Scripture, on the one hand, is the objective content of God's revelation, containing the *indicia* of truth and divinity.[38] The testimony of the Spirit, on the other hand, renews the mind and heart of believers, implanting spiritual sense to perceive the *indicia* of Scripture (*Inst.* 3.1.1).[39] The two are ineffective without the other in opening access to the knowledge of God[40] because a person can neither see God without Scripture because there would be nothing to see nor

demonstrate how the sacraments (signs) and the reality of grace (thing) in union with Christ through the Spirit are distinct, but inseparable when a person partakes the elements by faith.

37. Warfield, *Calvin and Augustine*, 69–70, 76.

38. "The *indicia* are supreme in their sphere; they and they alone give objective evidence" (Warfield, *Calvin and Augustine*, 86).

39. Warfield, *Calvin and Augustine*, 78, 90.

40. Warfield writes, "If [Calvin] holds that the revelation of God is ineffective without the testimony of the Spirit, he holds equally that the testimony of the Spirit is inconceivable without the revelation of God embodied in the Word. ... the Spirit is no more the agent by which the Word is impressed on the heart than the Word is the means by which the illumination of the Spirit takes effect. 'If apart from the Spirit of God' we 'are utterly destitute of the light of truth,' he says (I.ix.3, *ad fin.*), equally 'the Word is the instrument by which the Lord dispenses to believers the illumination of the Spirit'" (Warfield, *Calvin and Augustine*, 80–81).

know God apart from the Spirit because the mind's eyes would be closed to the *indicia* of God's word.[41] The Spirit allows the person to see Scripture, as it truly is, the word of God concerning Christ, so the person may become more like Christ.

If we use the analogy of physical light for Calvin's spiritual light of illumination, then the ray of light that illumines our eyes to the *res* is the *signum* of Scripture, the warmth of light that affects our soul and allows us to connect to the light of Christ is the Spirit, and the wave-particle of the substance of light (to use an Einsteinian term) is Christ—light from light, so in his light, we see light, the Father. In union with Christ, the doctrine of Scripture is neither cold nor abstract, but a reality that we taste and know by experience that the Lord is good. In Calvin's hands, Christ, the divine teacher in Augustine's theory, has the light of Scripture and the testimony of the Spirit, with which he daily illumines our hearts from heaven. Calvin's theory is crucial in showing us that there is no light to the glory of God in Christ without Scripture: the light in the economy of illumination comes to those in darkness from Scripture through the Spirit in Christ.

JOHN OWEN (1616–1683)

Standing on the tradition Cavin laid, John Owen viewed union with Christ as the foundation of communion with God: "Our communion ... with God consisteth in his *communication of himself unto us, with our returnal unto him* of that which he requireth and accepteth, flowing from that *union* which in Jesus Christ we have with him."[42] If communion with God is to receive what God communicates and gives, then union with Christ is the wellspring of communion[43]

41. Warfield puts it this way: "Only in the conjunction of the two can an effective revelation be made to the sin-darkened mind of man. The Word supplies the objective factor; the Spirit the subjective factor; and only in the union of the objective and subjective factors is the result accomplished. The whole objective revelation of God lies, thus, in the Word. But the whole subjective capacitating for the reception of this revelation lies in the will of the Spirit. Either, by itself, is wholly ineffective to the result aimed at—the production of knowledge in the human mind. But when they unite, knowledge is not only rendered possible to man: it is rendered certain" (Warfield, *Calvin and Augustine*, 82–83).

42. John Owen, *Communion with God*, vol. 2 of *The Works of John Owen*, ed. William H. Goold (1850–1853; repr., Edinburgh: Banner of Truth, 1965), 8–9; hereafter cited as *Works* 2:8–9. Simply put, communion "is a communication and receiving between God and us; so near are we unto him in Christ" (*Works* 2:19), a "mutual communication in giving and receiving ... between God and the saints while they walk together in a covenant of peace, ratified in the blood of Jesus" (*Works* 2:9).

43. To put it another way, union is the ground and communion is the purpose of the salvific work of the "whole blessed Trinity," the "kindness and love of" the Father as the fountain, the Son as the "procuring cause of the application of the love and kindness," and the Spirit as the "immediate efficient cause in the communication of the love and kindness of the Father,

because God communicates and gives all things *in* the Son[44] through the Spirit.[45] The economy of illumination, for Owen, is a means to participate in Christ and receive what God communicates in Christ because it is the work of the Spirit who is the "immediate efficient cause in the communication of the love and kindness of the Father" to us procured in Christ.[46] Owen's version of illumination offers insights on the work of the Spirit, which enables us to receive what the Father communicates in the Son,[47] and into the relationship between preparatory and saving illuminations for Part III of our study.

THE AGENCY OF THE HOLY SPIRIT IN ILLUMINATION

The Holy Spirit is the "author"[48] and "foundation of all illumination."[49] In 2 Cor 3:13–18, Owen perceived that there are two veils, one over the Old Testament, which the gospel takes away, and the other over our hearts, which "is to be removed only by an *effectual work of the Spirit of Christ*, in the conversion of the souls of men unto God."[50] The second veil represents "ignorance, darkness, blindness, that is on men by nature."[51] Spirit removes the second veil by "the *effectual illumination* of our minds, or the enlightening of the eyes of our understandings."[52] To aid in understanding what this means, let me begin by explaining what it is not.

The effectual illumination of the Spirit is not the Spirit's preparatory illumination, which aids "our natural abilities" to discern and understand

---

through the mediation of the Son, unto us" (John Owen, ΠΝΕΥΜΑΤΟΛΟΓΙΑ or *A Discourse Concerning the Holy Spirit*, vol. 3 of *The Works of John Owen*, ed. William H. Goold [1850–1853; repr., Edinburgh: Banner of Truth, 1965), 209; hereafter cited as *Works* 3:209].

44. Cf.: "The mutual love of God and the saints agrees in this,—that the way of communicating the issues and fruits of these loves is *only in Christ*. The Father communicates no issue of his love unto us but through Christ; and we make no return of love unto him but through Christ" (*Works* 2:26–27).

45. According to Kelly M. Kapic, *Communion with God: The Divine and the Human in the Theology of John Owen* (Grand Rapids: Baker Academic, 2007), 152–57, while we are never at risk of losing our union, we can hinder our intimacy with God in communion by sin. See also *Works* 3:466.

46. *Works* 3:209. In his later writing, Owen would refer to the Spirit as the "author or principal efficient cause of" illumination (John Owen, *Causes, Ways, and Means of Understanding the Mind of God*, vol. 4 of *The Works of John Owen*, ed. William Goold [1850–1853; repr., Edinburgh: Banner of Truth, 1967], 135; hereafter cited as *Works* 4:135).

47. *Works* 2:10.

48. *Works* 4:130.

49. *Works* 3:236.

50. *Works* 4:132 (emphasis original).

51. *Works* 4:131.

52. *Works* 4:132–133 (emphasis original).

more clearly the "doctrine of the gospel as the way of righteousness."[53] Those who experience preparatory illumination will either remain for a time in preliminary faith (John 8:30–31; Acts 8:13) and then fall away (Heb 6:4) or move unto saving faith and persevere in the course to glory.[54]

Contrary to preparatory illumination, which only uses and enhances our natural abilities, saving illumination from the Spirit creates a new heart and mind in Christ through the gospel.[55] "The true nature of saving illumination," as Owen understands it, "is this, that it gives the mind such a direct intuitive insight and prospect into spiritual things as that, in their own spiritual nature, they suit, please, and satisfy it, so that it is transformed into them, cast into the mould of them, and rests in them, Rom. vi. 17, xii. 2; 1 Cor. ii. 13–15; 2 Cor. iii. 18, iv. 6."[56] This light, which the Spirit introduces in saving illumination, "is a spiritual ability to discern and know spiritual things, as is declared, 2 Cor. iv. 6,"[57] and "[w]ithout this *light* no man can understand the Scripture as he ought"[58] because after the fall, human beings "are in a *state of darkness and blindness* with respect unto God and spiritual things, with the way of pleasing him and living unto him."[59]

53. *Works* 3:232.
54. *Works* 3:232.
55. *Works* 4:172; cf. *Works* 3:224.
56. *Works* 3:238.
57. *Works* 4:171.
58. *Works* 4:172.
59. *Works* 3:244 (emphasis original).

SPECIAL ILLUMINATION: BEING IN THE LIGHT OF NEW CREATION

Similar to Aquinas, Owen understood the light of new birth as an infusion of the habit of grace,[60] a habit not acquired by what we do,[61] but implanted and created in us by the "holy habitation" of the Spirit,[62] so the habit or principle of "grace, as a quality, remains in us, as in its own proper subject."[63] The indwelling of the Spirit affects and infuses the habit of grace in our hearts and minds by uniting us to Christ.[64]

> Whatever is wrought in believers by the *Spirit of Christ*, it is in their *union* to the person of Christ, and by virtue thereof. ... the Holy Spirit is the immediate efficient cause of all grace and holiness ... the end why the Holy Spirit is sent ... is to glory Christ; and this he doth by receiving from Christ, and communicating thereof unto others, John xvi. 13–15. And there are two works of this kind which he hath to do and doth effect:—first, To unite us to Christ; and secondly, To communicate all grace unto us from Christ, by virtue of that union.[65]

Illumination is not only the cause but also the fruit of union with Christ because it is the work of the Spirit administering what is in Christ,[66] and the formal effect of union with Christ[67] because whoever is in Christ *is*

---

60. For example, Owen writes, "He [the Spirit] gives us *habitual grace*;—a principle of grace, opposed to the principle of lust that is in us by nature. This is the grace that dwells in us, makes its abode with us; which, according to the distinct faculties of our souls wherein it is, or the distinct objects about which it is exercised, receiveth various appellations, being indeed all but one new principle of life. In the understanding, it is light; in the will, obedience; in the affections, love; in all, faith" (*Works* 2:172). See Andrew M. Leslie, *The Light of Grace: John Owen on the Authority of Scripture and Christian Faith* (Göttingen: Vandenhoeck & Ruprecht, 2015), 110; cf. *Works* 2:199–200.

61. *Works* 3:476.

62. *Works* 3:476; *Works* 2:200.

63. *Works* 2:200.

64. Cf.: "The *fountain* of this life being in God, and the *fulness* of it being laid up in Christ for us, he communicates the power and principle of it unto us by the Holy Ghost, Rom. viii. 11. That he is the immediate efficient cause hereof. ... But yet he doth it so as to derive it unto us from Jesus Christ, Eph. iv. 15, 16; for he is 'the life,' and 'without him,' or power communicated from him, 'we can do nothing,' John xv. 5" (*Works* 3:292; cf. *Works* 2:42).

65. *Works* 3:516 (emphasis original).

66. *Works* 3:464.

67. Cf.: "Originally and *efficiently* the Holy Spirit dwelling in him and us is the cause of this union; but *formally* this new principle of grace is so. It is that whereby we become 'members of his flesh and of his bones,' Eph. v. 30" (*Works* 3:478; emphasis original).

a new creation, formed into Christlikeness (2 Cor 5:17).[68] To be in Christ is to be in light, to receive light, and to become a light.

Illumination does not reveal anything new, but only subjectively what has been revealed objectively by the Father in the Son through Scripture.[69] "By subjective revelations," Owen wrote, "nothing is intended but that work of spiritual illumination whereby we are enabled to discern and understand the mind of God in Scripture."[70] The way the Spirit reveals subjectively to us, what is revealed objectively in Scripture, is by molding and forming our mind to the mind and perspective of God in Scripture. Owen viewed the Spirit's illumination as the inscribing of the law on the heart from the new covenant promise (Jer 31:33)[71] to form and "mould" our minds to the shape of the gospel, so that "our minds and the word should answer one another, as face doth unto face in water."[72]

The light of renewal forms our minds to receive and experience the gospel by giving us "a *spiritual sense* of the *power and reality of the things believed*."[73] The effect of illumination, in other words, is a new mind to taste and see that the Lord is good (Ps 34:8).

> The work of the Holy Ghost ... consists in the saving *illumination* of the mind; and the effect of it is a *supernatural light*, whereby the mind is renewed: see Rom. xii. 2; Eph. i. 18, 19, iii. 16–19. It is called a "heart to understand, eyes to see, ears to hear," Deut. xxix. 4; the "opening of the eyes of our understanding," Eph. i. 18; the "giving of an understanding," 1 John v. 20. Hereby we are enabled to discern the evidences of the divine original and authority of the Scripture that are in itself, as well as assent unto the truth contained in it; and without it we cannot do so, for "the natural man receiveth not the things of the Spirit of God, for they are

68. *Works* 3:214. Owen wrote, "Our union with Christ is immediately in and by the *new creature* in us, by the divine nature which is from the Spirit of holiness, and is pure and holy" (*Works* 3:465; emphasis original).

69. *Works* 4:170; *Works* 3:333–334. Illumination is "an *internal subjective revelation*, whereby no *new things* are revealed unto our minds, or are not outwardly revealed *anew*, but our minds are enabled to discern the things that are revealed already" (*Works* 4:134).

70. *Works* 3:13.

71. *Works* 3:476.

72. *Works* 3:508. For further discussion, see Leslie, *Light of Grace*, 115–18.

73. *Works* 4:64.

> foolishness unto him, neither can he know them, because they are spiritually discerned," 1 Cor. ii. 14; and unto this end it is written in the prophets that "we shall be all taught of God," John vi. 45.[74]

To be illumined is then to see, taste, and experience the "power" and the "spiritual things" revealed,[75] rather than to have merely the notion or sense of these things in Scripture.[76] As our taste, sight, and experience convince us of natural things, the effect of the Spirit's illumination assures us of the truth of spiritual things by the implanting of a divine sense to enable us to know by personal experience the Lord's grace and holiness.[77]

In brief, the saving illumination of the Spirit gives us the mind and perspective of God to understand and see what God says in Scripture.[78] The economy of illumination is then the "*internal teaching* of the Holy Ghost,"[79] whereby the Father communicates himself "unto the saints whereof they are made partakers" of Christ for communion with God.[80] It enables us to participate in communion with God through union with Christ because it allows us to receive all the things that God desires to communicate to us in Christ,[81] producing "in us *returning*

---

74. *Works* 4:57.

75. *Works* 4:205

76. Owen made a distinction here between knowing the things of Scripture notionally and experiencing the things of Scripture personally: "There is a wide difference between the mind's receiving doctrine *notionally*, and its receiving the thing taught in them *really*. ... In the latter way they only receive spiritual things in whose minds they are so implanted as to produce their real and proper effects, Rom. xii. 2; Eph. iv. 22–24" (*Works* 3:260). Leslie, *Light of Grace*, 117, comments, "While Owen believes the literal words and propositions of the gospel are perspicuously accommodated to the 'common reason' of humanity, so that even someone of the 'meanest capacity' can grasp their 'sense' without the Spirit's special illumination, natural reason is unable to detect the spiritual truth actually signified by those words. That is, the gospel will never be regarded as anything more than an object of reproach or indifference. ... when the gospel is described in scripture as a 'wondrous light' (φῶς θαυμαστόν) does not merely refer to the doctrine as objective propositions, but the spiritual light through which the glory of God signified in those propositions may be rightly perceived."

77. *Works* 4:64; 127.

78. *Works* 3:238.

79. *Works* 4:144 (emphasis original).

80. *Works* 2:15. Owen goes on to write, "This teaching, whereby we are translated from death unto life, brought unto Christ, unto a participation of life and love in him,—it is of and from the Father: him we hear, of him we learn, by him are we brought unto union and communion with the Lord Jesus. This is his drawing us, his begetting us anew of his own will by his own Spirit; and in which work he employs the ministers of the gospel, Acts xxvi. 17, 18" (*Works* 2:15–16).

81. Believers cannot "discern, receive, understand, or believe savingly, spiritual things, ... without an effectual, powerful work of the Holy Spirit, creating ... a new *saving light* into them" (*Works* 3:249).

praise, and thanks, and honour, and glory, and blessing to him, on the account of the mercies and privileges which we receive from him."[82] Owen's account highlights the vital role of illumination in sanctifying the mind. A natural person cannot understand the things of God in Holy Scripture because "they are spiritually discerned" (1 Cor 2:14), requiring spiritual and holy reasoning. To hear God, the person needs the "holy habitation" of the Spirit to infuse the habit of grace to make him holy. Without holiness, no one sees God (Heb 12:14).

JONATHAN EDWARDS (1703–1758)

The account of Jonathan Edwards draws our attention even further into the effects (faith and affection) of the Spirit on the soul of the elect in union with Christ her Savior. In his sermon on 2 Cor 3:18, titled, "A Sight of the Glory of Christ," Edwards illustrates the way the Spirit gives us a "true sight" of Christ, the glory of God.

> 'Tis the Spirit of Christ that is the immediate teacher and instructor, to give a true sight of Christ. ... Christ is the great teacher; we are the disciples of Christ, but he teaches by his Spirit. Christ is the luminary, he is the sun; but the spirit of Christ is as the rays, as the very light itself. The sun don't [*sic*] enlighten us immediately, but by his beams. 'Tis the rays of the sun that are sent forth, that do immediately enlighten. 'Tis Christ's face that shines into the heart, but 'tis the spirit of Christ are the rays by which it shines into them. The instructions and teachings that are given us, are Christ's; he is the great prophet and teacher sent from God: but the spirit of Christ opens the understanding to receive his instructions.[83]

The rays of the Spirit give us a true "sight" of the sun, the glory of Christ. Referencing 2 Cor 4:6, Edwards views this ray of sight as creative because it is "Creating of Eyes to see."[84] Faith and affection are awakened when what God reveals in the Son is illumined in the Spirit because the person senses

82. *Works* 2:271.

83. Jonathan Edwards, "A Sight of the Glory of Christ" (72. II Cor. 3:18 [1728]), in *Sermons, Series II, 1728–1729, Works of Jonathan Edwards Online*, vol. 43, n.p. http://edwards.yale.edu/archive?path=aHR0cDovL2Vkd2FyZHMueWFsZS5lZHUvY2dpLWJpbi9uZXdwaGlsby9nZRvplY3QucGw/Yy40MToxNC53amVv.

84. Edwards, "Sight," n.p.

and sees the glory and excellency of God in Christ. The illumination by the Spirit unites us to Christ because the Spirit imparts spiritual sight and sense to move and affect our souls in Christ, allowing us to see and taste what is in Christ, the glory and excellency of God. To demonstrate how the Spirit's illumination is an effectual means to unite us to Christ, I begin with Edwards's concept of participation and then show how illumination awakens faith in and affections for Christ and God.

ON THE NATURE OF PARTICIPATION IN GOD

Since the time Michael McClymond proposed, "Edwards taught a doctrine of divination,"[85] certain quarters of Edwards readers following his lead have employed *theosis* as a framework to understand Edwards's concept of participation in God.[86] However, in my reading, Edwards's concept of participation seems more in line with Augustine and Calvin's conception of participation because Edwards understood participation more in terms of the *person* of the Holy Spirit than the *energies* of God.[87]

Edwards perceived that the person of the Spirit is the bond of our union with God[88] because the Spirit is the mutual love between the Father and the

85. Michael J. McClymond, "Salvation as Divinization: Jonathan Edwards, Gregory Palamas and the Theological Uses of Neoplatonism," in *Jonathan Edwards: Philosophical Theologian*, ed. Paul Helm and Oliver D. Crisp (Burlington, VT: Ashgate, 2003), 153.

86. For discussion from those who follow McClymond's reading, see William Danaher, *The Trinitarian Ethics of Jonathan Edwards* (Louisville: Westminster John Knox, 2004), 6–7, 17–18; Oliver Crisp, *Jonathan Edwards on God and Creation* (Oxford: Oxford University Press, 2012), 166–73; and W. Ross Hastings, *Jonathan Edwards and the Life of God: Toward an Evangelical Theology of Participation* (Minneapolis: Fortress, 2015), 265–321. For an exploration of Edward's concept of grace in relationship to the theme of deification, see James R. Salladin, *Jonathan Edwards and Deification: Reconciling Theosis and the Reformed Tradition* (Downers Grove, IL: InterVarsity Press, 2022).

87. I acknowledge Kyle Strobel's reasoning: "While Edwards does not wield this specific terminology, he invokes the grammar of *theosis*, turning to the key biblical passages and doctrines to develop a robust account of 'divinization'" (Kyle Strobel, "Jonathan Edwards and the Polemics of *Theosis*," *Harvard Theological Review* [2012]: 260). Yet, I think this may not be the best way to understand what Edwards had in mind, when he wrote about participation. Since the reality that God became one with us (John 1:14), in order that we may become one with him is something that Scripture reveals (John 17:21; 2 Pet 1:4), every Christian tradition (whether Orthodox, Roman Catholic, or Reformed) will invariably share the same grammar, or parts of it, in their description or framework of this reality. Even in two incommensurable paradigms or frameworks such as the Ptolemaic and Copernican, for example, we find almost all the same parts of the solar system. The difference is in the arrangement, the configuration of the parts. So, to see which tradition or framework influenced Edwards, it may be better to see how he arranges and interprets the parts.

88. Edwards believed that the Holy Spirit is the bond of love or holy union between the Father and the Son and between believers and God: "all creature holiness consists essentially

Son. Before the fall, the Spirit inhabited the souls of Adam and Eve as his temples, enabling them to enjoy communication with God.[89] After the fall, however, the Spirit was only able to dwell in us through Christ.[90] The Spirit was the gift that Christ purchased for the elect through his work on earth.[91] "Christ Jesus has received the Spirit without measure, and he gives of that Spirit which he receives to those that are his, and that is his grace," wrote Edwards.[92] The Holy Spirit applies "Christ's redemption" to the elect by uniting her with Christ[93] and through her union with Christ she enters communion with God, the mutual love between the Father and the Son in the Spirit. The Spirit unites the elect to Christ by awakening in her faith and affection for Christ. Through affection and faith, the elect participates in what God has communicated to her in Christ.[94] At this

---

and summarily in love to God and love to other creatures; so does the holiness of God consist in his love, especially in the perfect and intimate union and love there is between the Father and the Son. But the Spirit that proceeds from the Father and the Son is the bond of this union, as it is of all holy union between the Father and the Son, and between God and the creature, and between the creatures among themselves. All seems to be signified in Christ's prayer in the *John 17*, from the *John 17:21*. Therefore this Spirit of love is the 'bond of perfectness' (*Colossians 3:14*) throughout the whole blessed society or family in heaven and earth, consisting of the Father, the head of the family, and the Son, and all his saints that are the disciples, seed and spouse of the Son" (Jonathan Edwards, "Treatise on Grace," in *Writings on the Trinity, Grace, and Faith*, ed. Sang Hyun Lee, *The Works of Jonathan Edwards*, vol. 21 [New Haven, CT: Yale University Press, 2003], 186). For discussion on the Holy Spirit as the bond of all holy unions in Scripture, see Robert W. Caldwell, *Communion in the Spirit: The Holy Spirit as the Bond of Union in the Theology of Jonathan Edwards* (Eugene, OR: Wipf & Stock, 2007), 8, who argues: "In the theology of Jonathan Edwards, the Holy Spirit's activity as the bond of the trinitarian union between the Father and the Son is paradigmatic for all the other holy unions in his theology."

89. Jonathan Edwards, "The Threefold Work of the Holy Ghost," in *Sermons and Discourses: 1723–1729*, ed. Kenneth P. Minkema, *The Works of Jonathan Edwards*, vol. 14 (New Haven, CT: Yale University Press, 1992), 378, writes, "The Holy Ghost dwelt in the hearts of men before his fall, and moved and influenced not through a savior."

90. "But since the fall, men are never any way made partakers of the Spirit but it is through a mediator, through the Son of God" (Edwards, "Holy Ghost," 378).

91. "The inheritance that Christ has purchased for the elect, is the Spirit of God; not in any extraordinary gifts, but in his vital indwelling in the heart, exerting and communicating himself there, in his own proper, holy and divine nature: and this is the sum total of the inheritance that Christ purchased for the elect" (Jonathan Edwards, *Religious Affections*, ed. John E. Smith, *The Works of Jonathan Edwards*, vol. 2 [New Haven, CT: Yale University Press, 1959], 236).

92. Edwards, "Sight," n.p.

93. Edwards continues, "Whatsoever in the work of redemption is done immediately in or upon men's souls is the work of the Spirit, whether it be actually making them partakers of this redemption, by converting them and uniting them to Christ, and carrying on [grace in their hearts] and making of them perfect in holiness in heaven, and filling them with happiness; but also convincing men of sin, making of them sensible [of their unworthiness]" (Edwards, "Sight," n.p.).

94. Caldwell, *Union*, 54–55, offers helpful definitions of communication, communion, and participation: "'Communication' ... refer[s] to the active transfer of divine riches, fullness and

point, Edwards's concept of participation seems to be a development of Calvin who emphasized the Spirit as the bond that unites us to Christ by faith and Augustine who singled out the Spirit as the gift of love,[95] but this will become clearer below.

THE UNION OF THE SOUL TO CHRIST HER SAVIOR

Why does the act of faith and affection unite the person to Christ as her Savior? The human person, Edwards believed, is "a bundle of affections that determine nearly everything that person feels, thinks, and does."[96] Our affection is what moves us toward the object of our love and away from what we hate.[97] According to Edwards, "the affections are no other, than the more vigorous and sensible exercises of the inclination and will of the soul."[98] Similar to Augustine who saw love as the weight that carries us to God,[99] Edwards understood the "religious affection" as the movement of the soul back to God, the object of our love.[100]

In his notebook, Edwards made 148 entries on faith over the span of almost three decades. On entry 106, probably after 1739, more than a decade

glories"; "'[c]ommunion' … 'is a common partaking of benefits, or of good, in union and society'"; and "'[p]articipation' … is the reception of good that is communicated from another and the common enjoyment of good with another."

95. See Augustine, *The Trinity*, trans. Edmund Hill (Hyde Park, NY: New City Press, 2012), 423 (*Trin.* 15.31).

96. Michael J. McClymond and Gerald R. McDermott, *The Theology of Jonathan Edwards* (Oxford: Oxford University Press, 2012), 311.

97. For example, Edwards writes, "the affections of men are the springs of the motion: take away all love and hatred, all hope and fear, all anger, zeal and affectionate desire, and the world would be, in a great measure, motionless and dead; there would be no such thing as activity amongst mankind, or any earnest pursuit whatsoever" (Edwards, *Affections*, 101).

98. Edwards, *Affections*, 96.

99. Augustine understood that that the movement of the Spirit is God's gift of love that moves us back to Him: "In your gift we find our rest. There are you our joy. Our rest is our peace. Love lifts us there, and 'your good Spirit' (Ps. 142:10) exalts 'our humble estate from the gates of death' (Ps. 9, 15). In a good will is our peace. A body by its weight tends to move towards its proper place. The weight's movement is not necessarily downwards, but to its appropriate position: fire tends to move upwards, a stone downwards. … My weight is my love. Wherever I am carried, my love is carrying me. By your gift [the Spirit] we are set on fire and carried upwards: we grow red hot and ascend" (*Conf.* 13.9.10).

100. The unitive love that the saints have for God comes from the Spirit: "the Spirit of God gives the evidence, by infusing and shedding abroad the love of God … in the heart" (Edwards, *Affections*, 239).

from his first entry on January 1728, Edwards views faith as the "most proper name" for active union with Christ:

> Faith is the proper active UNION of the soul with Christ as our Savior, as revealed to us in the gospel. But the proper active union of the soul with Christ as our Savior, as revealed to us in the gospel, is the soul's active agreeing and suiting or adopting itself in its act to the exhibition God gives us of Christ and his redemption, to the nature of the exhibition being pure revelation, and a revelation of things perfectly above our senses and reason; and to Christ himself in his person as revealed, and in the character under which he is revealed to us; and our states with regard to him in that character, and our need of him and concern with him; and his relation to us, [the] benefits to us with which he is exhibited and offered to us in that revelation; and the great design of God in that method and divine contrivance of salvation revealed. But the most proper name for such an active union or unition of the soul to Christ, as this, of any language, affords, is *faith*.[101]

Faith unites the soul to Christ *as* Savior because it is accepting the gospel, the object and content of faith that reveals who Christ is, Lord and Savior. Faith is an act of receiving Christ from God, participating in Christ and what he has accomplished for our redemption. Faith actively joins us in union with God because it is based on the "principle of divine love" that the Holy Spirit affects.[102]

DIVINE ILLUMINATION: NEW SPIRITUAL SENSE

The indwelling Spirit, the love of God in our hearts, engrafts us into Christ by stirring our religious affections and awaking us to faith in Christ as our Savior.[103] The Spirit reorients our affections toward God and implants faith into our heart by illuminating our soul to the truth of the gospel. Along with Calvin and Owen, Edwards believed that the light of illumination is not the light of revelation

---

101. Jonathan Edwards, "Faith," in *Writings on the Trinity, Grace, and Faith*, Sang Hyun Lee, *The Works of Jonathan Edwards*, vol. 21 (New Haven, CT: Yale University Press, 2003), 447–48.

102. Edwards, "Faith," 420.

103. By being engrafted into Christ, we organically become a part of Christ: "the sap of the true vine is not only conveyed into them, as the sap of a tree may be conveyed into a vessel, but is conveyed as sap is from a tree into one of its living branches, where it becomes a principle of life. The Spirit of God being thus communicated and united to the saints, they are from thence properly denominated from it, and are called spiritual" (Edwards, *Affections*, 200–201).

because it does not reveal any new things about God that are not in the Bible: "This spiritual light is not the suggesting of any new truths, or propositions not contained in the Word of God. ... it reveals no new doctrine, it suggests no new proposition to the mind, it teaches no new thing of God, or Christ, or another world, not taught in the Bible; but only gives a due apprehension of those things that are taught in the Word of God."[104] The "divine and supernatural light" allows us to have a "true sense of the divine and superlative excellency of the things of religion: a real sense of the excellency of God, and Jesus Christ, and of the work of redemption, and the ways and works of God revealed in the gospel."[105] The light of illumination is not obtained through nature, but through the Spirit who imparts it to our souls by virtue of his very presence.[106] Even after conversion, this divine light continues to illumine the eyes of our hearts to divine things, until faith turns into sight, the beatific vision of Christ.[107]

The indwelling Spirit illuminates and infuses a new spiritual sense or principle within our souls,[108] by which we apprehend and taste God's goodness that awakens faith and religious affections.[109] Similar to John Locke who thought that our sense of the things in the external world forms ideas in our minds of those things, Edwards believed that the new sense implanted in

---

104. Edwards, "Light," 412.

105. Edwards, "Light," 413.

106. Edwards defines the light of illumination for us here: "*There is such a thing, as a spiritual and divine light, immediately imparted to the soul by God, of a different nature from any that is obtained by natural means*" (Edwards, "Light," 410). There is nothing that we could do to attain the knowledge of divine things, but through divine illumination: "But as to the other, viz. a sense of divine things with respect to spiritual good and evil, because these don't consist in any agreeableness or disagreeableness to human nature as such, or the mere human faculties or principles, therefore man, merely with the exercise of these faculties and his own natural strength, can do nothing towards getting such a sense of divine things; but it must be wholly and entirely a work of the Spirit of God, not merely as assisting and co-working with natural principles, but infusing something above nature" (Edwards, "Sense of the heart," 463).

107. "By the things that have been said, we may see the difference between the influences of the Spirit of God on the minds of natural men in AWAKENINGS, COMMON CONVICTIONS, and ILLUMINATIONS, and his spiritual influences on the hearts of the saints at and after their conversion" (Edwards, "Sense of the heart," 463).

108. Caldwell, *Union*, 104–108, also follows Conrad Cherry's view that illumination and infusion are describing the same thing.

109. The Spirit does not act *upon* the mind of the saint as he does with an unbeliever, but *within* "the mind of a saint as an indwelling vital principle. ... he unites himself with the mind of a saint, takes him for his temple, actuates and influence him as a new, supernatural principle of life and action" (Edwards, "Faith," 411).

our hearts by the Spirit enables us to have an idea of divine things. Locke's concept of the "simple ideas" such as "*Pleasure* and *Pain*" was perhaps a catalyst for Edwards's "sense of the heart" for "religious affections" because Edwards believed that our sensible knowledge of divine things moves us to God.[110] But Edwards went beyond Locke's proposal of human understanding. For Locke, our minds do not have direct knowledge of the external world because we only know the world through ideas, which are representations of the world.[111] Edwards instead argued that the saints have direct knowledge of divine things, such as the excellency of Christ, because they do not perceive a representation of Christ's love, but the actual thing through "spiritual sensations,"[112] which transform them into the likeness of Christ.[113] The

110. John Locke, *An Essay Concerning Human Understanding*, ed. Peter H. Nidditch (Oxford: Clarendon, 1975), 229.

111. C. Stephen Evans, *Natural Signs and Knowledge of God: A New Look at Theistic Arguments* (Oxford: Oxford University Press, 2010), 29, for example, writes, "Philosophers such as Locke, who think of perception as rooted in sensations, typically see those special sensory 'ideas' as immediate objects of awareness that give us an *indirect* connection to extra-mental entities."

112. Edwards argued that "spiritual sensations" are entirely different from any other "kinds of sensation of the mind" because "something is perceived by a true saint" (Edwards, *Affections*, 205–6). Elsewhere, he writes, "To have an actual idea of any pleasure or delight, there must be excited a degree of that delight. So to have an actual idea of any trouble, or kind of pain, there must be excited a degree of that pain or trouble, and to have an idea of any affection of the mind there must be then present a degree of that affection. This alone is sufficient to show that, in great part, our discourses and reasonings on things, are without the actual ideas of those things of which we discourse and reason: for most of our discourses and reasonings are about things that belong to minds, or things that we know by reflection, or at least do involve some relation to them in some respect or other; but how far are we when we speak, or read, or hear, or think of those beings that have minds, or intelligent beings, or of their faculties and powers, or their dispositions, principles, and acts, and those mixed modes that involve relations to those things, from actually having present in our minds those mental things, those thoughts and those mental acts, that those spiritual things do consist in, or are related to." (Jonathan Edwards, "Ideas. Sense of the Heart. Spiritual Knowledge or Conviction. Faith," in *The "Miscellanies,"* ed. Ava Chamberlain, *The Works of Jonathan Edwards*, vol. 18 [New Haven, CT: Yale University Press, 2000], 455). In this respect, Edwards resonated more with Thomas Reid, a contemporary of his, who viewed our sensations as a means by which we perceive the things of the world: "The external senses have a double province; to make us feel and to make us perceive. They furnish us with a variety of sensations, some pleasant, others painful, and others indifferent; at the same time they give us a conception, and an invincible belief of the existence of external objects . . . This conception and belief which Nature produces by means of the sense, we call *perception*. The feeling which goes along with the perception we call *sensation*" (Thomas Reid, *Essays on the Intellectual Powers of Man: A Critical Edition*, ed. Derek R. Brookes [University Park: Pennsylvania State University Press, 2002], 210, cited in Evans, *Natural Signs*, 29.

113. In his unpublished sermon, "A Sight of the Glory of Christ" [72. II Cor. 3:18 [1728], n.p., Edwards teaches, "They see the excellency of the love of Christ, and it changes them into the same image, and makes them of a bright disposition. It fills their hearts with mutual love to

Spirit infuses divine love within the believers' hearts that transforms them and implants a new spiritual sense that opens the eyes of their hearts to taste divine things. This new sense through the illumination by the Spirit gives rise to religious affections. Without the illumination by the Spirit, the knowledge of God is only speculative, remaining in the head (the faculty of understanding).[114] The illumination by the Spirit gives rise to the religious affection because it gives a sensible knowledge of God that moves our souls, will, and heart toward God, the object of our affection.

The illumination by the Spirit also awakens faith, the active union of the soul with Christ. Faith does not come from the natural man's ability to judge rightly the truthfulness of the gospel: "'for if faith is a mere act of the mind judging upon motive of credibility, it is as reasonable to exhort a man to see with his eyes, as to judge with his understanding.'"[115] It is the illumination by the Spirit that awakens us to behold the "great things of the Word of God" and convinces us of its truths.[116] It indirectly persuades us of the truths of the gospel by removing the "prejudice" in our hearts that blinds us from the gospel[117] and directly convinces us of the gospel by fixing the eyes of our hearts on the truths of the gospel through shining its light, "so that the mind can better judge of them."[118] Without the illumination of the Spirit, the light of the gospel of Jesus Christ would not shine in our hearts because the eyes of our hearts remain shut. Without the light of the gospel, there would not be faith, which

Christ, and it fills them with tender love and charity towards those that are Christ's, those that Christ died for."

114. Jonathan Edwards, "Christian Knowledge," in *Sermons, Series II, 1739*, *Works of Jonathan Edwards Online*, vol. 54, n.p. http://edwards.yale.edu/archive?path=aHR0cDovL2Vkd2FyZHMueWFsZS5lZHUvY2dpLWJpbi9uZXdwaGlsby9nZXRvYmplY3QucGw/Yy41MjoyNS53amVvLjE2ODkxMjguMTY4OTE0MS4xNjg5MTQ0LjE2ODkxNDg=.

115. Edwards quoted Thomas Sherlock's *Several Discourses Preached at Temple Church* to make this point ("Faith," 466).

116. Jonathan Edwards, "Profitable Hearers of the Word," in *Sermons and Discourses: 1723–1729*, ed. Kenneth P. Minkema, *The Works of Jonathan Edwards*, vol. 14 (New Haven, CT: Yale University Press, 1992), 254.

117. Edwards, "Light," 415.

118. Edwards, "Light," 415.

unites us to Christ[119] because faith inclines and motions our hearts "towards Christ as a Savior."[120]

To conclude, Edwards viewed the illumination of the Spirit as a means by which we partake in Christ for communion with God. The divine and supernatural light of God is the new spiritual sense to see and taste God's goodness and excellency. With this new sense, participation with Christ in God is possible because the new sense allows us to sense, touch, and enjoy contact with God and to be affected by God, drawing us to God because we are moved to that which affects us. Along with Calvin and Owen, Edwards drew out the depravity of the human heart and mind. So divine light is required because God's light allows us to see things from God's "sight," see Christ, Scripture, and ourselves truly—sinners saved by grace. The economy of illumination draws us into union with Christ for communion with God because it is the rays of the Spirit unveiling our hearts to receive Christ as our Savior by faith and draws us into God with religious affection, which arises from knowing and tasting the excellency of God as we would the sweetness of honey.

KARL BARTH (1886-1968)

We now turn to our last Reformed theologian, Karl Barth. Similar to Balthasar, his Catholic counterpart, Barth understood participation in God in terms of an objective and subjective movement between revelation and illumination. Light, for Balthasar, is the splendor and beauty of God in cruciform, drawing us into God with the beauty of Christ, but light, for Barth, is the knowledge of reconciliation, where God makes himself known as Lord and Savior, claiming us as his own (*CD* IV.3.2., p. 81). According to Barth, "Revelation is reconciliation, as certainly as it is God Himself: God with us; God beside us, and chiefly and decisively, God for us."[121] Revelation in and of itself, to be precise, is not reconciliation, but it "takes place as reconciliation takes place; as it has in it its

119. For Edwards, *Affections*, 176, faith must always have as its content the gospel: "They into whose minds 'the light of the glorious gospel of Christ, who is the image of God,' does not shine: they believe not (II Cor. 4:4). That faith, which is without spiritual light, is not the faith of the children of the light, and of the day; but the presumption of the children of darkness."

120. Edwards, "Faith," 426.

121. Karl Barth, *God in Action*, trans. E. G. Homrighausen and K. J. Ernst (New York: Round Table Press, 1936), 17. Cf.: "Now revelation is no more and no less than the life of God Himself turned to us, the Word of God coming to us by the Holy Spirit, Jesus Christ" (Karl Barth, *The Doctrine of the Word of God*, vol. 1.2 of *Church Dogmatics*, ed. G. W. Bromiley and T. F. Torrance [1956; repr., Peabody, MA: Hendrickson, 2010], 483; hereafter cited as *CD* I.2, p. 483).

origin, content and subject; as reconciliation is revealed and reveals itself in it" (*CD* IV.3.2., pp. 8–9). Barth further distinguished reconciliation, the reality of revelation, into two correlated events: (1) the history of reconciliation in Jesus Christ *illic et tunc*, there and then, and (2) the history of Christian knowledge, which participates in Christ *hic et nunc*, here and now (*CD* IV.3.1., p. 213).[122] So, the reality of revelation is actualized *objectively* in the historical event of God reconciling the world in his Son (2 Cor 5:19), but *subjectively* in the history of believers by the Spirit who leads them into all truth concerning Christ (John 14:17, 26; 16:13; 1 John 5:6). Herein lies what I now refer to as Barth's conception of the economy of illumination: the light of knowledge that God reveals objectively in the Son becoming subjectively ours through the Spirit in union with Christ.

VOCATION OF MAN IN THE LIGHT OF LIFE

In *Church Dogmatics*, we find the most real estate for the concept of illumination in § 71.1–2, where Barth reflects on the vocation of man. Vocation is the event, in which the Word of God encounters us here and now. The "formal character" (*CD* IV.3.2., p. 511) or "primary form" of this event, Barth argued, is

> illumination (φωτισμός, *illuminatio*). ... Illumination means that the light of life carries through its work in a particular man to its conclusion. ... The distinctive element in the event of his vocation, in which Jesus Christ in person meets him as a person and becomes a known and conscious element in his life-history, is that the light, Jesus Christ as the light of the world, illuminates this man. It does not now merely shine for him in general. It now shines for him in such a way that his closed eyes are opened by its shining, or rather his blind eyes are healed by its shining and made to see. This is the process of vocation. Man is called and becomes a Christian as he is illuminated. ... We are confronted rather by the work of the wholly new and strange light of life shining on him wholly from without but now also lighting him within, making

122. Jesus "does not exist only primarily in His *illic et tunc*, but also secondarily with this man in His *hic et nunc*. He makes Himself the object, and as a living and acting 'object' the basis, and as a basis which underlies knowledge of Himself the content, of the contemplation and apprehension of this man" (Karl Barth, *The Doctrine of Reconciliation*, vol. 4.3.1 of *Church Dogmatics*, ed. G. W. Bromiley and T. F. Torrance [1961; repr., Peabody, MA: Hendrickson, 2010], 217; hereafter cited as *CD* IV.3.1., p. 217).

> itself known in its newness, commending itself in its strangeness, becoming inward in its outwardness. (*CD* IV.3.2., p. 508)

The light of illumination is outside us because it is in Christ, but it becomes a light within us through the presence of the Spirit of Christ (*CD* I/2, p. 512–13). Like Clement (*Paed.* 1.1.1–2) and Augustine (*Mag.* 11.38), Barth referred to Jesus Christ as the agent of divine illumination because he is the light of life,[123] but he only becomes our light and "*interior magister* by the Spirit" (*CD* I.2., p. 242).[124] To understand the correlating roles of Jesus and the Spirit in greater detail, we need to understand what illumination entails.

Both the command of God and the response of man are involved in illumination. "[I]n the illumination of man," Barth writes, "we have an act of dynamic command from the standpoint of God's revelation and of equally dynamic obedience from the standpoint of man's knowledge" (*CD* IV.3.2., p. 512). The dynamic command is the Word of God, confronting us externally through the preaching of the words of the prophets and apostles in Scripture (*CD* IV.3.2., p. 516), which bear witness to the Word of God through the inspiration of the Holy Spirit.[125] Our response in the dynamic obedience of faith

---

123. Cf.: "As Jesus Christ lives, He also shines out, not with an alien light which falls upon Him from without and illuminates Him, but with His own light proceeding from Himself. He lives as the source of light whose shining gives light without. He does not need to receive light from without, from men, the world, or the faith of His community. On the contrary, as He lives He is Himself the light which shines on men, in His community and over the world, revealing Him to men, and men to themselves and also the world to men. As He lives, He is the light which comes and gives sight to all the eyes which as such are created and destined to see Him and everything which He discloses" (*CD* IV.3.1., p. 46).

124. Cf.: "The living Lord Jesus Christ in the power of His Word and therefore in His Holy Spirit is the Subject who acts in this event" (Karl Barth, *The Doctrine of Reconciliation*, vol. 4.3.2 of *Church Dogmatics*, ed. G. W. Bromiley and T. F. Torrance [1961; repr., Peabody, MA: Hendrickson, 2010], 519; hereafter cited as *CD* IV.3.2., p. 519).

125. Scripture, for Barth, is the second of the three forms of revelation because it bears witness to the objective reality of the Word of God (*CD* I/2, p. 463). Inspiration, on the one hand, is *opus perfectus*, a perfect event, because the "original written document of Scripture" (*αὐτόγραφη*) is breathed out by the Holy Spirit (*CD* I/2, p. 502). On the other hand, it is an ongoing operation of the Spirit, *actus perpetuus de Spiritu*, because Scripture becomes the Word of God again and again through the inspiration of the Spirit (Karl Barth, *The Doctrine of the Word of God*, vol. 1.1 of *Church Dogmatics*, ed. G. W. Bromiley and T. F. Torrance [1936; repr., Peabody, MA: Hendrickson, 2010], 109–10; hereafter cited as *CD* I.1, p. 109–10; cf. *CD* I.2, p. 524–25). According to George Hunsinger, *How to Read Karl Barth: The Shape of His Theology* (New York: Oxford University Press, 1991), 31, inspiration for Barth was never "self-initiating and self-sustaining" because it is an event of God and from God. Barth framed inspiration within his concept of actualism to safeguard God's sovereign freedom in revelation. God is not contained in the "written document of Scripture" (*γραφή*) as a genie in a bottle, whom we can control once we have the bottle. Rather,

arises from the freedom that the Spirit brings.[126] Through the Spirit, the call of Jesus is not only *vocatio externa*, an external call, but becomes *vocatio interna*, an internal call: "it is very 'internally,' existentially and totally man himself who through the Holy Spirit, i.e., through the power of what Jesus Christ says to him, becomes another man, called instead of uncalled" (*CD* IV.3.2., p. 516). The freedom that comes in the presence and power of the Spirit is also what makes the call of Jesus Christ to the person an "effectual call" (*vocatio efficax*, *CD* IV.3.2., p. 538) because the Spirit unites the person to the one who calls him into fellowship with light (*CD* I/1, p. 453).[127]

The Son and the Spirit work together to lead the person to the knowledge of the Father. On the one hand, Jesus is the subject and object of illumination because he is the one who illumines us to the Father in himself, but he never does so apart from the "power of the Holy Spirit" (*CD* IV.3.2., p. 609). The Spirit, on the other hand, never illumines us "beyond Christ, beyond the Word," but only "through the Word and for the Word" (*CD* I/1, pp. 452–53), illuminating us to our truth and reality in Christ (*CD* I/2, pp. 240, 277).

BEING IN LIGHT

The effect of illumination is an awakening.[128] "Awake, O sleeper, and arise from the dead, and Christ will shine on you" (Eph 5:14). The concept of "awakening" highlights the "dynamic character of illumination," underlining the "turning

---

God is Lord, free to reveal and give himself, to whom *he* pleases. The ecclesial readers are taken subjectively into the reality of revelation as they encounter and are awakened by the call of the Word through the presence and power of the Spirit (*CD* IV.3.2, p. 519).

126. Concerning freedom, Karl Barth, *The Humanity of God* (Louisville: Westminster John Knox, 1960), 82, writes, "Human freedom is the God-given freedom to obey. *Faith* is the obedience of the *pilgrim* who has his vision and his trust set upon God's free act of reconciliation. This obedience confirms and evinces the transition from sin to righteousness, from the flesh to the spirit, from the law to the sovereignty of the living God, from death to life in the small and preliminary, yet determined, steps of the daily journey. *Love* is the obedience of the *witness* who is summoned to announce this transition. ... This obedience in love and faith is the human response to the divine offer of justification, sanctification, and calling in Jesus Christ."

127. Cf.: "in the divine power of His Spirit He unites Himself with them" (*CD* IV.3.2., p. 542).

128. Barth writes, for instance: "the process of vocation ... comes about ... by his illumination to active knowledge which as such is awakening. Since this is an act of God, of Christ, of the Holy Spirit; since it is the active Word of God effectively spoken to him" (*CD* IV.3.2., p. 531), and similarly, "we are dealing with the process which as his illumination is effective revelation and active knowledge, which is thus fruitful illumination, and which has thus to be described as awakening. How could it be the living Jesus Christ who makes Himself known to man in his vocation, if this were not his awakening and did not therefore include his awaking?" (*CD* IV.3.2., p. 514)

and transition" from darkness to light (*CD* IV.3.2., p. 513), from a spiritual slumber to a knowledge of the Lord (*CD* IV.3.2., p. 352; cf. 205). To know God in this way is to understand him not from afar, but to see all things new and have our whole being "seized and refashioned" *in* Christ (*CD* IV.3.2., p. 519):

> the knowledge of God given to man through his illumination is no mere apprehension and understanding of God's being and action, nor as such a kind of intuitive contemplation. It is the claiming not only of his thinking but also of his willing and work, of the whole man, for God. It is his refashioning to be a theatre, witness and instrument of His acts. Its subject and content, which is also its origin, makes it an active knowledge, in which there are affirmation and negation, volition and decision, action and inaction, and in which man leaves certain old courses and enters and pursues new ones. As the work of God becomes clear to him, its reflection lights up his own heart and self and whole existence through the One whom he may know on the basis of His own self-declaration. Illumination and therefore vocation is the total alteration of the one whom it befalls. (*CD* IV.3.2., p. 510)

Illumination enables us to know Christ and our true self, awakens us to faith, and reorients and puts us in a different trajectory and terminus because it is to partake, to be taken up and to be made new in the reality of the Word made flesh. The process of illumination, for Barth, does not take place in different stages or in parts, but it is "the totality of what makes a man a Christian" (*CD* IV.3.2., p. 511; cf. 526).

That does not mean, however, that the person illumined and awakened cannot fall asleep again. The point is: the person stands in constant need of Christ again and again.

> What makes a man a Christian is that the One who has wakened him once is not content with this, but as the faithful One He is (1 Thess. 5:24) wakens him again and again, and always with the same power and severity and goodness as the first time. What makes him a Christian is that he has a Lord who to his salvation will not leave him in peace but constantly summons him to wake up again" (*CD* IV.3.2., p. 512).

The call of Jesus, therefore, is not only *vocatio unica*, a once-for-all call, but also *vocatio continua*, a continual call through the Spirit (*CD* IV.3.2., pp. 518, 536). It is the call to be our true self, to be in fellowship with God (*CD* IV.3.2., p. 554).[129] The call to be awakened, in other words, is a call to be reconciled to God.

Reconciliation takes place first in the history of Jesus Christ before it becomes our history (*CD* IV.3.2., p. 38). The history of Jesus Christ is revelation[130] because God reveals himself as Father, Son, and Holy Spirit for us: God reconciling the world to himself in the Son through the Spirit (2 Cor 5:19; *CD* IV.3.2., p. 72–82; *CD* I.1., p. 370).[131] Reconciliation, the reality of revelation, becomes a true reality for us through the Spirit:[132] "reconcili-

---

129. The freedom that the Spirit offers is for us to see God (*CD* IV.3.1., p. 90), our true self (*CD* IV.3.1., p. 250), and "everything which [God] discloses" in his light (*CD* IV.3.1., p. 46). Apart from God, we are alienated from our true self and terminus as being in fellowship with God (Barth, *Humanity of God*, 80). In his section on the "Real Man (§ 44.3)," for example, Barth argued that a human being is "a being with God" and a being "that derives from God" (Karl Barth, *The Doctrine of Creation*, vol. 3.2 of *Church Dogmatics*, ed. G. W. Bromiley and T. F. Torrance [1960; repr., Peabody, MA: Hendrickson, 2010], 157; hereafter cited as *CD* III.2., p. 157) because a human being is a being who "rests upon the election of God" and "consists in the hearing of the Word of God" (*CD* III.2., p. 142). Barth wrote, "When we say that the being of man rests on the election of God, we say that it springs from a history which has its prototype and origin in God Himself" (*CD* III.2., p. 163). Human beings are determined to be God's covenant partner because they are elected to be with Christ (*CD* III.2., p. 145). At first glance, Barth's doctrine of election may have a Reformed ring to it, but a closer look shows that it has a rather unique twist. For Barth, election is the election of Jesus Christ first and foremost. He is the object of God's election (*CD* III.2., p. 163). Human beings are elected only *in* the election of Jesus Christ (*CD* III.2., p. 162). This eternal election of God is actualized in the "history" of Jesus Christ, the history in which God's kingdom, revelation, and grace come into the sphere of humanity with the speech and action of Jesus Christ (*CD* III.2., p. 147–48). This history breaks into the "state" of humanity (*CD* III.2., p. 158), the breaking in of God's gracious Word to summons human beings to hear and respond (*CD* III.2., p. 150–60, cf. 142, 167). Humanity find their being summoned by this Word because this Word is the truth of their being (*CD* III.2., p. 152), the "uncreated prototype" of humanity (*CD* III.2., p. 155). The summons of the Word of grace requires human beings to respond in obedience and in gratitude (*CD* III.2., pp. 167–72). Through obedience and gratitude, the being of humanity "continues to be, as it allows itself to be called" (*CD* III.2., p. 165). The being of human is simply a response, a "word of thanks" to the "Word of grace" (*CD* III.2., p. 175). In sum, as a being in response, humanity has the characteristics of "the knowledge of God" (*CD* III.2., p. 176), "obedient to God" (*CD* III.2., p. 179), "an invocation of God" (*CD* III.2., p. 186), and "the freedom which God imparts to it" (*CD* III.2., p. 192).

130. It is a history, which encompasses all history, because it is the history of salvation of all humanity (*CD* IV.3.2., p. 43).

131. Eberhard Jüngel, *God's Being Is in Becoming: The Trinitarian Being of God in the Theology of Karl Barth*, trans. John Webster (Grand Rapids: Eerdmans, 2001), 35, 115–16.

132. Reconciliation as revelation comes to us again and again through the illumination of the Spirit: "It can only be repeated on the basis of the fact that in the enlightening power of the Holy Spirit it has been previously declared to us as the central statement of the biblical witness" (*CD* IV.3.2., p. 44).

ation in itself and as such is not only real but true, proving itself true in the enlightening work of the Holy Spirit, but first true as well as real in itself, as disclosure, declaration and impartation. This is the basis of certainty and clarity when it is a matter of the knowledge of Jesus Christ and His work through the work of the Holy Spirit" (*CD* IV.3.2., p. 11).[133] If the objective reality of revelation is the person and work of Christ, then our union with Christ is the subjective reality of revelation: "The very common Pauline formula *ἐν πνεύματι* describes man's thinking, acting and speaking as taking place in participation in God's revelation. It is an exact subject correlate of ἐν Χριστῷ, which denotes the same thing objectively" (*CD* I/1, p. 453; cf. *CD* I/2, p. 251; *CD* IV.3.1., p. 218, 224).[134] To be illumined, therefore, is to be taken up into revelation, the history of God in Christ.[135]

In his concept of the economy of illumination, Barth offers a view of Paul's encounter with Christ on the road to Damascus as an encounter with Jesus's victorious light over darkness. Barth interpreted 2 Cor 4:6 as both the Christian experience of being made a "new creation" in Christ[136] and Paul's encounter with Christ: "The God 'who commanded the light to shine out of darkness' (*ἐκ σκότους*) by His Word had spoken to him [Paul] the same creative Word with the same effect" (*CD* IV.3.1., p. 198). The encounter took Paul into the life of light, making Paul a "new man" and moving him "from an old way to a new. ... [Paul's] knowledge has the power not merely to give him new information, but radically to transform his life, himself. This is why his knowledge itself is genuine history, and especially history which is teleologically orientated, the history of warfare, history which from the very outset is victorious" (*CD* IV.3.1., p. 198). The economy of

133. Adam Neder, *Participation in Christ: An Entry into Karl Barth's Church Dogmatics* (Louisville: Westminster John Knox, 2009), 56, puts it succinctly here: "When, by the power of the Holy Spirit, faith, love, and hope are offered as responses to the divine verdict, direction, and promise, that which is objectively true becomes subjectively true."

134. Barth viewed Jesus as the objective side and the "Holy Spirit as the subjective side of the event of revelation" (*CD* I.1., p. 449).

135. Similar to how the dynamic command of God and response of man form Barth's concept of illumination, Barth wrote that *unio cum Christo* consists in the "confrontation" of God and the response of man: "the former kindling the latter and the latter kindled by it" (*CD* IV.3.2., p. 546).

136. Cf.: "Between this foolishness of Christ known after the flesh (2 Cor. 5:16) and the salvation, which He has effected, of those who believe, and therefore the fulfilled knowledge of God in the His face (2 Cor 4:6), there stands, objectively, His resurrection, and subjectively, the outpouring of the Holy Spirit, through which believers are what they are—a new creation (2 Cor. 5.17)" (*CD* II.1., p. 56).

illumination is the act of God, which makes his claim on our life a reality by drawing us interiorly through the Spirit by faith into the substance of faith, the history of Christ, the objective reality of our reconciliation. To participate in union with Christ, we may say, is to be claimed by God, our whole existence belonging now to him.

CONCLUSION

While the theory of illumination from the Catholic and Reformed traditions share the same Augustinian root, the emphasis of the former is the mind's ascent into God, but the accent of the latter is redemptive—the way God claims an elect sinner as his own, making her a Christian, heart and mind anew to sense and know Christ as Lord and Savior: "That [she is] not [her] own, but belong[s]—body and soul, in life and in death—to [her] faithful Savior, Jesus Christ" (Heidelberg Catechism A1). The Reformed tradition construes redemption as accomplished by Christ and applied to the elect in union with Christ. And the economy of illumination is the means by which God applies to the elect what Christ has accomplished in the history of redemption because it makes the call of the gospel *effective*, so the elect can participate in union with Christ. To put it another way, the economy of illumination is the process of God awakening the elect from sin and death through the Spirit to life with God in union with Christ because it is the light of the Father in Christ renewing her heart and mind through the habitation of the Spirit, implanting spiritual senses in the elect to be affected by the truth of Scripture of who she is and what is hers in Christ.

For the Reformed tradition, the light of the Spirit and the light of Scripture always work in tandem to make the light of Christ sensible to a person's heart and mind. Without Scripture, the Spirit has nothing to reveal; but without the Spirit, the light of Scripture does not enter a person's heart. The light of Christ comes to a person from Scripture, but it comes into a person's heart through the Spirit. The economy of illumination makes what God reveals objectively in Christ through Scripture subjectively ours by faith and affection. So, for a person illumined, the doctrine of Christ in Scripture is no longer cold and distant, but becomes warm and personal, moving her in Christ to God, the object of her affection.

While the Reformed tradition focuses on the operation of the Spirit, the operations of the Father and the Son are always assumed with the

Spirit because, when we are illumined, we behold the Son, the image of God, through the Spirit, the light of God, from the sight of the Father. The Reformed tradition offers implications for the component of divine "sight" to complete the components of "image" and "light" in the economy of illumination that I have retrieved from the Orthodox and Catholic traditions. In John 6:44–45, Jesus says that whoever comes to him is taught by his Father. To be taught by the Father is to see Jesus from the "sight" (or perspective) of the Father. In the next and final part of the study, I will employ these three components of image, light, and sight to construct a trinitarian operation of the economy of illumination in contemplative union with Christ.

Part 3

—

ECONOMY OF ILLUMINATION: A DOGMATIC ACCOUNT

7

COMMUNION WITH GOD

In Part I of the study, I sketched a biblical outline of the economy of illumination as the initial lighting that brings us into "covenant union with Christ," the head of new humanity, and the ongoing lighting, by which God enables us to enjoy communion with God in "contemplative union with Christ" from glory to glory. I will now flesh out this sketch in Part III with the theological materials, principles, and interpretations retrieved from the Orthodox, Roman Catholic, and Reformed traditions in Part II. I retrieved from the Orthodox and Catholic traditions as an exercise of "Reformed Catholicity" to thicken my Reformed understanding of what it means to participate in union with Christ for communion with God through the economy of illumination.[1]

To grasp how the economy of illumination draws us into communion with God through union with Christ, I begin my account with what communion with God is. The shared principles and different emphases from our three traditions will provide a basic structure and possible ways to construct my account of communion with God. Our three traditions converge on the following principles that form the bases for our structure: (1) communion with God takes place in the Son through the Holy Spirit, (2) it is distinct from the participation of the world in God; and (3) it flows from the communion of the Father, Son, and Spirit, but it is distinct from God's intra-Trinitarian communion. In other words, the church does not relate to God as one with light and love in herself (as though she was autonomous or self-sufficient

1. It is "an exercise in theological remembrance and retrieval, seeking to recover the habits of theological thought and argumentation belonging to an older confessional dogmatics, and to the broad churchly tradition of biblical interpretation that lies both behind and beside it, for the sake of contemporary theological renewal" (Michael Allen and Scott R. Swain, *Reformed Catholicity: The Promise of Retrieval for Theology and Biblical Interpretation* [Grand Rapids: Baker Academic, 2015], 96).

in her powers), but only as one who participates in God who pours the light and love in himself on her.

The places where the three traditions diverge offer different vantage points to view communion with God. The Orthodox tradition identifies the light, which allows us to participate in communion with God, as God's uncreated energies, flowing from God's essence but in a certain way are distinct from his essence (even while being divine). This light does not change but intensifies from glory to glory, drawing us infinitely deeper into God from faith to sight. The Catholic tradition, on the other hand, teaches that we participate in God through the different lights of nature, grace, and glory from God. The first two lights prepare and lead us to the light of glory, which occurs only in heaven to empower the blessed to enjoy the beatific vision of God's *essence*. For the Reformed tradition, the light that enables us to participate in God is covenantal and communicative because it refers to God's communicative action in the gospel. Do we participate in God's essence (mind and will), energies (activities), or communicative actions in the gospel? To a certain extent, I would say all three. We do not participate in the mind and will of the Father, Son, and Spirit as they are by nature, but we share their mind and will as they open themselves to us in the Word made flesh and unveil our hearts and minds to the words of the gospel. In communion with God, we participate in the knowledge and love of the Trinity.

Let me now put the convergent principles and divergent emphases from our three traditions to offer the following account: communion with God is a new covenant fellowship with God through union with Christ, which flows from the mind and will of God in eternity and is actualized through the person and work of the Son in the history of redemption for elect sinners who receive the gospel by faith through the Holy Spirit. The *source* of communion with God is then the covenant of redemption (or *pactum salutis*), whereby the triune God made a pact in themselves from eternity to be God for us in Jesus Christ, the mediator. From eternity, the triune God has set in motion for the fullness of time to recapitulate and "'bring everything under the headship of'" Jesus Christ (ἀνακεφαλαιώσασθαι, Eph 1:10, cf. vv. 22–23).[2] The *substance* of communion is the person and work of Jesus Christ because

2. Translation of Eph 1:10 comes from Clinton E. Arnold, *Ephesians*, ZECNT (Grand Rapids: Zondervan, 2010), 88.

Jesus has actualized the eternal plan of God in himself as the new Adam, making the new covenant a reality in himself as the head of new humanity, so elect sinners can enjoy new covenant fellowship with God in him as their head. So, communion with God is a new covenant fellowship with God who graciously communicates, interprets, and gives himself in the person and work of Jesus Christ to elect sinners who are in union with him as his body, the church. The church, therefore, does not participate in God in the same way the world as such participates in God because her communion with God takes place in union with Christ, which God has decreed for her before the foundation of the world.

Since the dogmatic task is to assist the church in her proclamation of the gospel today, I begin this chapter with two models of participation in contemporary theology to show what happens when theology transgresses the distinctions between the immanent communion of God in himself and the church's communion with God in Christ and between her communion with God and the world's participation in God. The two models will function as foils to my dogmatic model, which seeks to order the theological distinctions rightly according to Scripture and the doctrines handed down to the church.

CONTEMPORARY MODELS OF PARTICIPATION IN GOD

In contemporary theology, Jürgen Moltmann and John Milbank have responded to the secularization facilitated by modernity that seeks to take God out of the natural process and understand reality apart from religion.[3] While both theologians reach similar conclusions of participation in the *being* of God, they take different routes there. Moltmann takes the route of the particular-concrete event of the cross, where God emptied himself to make space in himself for us, because God could not embrace us in love without suffering deep loss in himself. Milbank goes the speculative (or contemplative) route to present a God who continually gives himself to us without suffering any loss in himself. These two models represent the spectrum of participation that does not make distinctions between the way triune God

3. John G. Stackhouse, "Religious Diversity, Secularization, and Postmodernity," in *The Oxford Handbook of Religious Diversity*, ed. Chad Meister (Oxford: Oxford University Press, 2011), 240, writes, "it would be better to say that several processes of modernization act not as *carriers* of secularization (too strong a term, implying inevitability) but as *facilitators* of it."

relates with us and the way the three divine persons are in one being and between the general participation of the world in God and the redemptive participation of the church in God. By blurring these lines, they limit God's freedom and distort our understanding of the church's participation in God, which should be derived from Scripture.[4]

JÜRGEN MOLTMANN: A PANENTHEISTIC MODEL

Panentheists in general hold to *creatio ex Deo* (creation out of God) rather than *creatio ex nihilo* (creation out of nothing) because they believe that nothing is outside of God, since all things are in God.[5] Moltmann, however, is unique in this respect. While maintaining it is "'counter' to God" to create outside of himself because it would imply that there is a space outside of God, co-eternal to God,[6] Moltmann holds to the doctrine of *creatio ex nihilo* but gives it a panentheistic twist.[7] Employing the "Jewish kabbalistic doctrine of God's 'self-limitation' (*zimzum*)," Moltmann bypasses the apparent contradiction between the traditional doctrine of *creatio ex nihilo* and his panentheistic stance with this conjecture:

> In order to create a world "outside" himself, the infinite God must have made room beforehand for a finitude in himself. It is only a withdrawal by God into himself that can free the space into which God can act creatively. The *nihil* for his *creatio ex nihilo* only comes into being

4. If we have learned anything from our theologians in the second moment, it is this: the three divine persons do not relate to us the same way they relate to themselves, but they made us in their image to relate to them in the likeness of the way they relate to themselves, and the church does not participate in God in the same way the world participates in God.

5. For a brief description of panentheism, see John W. Cooper, *Panentheism: The Other God of the Philosophers* (Grand Rapids: Baker Academic, 2006), 18; 341–42.

6. So Jürgen Moltmann, *God in Creation: A New Theology of Creation and The Spirit of God* (San Francisco: Harper and Row, 1985), 86, is against the notion of "*operatio Dei ad extra, opus trinitatis ad extra, actio Dei externa.*"

7. More precisely, Moltmann wraps *creatio ex nihilo* within the panentheistic framework: "if creation *ad extra* takes place in the space freed by God himself, then in this case the reality outside God still remains *in* the God who has yielded up that 'outwards' in himself. ... God is all in all" (Moltmann, *Creation*, 88–89). He also switches the paternal metaphor for a maternal metaphor for the doctrine of *creatio ex nihilo*: "God does not create merely by calling something into existence, or by setting something afoot. In a more profound sense he 'creates' by letting-be, by making room, and by withdrawing himself. The creative making is expressed in masculine metaphors. But the creative letting-be is better brought out through motherly categories" (Moltmann, *Creation*, 88).

> because—and in as far as—the omnipotent and omnipresent God withdraws his presence and restricts his power.[8]

God has made space in himself for the world by emptying himself, becoming nothing.[9] The emergence of "Nothingness" in God, however, is distinct from the "annihilating Nothingness" (*annihilatio nihili*) from sin.[10] The former is creative, life giving; the latter destructive, leading to death.[11] In the end, the former will swallow up the latter because "[c]*reatio ex nihilo* in the beginning is the preparation and promise of the redeeming *annihilatio nihili*, from which the eternal being of creation proceeds."[12]

Because Moltmann believes the eschatological "future is 'ontologically prior' to the present and the past," he argues that the future moves and transforms the present and the past in God.[13] Creation is a dialectical process toward the future in God because God is the "'God of hope' (Rom. 15.13), a God with 'future as his essential nature.'"[14] On the cross, God enters our present situation to bring us into his future: "the trinitarian God-event on the cross becomes the history of God which is open [*sic*] to the future and which opens up the future."[15] This future is the possibility of the world in

8. Moltmann, *Creation*, 86–87.

9. Moltmann, *Creation*, 87.

10. Moltmann, *Creation*, 88–90.

11. The former gives life because it is God "making room" in himself for creation to participate in his life: "God 'withdraws himself from himself to himself' in order to make creation possible" (Moltmann, *Creation*, 88).

12. Moltmann goes on to elaborate, "The creation of the world is itself a promise of resurrection, and the overcoming of death in the victory of eternal life (1 Cor. 15.25, 55–57)" (Moltmann, *Creation*, 90).

13. Cooper, *Panentheism*, 240.

14. Jürgen Moltmann, *Theology of Hope* (Minneapolis: Fortress, 1993), 16. For Moltmann, "God's activity in history" then is not merely to preserve the world as we have it, but to open up the "closed systems" of our given world, shaped by sin and death, to the possibilities of the new heaven and earth *in* God, where "glorified creation is wholly free in its participation in the unbounded existence of God" (Moltmann, *God in Creation*, 210–13).

15. Jürgen Moltmann, *Crucified God* (New York: HarperCollins, 1974), 255. The cross is "the event of the love of the Son and the grief of the Father from which the Spirit who opens up the future and creates life in fact derives" (Moltmann, *Crucified God*, 247). The cross opens the world to new life in God because the cross is the culmination of the self-emptying of God in creation to bring the godforsaken world to new life in God. So, "it is not the ascent of man to God but the revelation of God in his self-emptying in the crucified Christ which opens up God's sphere of life to the development of man in him" (Moltmann, *Crucified God*, 275). As in creation, God makes space by emptying himself for us in new creation (cf. Moltmann, *God in Creation*, 87).

God,[16] and the cross is the way to it[17] because God is the event of the cross.[18] The cross is the event where God becomes God for us (*pro nobis*) and toward us (*quoad nos*) in himself (*in se*) because God becomes who he is in himself on the cross, which is a God for us—the Father forsaking his Son who is forsaken *for* us to bring us into new life with him in the Spirit.[19]

So instead of holding to "the distinction made in the early church and in tradition between the 'God in himself' [i.e., immanent Trinity] and the 'God for us' [economic Trinity]," Moltmann develops the doctrine of the Trinity on the event of the cross:

> We cannot say God who is of himself and in himself; we can only say who [God] is for us in the history of Christ which reaches us in our history. ... We would have to find the relationship of God to God in the reality of the event of the cross and therefore in our reality, and consider it there. In practice that would amount to a "complete reshaping of the doctrine of the Trinity", because in that case the nature of God would have to be the human history of Christ and not a divine "nature" separate from man.[20]

Moltmann is afraid the traditional distinction between the economic Trinity and the immanent Trinity will lead us to a "theological speculation with no relevance for life," detaching God from the suffering of the world.[21] To see God instead in the event of the cross is to understand the suffering of the world in the suffering of God. Moltmann writes,

> The concrete "history of God" in the death of Jesus on the cross on Golgotha therefore contains within itself all the depths and abysses

16. Moltmann, *Crucified God*, 219.

17. The cross of Jesus Christ is the event, in which God brings the world into his future, because it is the "ground of [God's] new creation" (Moltmann, *Crucified God*, 217), the "transition" in Christ from death to life with God because God is this event and this life with God is communication in communion with God (Moltmann, *Crucified God*, 266). What Moltmann wants to highlight is God, the Son, will always be the ground and condition of our participation in God, even in the eschaton.

18. Moltmann, for example, writes, "The Christ event on the cross is a God event. And conversely, the God event takes place on the cross of the risen Christ" (Moltmann, *Crucified God*, 205).

19. Paradoxically: "In the cross, Father and Son are most deeply separated in forsakenness and at the same time are most inwardly one in their surrender" (Moltmann, *Crucified God*, 244).

20. Moltmann, *Crucified God*, 238–39.

21. Moltmann, *Crucified God*, 237.

> of human history and therefore can be understood as the history of history. All human history, however much it may be determined by guilt and death, is taken up into this "history of God", i.e., into the Trinity, and integrated into the future of the "history of God". There is no suffering which in this history of God is not God's suffering; no death which has not been God's death in the history of Golgotha. ... To "think of history in God" however, first means to understand humanity in the suffering and dying of Christ, and that means all humanity, with its dilemmas and its despairs.[22]

Moltmann's view led him to conclude the universal participation of all creation in the suffering of God, a birth pain that produces new life in God for all creation.[23]

We are "taken up into the inner life of God" because "the Trinity is no self-contained group in heaven, but an eschatological process open for men on earth, which stems from the cross of Christ."[24] To put it more radically, we participate in the "substance" of God.[25] God is a God for the world in himself at the cross because the event of the cross is all inclusive, encompassing all world history and all creation. So, for Moltmann, there is now no longer any distinctions between the way God relates to himself and the church and between the way God relates to the church and the world, but all is one in the cross of Jesus Christ.

JOHN MILBANK: A RADICAL ORTHODOXY MODEL

Similar to Moltmann, Milbank also holds to a version of *creatio ex nihilo*,[26] submitting that there is nothing "outside of God, who is replete Being," so for creation "to be possible, God must have gone outside of himself, and yet

22. Moltmann, *Crucified God*, 246.

23. This life is "communication in communion" with God (Moltmann, *Crucified God*, 3).

24. Moltmann, *Crucified God*, 249 (cf. Moltmann, *God in Creation*, 77–78).

25. Moltmann writes, for example, "John sees the very existence of God himself in this event of love on the cross of Christ: 'God is love' (4.16). In other words, God does not just love as he is angry, chooses or rejects. He *is* love, that is, he exists in love. He constitutes his existence in the event of his love. He exists as love in the event of the cross. Thus in the concepts of earlier systematic theology it is possible to talk of a *homoousion*, in respect of an identity of substance, the community of will of the Father and the Son on the cross" (*Crucified God*, 244).

26. See Christiane Alpers, *A Politics of Grace: Hope for Redemption in a Post-Christendom Context* (London: Bloomsbury Academic, 2018), 73–76.

there is no exterior to God, no sum which might add to his amount."[27] Unlike Moltmann, however, Milbank holds to a belief in an actual "nothingness,"[28] viewing creation as a "movement of finite beings through time," so "the finality of each moment is cancelled out by the next."[29] Creation is, in other words, a "reality suspended between nothing and infinity," always in "flux"—moving each moment from nothing to God.[30] If Moltmann views creation as already *in* God, then Milbank perceives it as perpetually returning *to* God.

Milbank construes participation in God as a gift exchange, a "*methexis* of donation."[31] He develops his concept with Plato's notion of *methexis*[32] and Marcel Mauss's idea of gift,[33] presenting participation in God as a kind of gift exchange, which understands the notion of gift on the basis of a return. "Creation," Milbank writes, "is in one sense an entirely one-way gift, in another it is an absolute exchange, since the gift is only received in its return to God, just as deified humanity comes more and more to participate in the Son's return to the Father within the Trinity."[34] So we receive ourselves as a gift only in our return to God.[35] "Because gift is gift-exchange," Milbank

27. John Milbank, *Being Reconciled: Ontology and Pardon* (London: Routledge, 2003), 63.

28. Milbank, for example, argues that creation "is of itself nothing, and only exists by participation" (Milbank, *Being Reconciled*, 114).

29. Alpers, *Grace*, 75.

30. John Milbank, *The Future of Love: Essays in Political Theology* (Eugene, OR: Cascade, 2009), 339.

31. Milbank, *Being Reconciled*, xi.

32. Plato's *methexis* refers to the relationship between the form and particular objects in the world. Plato believed, for example, that objects in the world are beautiful because they participate in the form of beauty. The Neoplatonic version of Proclus, which Milbank has in mind in particular, stresses "a kind of kenotic descent of the divine powers into the cosmos" (Milbank, *Being Reconciled*, 114). However, by contrast to Neoplatonism, "for Christian theology the hyper-diverse and eminently intellectual essence of God can, by the contradictory hyperbole of glory (para-doxa), be imparticably participated" (Milbank, *Being Reconciled*, 115).

33. In his essay, "Essai sur le Don," Mauss argues that the notion of gift as something free, given without expectation of anything in return, is a modern one because ancient society has always used gift within the context of contract and social exchange. Mauss highlighted that a gift is not an impersonal object separated from its giver, but it contains a personal aspect of its giver, so it is only properly received with a counter gift from the recipient. Mauss wrote, "to make a gift of something to someone is to make a present of some part of oneself," so the recipient "must give back to another person what is really part and parcel of his nature and substance, because to accept something from somebody is to accept some part of his spiritual essence, of his soul" (Marcel Mauss, *The Gift: The Form and Reason for Exchange in Archaic Societies*, trans. W. D. Halls [New York: Norton, 1990], 12).

34. Milbank, *Reconciled*, 66. God "is replete Being" (Milbank, *Being Reconciled*, 63) and creative in himself (idem, *Theology and Social Theory*, 2nd ed. [Oxford: Blackwell, 2006], xxvii, 430).

35. Milbank writes that realizing myself is accomplished "by orientating myself beyond myself to the other; my realizing myself by expressing myself and letting myself go, and receiving back

writes, "participation of the created gifts in the divine giver is also participation in a Trinitarian God."[36] Similar to Moltmann, Milbank does not preserve the distinctions of participation handed down from our three traditions.

Milbank views the fall as a glitch in our participation with God. Whereas Moltmann understands original sin as despair,[37] Milbank views it in light of gift-exchange as a refusal to receive by returning to God, a refusal to recognize God as God.[38] To overcome our refusals and restore gift exchange with us, God continues "giving in and through our refusals of the gift, to the point where these refusals are overcome."[39] A key gift God gives to restore the exchange is forgiveness[40] because the aim of forgiveness is "reconciliation, where the bond of love is an exchange of infinite love."[41] Interestingly, Milbank does not think God needs to be reconciled to us because God is always and eternally reconciled to us.[42] "Therefore divine redemption is not God's forgiving us, but rather his giving us the gift of the capacity for forgiveness."[43] We receive the gift of forgiveness in the Son,[44] in his return to God.[45]

---

from the other a new interpretation of myself" (Milbank, *Reconciled*, 57). To receive ourselves from God is to participate in God, who gives us himself in his gift. Since God cannot give us anything, he gives us everything—himself. That is to say, God cannot give *outside* of himself, so he must give himself for us to receive by returning to him (cf. Milbank, *Being Reconciled*, 65–66).

36. Milbank, *Being Reconciled*, xi.

37. Jürgen Moltmann, *Theology of Hope* (Minneapolis: Fortress, 1993), 121, cf. 22.

38. "The kingdom is really offered by Christ to humanity, and the cross is the result of a rejection of this offer. However, this very rejection tends to suggest the 'original' character of human sin; to sin, theology has speculated, is to refuse the love of God, and so to render oneself incapable of recognizing God, by substituting the goals of human pride in his place the putting to death of God shows what evil is: its nihilistic pointlessness, its incomprehensibility (Schwäger)" (Milbank, *Future of Love*, 344; cf. idem, *Reconciled*, 150).

39. Milbank, *Being Reconciled*, 100.

40. For instance, Milbank writes, "to forgive is to restore that order of free unlimited exchange of charity which was interrupted by sin" (Milbank, *Being Reconciled*, 57).

41. Milbank, *Being Reconciled*, 47.

42. Milbank, *Being Reconciled*, 62, 64.

43. Milbank, *Being Reconciled*, 62.

44. Milbank writes, "the gift of intrahuman forgiveness offered by the whole Trinity to Christ's humanity is passed on by Christ to us as the hypostatic presence amongst us in time of the Holy Spirit, the bond of exchange and mutual giving within the Trinity" (Milbank, *Being Reconciled*, 62). Put otherwise, our gift exchange with God is restored in the "perpetual eucharist," which is "a living through the offering (through the offering, through the offering) of the gift given to us of God himself in the flesh" (John Milbank, "Can a Gift be Given?: Prolegomena to a Future Trinitarian Metaphysic," *Modern Theology* 11, no. 1 [1995]: 152).

45. Cf.: "forgiveness has become literally for-giving, giving the gift on behalf of the other; in this Christological instance it is the divine Son through his assumed human nature making

To receive the Son is to return with him to God, for in a gift exchange, a gift is only received in our return. The Son returns us to the Father by restoring the knowledge of God as the divine Word enfleshed, *Verbum Dei incarnatum*: the incarnate Word has become the "sole ground for the restoration of our participation in the divine understanding."[46] God's knowledge, Milbank writes, "is God's perpetual return to Himself. ... For God, in knowing His own essence, also knows other things in which He sees a likeness of Himself, since He grasps Himself as participable, and so He here returns to His essence."[47] God knows himself along with all things in his essence. So, we likewise know God and all things in God's essence. Since knowledge for us begins in our senses, Jesus took on flesh to redirect our sensory knowledge to God in himself because, in his incarnation, "a new ontological state for Creation" arises, namely, the fusion of the finite with the infinite, the visible with the invisible.[48] As a result of this "fusion," Jesus's humanity (i.e., his body, physical actions, and "especially his transmission of the substance of his body to the eucharistic elements") reveals his divinity.[49] So our knowledge of truth, which is a participation in God,[50] now comes through Christ. "*Analogia entis*," therefore, "becomes *analogia Christi*, and the former ... is only available for fallen humanity through the latter."[51]

On the cross, Jesus offers a "defence of the truth he has secretly proclaimed to [his disciples] through mysterious deeds and enigmatic words;

---

the return offering of true worship to the Father—return which humanity should make, but since the Fall can make no longer" (Milbank, *Reconciled*, 46). Again, he writes, "Before a gift can be given, it must already have started to be received. ... gift-giving is a mode ... of social being" (Milbank, *Being Reconciled*, 156).

46. John Milbank and Catherine Pickstock, *Truth in Aquinas* (London: Routledge, 2001), 60.

47. Milbank and Pickstock, *Truth in Aquinas*, 12; cf. Milbank, *Reconciled*, 73.

48. Milbank and Pickstock, *Truth in Aquinas*, 63. See also Milbank, *Reconciled*, 114–15.

49. Since knowledge for us begins in our senses, the incarnation of the Son restores "our participation in the divine understanding" (Milbank and Pickstock, *Truth in Aquinas*, 60) by instructing "our intellect in divine matters by our senses, to correct the turning of the intellect to sensory ends rather than divine ends after Adam" (Milbank and Pickstock, *Truth in Aquinas*, 64).

50. To know the truth of a thing, "we are catching it on its way back to God. One could even say ..., knowledge is God's perpetual return to Himself. This is not a movement in the sense of a discursive passage from known to unknown, but a kind of encircling, a movement out of Himself and returning to Himself, always already completed from the beginning of eternity. For God, in knowing His own essence, also knows other things in which He sees a likeness of Himself, since He grasps Himself as participable, and so He here returns to His essence" (Milbank and Pickstock, *Truth in Aquinas*, 12).

51. Milbank and Pickstock, *Truth in Aquinas*, 61.

the truth of which is the absolute creative power of the Father, a truth only maintained and indeed fully taught in Christ's resurrected return."[52] Jesus reveals the truth that to offer oneself and return to God is to receive oneself more abundantly from God.[53] In giving himself to God on our behalf, Jesus also receives us back for God. "In dying, as God, he already receives back from us, through the Holy Spirit which elevates us into the life of the Trinity, our counter-gift of recognition."[54] To recognize God is a counter-gift, a return to God, because our recognition of God is itself "formed and measured by participation in the divine understanding."[55] Jesus's offering and return raise us "up into the eternal gift-exchange of the Trinity."[56]

While Milbank offers insights into the purpose of God's gift, which is to return us to God, I think he oversteps by saying that God's gift is on the basis of our return. We are sinners who do not return to God—moreover, what are we returning exactly, if we are but a gift?[57] And as intriguing as the insights of Milbank and Moltmann are, they both transgress the distinctions between the inner life of God in himself and our life in God and between the participation of the world in God and the communion of the church with God, which our three traditions have taught from Scripture. There are consequences to their transgressions. By taking away the distinction between the participation of the world and the communion of the church with God, they are led to conclude a universal participation of all humanity in the redemptive work of Christ. While participation in God is a fundamental reality of all creation because God sustains and knows all creation providentially,[58] the church's

52. Milbank, *Reconciled*, 160.

53. Milbank, for example, writes, it is "an offering of self (soul and body) to a personal God which implicitly involves a trust in a return of self as a more abundant living soul and body" (Milbank, *Reconciled*, 158).

54. Milbank, *Reconciled*, 100.

55. Milbank and Pickstock, *Truth in Aquinas*, 24.

56. Milbank, *Reconciled*, 100.

57. As Augustus Toplady reminds us: "'Nothing in my hand I bring; Simply to your Cross I cling; Naked, come to you for dress; Helpless, look to you for grace; Foul, I to the fountain fly; Wash me, Saviour, or I die'" (quoted by John Stott, *The Cross of Jesus Christ* [Downers Grove, InterVarsity, 2006], 162).

58. "For in him [ἐν αὐτῷ]," Paul tells us, "all things were created: things in heaven and on earth, visible and invisible, whether thrones or powers or rulers or authorities" (Col 1:16 NIV; cf. John 1:3). Not only are all things created in God but continue to move and exist in God every moment (Heb 1:2–3). When Paul sought to establish a common ground with those outside of Christ in the midst of the Areopagus, for example, he pointed to this reality, "In him we live and move

communion with God is reserved for the elect whom God knows covenantally in Christ from eternity and who receives the gospel by faith in time.[59]

The distinction between God *in se* and God *pro nobis* (or *quoad nos*) concerns the way the Father, Son, and Spirit relate to one another in their intra trinitarian life and the manner the three divine persons relate and become God for us on the cross of Jesus Christ and through the indwelling of the Holy Spirit.[60] Moltmann, on the one hand, conflates this distinction, arguing that we can only understand "the relationship of God to God in the reality of the event of the cross."[61] By doing so, God is no longer truly the God of hope, as Moltmann had hoped to present him, because God is not free from the history of suffering, and a God who is not free, but bound to the event of the cross is not a God who can free us from suffering. One who is drowning cannot save another from drowning. A God in whom we can hope in the face of sin, suffering, and death, must be free from these things. Milbank, on the other hand, blurs this distinction by submitting that we can participate in God *in se* on our return to God. But the opposite is true because it is God who graciously comes to communicate and make himself present with us. As Ingolf Dalferth says,

> ... it is all-important here to see that it is not the creature that participates in the Trinitarian God but God who becomes present to the

---

and have our being" (Acts 17:28). A reason why all things are *in* God is because God has made his presence and his goodness available everywhere and to everyone in creation, making his sun to rise and sending his rain to bless the just and the unjust (Matt 5:45). So, God's providential presence is over all, allowing all to subsist and have their being *in* God.

59. Karl Barth and his student T. F. Torrance claim that Scripture teaches that all are elected in Christ. But if God's truth for the elect in Christ only actualizes by faith, then why doesn't everyone believe?

60. Kevin J. Vanhoozer, *Remythologizing Theology: Divine Action, Passion, and Authorship* (Cambridge: Cambridge University Press, 2010), 293, believes, "Communicants do not become one with the divine essence but participate in God's communicative work (i.e., the economy of revelation and redemption)." This distinction should also help us think of *how* we relate to God, rather than force us to ask in *what* Trinity, immanent Trinity or economic Trinity, do we participate. To think in the form of a *what* question, in other words, may turn talk of the Trinity unnecessarily into "two Trinities," in which we must pick. The distinction should instead allow us to ponder *how* we are able to participate in God who dwells in unapproachable light, beyond our creaturely reality in himself. For more discussion on the possible setbacks of employing the distinction between the immanent Trinity or economic Trinity, see Fred Sanders, *The Triune God* (Grand Rapids: Zondervan, 2016), 144–53.

61. In other words, "the nature of God would have to be the human history of Christ and not a divine 'nature' separate from man" (Moltmann, *Crucified God*, 238–39).

> creature. God "participates" in created reality and not the other way round; and God does so by opening up his divine life and makes space for created reality to be present in a way that cannot be described in terms of "gift-exchange" since the only one who gives here is God and not the creature: Both *that* and *what* the creature can return is God's gift, and only God's gift. Throughout his argument Milbank's [*sic*] obfuscates the important difference between a divine love that hopes for reciprocity and a God who loves only where there is reciprocity.[62]

A human person participates in God only as God draws near and makes himself present to her. A human person, in other words, does not participate in communion with God as the three divine persons are one *by nature*, but she participates in communion with them only as they communicate and open their life of light and love to her *by grace*.

A REFORMED MODEL OF COMMUNION WITH GOD: COVENANTAL AND COMMUNICATIVE

If, as Oliver O'Donovan writes, "the validity of a concept depends for theology not only on whether it seems to fit experience, but on whether it illuminates, and is illuminated by, the scriptural text,"[63] then the validity of a theological concept of communion with God depends on how fittingly it makes sense of what Scripture has revealed through the church. To understand communion with God properly from Scripture, we need to preserve these distinctions and order them rightly to each other. What follows is an attempt to do just that, to present the communion of the church with God as covenantal and communicative in nature because it is new covenant fellowship with God, which has as its source the covenant of redemption in the intra trinitarian life of God and its substance the person and work of the Word who became flesh (Col 2:17; cf. John 1:14; Heb 10:1–20).

Communion with God is new covenant oneness with God. In chapter 4, Dumitru Staniloae distinguished knowing a person from knowing a thing, which offers a way to begin thinking about our covenantal oneness with God. Unlike a thing, which has no depth, neither concealing nor revealing

62. Ingolf U. Dalferth, *Becoming Present: An Inquiry into the Christian Sense of the Presence of God* (Leuven: Peeters, 2006), 178.

63. Oliver O'Donovan, *Self, World, and Time: Ethics as Theology 1* (Grand Rapids: Eerdmans, 2013), 6.

what is within, to know a person takes place in a kind of covenant fellowship, an agreement to disclose oneself to the other person and to know the other person as one knows oneself.[64] Eleonore Stump defines oneness similarly as a "mutual *within-ness* of individual psyches or persons," involving a "mutual closeness and mutual personal presence of the most significant kind."[65] Mutual closeness is to trust and disclose to another person what is within oneself, and personal presence is knowing what is inside the other person. The Father, Son, and Holy Spirit are eternally and perfectly one in this way by "reciprocal immanence" (or "within one another" [John 10:30, 38; 14:10–11; 17:21]) because of their divine nature, subsistent relation, and eternal processions.[66] A human person, on the other hand, enjoys oneness with the three divine persons not by nature but by *covenant*. "A covenant," writes Daniel Block, "is a formally confirmed agreement between two or more parties that creates or governs a relationship that does not exist naturally."[67] To reflect on the distinction between a human person's communion with the three divine persons and the intra-Trinitarian communion of the Father, Son, and Spirit within themselves, we need a definition of person.

At the close of antiquity, Boethius tendered this classic definition:[68] "'A person is an individual substance of rational nature (*naturae rationabilis individua sustantia*).'"[69] Boethius's definition shows both the similarities and the profound differences between what a person is when it is applied to God and when it is applied to a human being. In a human being, a person is a singular subject who subsists on her own with a nature capable of

64. Dumitru Staniloae, *Revelation and Knowledge of the Triune God*, vol. 1 of *The Experience of God: Orthodox Dogmatic Theology*, trans. and ed. Ioan Ionita and Robert Barringer (Brookline, MA: Holy Cross Orthodox, 1998), 202–3.

65. Eleonore Stump, *Atonement* (Oxford: Oxford University Press, 2018), 117.

66. Gilles Emery, *The Trinitarian Theology of Saint Thomas Aquinas*, trans. Francesca Aran Murphy (Oxford: Oxford University Press, 2010), 298, 307. Cf. Staniloae, *Triune God*, 202–3, 259–64.

67. Daniel I. Block, *The Triumph of Grace: Literary and Theological Studies in Deuteronomy and Deuteronomic Themes* (Eugene, OR: Cascade Books, 2017), 98.

68. Though the persons and the essence of God are identical because the Father *is* God, the Son *is* God, and the Spirit *is* God, Boethius's definition allows us to differentiate between them in our way of thinking (cf. *ST* I, q.39, a.1, ad.2) and, correspondingly, to understand how Jesus is one person in two natures, fully God and fully man, distinct and unmixed. The person of the Son is more than his human nature because the person of the Son is the subject and underlying reality, in which his human nature subsists.

69. Gilles Emery, *The Trinity: An Introduction to Catholic Doctrine on the Triune God*, trans. Matthew Levering (Washington: Catholic University of America Press, 2011), 102.

reasoning and willing. The human person is like the three persons of God because God has made her nature in the image of God,[70] so she can relate to God like no other creatures can.[71]

In the retrieval moment, our patristic theologians were divided on whether the human mind or body is created in God's image. Scripture, however, does not narrow God's image to one aspect of our nature. Since we are created to know, love, and reflect God with all that we are, all aspects of us are created after God's image—our heart, mind, and body (Deut 6:4–5; Mark 12:30; Rom 12:1). The heart is the core of our being, the seat of our intellect, will, and emotion. The human mind, Augustine said, is "the interior eye of the heart" (*Serm.* 67.15) because it allows the heart to see intellectual and spiritual things (Eph 1:18). The body is what individualizes one person from another person,[72] and it functions as the instrumental means of a person's heart because it enables her heart to sense through her mind the world outside and enact what is in her heart freely out into the world (Luke 6:45; Matt 12:35; cf. Ps 19:14). Since a human person's heart and mind are embodied, the person can conceal her heart and mind or reveal them to another person with her body. She communicates and shares her heart and mind to another person with words and actions through her body and conversely receives what is in the other person's heart and mind by that person's words and actions. While a human person relates independently to another person outside of herself, and her nature is distinct from her existence because what she is and that she is are distinct from each other, the three persons of God are subsisting relations[73] and their nature is identical to their very existence as God, "as the doctrine of the divine simplicity reminded us."[74] What they are (nature) and that they are (act of existence) as the Father, Son, and Spirit are one and the same.

The three persons are one by nature. The Father is God, the Son is God, and the Spirit is God, yet they are together one God. They are distinct in

70. Following Thomas Aquinas, Emery writes that the nature of the person "is precisely what the theme of the image of God expresses" because "the human being has been created to the 'image' of God, which means that the human being 'is endowed with intelligence and free will, and has the power to act by itself'" (Emery, *The Trinity*, 104).

71. Emery, *The Trinity*, 103.

72. Emery, *The Trinity*, 105–6.

73. Emery, *The Trinity*, 108.

74. Emery, *The Trinity*, 106.

their oneness because they are subsisting relations. The Father is Father in relation to the Son, the Son is Son in relation to the Father, and the Spirit is Spirit in relation to the Father and the Son. They subsist eternally in relation. We can also see their immanent oneness in their relation of origin (or eternal processions). The Father is the source, the innascible One, who relates to the Son through eternal generation (John 8:42) and to the Spirit with the Son through eternal spiration (Rev 22:1; cf. John 7:37–39).[75] As our word is conceived in our mind, the Father, the Mind of all minds, conceived the Son, his eternal Word, in himself in such a way that the Son has the fullness of his nature, his Mind. As our love is a movement within our heart (or will) toward what is good, the eternal movement of the Father and the Son toward each other breathes out the Holy Spirit, the perfect love of their will toward one another. The Father, Son, and Spirit relate to each other perfectly in one divine nature. The three persons, we can say, are one mind and one will in their divine nature (see Origen, *Cels.* 8.12).[76]

Since a human person is not one with God in mind and will by nature, God communicates his mind and will to her in covenant. In the garden of Eden, God communicated to Adam in the first covenant (cf. Hos 6:7). According to the Westminster Confession of Faith (WCF 7:2): "The first covenant made with man was a covenant of works, wherein life was promised to Adam; and in him to his posterity, upon condition of perfect and personal obedience."[77] In the first covenant, God gave Adam a command, "From any tree of the garden, you may eat freely; but from the tree of the knowledge of good and evil you shall not eat, for in the day that you eat from it you shall surely die" (Gen 2:16–17), to set before Adam an opportunity to respond to God with his "Yes" or "No." There was an implicit agreement in the command that, if

75. Thomas Joseph White, *The Trinity: On the Nature and Mystery of the One God* (Washington: Catholic University of America Press, 2022), 421, writes: "The Father eternally knows and loves himself in the simplicity and perfection of his pure actuality (in virtue of his divine nature as God) and in so doing he eternally generates the Word as the fruit of his self-understanding. So too, the Father and Son, knowing one another fully (in virtue of the simple perfection of the divine nature), also love one another fully, and in doing so spirate the Holy Spirit."

76. Rowan Williams, *On Augustine* (New York: Bloomsbury, 2016), 185, writes, "the 'content' of what these subjects are conscious of is formally identical."

77. See J. V. Fesko, *Adam and the Covenant of Works* (Fern: Mentor, 2021), who offers a historical, exegetical, and doctrinal analysis of the first covenant.

Adam would continue in his "yes," he would grow in his oneness with God, sharing more and more God's mind and will.[78]

Eden was the first temple, where God was close and personally present with man (Gen 2:8; 3:8).[79] In the retrieval moment, Irenaeus, Athanasius, Cyril, and Edwards argued that, even from the beginning, communion with God came through the Holy Spirit because he is the presence of God, the one who makes God close and present with man.[80] In the New Testament, Jesus is the eschatological temple because he has the Spirit without measure, so he can give the Spirit without measure (John 3:34), and the church is the temple of God because she receives the Spirit from Jesus (John 14:17). "Destroy this temple," Jesus said, "and in three days I will raise it up" (John 2:19), and "the Spirit," wrote Paul, "who raised Jesus from the dead dwells in you" (Rom 8:11) because we are the temple of God (1 Cor 3:17; 6:19; 2 Cor 6:16; Eph 4:21–22). So, God placed Adam and Eve in the garden to live *coram Deo*, in the presence of God, through the Holy Spirit who gave the first couple freedom for oneness with God.

78. We can observe this oneness that Adam had with God and Eve before the fall. God was personally present with the first couple. God knew them as reflections of himself because God made them in his image (Gen 1:27). God knew Adam needed a helper, even before Adam realized he needed one. After God made Eve out of Adam, God brought her to him, and when he saw her, he exclaimed that she was bone of his bone and flesh of his flesh (Gen 2:23). Like God, Adam saw Eve as a reflection of himself (1 Cor 11:7). God was also close to them as he made his mind and will plain to them through his command, and they were naked before God and each other and were unashamed because they had no sin, guilt, and shame to hide from each other and from God. God made the two out of one, so they may be one in their marriage covenant. "For this reason a man shall leave his father and his mother, and be joined to his wife; and they shall become one flesh" (Gen 2:24 NASB). Their marriage covenant points to their oneness with God in the first covenant and ultimately to a more profound oneness between Christ and the church in the new covenant as Christ loves the church as his own body and gave himself up for her (Eph 5:25–33).

79. The prophet Ezekiel explicitly refers to Eden as a temple, "'the garden of God … the holy mountain of God' containing 'sanctuaries' (Ezek 28:13–14, 16, 18). 'Mountain' and 'sanctuaries' are both references elsewhere to the temple" in Scripture (G. K. Beale and Mitchell Kim, *God Dwells among Us: Expanding Eden to the Ends of the Earth* [Downers Grove, IL: InterVarsity Press, 2014], 18). The imagery of "the Lord God walking in the garden in the cool of the day" (יְהוָה אֱלֹהִים מִתְהַלֵּךְ בַּגָּן לְרוּחַ הַיּוֹם) further illustrates that God's holy presence was in Eden (Gen 3:8; cf. Lev 26:12; Deut 23:14; 2 Sam 7:6 [Beale and Kim, *God Dwells among Us*, 18])

80. The presence of the Spirit allows us to enjoy mutual closeness and mutual personal presence with God because the Spirit leads us into all truth concerning God (John 16:13–14), even the deep things of God (1 Cor 2:10), and the Spirit knows what is inside our hearts and minds even more than we can (Rom 8:26–27; cf. Acts 5:3–4).

THE FALL: A BROKEN COMMUNICATION

Adam, however, broke covenant with God through disobedience and, as a result, was banished from Eden and so lost the Spirit, the presence and closeness with God. Since Adam was the covenant head of humanity, his action affected all humanity.[81] So when Adam turned from God's word (which gave life with God) to the serpent's lie (which brought death and alienation from God), all died (Rom 5:12, 17–18) because all were in Adam when he sinned (Rom 3:23; 5:12; 1 Cor 15:22; Eph 2:1; Ps 51:5).[82] If covenantal oneness with God comes through a free-flowing communication of opening ourselves to God and receiving God into ourselves (Augustine, Owen, Staniloae, etc.), then sin is a barrier to our oneness with God.[83]

Sin not only breaks our communication with God but also bars us from it because sin is a "self-confinement within," confining us from opening our hearts to receive God into our hearts.[84] Sin turns the desires of our hearts and minds to the flesh: "For the mind that is set on the flesh is hostile to God, for it does not submit to God's law; indeed, it cannot. Those who are in the flesh cannot please God" (Rom 8:7–8). Sin makes us a paradox to ourselves, for on the one hand, we desire God most deeply because God has made us with himself as our highest good (the object of our knowledge and love), but on the other hand, we desire what is not God because of sin.[85] Our divided desires make us restless because we do not desire God, whom our hearts desire most (*Conf.* 1.1.1).[86] Our hearts long to return to God, but sin makes our return to God impossible, as it forges a chain binding our will from God

81. God made Adam not only to image God on earth, but also the "representative head" of the human race in God's "covenant with creation" (Peter J. Gentry and Stephen J. Wellum, *Kingdom through Covenant: A Biblical-Theological Understanding of the Covenants* [Wheaton, IL: Crossway, 2012], 177–221, 611–28). Another case for Adam as the head of the covenant of creation is Scripture pointed to Adam, rather than Eve who ate the fruit first, as the one responsible for the fall of humanity (cf. Romans 5).

82. In Heb 7:9–10, we find a similar concept of Levi paying a tenth to Melchizedek through Abraham because Levi was in Abraham's loins.

83. See Stump, *Atonement*, 117.

84. Dumitru Staniloae, *The World: Creation and Deification*, vol. 2 of *The Experience of God: Orthodox Dogmatic Theology*, trans. and ed. Ioan Ionita and Robert Barringer (Brookline, MA: Holy Cross Orthodox, 2000), 166.

85. As a result, our heart and mind become a factory of idolatry (*Inst.* 1.11.8).

86. Since God has made us with himself as our highest good, God is the object of our deepest desire, but we cannot return to God, whom our heart and mind long for, because of sin. So therein lies our restlessness (*Conf.* 1.1.1).

(*Conf.* 8.5.10). We are at odds with our self, a disintegrated and fragmented self; torn within, we resist our very self (*Conf.* 8.9.21; 8.10.22). We are, therefore, divided against ourselves.[87] "To the extent to which a person is divided against himself," Eleonore Stump writes, "to that extent he cannot be at one with others either. The lack of internal integration is therefore inimical to the union desired in love."[88] If we cannot be at one with ourselves, then we cannot be one with God, but unless we are one with God, we cannot be one with ourselves because we are restless. We are thus at an impasse.

THE SOURCE OF COMMUNION WITH GOD

If the first covenant is the source of communion with God, then the prospect of it would have been lost in Adam, whose act of disobedience as the head of humanity broke covenant with God and separated us from the presence of God in the Spirit, rendering us no longer free to return to God because of sin. But from eternity, God has determined in himself to be God for us in Jesus Christ. The source of the church's communion with God, therefore, is the covenant of redemption (or *pactum salutis*).[89] In the intra trinitarian life of light and love, the Father and the Son made a pact in the Spirit to redeem elect sinners and make them his sons and daughters for communion through the new covenant in the person of the Son.

In their agreement to become God for us from eternity, the Father agreed to glorify the Son by sending him into the world, the Son agreed to glorify the Father by coming into the world to actualize and become mediator of the new covenant, and the Spirit agreed to glorify the Father and the Son by perfecting the Son in his human nature as the head of new humanity. The eternal agreement of the three divine persons makes communion or new covenant fellowship with God a *certainty* because it is based on the eternal decree of

87. For we do not do what we want, but the opposite of what we want (Rom 7:15–20).

88. Stump, *Atonement*, 125.

89. J. V. Fesko, *The Covenant of Redemption: Origins, Development, and Reception* (Göttingen: Vandenhoeck & Ruprecht, 2016), 15, defines the *pactum salutis* as "the eternal intra-trinitarian covenant to appoint the Son as covenant surety of the elect and to redeem them in the temporal execution of the covenant of grace." See also idem, *The Trinity and the Covenant of Redemption* (Fern: Mentor, 2016), where Fesko presents the doctrine of the *pactum salutis* in relation to the doctrine of the Trinity, predestination, imputation, and the *ordo salutis*. For a more concise treatment of the *pactum salutis*, see Scott Swain, "Covenant of Redemption," in *Christian Dogmatics: Reformed Theology for the Church Catholic*, ed. Michael Allen and Scott R. Swain (Grand Rapids: Baker Academic, 2016).

God who chose them to be in union with his Son out of his great love and good pleasure of his will (Eph 1:4–5).[90] So contrary to Moltmann, God is not so moved, determined, and bound to world history as he is the one who moves, determines, and directs world history from his own freedom, purpose, and love in the Son through the Spirit from eternity.

While the church's oneness with God is distinct from the oneness of the Father, Son, and Spirit in themselves, her oneness with God flows from their oneness[91] because before the foundation of the world, the three persons of God have determined in themselves to communicate outside of themselves to her. In the fullness of time, the Father sent his Son, speaking the Word incarnate, into the world, and, through his Son, breathed out his Spirit into his church, so she may partake in "a second communication, far more amazing than the first" enjoy new covenant communion with God (Gregory of Nazianzus, *Or.* 38.13). The communion of the church with God flows from the oneness of knowledge and love that the Father and the Son share in the Spirit from eternity, into which the Father calls the church when she hears and receives the word of truth, the gospel of Jesus Christ through the Spirit (John 14:26; Rom 8:16; 1 Cor 2:10–13; Eph 1:13; 3:3–5).[92]

THE SUBSTANCE OF COMMUNION WITH GOD

What God had in mind and willed from eternity, the Son actualized in time (Eph 1:10; John 1:14).[93] God's eternal decree is the source, the principal cause, by which God set the church's communion with him into "motion" for the fullness of time when Jesus Christ came to actualize the new covenant in

---

90. The church can know and love God in time because God has known and loved her in the Son from eternity. Hans Urs von Balthasar went so far as to say, "we would never come to a knowledge of the triune life in Jesus Christ ..., unless we had also been participants, from all eternity, in the subjective relationship of the incarnate Son with his heavenly Father in the Holy Spirit" (Hans Urs von Balthasar, *Prayer*, trans. Graham Harrison [San Francisco: Ignatius Press, 1986], 178, cf. 78).

91. Richard Bauckham, *Gospel of Glory: Major Themes in Johannine Theology* (Grand Rapids: Baker Academic, 2015), 13, describes our communion with God as "the in-one-anotherness of the Father and the Son" (cf. John 6:56; 10:38; 14:10, 17, 20–23; 15:4–7; 17:21–26).

92. Bauckham writes: "The love between the Father and the Son, their unsurpassable intimacy, is the source from which relationship between God and human derives" (Bauckham, *Gospel of Glory*, 19).

93. The Son is, as Gregory of Nyssa says, the perfect effect of the principal cause of God for communion with her (Khaled Anatolios, *Retreiving Nicaea: The Development and Meaning of Trinitarian Doctrine* [Grand Rapids: Baker Academic, 2011], 190–91).

himself.[94] Jesus is the substance of new covenant fellowship with God because he is the reality on which the church stands for her communion with God. To paraphrase the apostle Paul, the life of the church is hidden with Christ in God (Col 3:3). New covenant fellowship with God was realized in Jesus Christ first (Gal 4:4; Eph 1:10) and then flows to us when we come into union with him (John Owen, *Works* 2:8–9). How did Jesus make new covenant fellowship a reality in himself for us? Let's consider this closely.

Jesus Christ: The Word Incarnate

To realize the Father's eternal decree for communion with us, the Son came close and became personally present with us in a new way through the Spirit. What sort of communion would we have if God were absent? For us to have communion with God who dwells in unapproachable light (1 Tim 6:16), he must first come close and make himself present with us (Matt 1:23). As I mentioned earlier, to be present with another person is to attend and know what is in the mind and heart of that person. We see the connection between divine knowledge and presence in Psalm 139.[95] There is nowhere that the psalmist can go physically, emotionally, and spiritually from God's presence because darkness is as light to God (Ps 139:11–12).[96] God is always present with the psalmist because God knows him from beginning to end (Ps 139:13–18).

As an author knows his characters in the story from his mind God knows us in *himself*. God, however, can only know our sin, shame, and suffering in our *persons*. Let me explain. God knows all things in his essence because God made them out of nothing and gave them being and life from his fullness, so they model themselves after God as a very good reality (Gen 1:31).[97] God cannot know things that arise from sin and evil in himself because God did not create or author them. They are non-beings, parasites that latch onto and

94. The principal cause, in other words, is "the *source of motion*" (*Metaph.* 5.2.4 [Tredernnick, LCL).

95. In Psalm 1, the righteous and not the wicked will be in God's presence (Ps 1:4–5), and the reason is God knows (MT: ידע; LXX: γινώσκω) the way of the righteous (Ps 1:6). Scripture also employs ידע (LXX: γινώσκω), a word for knowledge, to describe Adam being intimately present with Eve, consummating his union with her (Gen 4:25).

96. In other words, God is always present with the psalmist because God knows him, none of psalmist's thoughts are ever hidden from God (Ps 139:4, 17–18, 23). We also find the connection between the knowledge and presence of God in Isaiah, where God's presence with the contrite and humble (Isa 57:15) is God looking after them with favor (Isa 66:1–2).

97. See James E. Dolezal, *God without Parts: Divine Simplicity and the Metaphysics of God's Absoluteness* (Eugene, OR: Pickwick, 2011), 171, and White, *The Trinity*, 326.

corrupt beings. Though God cannot know evil and sin in himself (Hab 1:13), he knows them in our persons. God sees what is in our hearts and minds when we cause or experience sin and evil (1 Sam 16:7; Jer 17:10; Ps 44:21; Luke 16:15; Acts 1:24). Even when we move away from God in sinful deed and thought, we are still in God in whom we move and have our being (Acts 17:28), so God knows our every move and thought (Ps 139:2–4).

When the Word became flesh (John 1:14), God became present with us in a new way (Isa 7:14; Matt 1:23). In the mystery of the hypostatic union, God, the Son, was able to sympathize (συμπαθῆσαι) with us and understand the effect of our sins in his own *person* (Heb 4:15).[98] Though Jesus did not sin and was without guilt (Luke 23:4, 22; John 18:38; 19:4, 6; Acts 13:28),[99] he suffered (Mark 8:31; 9:12; Luke 9:22; Heb 12:2) and experienced our death, our forsakenness from God, in his human nature (Ps 22:1–2; Matt 27:46; Mark 15:34).[100] In the incarnation, God became present with us in a new and personal way because he knew our suffering and temptation from sin in person through his human nature.

God also came close to us, disclosing his innermost to us in the Son. The Son opened the heart of God's love for the world in bodily form (John 3:16; Rom 5:8; 1 John 4:9).[101] "No one has ever seen God. It is God the only Son, who is close to the Father's heart, who has made him known" (John 1:18 NRSV). The Son embodied and manifested the mind and will of God fully in his human nature "as our thoughts are in our words" and our love is in our actions because the Son taught and "did nothing on [his] own but speaks just what the Father has taught" (John 8:28 NIV; cf. 5:30; 6:38).[102] In the incarnation,

98. I want to highlight that Jesus experienced the *effect* of our fallen condition to maintain that Jesus did not have original sin and guilt. If he had original sin and guilt, then his death was not guiltless and therefore cannot save us. Although Jesus did not have original sin and guilt like us in Adam, he experienced the full *effect* of our fallen condition in his humanity. Jesus felt tiredness, sorrow, temptation, guilt, and even shame. See Oliver D. Crisp, *Divinity and Humanity: The Incarnation Reconsidered* (Cambridge: Cambridge University Press, 2007), 90–117, who argues from an Augustinian view, "Christ is sinless and yet possesses a human nature affected by the Fall. And this makes sense of those biblical passages where Christ is tired, weeps and is sad" (cf. John 4:6; 11:33, 35).

99. He was tempted in every way like us in his humanity, but he did not sin because he submitted himself fully to the will of his Father in his human nature.

100. Death, in other words, is the consequence of sin and being forsaken by God (Rom 6:23).

101. We cannot understand another person, unless the person opens up himself and allows us to share in his innermost thoughts and feelings. In Christ, the Father opens up himself to us, in order to allow us in the triune life in the Son through the Spirit.

102. Williams, *Augustine*, 44. All Jesus has done in creation (John 1:3; Col 3:15) and new creation (John 14:10–20; cf. 5:36–37; 10:25–30, 34–38) images and, therefore, reveals the Father, whom

God disclosed his mind and will to us in the human words, actions, and life of the Word who became flesh (John 1:14). Jesus, the Word of God, unveiled and opened the mind and will of God as the self-expression of the knowledge and love of God in human form.

In his resurrection and return to the Father, Jesus came closer still, becoming more present with the church through the Spirit.[103] Jesus's "going to the Father" is his "coming to" the church more intimately (John 14:12, 18, 28)[104] because Jesus is now united to the church, his body, as her head, through the indwelling of the Spirit. Jesus is closer to the church after his ascension because the Spirit now dwells in her heart and discloses all truth concerning Jesus (John 14:26; 16:13–15), so she may know that Jesus is in his Father, she is in him, and he is in her (John 14:20). Through the indwelling Spirit, Jesus is personally present with the church (Matt 28:20), knowing and identifying with her as his *body* (Acts 9:4–5; Eph 5:23, 29–32), so he can even say to Saul who was persecuting his church, "Why are you persecuting me?" (Acts 9:4).

Jesus Christ: The Mediator and Sacrifice of the New Covenant

Jesus not only came close and tabernacled among us but also established new covenant fellowship with God in himself. As we may recall from chapter 2, the Servant is himself a "covenant" and "light" (Isa 42:6) because "in him covenant blessings are enjoyed"[105] and through his work those in darkness will come to light (Isa 42:7, 16). The work of the Servant brings light because the Servant knows and accomplishes God's will, which is to crush him, to make many righteous (Isa 53:10–11). In John 4:34, Jesus says that his food is to do his Father's "will" and accomplish his Father's "work," which is to go to the cross (Matt 26:39; Mark 14:36; Luke 22:42; Phil 2:8) and establish the new covenant in his blood (Luke 22:20; 1 Cor 11:25; Heb 9:15; 12:24). According

---

he indwells, knows, and loves from eternity in the Spirit.

103. In Rom 10:6–8, Paul refers to the "commandment" (מִצְוָה) of God in Deut 30:11 as the second person of the Trinity because we confess him not only with our mouth, but with our heart, our innermost, by faith (Deut 30:14; Eph 3:17). It is another way of saying that the Word of God now dwells in our hearts richly by faith (Eph 3:17; cf. Rom 8:10; Gal 2:20; 4:19; Col 1:27).

104. Raymond E. Brown, *The Gospel According to John II, 13–21*, AB (Garden City, NY: Doubleday, 1970), 645, writes that this "is John's way of telling the reader that the presence of Jesus after his return to the Father is accomplished in and through the Paraclete."

105. J. Alex Motyer, *Isaiah: An Introduction and Commentary*, TOTC 20 (Downers Grove, IL: InterVarsity Press, 1999), 294.

to Richard Bauckham, the New Testament writers read the cross of Jesus Christ back into the Old Testament "in a process of mutual interpretation from which some of their profoundest theological insights sprang," and to them the most significant part of the Old Testament was Isaiah 40–55, where we find the prophecy of the suffering servant.[106] What if we read the prophecy of the suffering servant in light of its fulfillment in the New Testament?

Like the ending of a great mystery that makes sense and connects the details leading up to it, reading the prophecy in light of its fulfillment can do the same. By reading the prophecy of the Servant in this way, we can understand the "will" of God in the Servant as the unfolding of "the mystery of [God's] will, according to his purpose, which he set forth in Christ as a plan [the economy, οἰκονομίαν] for the fullness of time" (Eph 1:9–10); the knowledge of the Servant as the knowledge of the Son in the *pactum salutis*; and how the Servant established the everlasting covenant of peace in himself (Isa 54:10; 55:3; 61:8; Jer 32:40; 50:5; Ezek 16:60; 37:26) as the eternal mediator and perfect sacrifice of the new covenant (Heb 5:8–10; 9:12–14; 10:12–14).

Knowledge is one of the key themes of redemption in Isaiah, which opens with the ignorance of Israel[107] and closes with the knowledge of the Lord.[108] Because of Israel's ignorance, exile looms over her: "my people go into exile without knowledge" (Isa 5:13; cf. Hos 4:6, 14; Prov 10:21). Exile is the judgment of God (Deut 28:15–68; 29:26–30:5), the consequence of Israel's ignorance, doing what is right in her own eyes, calling good evil and evil good, darkness light and light darkness (Isa 5:20). Chapters 40–55 form the great reversal of the book and have as their climax the prophecy of the suffering servant. The prophecy reveals how the Lord will act in *person*, to turn the darkness before his people into light (Isa 42:16).[109] "And to whom has the arm of the

---

106. Richard Bauckham, *God Crucified: Monotheism and Christology in the New Testament* (Grand Rapids: Eerdmans, 1999), 47. In the NT, the cross is the fulfillment of prophecy of the suffering servant (Matt 8:17; 26:63; Mark 14:16; John 12:38; Acts 8:32; Rom 4:25; 5:18–19; 10:16; 1 Cor 5:3–4; 2 Cor 5:21; Phil 2:6–8; Col 2:14; Heb 9:28; 1 Pet 1:11; 2:22–25; 1 John 3:5).

107. Cf.: "The ox knows its master, the donkey its owner's manger, but Israel does not know, my people do not understand" (Isa 1:3 NIV).

108. Cf.: "the hand of the Lord shall be known to his servants" (Isa 66:14). Isaiah also gave a vision of a time when the world will be full of the knowledge of the Lord as the waters cover the sea (Isa 11:9) because the Lord will be our everlasting light (Isa 60:19–10).

109. Motyer, *Isaiah*, 376. In light of the New Testament, the reason why the Servant is able to reveal the "arm of the Lord" is because he is the second person of the Trinity who took "the form of a servant" (Phil 2:7).

Lord [זְרוֹעַ יְהוָה] been revealed" (Isa 53:1 NRSV)? The "arm of the Lord" paints a picture of God personally rolling up his sleeves to deliver his people from darkness, spiritual ignorance (Isa 51:5, 9; 52:10; 59:16; 62:8; 63:5).[110]

Israel's ignorance is her idolatry and hostility against God's truth.[111] Like Adam before her, Israel broke covenant with God and so deserves death. Instead, the Servant, in whom there is no deceit (מִרְמָה), dies in her place (Isa 53:9), becoming a substitutionary atonement for her (Isa 53:4–8). Remarkably, as we read on, it was the "will" of the Lord to crush him, and the "will of the Lord will prosper in [the Servant's] hand" (Isa 53:10 NIV; cf. Acts 2:23–24) because the Servant will not act on his own accord (Isa 11:3–4), but submit wisely to the will of the Lord even unto death (Isa 52:13; Matt 26:39–42; Phil 2:8). What made the death of the Servant effective, we are told, is the Servant's knowledge: "by his knowledge shall the righteous one, my servant, make many to be accounted righteous" (Isa 53:11) because the Servant knows what is required of him "to fulfill all righteousness" (Matt 3:15). In light of Eph 1:5–7, what the Servant knows precisely is the "purpose of [God's] will" from eternity to adopt and redeem elect sinners in himself through "his blood" for the "forgiveness of [their] trespasses" (cf. Heb 9:12). The Servant knows the mind of God from eternity because he is the eternal Son of God (Isa 40:13; Rom 11:34; 1 Cor 2:16).[112] It was the Father's will to make many righteous, to draw them into new covenant fellowship with him; the Son knew and obliged, taking on the form of a servant to make many righteous by bearing "their iniquities" in himself (Isa 53:11; Phil 2:7–8). So, those in him may receive the "forgiveness of sin" (Eph 1:7), which the prophet Jeremiah states is the *basis* of the new covenant with the causal conjunction כִּי (Jer 31:34).

110. Motyer, *Isaiah*, 376. New Testament scholars often refer to it as "Isaianic new exodus," God's deliverance of Israel from exile and darkness (Isa 11:11–16; 43:16–20). See David W. Pao, *Acts and the Isaianic New Exodus* (Grand Rapids: Baker Academic, 2002), 10–17; and Scott W. Hahn, *Kinship by Covenant: A Canonical Approach to the Fulfillment of God's Saving Promises* (New Haven: Yale University Press, 2009), 202–5.

111. In Scripture, ignorance is not a neutral matter, but a kind of resistance and hostility against the truth of God because God has plainly revealed himself in creation (Rom 1:18–32; Ps 14:1–4).

112. So how did the Servant know the eternal decree from God? In 1 Cor 2:11, Paul writes, "No one comprehends the thoughts of God except the Spirit of God." Since only God can know God, only God can make God known. From this logic, Basil of Caesarea, as we may recall, concludes that the Spirit can make God known because he is God.

As a result of the Servant's suffering, God heals (Isa 53:5) and establishes with those whom the Servant gave himself a sacred marriage (Isa 54:5–6) and a "covenant of peace" (MT: בְּרִית שָׁלוֹם; LXX: διαθήκην εἰρήνης, Isa 54:10; cf. Num 25:12; Ezek 34:25; 37:26). The outcome of this marriage union will produce in the "barren one" many children (Isa 54:1–3) who "will all be taught by YHWH" (כָּל־בָּנַיִךְ לִמּוּדֵי יְהוָה, Isa 54:13). In other words, those in the Servant, as their covenant and light, will have the divine Teacher in them[113] because the Spirit of Christ will dwell in them (Isa 11:2; 59:21; Jer 31:34; Ezek 39:29; John 14:17, 26; 15:26; 16:13; Eph 1:17).[114] To have the Spirit of Christ is not only to have the "mind" of Christ (1 Cor 2:16), but also to have Christ dwell in our heart richly as the object of faith and love (Col 3:16; 2 John 2). It is the reality of union with Christ, Christ becoming present to us as the object of our heart and mind, and us sharing his heart and mind to know and love what he knows and loves: namely, God—his Father.

The question still lingers. How does the Servant establish in himself a "covenant of peace," which is "everlasting" (Isa 55:3; 61:8; Jer 32:40; 50:5; Ezek 16:60; 37:26)? From the logic of Hebrews, we can see that Jesus, the Servant, was able to establish the "new covenant" or "eternal covenant" in himself (Heb 9:15; 12:24; 13:20) because he is the eternal Son, whom the Father has appointed as a mediator forever: "Christ .... was appointed by him [God] who said to him, 'You are my Son, today I have begotten you'; as he says also in another place, 'You are a Priest forever, after the order of Melchizedek'" (Heb 5:5–6).[115] So, unlike "former priests [who] were many in numbers, because they were prevented by death from continuing in office"

113. Isaiah prophesied of a time after the exile, when God, Israel's divine Teacher, will speak again to his people, but this time they will respond to his word and walk in his way: "Though the Lord may give you the bread of adversity and the water of affliction, yet your Teacher will not hide himself any more, but your eyes shall see your Teacher. And when you turn to the right or when you turn to the left, your ears shall hear a word behind you, saying, 'This is the way; walk in it'" (Isa 30:20–21 NRSV).

114. To have the divine Teacher is one of the promises of the new covenant to those in exile. It is another way of saying that God has put his Spirit in his people (Ezek 36:27; 37:14), so they may be "taught by the Spirit" (1 Cor 2:13). See J. Alec Motyer, *The Prophecy of Isaiah: An Introduction and Commentary* (Downers Grove, IL: InterVarsity Press, 1993), 441–42, 424; and Barry G. Webb, *The Message of Isaiah*, BST (Downers Grove, IL: InterVarsity Press, 1996), 213.

115. According to Origen, "[t]his is an eternal and everlasting begetting as brightness is begotten from light" because Jesus is the "Son by nature" (*Princ.* 1.2.4). Similarly, Richard Bauckham, "The Divinity of Jesus Christ in the Epistle to the Hebrews," in *The Epistle to the Hebrews and Christian Theology*, ed. Richard Bauckham et al. (Grand Rapids: Eerdmans, 2009), 34, interprets "today" as "the eternal today of the divine eternity." We also find this interpretation in Philo, a

(Heb 7:23), the Servant can establish the "everlasting covenant" in himself once for all because he is *eternal* (Isa 55:3; 61:8; Jer 32:40; 50:5; Ezek 16:60; 37:26). The Servant is both a light and covenant because he is the perfect sacrifice, the blood of the eternal covenant that speaks a better word (Heb 12:24; 13:20; cf. Luke 22:20; 1 Cor 11:25), and the eternal "mediator" of the new covenant, in whom we enjoy God forever (Heb 12:24),[116] because he entered heaven to appear before God on our behalf (Heb 9:24). In him, a new and living way is opened to God (Heb 10:20).

Jesus Christ: The Head of New Covenant and New Creation

While the passive work of Jesus on the cross fulfills what God has required to offer the forgiveness of sin and inaugurate the new covenant, the active work of Jesus recapitulates the work of Adam to become the head of new creation. To understand how God "summed up all things under the headship of Christ" (Eph 1:10),[117] I turn to Irenaeus's doctrine of recapitulation.[118] "Like the apostle Paul, Irenaeus is concerned to emphasize Christ as the second Adam who does what Adam failed to do, down to 'the transgression which occurred through the tree' of the knowledge of good and evil in Eden, which was 'undone by the obedience of the tree'—that is, the obedience of Christ to God's will in being crucified."[119] In recapitulating what Adam had failed to do, Jesus renews not only the heart and mind of elect sinners in his human nature but also their narrative and script in Adam, renewing them from the inside out.

---

first century Jewish philosopher living in Alexandria: "the unerring proper name of eternity is 'today'" (*Flight* 1:57).

116. Jonathan Edwards, "Consummation of All Things: Christ's Delivering up the Kingdom to the Father," in *The "Miscellanies,"* ed. Ava Chamberlain, *The Works of Jonathan Edwards*, vol. 18 (New Haven, CT: Yale University Press, 2000), 362, argues, "Christ will to all eternity continue the medium of communication between God and the saints. 'That God, who gathers all the things in heaven together in Christ, will doubtless continue him, as an everlasting bond of union, and medium of communion, betwixt himself and the glorified saints.'"

117. Above is my English translation of ἀνακεφαλαιώσασθαι τὰ πάντα ἐν τῷ Χριστῷ.

118. Ivor J. Davidson, "Atonement and Incarnation," in *T&T Clark Companion to Atonement*, ed. Adam J. Johnson (New York: Bloomsbury T&T Clark, 2017), 49, provides this clear and concise definition of the doctrine of recapitulation: "the Savior passes through each stage of the human journey, perfectly fulfilling the broken covenant; this way, he reorders the human situation—Adam's story of fall, Israel's story of exile—by reenacting it, restoring not only the human creature but creation itself to God."

119. Oliver D. Crisp, *Approaching the Atonement: The Reconciling Work of Christ* (Downers Grove, IL: InterVarsity Press, 2020), 37.

Irenaeus teaches that even in the state of sinlessness, Adam was not perfect but had to mature as the image and glory of God. Because Adam sinned, all sinned and fell short of God's glory (Rom 3:23). So, the narrative of all humanity finds its conclusion in death (1 Cor 15:21–22). This conclusion governs the logic of our narrative identity in Adam.[120] Scripture tells us, we are by nature children of wrath (Eph 2:3), enemies of God (Rom 5:10), and separated from God (Col 1:21), "having no hope and without God in the world" (Eph 2:12).

Like the first Adam, Jesus had to mature and become perfect in his humanity because, in bringing many sons to glory, it was fitting for God to make Jesus, the founder of our salvation, perfect through suffering (Heb 2:10; 7:26–28; Luke 24:26). In his earthly life, Jesus perpetually conformed and attuned his human mind and will to the divine mind and will of the Father through the Holy Spirit (Isa 11:2; 61:1–2; Luke 4:18). At baptism, Jesus received the Spirit to begin his earthly ministry and then walked by the Spirit into temptation and succeeded, whereas Adam had failed in the Garden and Israel had failed in the wilderness (Matt 4:1–4). In his death, the climax of his life of obedience, Jesus perfected human nature in himself because he forged and welded his human mind and will perfectly to the will and mind of God, completely submitting himself to God on the cross (Heb 2:10). Because Jesus submitted himself to God in his human nature (Matt 26:39; Mark 10:38; Luke 22:42; Heb 10:9; cf. Ps 40:8), he restored in himself the duplexity of the human mind and will, which were divided against themselves, by making them undivided to God.

The new covenant between God and man, therefore, has become a reality because God's law was written perfectly on the tablet of the heart and mind of a man for the first time in history (Heb 10:16; Jer 31:33). The human mind and will of Jesus were perfectly one with the will and mind of God on the cross; the bond of the new covenant between God and man was unbroken even to the point of death (Phil 2:8). New covenant fellowship with God has taken place first in Jesus, the new Adam, and then in those in union with him, as their head. As God created Adam and made him the head of creation,

120. The end of the plot, in other words, makes sense of the whole. See Paul Ricoeur, *Time and Narrative*, trans. Kathleen McLaughlin Blamey and David Pellauer (Chicago: University of Chicago Press, 1984–1988), 1:66–68.

God raised Jesus from the dead through the Holy Spirit to become the head of new creation (Col 1:18; cf. Rom 1:4). Adam disobeyed and brought death to all humanity, but Jesus obeyed and brought life to new humanity.

Jesus restores the Holy Spirit, whom Adam lost, to elect sinners and, through the Holy Spirit, renews their hearts and minds in union with him for new covenant fellowship with God, transforming them into his image from glory to glory (2 Cor 3:18). New covenant and new creation go hand in hand because, to enjoy communion with God, we need a new heart and mind in Christ through the Spirit.[121] By receiving the Spirit first in himself as a man (Isa 42:1; 61:1–2), Jesus was able to purify and sanctify the human heart and mind in himself by walking perfectly in the Spirit even unto death, and so, can breathe out the Spirit without measure to the church as God (John 1:32–34; 3:34; 20:22; cf. Matt 3:11, 16; Luke 3:22; Acts 1:5; 2:33). In this way, Athanasius wrote, the Spirit was able to indwell the church permanently as new humanity in the Son (*C. Ar.* 1.47–48; 2.41; *Decr.* 7.31; *Ep. Afr.* 11).

God not only renewed the heart and mind of the church, but also her narrative identity and script in Christ. Like Israel (Hos 6:7), we have clothed ourselves in the narrative of Adam, following and repeating his pattern of disobedience (Eph 4:22–23). But Jesus entered and recapitulated our narrative in Adam in his life, death, and resurrection to transform our narrative, bestowing on us a new identity, a new name, and a new script in the world (Isa 62:2; cf. 56:5; 65:15; Rev 2:17). The life, death, and resurrection, we can say, form not only the gospel narrative of Jesus Christ, but also the narrative of our lives because he came, suffered, died, and was raised *for* us. The gospel of Jesus Christ gives us a new script to direct our life under the headship of Jesus Christ, so to those in Christ, Paul exhorts us to live our life in a manner worthy of the gospel narrative of Jesus Christ (Phil 1:27; cf. Gal 2:20; cf. Rom 6:4–8; 2 Cor 5:14–15; Eph 2:5; 1 Pet 4:1–2).[122]

---

121. Creation and covenant are closely related in Scripture. God created Adam and made a covenant with him (Hos 6:7). God made a new world with Noah and made a covenant with Noah (Gen 9:7–10). God called Abraham out to make a nation out of him and made a covenant with him (Gen 12; 15). God made a people for himself out of Israel through the exodus and made a covenant with them through Moses (Exod 19–20; 24). In Jer 31:22, before God announces his new covenant promise, God declares that he will create (בָּרָא) "a new thing on earth." The verb בָּרָא is a theological term, which always has as its subject God, suggesting that there will be a new covenant for new creation.

122. G. Walter Hansen, *The Letter to the Philippians*, PNTC (Grand Rapids: Eerdmans, 2009), 94, writes, "The good news of Christ, the story of Christ, is the rule for the community of believers.

CONCLUSION

In this chapter, I offered a dogmatic account of the nature, source, and substance of our communion with God. The nature of our communion with God is new covenant fellowship with God, because the covenant of redemption is the source and the person and work of Jesus Christ in redemptive history is the substance of our communion with God. What the triune God has set forth in eternity (Eph 1:4–6), the Son has actualized through his humanity in time (Eph 1:7–9), recapitulating and uniting all things, on heaven and earth, in himself as the head of new creation (Eph 1:10). The church's communion with God stems from what God has eternally decreed for her in union with Christ, the covenant head of new humanity, so what is true of him is also true of her by grace (Eph 1:4–12; 5:32; Rom 6–8). The church enters new covenant fellowship with God in union with Christ because to participate in Christ is to have the person of Christ dwell in our hearts as the object of our love and faith (Eph 3:17),[123] to enjoy all the benefits of what Christ has done as the head of the new covenant (Rom 5:12–21),[124] and to share the "mind of Christ" through the Spirit, so we may know and love what he knows and loves, namely the Father (1 Cor 2:16). Christ is the substance, the underlying reality, of our life with God because he has realized new covenant fellowship with God in himself as the second Adam, the head of new creation. So, in him, we enjoy new covenant fellowship with God through receiving the gospel by faith (*Inst.* 3.1.1).

... The *gospel of Christ* provides the motive and the pattern for all Christian behavior."

123. It is hearing the Father speak to our hearts in the Son (John 6:45; cf. 2 Cor 4:6) through the presence of Spirit (John 16:13–15; cf. 14:16–17; 26).

124. In Christ, we receive the forgiveness of sin (Eph 1:7; Col 1:14; Acts 2:38), right standing with God (Rom 4:25), and adoption as sons for new covenant fellowship with God (Heb 2:10).

8

THE ECONOMY OF ILLUMINATION: BEING IN TRIUNE LIGHT AD EXTRA

The present chapter puts dogmatic flesh on the initial lighting in the economy of illumination from the biblical sketch in Part I by reflecting on Saul's encounter with Jesus Christ on the road to Damascus. This encounter provides a thick description from Scripture of the initial lighting, by which God brings a person from darkness to light. We have on the one hand Luke's narrative account of the encounter in Acts 9 (cf. 8:3; 22:3–16; 26:9–18) and on the other hand Paul's personal account of it in 2 Cor 4:6.[1] The former narrates the economy of illumination at work on a person in narrative space and time; the latter zooms in on the operation of the triune God that causes a heart and mind darkened by sin to be alight with the knowledge of the Father in the Son through the Spirit. While Paul's encounter is unique because it concerns his conversion and call to be the apostle of the gentiles, it also describes the general experience of those in Christ, the experience of the way the triune God restores communication with those in darkness with the light of new creation in Jesus Christ.[2]

In the evangelical circle, we often view illumination as the operation of the Spirit that convicts and allows our minds to understand the truth of

1. Exegetes often interpret 2 Cor 4:6 as Paul's description of his Damascus Road experience. Murray J. Harris, *The Second Epistle to the Corinthians*, NIGTC (Grand Rapids: Eerdmans, 2005), 336, for instance, notes, "What makes an allusion to Paul's Damascus encounter with the risen Christ likely are the many similarities in thought and diction between 2 Cor. 4:6 and the three Lukan accounts of Paul's conversion in Acts." See also Richard Bauckham, *The Christian World around the New Testament* (Tübingen: Mohr Siebeck, 2017), 242; Mark A. Seifrid, *The Second Letter to the Corinthians*, PNTC (Grand Rapids: Eerdmans, 2014), 203–4; Margaret E. Thrall, *A Critical and Exegetical Commentary on the Second Epistle to the Corinthians*, ICC (Edinburgh: T. & T. Clark, 1994), 1:317; Seyoon Kim, *The Origin of Paul's Gospel* (Grand Rapids: Eerdmans, 1981), 6–7, 123–39; and N. T. Wright, *Paul: A Biography* (San Francisco: HarperOne, 2018), 53.

2. Notice: Paul employed the plural, ταῖς καρδίαις ἡμῶν, to indicate that it is a universal experience of those who have been affected by the light of the gospel of Jesus Christ (2 Cor 4:6).

Scripture.[3] What I want to draw out from Paul's encounter instead are the trinitarian operations and the dual effects of the economy of illumination. The economy of illumination produces both cognitive (knowing) and cardiac (being transformed) effects with the triune light of the Father, Son, and Holy Spirit, which transforms a person to know God in covenant union with Christ. Knowledge from the economy of illumination is covenantal, so transformation is required. Because without a new heart, mind, and way of life, no one will see God (Heb 12:14; cf. Matt 5:8). This knowledge, which requires a new heart and mind from God (Ezek 11:19; 36:26; 2 Cor 3:3), is the one God promised in the new covenant: "I will be their God, and they shall be my people" (Jer 31:33).[4] The economy of illumination is the concerted operations of the Father, Son, and Holy Spirit that allow the church to experience new creation reality in Christ for new covenant fellowship with God.

SAUL: A MAN IN CHRIST

Our three Christian traditions from the retrieval moment allow us to see in Luke's account the different ways the economy of illumination unites a person in Christ for communion with God. In chapter 5, the Catholic tradition teaches that the coming of light from the invisible missions of the Son and the Spirit draws a person into light. We can see likewise in Luke's account how a man outside of Christ becomes "a man in Christ" through his encounter with light (2 Cor 12:2). The Reformed tradition, which was covered in chapter 6, shows that a new divine sense or sight is required after the fall to hear and respond to God in the gospel.[5] Luke's narrative also offers a picture of

3. See, for example, Bernard Ramm, *The Witness of the Spirit: An Essay on the Contemporary Relevance of the Internal Witness of the Holy Spirit* (Grand Rapids: Eerdmans, 1960), Kevin D. Zuber, "What Is Illumination?: A Study in Evangelical Theology Seeking a Biblical Grounded Definition of the Illuminating Work of the Holy Spirit" (PhD diss., Trinity Evangelical Divinity School, 1996); Michael X. Seaman, *Illumination and Interpretation: The Holy Spirit's Role in Hermeneutics* (Eugene: Wipf & Stock, 2013); and John Webster, "Illumination," *JRT* 5 (2011): 325–40.

4. Sin has hardened and darkened our heart and mind (2 Cor 3:14; Eph 4:18), rendering us unresponsive to God and incapable of thinking God's thoughts after him (1 Cor 2:14). As God called light out of darkness to put order and give life to creation, God now shines the light of new creation to reorder our hardened heart and attune it to turn our mind to God for life with him in the Son through the Spirit (2 Cor 4:6; Eph 4:20–24; Col 3:10). In Eph 4:17–18, the hardened heart is the source of the darkened mind and alienation from communion with God.

5. The elect, illumined by the Spirit to the revelation of Scripture, knows God in a suprarational way: "It is a persuasion which does not require reasons—that is to say, it is a state of conviction not induced by arguments, but by direct perception" (B. B. Warfield, *Calvin and Augustine* [Philadelphia: Presbyterian & Reformed Publishing Company, 1956], 79). Believers and

a person who was blind and unresponsive to the truth of the Messiah made responsive with a new heart and mind in the light of the Messiah. In chapter 4, the Orthodox tradition features the transformation of those in enhypostatic or deifying light of the Son. Luke narrates the transformation of Saul into the gospel narrative (life, death, and resurrection) of Jesus Christ through the economy of illumination. I will refer to enhypostatic light as the light of new creation in Christ because it is the truth of which reality is in Christ—namely, the new life that God has established for the church in the death and resurrection of Christ as the head of the new creation (2 Cor 5:14–17).[6]

Let's turn now to Luke's account of Paul's encounter with Christ and examine the movement and transformative effect of the economy of illumination on a person in narrative space and time. Before Paul was "a man in Christ" (2 Cor 12:2), and an apostle to the gentiles (Gal 1:16; 2:2–9), he was Saul, a persecutor of the church, outside of Christ—in darkness (Acts 8:1–3; 9:1–2; 1 Cor 15:9; 2 Cor 5:16b; Gal 1:13; Phil 3:6; 1 Tim 1:13–16). The turning point of Saul's life occurred in his encounter with the risen Lord on the way to Damascus. The encounter reconfigured his understanding of Scripture, identity, and way of life. What was the nature of this encounter, and how do we make sense of Saul's transformation?

Discussions on Saul's encounter often center on whether it was a call or a conversion account and have extended more recently to the debate of the new perspective on Paul.[7] I want to move beyond these discussions and

unbelievers can see the same events or things, but perceive them differently because believers see things as God perceives them and as they truly are in God, Christ as the Word of God and Scripture as the word of God (Randall C. Zachman, *Image and Word in the Theology of John Calvin* [Notre Dame, IN: University of Notre Dame Press, 2007], 79).

6. On 2 Cor 5:14–17, G. K. Beale, "The Old Testament Background of Reconciliation in 2 Corinthians 5–7 and Its Bearing on the Literary Problem of 2 Corinthians 6.14–7.1," *New Testament Studies* 35 (1989): 552, writes, "Paul states that an effect (ὥστε) which Christ's death and resurrection (vv. 14–15) have upon the readership is that they are a new creation ... this idea of the new creation may even be incipient in the mention of Christ's death and resurrection of vv. 14–15, so that the new creation theme also provides the basis for Paul's exhortation in v. 16."

7. For a reading contrary to the Lutheran or Augustinian reading, see Krister Stendahl, *Paul Among Jews and Gentiles* [Philadelphia: Fortress, 1976). For a conversion and traditional perspective on Paul, read Peter T. O'Brien, "Was Paul Converted," in *Justification and Variegated Nomism*, vol. 2, ed. D. A. Carson et al. (Grand Rapids: Baker Academic, 2004), 361–91, 390. For readings, which hold to both sides of the debate, see Joseph A. Fitzmyer, *The Acts of the Apostles* (New Haven: Yale University Press, 1998), 420, who concurs with Stendahl that Acts 9 was a call narrative and that Paul's conversion is not "a psychological experience in the Augustinian sense," but he agrees with O'Brien that it is a conversion in a sense of the transformation of Saul "from a persecutor to a witness of the risen Christ"; and C. K. Barrett, *A Critical and Exegetical Commentary of the Acts of*

submit that the encounter was a new creation event of how the economy of illumination overcame the darkness of Saul's ignorance with the light of new creation.[8] By viewing the encounter of Saul as a transformation in the light of new creation, we can account for both aspects of conversion and call. In the new creation light of Jesus Christ, Saul was made new and so was converted (2 Cor 5:17). Saul joined and identified himself with those he previously persecuted (Acts 9:18–20, 26–30), and through them (Acts 9:12, 17), he answered his call to become an "instrument" of God to carry the name of Jesus "before the Gentiles and kings and the children of Israel" (Acts 9:15; cf. 13:2–3).

CONVERSION TO THE "WAY"?

According to Krister Stendahl, those who hold Saul's encounter as a conversation commit an anachronistic fallacy because "people in those days did not think about 'religions.' And, furthermore, it is obvious that Paul remains a Jew as he fulfills his role as an Apostle to the Gentiles."[9] A way to see if this fallacy was committed is to see whether Luke had a definition of conversion. If Luke had one, then we could see if it aligned with his narrative of Saul's encounter (Acts 9:3–8; 22:6–11; 26:12–18).

In Luke-Acts, we find the noun, "ἐπιστροφή," for conversion (Acts 15:3), and eighteen occurrences of the verb, "ἐπιστρέφω," which can mean to convert, turn, or return (Luke 1:16–17; 2:39; 8:55; 17:4, 31; 22:32; Acts 3:19; 9:35, 40; 11:21; 14:15; 15:19, 36; 16:18; 26:18, 20; 28:27).[10] While Luke used the verb, "ἐπιστρέφω," more often than the noun, "ἐπιστροφή," the meaning of the verb is elusive, with the exception of perhaps Acts 26:18,[11] which according to Beverly Roberts Gaventa means to convert because of the phrase "from darkness to light," a standard

---

the Apostles, vol. 1, ICC (Edinburgh: T. & T. Clark, 1994), 442, who adds that you cannot have one without the other. In other words, Saul was converted, in order to fulfill his call.

8. Like Nicodemus, a Pharisee before him, Saul was in the dark and needed to be born again to see the "kingdom of God" (John 3:3; Acts 19:8; 28:23, 31). See D. A. Carson, *The Gospel According to John*, PNTC (Grand Rapids: Eerdmans, 1991), 189–90.

9. Stendahl, for example, argued that if a conversion means a change from one religion to another, then a fallacy of anachronism has been committed in calling Paul's encounter a conversion (Stendahl, *Paul*, 11).

10. The verb occurs seventeen other times in the New Testament (Matt 10:13; 12:44; 13:15; 24:18; Mark 4:12; 5:30; 8:33; 13:16; John 21:20; 2 Cor 3:16; Gal 4:9; 1 Thess 1:9; Jas 5:19–20; 1 Pet 2:25; 2 Pet 2:22; Rev 1:12).

11. In Acts 26:18, Jesus tells Saul he is sending him " '... to open their eyes, so that they may turn from darkness to light and from the power of Satan to God, that they may receive forgiveness of sins and a place among those who are sanctified by faith in me.' "

image of conversion.[12] If "ἐπιστρέφω" means to convert in Acts 26:18, then not only do gentiles need to be converted, but also Jews because "ἐπιστρέφειν" was applied two verses later to both Jews and gentiles (Acts 26:20).[13]

In Acts 15:3, the noun "ἐπιστροφή" describes the conversion of gentiles to Christianity. But who were these gentiles? The answer will delineate what kind of conversion Luke had in mind. These gentiles consisted of "God-fearing proselytes" (Acts 13:43 NASB) or those, like Cornelius, "who worship the true God and are to some degree adherents of Judaism," with exception to the ritual laws.[14] It is important to note that within Judaism there are different sects or subgroups with divergent interpretations of the Old Testament (OT) Scripture.[15] So the noun "ἐπιστροφή" does not simply mean from paganism to Christianity, but from one subgroup (e.g., Pharisee or Sadducee) within Judaism to another subgroup (e.g., Christians, those belonging to the Way).[16] These God-fearing gentiles were converted to Christianity by the gospel of Jesus Christ (Acts 13:48; cf. 4:12), which proclaims that the event of Jesus's death and resurrection was according to Scripture (Acts 13:28–41).

This conversion experience describes a paradigm shift in how these gentiles understood the OT Scripture and their world.[17] They now read and understand parts (e.g., the Torah, events, promises, prophecies, Messiah,

12. Beverly Roberts Gaventa, *From Darkness to Light: Aspects of Conversion in the New Testament* (Philadelphia: Fortress, 1986), 86. *On Virtues* 179. For example, Philo described the proselytes' conversion experience as follows: "though blind at the first they had recovered their sight and had come from the deepest darkness to behold the most radiant light." Aseneth's conversion was also described in a similar way: "Blessed is the Lord God, who sent you to deliver me from darkness and to lead me up into the light" (*Jos. Asen.* 15.13).

13. The general definition for the verb is, "to change one's mind or course of action, for better or worse" ("ἐπιστρέφω," BDAG, 382). The concept of "conversion" involves some sort of change, whether it is a religious (Stendahl), social (see Bruce J. Malina and John J. Pilch, *Social-Science Commentary on the Book of Acts* [Minneapolis: Fortress, 2008], 67), perceptual (see O'Brien, "Paul Converted," 361–91), or directional change in life (see A. D. Nock, *Conversion: The Old and the New in Religion from Alexander the Great to Augustine of Hippo* [Baltimore: Johns Hopkins University Press, 1998], 7).

14. Ben Witherington III, *The Acts of the Apostles: A Socio-Rhetorical Commentary* (Grand Rapids: Eerdmans, 1998) 344. But "if we compare Acts 13:16 to 13:43 it would appear form this text that the term 'proselyte' means the same as the phrase 'those who fear God'" (Witherington, *Acts*, 343).

15. See J. Andrew Overman and William Scott Green, "Judaism in the Greco-Roman Period," *AYBD* 3:1037–54.

16. This may be like the conversion experience in science, which is not always a conversion of a whole group, but sometimes of a "subgroup" (Thomas Kuhn, *The Structure of Scientific Revolutions*, 3d ed. [Chicago: University of Chicago Press, 1996], 144).

17. According to Kuhn, "The transfer of allegiance from paradigm to paradigm is a conversion experience" (Kuhn, *Scientific Revolutions*, 151).

etc.) of the OT in light of their fulfillment in Jesus the Messiah (Luke 24:25–27, 46–47; cf. Gen 3:15; Num 21:9; 2 Sam 7:12–16; Isa 53:1–12; Jer 32:5–6; Mic 5:2; John 5:39–47). The paradigms of the Pharisees and the Sadducees would not have allowed them to read Scripture this way. To understand Scripture this way, they must be converted to the Christian paradigm. In the Christian paradigm, "[t]he old parts were still there—the Jewish scriptures remained essential to the new story—but they were no longer 'parts' in the same sense, because their meaning had been redefined in terms of a new and different constitutive pattern: the Jewish scriptures had become the Old Testament."[18] Those who shift to the Christian paradigm no longer read the OT and conclude, "[u]nless you are circumcised according to the custom of Moses, you cannot be saved" (Acts 15:1), but rather they now believe, "there is salvation in no one else, for there is no other name under heaven given among men by which we must be saved" (Acts 4:12).[19]

Conversion, for Luke, is to turn and join the community belonging to the "Way" (Acts 9:2), who were later called, Christians (Acts 11:26).[20] It means to receive the gospel message and to identify oneself with those whom Jesus Christ saw as his body (Acts 9:5; 22:8; 26:15). Saul was from the Pharisaical sect within Judaism. This sect was antagonistic to the new Christian sect, and Saul was one of their most zealous practitioners. So, for Saul not only to identify himself with the Way, but also to become a witness of the Way was nothing short of a conversion. But how did this shift take place? How did the encounter with the risen Lord set Saul on a new course and way of being in the world?

BEHOLDING AND BECOMING LIGHT

With Luke's definition of conversion, a closer look at Saul's encounter is in order. Before Saul's encounter, he was outside of Christ, in darkness, veiled from the gospel of light, but something occurred during his encounter with Jesus. The light of Christ confronted his blindness, overcame his darkness, brought him into light, and made him a light (Acts 26:16–18).

---

18. Garrett Green, *Imagining God: Theology and the Religious Imagination* (San Francisco: Harper & Row Publishers, 1989), 124.

19. Salvation in fact has always been in and through Jesus Christ, to whom all Scripture points (Luke 24:26; cf. Isa 52:13–53:12; Heb 10:1–18; John 5:39).

20. David W. Pao, *Acts and the Isaianic New Exodus* (Grand Rapids: Baker Academic, 2002), 63.

When Saul first came on the scene in Acts, it was during the execution of Stephen (Acts 7:58). The Jews stoned Stephen because he accused them of being stiff-necked and uncircumcised in heart, always resisting the Spirit (Acts 7:51). In other words, they were spiritually blind to the truth of the Messiah, and Saul was among them, approving Stephen's execution (Acts 8:1). The death of Stephen did not quench Saul's rage but fueled it. Saul went to the high priest for a warrant, so he might bring those from the "Way" bound to Jerusalem (Acts 9:2; 26:9). On his way to Damascus, Saul encountered the light of Jesus Christ. This light shook Saul to the core and shifted his whole trajectory in life. This light, Gregory of Palamas tells us, is neither symbolic nor merely physical, but enhypostatic light (φῶς ἐνυποστάτως), the light of the glory, splendor, and power of God in the person of the Son (*Triad* 1.3.23; 2.3.66). "This mysterious light, inaccessible, immaterial, uncreated, deifying, eternal, this radiance of the Divine Nature, this glory of the divinity, this beauty of the heavenly kingdom, is at once accessible to sense perception and yet transcends it" (*Triad* 3.1.22). This light left Saul blind three days.

Saul's physical blindness reveals his spiritual blindness.[21] "Given the pervasive physiognomic consciousness," Chad Hartsock writes, "it is not surprising that the Greco-Roman world developed something of a literary *topos* for the blind character that equated physical blindness with spiritual blindness."[22] Hartsock "also found that in Luke-Acts, the blind *topos* is standard in every case and provides an interpretive key to the meaning of the text."[23] If Hartsock is right, then the reason why Luke highlighted Saul's physical blindness was to draw out Saul's spiritual blindness to who Jesus, the Messiah, was:

> [Pharisaical Judaism] is the truth as [Saul] knows it, but the reader knows that Saul is in actuality blind to the truth—he fails to recognize the Messiah who has been in their very midst. Saul, then, is spiritually blind to the work of God in his world, and when he encounters Christ, the world as he knows it is shattered and his error is exposed. Everything he *thought* to be true is no longer true. To make things

21. Thrall, *Corinthians*, 1:318.

22. Chad Hartsock, *Sight and Blindness in Luke-Acts: The Use of Physical Features in Characterization* (Leiden: Brill, 2008), 207–8.

23. Hartsock, *Sight and Blindness*, 207.

> worse, his physical condition is made to mirror his now-exposed spiritual condition—he is blind on both counts.[24]

Like Israel who was blind to "Yahweh's acts and word" (Isa 42:16–25; cf. 9:2; 29:18; 35:5–8; 50:10; 60:1–3), Saul was blind to God's final and definitive act and word in the Son (Heb 1:2).[25]

We can pick up on Saul's spiritual condition from the subtlety in Luke's narration as we zoom into Saul's dialogue with Jesus. Jesus's question, "Saul, Saul, why are you persecuting Me" (Acts 9:4), for instance, reveals that Saul has "a zeal for God, but it [was] not enlightened" (Rom 10:2 NRSV). Saul's inability to recognize Jesus further illustrates that he was indeed in the dark: "Who are you, Lord" (Acts 9:5a)? The initial light of the knowledge of God's glory in the face of Christ, however, met Saul at that moment: "I am Jesus, whom you are persecuting" (Acts 9:5b NRSV). Jesus, whom Saul was persecuting, is "the radiance [ἀπαύγασμα] of the glory of God and the exact imprint of his nature" (Heb 1:3; cf. 2 Cor 4:4; Col 1:15; Phil 2:6). The light of Jesus overcame Saul's ignorance with the knowledge of God, shattering Saul's conception of YHWH, the church, and his very self. "Confronted with [the light of Jesus]," Karl Barth wrote, "the false and pretended light of [Saul's] whole seeing, understanding, thinking and willing has been changed into darkness" (*CD* IV.3.1., p. 204). It was the realization that he was in the dark that allowed Saul to take another step into the light (*CD* IV.3.1., p. 205).

If Saul's physical blindness revealed his spiritual blindness, then Saul being restored to sight, baptized, and filled with the Holy Spirit (πλησθῇς πνεύματος ἁγίου) now communicates that he is illumined (Acts 9:17–18; 22:13–16; cf. 2 Cor 3:18).[26] The scale of blindness has fallen off the eyes of his heart; Saul now sees the light of the gospel and loves Jesus Christ because the beauty, goodness, and love of Christ, revealed in the gospel, move his heart, mind, and life in the deepest way (2 Cor 5:14–15). No longer seeing Christ according to the flesh, Saul sees himself, the world, and God anew in the light of new

24. Hartsock, *Sight and Blindness*, 185.

25. Klaus Baltzer, *Deutero-Isaiah: A Commentary on Isaiah 40–55*, ed. Peter Machinist, trans. Margaret Kohl, vol. 23C of Hermeneia: A Critical and Historical Commentary on the Bible (Minneapolis: Fortress, 2001), 146.

26. Peterson puts it thus, "the moment that the Spirit enters is the moment that he will be able to see/understand the truth of the Christian gospel" (David Peterson, *The Acts of the Apostles*, PNTC [Grand Rapids: Eerdmans, 2009], 191).

creation (2 Cor 5:16–17). God has awakened Saul from death with the light of new creation in Jesus Christ: "Awake, O sleeper, and arise from the dead, and Christ will shine on you" (Eph 5:14).

LIGHT OF NEW CREATION IN CHRIST

What can we take away from Saul's encounter for our dogmatic construction of the economy of illumination? Knowledge and transformation are integral in Saul's experience of being illumined because a person blind and in darkness comes into light (covenant knowledge of God) by being transformed (receiving a new heart and sight) in the light of the knowledge of God in the face of Jesus, the Messiah (2 Cor 4:6). The economy of illumination, in other words, is both a cognitive and a cardiac process, involving knowledge and transformation (2 Cor 3:18; 1 John 3:2). To analyze Saul's encounter further, the economy of illumination is the act by which God (1) draws a person into light with light; (2) forms him in light through light, and (3) directs him in light to reflect light. Let's look more closely at these three components of the initial lighting in the economy of illumination from Luke's account.

First, Luke's account shows how the initial lighting in the economy of illumination is the effectual cause that draws a person from darkness to light because it narrates how a man outside of Christ, in Adam, becomes a man in Christ. In Adam, Saul read Scripture by the letter rather than the Spirit (2 Cor 3:6). Scripture points to Christ (Luke 24:27, 44), but Saul was veiled from the glory of God in Christ (2 Cor 3:14) because he viewed Christ according to the flesh (2 Cor 5:16). Saul was in the dark, outside of light, so he cannot see light because only in light can he see light (Ps 36:9). In his encounter, the light of Christ shone not only around him but inside his heart when these words were spoken: "I am Jesus" (Acts 9:5), which Saul would later describe as God shining in his heart "the light of the knowledge of the glory of God in the face of Jesus Christ" (2 Cor 4:6).[27] In the personal light of Jesus, Saul was brought into light. God came close, manifesting his innermost to Saul, became personally present, knowing Saul's spiritual

---

27. These were Jesus's words in response to Saul's question, "Who are you, Lord" (κύριε, Acts 9:5). Because Saul was a devout Jew, a Pharisee (Acts 23:6; 26:5; Phil 3:5), it's safe to assume that he recognized the flash of light as an epiphany, so the purpose of his question was to know the identity of YHWH or his messenger. See Peterson, *Acts*, 304–5 and Eckhard J. Schnabel, *Acts*, ZECNT (Grand Rapids: Zondervan, 2012), 444–45.

condition, and made himself present to Saul's innermost, becoming the *object* of Saul's knowledge and love, more intimate to Saul than he is to himself (Augustine, *Conf.* 3.6.11; Aquinas, *ST* I, q. 43, a.3, *resp.*).

To be illumined is to receive what God communicates and gives in union with Christ (John 6:44–45; Eph 4:20–21), who has become "to us wisdom from God, righteousness and sanctification and redemption" (1 Cor 1:30). To put it another way, it is to have the word of Christ dwell richly in our hearts (Col 3:16). "'The word is near you ... in your heart,'" Paul would write in Romans 10:8, because God has not only *revealed* but also *illumined* Saul to Christ (Acts 9:17–18). "In revelation," Herman Bavinck writes, "God becomes knowable,"[28] and Gregory of Palamas adds, "participable" (*Triad* 2.3.66; cf. Irenaeus of Lyons, *Haer*. 4.20.1–4),[29] but a person does not know and participate in God until he is illumined to the gospel by God. God illumines by coming to us in the light of Christ, and we come to God by being illumined in Christ. God comes to us and draws us into himself by making himself present to us as the object of our knowledge and love. God comes to be the object of our knowledge and love through the invisible missions of the Son and the Spirit because God shines into our heart his light in the Son through his love in the Spirit. So, we may come to him in the Son, light from his light (1 John 4:9; John 3:16), through the Spirit, the love of God's light poured into our hearts (Rom 5:5; Eph 3:16–17), because we move to what we love (*Conf.* 13.9.10). The economy of illumination, as Barth and Balthasar said, is the initial act by which the Father causes the light of his glory revealed *objectively* in the Son to become *subjectively* ours through the Spirit, so we may be conscious of God's love in Christ and be in the light of his love.

Second, the initial lighting of the economy of illumination is a creative act by which the triune God turns a heart of stone to a heart of flesh by imparting the light of new creation into the darkness of the person's heart (2 Cor 3:3). Let me draw out this cardiac effect of the economy of illumination by examining the placement of Saul's encounter in Acts. As we read the surrounding context, we may notice something peculiar taking place literarily. The narrative transitions from the scene with Saul (Acts 8:1–3) to the scene

28. Herman Bavinck, *Prolegomena*, vol. 1 of *Reformed Dogmatics*, ed. John Bolt, trans. John Vriend (Grand Rapids: Baker Academic, 2003), 341–42.

29. See A. N. Williams, *The Ground of Union: Deification in Aquinas and Palamas* (New York: Oxford University Press, 1999), 117.

with "Philip the evangelist" (Acts 8:4–40) and then back to the scene with Saul (Acts 9:1–2). Why did Luke not develop Saul's scene all the way through, but instead skipped it, just to return to it again? Luke was using a literary device known as an *inclusio*[30] to envelop Acts 8:4–40 with Acts 8:1–3 and 9:1–2, the two scenes that have Saul persecuting the church. What is more, Luke then formed another *inclusio* to bracket the unit of Saul's encounter (Acts 9:1–31) with the theme of conversion and the gift of the Spirit to those outside of Jerusalem in Acts 8:4–40 and 9:32–10:48.

Why did Luke go through all this trouble to curate two overlapping units by way of *inclusios*? As we break down the two units and put them back together, our answer emerges. The first unit concerns *the spread of the gospel message from Jerusalem to the world through persecution* (Acts 8:4–40), and the second unit narrates *the way Saul saw the light of Christ, the Servant, and became a light for Christ* (Acts 9:1–31). Together the two units function as a transition in the book of Acts on how the gospel spread to the world. The gospel spread under persecution and through a persecutor, demonstrating that the gospel went forth not because of the will of man, but by the will of God that overcame the darkness of Saul's heart with light. To turn people from darkness to light, God had to turn Saul's heart of stone to a heart of flesh with the light (Acts 26:16–18). In 2 Cor 4:5–6, Saul, who now goes by Paul, says the reason he proclaimed, "Jesus Christ as Lord," is because "God, who said, 'Let light shine out of darkness,' has shone in our hearts to give the light of the knowledge of the glory of God in the face of Jesus Christ." The light of Christ turned Paul into a new creation—a Christian and a minister of the new covenant (2 Cor 3:6; 5:17).

Before Paul received the light of the new creation, he had a heart of stone (2 Cor 3:14–15; Eph 4:18). A person's heart is who he is at the core and what moves him to the object of his love. A heart unmoved and unresponsive to God and what he has done in Christ cannot enjoy new covenant fellowship with God. The light of new creation gave Paul both the knowledge of God and the transformation Paul needed for oneness with God in knowledge and love. This light turned Paul's heart of stone to a "heart of flesh" (Ezek 36:26), so the Spirit can write God's word on his heart (2 Cor

30. An *inclusio* is a literary device, which biblical writers employ to bracket a unit with the same phrases (cf. Ps 8:1, 9; 42:5, 11) or ideas (cf. Ruth 1:3, 5; 1 Sam 2:1, 10; 16:1, 13; John 1:1, 18).

3:3) and fill it with "the knowledge of the glory of God in the face of Jesus Christ" (2 Cor 4:6; cf. Col 3:10). To have this light is to receive what God has accomplished for us in the death and resurrection of Jesus Christ, to experience the new creation reality in Christ because this light gave Paul a "new mind" (רוּחַ חֲדָשָׁה) and an "undivided heart" (לֵב אֶחָד) to respond to God in new covenant fellowship (Ezek 11:19; 36:26–27; cf. Deut 30:6; Jer 31:33; 32:39). It gave Paul the "mind of Christ" (1 Cor 2:16) and made his divided heart in Adam undivided for God in Christ whose oneness with God was unbroken to the point of death on the cross (Phil 2:8).

In the economy of illumination, the light of the Son administered by the Father effected through the Spirit has both a cognitive (knowing) and a cardiac (being and doing) effect on the person. "Thus," Augustine said, "when God teaches through the grace of the Spirit rather than the letter of the law, the result of his teaching is not simply that a person is aware of what he has learned by knowing but also that he seeks it by willing and accomplishes it by acting" (*Grat. Chr.* 14.15). To have the light of new creation shine into our heart through the unveiling of our minds is to have a new perspective and disposition to see, will, and act out the word of God (Phil 2:13), so we may know the truth of God personally and tacitly.

This leads me to my final point. The economy of illumination is the operation by which God enables us to understand ourselves anew and redirects our life narrative to glory in Christ as children of light (Eph 5:8; 1 Thess 5:5). In his third missionary journey, the life of Paul became a recapitulation of Jesus Christ. Charles Scobie writes, for example,

> The third missionary journey to Jerusalem, as has often been observed, closely parallels Jesus' last journey to Jerusalem in Luke's Gospel. Like Jesus, Paul resolves to go to Jerusalem (Lk. 9:51; Acts 19:21); this despite the fact that his death is foretold (Lk. 13:33; 17:25; 18:31–33; Acts 20:22–23; 21:4, 11; cf. 21:13). Initially he has a good reception (Lk. 19:37; Acts 21:17–20); he enters the temple (Lk. 19:45; Acts 21:26); but then, like Jesus, he is arrested and undergoes four trials (Jesus: before the Sanhedrin, Pilate, Herod, and Pilate; Paul: before the Sanhedrin, Felix, Festus, and Agrippa).[31]

31. Charles H. H. Scobie, "A Canonical Approach to Interpreting Luke: The Journey Motif as a Hermeneutical Key," in *Reading Luke: Interpretation, Reflection, Formation*, ed. Craig G.

In the encounter, the light of Jesus transformed Paul's self-understanding and his script for life in the gospel narrative.

The economy of illumination enables us to understand God, his love, and ourselves anew in Christ, allowing us to see our whole existence in the life, death, and resurrection of Jesus (cf. Barth, *CD* IV.3.2., p. 38). We see his narrative as ours because we understand that he came, died, and rose again for us. To be illumined is to see God's eternal purpose for our life, "revealed by the appearing of our Savior Jesus Christ, who has abolished death and brought life and immortality to light through the gospel" (2 Tim 1:10; Eph 1:9). Death, the conclusion of our narrative in Adam, no longer has the last word because we have a new conclusion from our narrative in Christ, the hope of glory (Col 1:27). We see what is true of Christ as true of us by grace (Rom 6:6–8). So, we understand the recapitulation of Christ, his obedient life and death, as our restoration from sin and death in Adam for communion with God. Being illumined by God, we no longer see ourselves in the story of Adam, but in the narrative in Christ, a new self-understanding that directs us to live in a manner worthy of the gospel script of Christ (Phil 1:27).

THE TRIUNE LIGHTING OF NEW CREATION IN OUR HEART

While contemporary accounts of illumination focus on the operation of the Holy Spirit, I follow the trinitarian framework of the ante-Nicene and pro-Nicene theologians in the retrieval moment to construe the economy of illumination as the inseparable operations of the Trinity. Paul's account in 2 Cor 4:6 offers a look inside Paul's heart during his encounter with Christ that enables us to observe the trinitarian operations of the Father, Son, and Holy Spirit in the economy of illumination. "For it is God who said, 'Let light shine out of darkness,' who has shone in our hearts to give the light of the knowledge of the glory of God in the face of Jesus Christ" (2 Cor 4:6 NRSV).

Bartholomew et al. (Grand Rapids: Zondervan, 2005), 340. If Joel B. Green, "Learning Theological Interpretation from Luke," in *The Journey Motif as a Hermeneutical Key,*" in Bartholomew et al., *Reading Luke: Interpretation, Reflection, Formation* (ed. Craig G. Bartholomew et al.; Grand Rapids: Zondervan, 2005), 55–78, 65–66, is right in saying that Luke is seeking to form readers' identity through his narrative, then Paul's account offers us an example and invitation of how we are to become a light like Paul (Acts 13:47), recapitulating the message of Jesus Christ, in order to become a light to bring others to the true light—Jesus Christ.

THE FATHER: PRIME ADMINISTRATOR OF LIGHT

The Father is the prime administrator in the economy of illumination that restores communication with us, so we may share in his glory, the mutual knowledge and love between him and the Son in the Spirit (John 17:21–26). To borrow Irenaeus's metaphor, the Father uses his "two hands," the Son and the Holy Spirit, to administer his light into our hearts. As mentioned, this light in 2 Cor 4:6 does not refer to the light of creation, but the light of new creation from Isaiah 9:2.[32] To receive this light is to be "taught by God," the Father—to learn to see what the Father sees in the Son (Isa 54:13; John 6:44–45; Eph 4:20; 1 Thess 4:9). It is to have the Father's "sight" and perspective to see the way he sees his Son, the object of his love and knowledge in the Spirit from eternity. The Father shines the light of his perspective into our hearts through the invisible missions of the Son and the Spirit. While "the two missions have grace as their common root, they are distinct as to the effects grace has, i.e., the enlightenment of the mind and the enkindling of the affection [*illuminatio intellectus et inflammatio affectus*]" (*ST* I, q.43, a.5, ad.3).

THE SON: LIGHT FROM LIGHT

Jesus is the object of illumination, "in whom are hidden all the treasures of wisdom and knowledge" (Col 2:3),[33] because the light that illumines our heart "arises from knowing God's glory as it comes into clear focus on Christ's countenance."[34] So, we are illumined to God in the Son, light from light, the

32. According to Murray J. Harris, *The Second Epistle to the Corinthians*, NIGTC (Grand Rapids: Eerdmans, 2005), 333–35, the modification from Γενηθήτω φῶς in LXX Gen 1:3 to φῶς λάμψει in 2 Cor 4:6 suggests that it is the light of new creation that Isaiah had prophesied, "φῶς λάμψει ἐφ' ὑμᾶς" [LXX Isa 9:1]; "light will shine on you" [Isa 9:2 NET]).

33. Harris, *Corinthians*, 335, argues: "The parallelism between τῆς γνώσεως here and τοῦ εὐαγγελίου in 4:4, both after τὸν φωτισμόν, suggests that τῆς γνώσεως also is genitive of source (or subjective genitive) and that the knowledge that produces illumination is nothing other than knowledge of the gospel." Similarly, Victor P. Furnish, *II Corinthians*, AB 32A (New York: Doubleday, 1984), 224, offers this gloss, "*the enlightenment coming from the knowledge*" (emphasis his), for φωτισμὸν τῆς γνώσεως (2 Cor 4:6).

34. Harris, *Corinthians*, 337. The OT background for the theme of glory in 2 Cor 3:18 and 4:6 is Exod 33. In Exod 33:18, glory can refer to the identity of God as seen in Moses' prayer to see glory and the Lord replied my "face" (another word for identity) you cannot see (Exod 33:20). According to Richard Bauckham, *Glory: Major Themes in Johannine Theology* (Grand Rapids: Baker Academic, 2015), 50, "A person's identity is made visible in the person's face." The medieval Jewish commentators, Rashi, Rashibam, Nahmanides, and Ibn Ezra, however, interpret the "glory" as the very "presence" of God (Michael Carasik, ed., *The Commentator's*

image of the invisible God (Col 1:15). Jesus is not merely an earthly image of God, as a *signum* is to a *res*, but the fullness of God's glory in bodily form because he is the Son of God by nature (cf. Origen; Col 2:9; cf. 1:19; Eph 3:19; 4:21).[35] When Philip asks to see the Father directly (i.e., "the *visio Dei*"),[36] for example, Jesus replies,

> Whoever has seen me has seen the Father. How can you say, "Show us the Father"? Do you not believe that I am in the Father and the Father is in me? The words that I say to you I do not speak on my own authority, but the Father who dwells in me does his works. Believe me that I am in the Father and the Father is in me, or else believe on account of the works themselves. (John 14:9–11)

To see Jesus is to see the Father because we see the Father in him. We never go past the Son to the Father, but always *in* the Son to the Father (John 14:6) because the reality of the Father and the Son in the Spirit are indivisible, a subsisting relation.[37] To know the truth of one is then to know it in and through the other (Matt 11:27; Luke 10:22).

Bible: Exodus שמות JPS Miqra'ot Gedolot [Philadelphia: The Jewish Publication Society, 2005], 299). Glory as a reference to divine presence finds support from the lexical analysis of "כָּבוֹד." The word, "כָּבוֹד," is rich in meaning. Other than meaning glory, honor, splendor, majesty, and favor from the LXX translation (Takamitsu Muraoka, *A Greek-English Lexicon of the Septuagint* [Louvain: Peeters, 2009], 175–76), it can also connote the "name" or attribute of God (see C. John Collins, "כבד," *NIDOTTE* 2:574) and denote the "manifestation of Yahweh," the presence of God to the leaders of Israel (Deut 5:24; Isa 24:23), to Israel (Exod 16:7; 24:17), in the sanctuary (Pss 26:8; 63:3; 102:16; Isa 59:19), and in the clouds (Exod 16:10; Num 14:22; Isa 60:2; 66:18; Ps 97:6; see "כָּבוֹד," *HALOT*, 2:458 and " כָּבוֹד," *DCH* 4:353). There is also a phenomenological element in "glory." That is, the beholder senses or experiences the manifestation of God or "a touch of luminescence" of God's glory ("δόξα," *TLNT* 1:366; Gerhard Kittel, "δόξα," *TDNT* 2:249–50. cf. Isa 40:5; Ezek 33:22; Acts 22:11). For discussion on כבד as the manifestation of God's glory from German scholarship, see Sverre Aalen, *Die Begriffe Licht und Finsternis im Alten Testament* (Oslo: J. Dybwad, 1951), 73–76. In 2 Corinthians 3:18, glory, "δόξα," has a salvific and eschatological aspect, God's power of salvation in transforming believers in Christ (see Sverre Aalen, "Glory, Honour," *NIDNTT* 2:47–48).

35. Jesus is the image (εἰκών) of the invisible God because he reveals God's very presence on earth ("εἰκών," BDAG, 282). In his life, death, and resurrection, Jesus manifests "who God is in himself" (Ralph P. Martin, *2 Corinthians*, 2nd ed., WBC 40 [Grand Rapids: Zondervan, 2014], 223).

36. Carson, *John*, 494.

37. In John, Jacques Dupont, *Essais sur la christologie de saint Jean: Le Christ, parole, lumière et vie: La glorie du Christ* (Bruges: Éditions de l'Abbaye de Saint-André, 1951), 63, highlights that there are three main themes of John's christological description of Jesus as light: (1) moral theme, (2) didactic theme, and (3) eschatological salvific theme. So Jesus came as light to show the way of God and the way to God.

THE HOLY SPIRIT: THE WARMTH OF LIGHT IN OUR HEART

If Jesus is the light of the world because he manifests God's love to the world (Rom 5:8; John 3:16), then the Holy Spirit is the presence and warmth of light in our hearts because he is the love of God poured into our hearts (Rom 5:5).[38] The Spirit emits into our cold hearts a personal knowledge of God in union with Christ to transform us for communication with God (Jer 24:7). The presence of the Spirit not only makes the Father and the Son present in our hearts by faith, but also frees us from sin and falsehood for "communicative relation with God"[39] because the Spirit operates as the "efficient cause in [our] communication" with God (John Owen, *Works* 3:209).[40] The indwelling of the Spirit makes us sensible to receive and respond to what the Father gives and communicates to us in the Son.

Paul illustrated the operation of the Spirit in the economy of illumination through the new covenant metaphors from Jeremiah and Ezekiel. "And you show that you are a letter from Christ delivered by us, written not with ink but with the Spirit of the living God not on tablets of stone but on tablets of human hearts" (2 Cor 3:3, 6; cf. Jer 31:33; Ezek 36:26).[41] The Spirit is the living ink that the Father uses to write his Son on the tablet of our hearts. Before God gave us a "new heart" in Christ, we had a "heart of stone" like Paul in Adam (Ezek 11:19; cf. Deut 30:6). We were unresponsive to God, so communication with God could not take place. There was a barrier symbolized by a veil over us (2 Cor 3:14). Similar to the veil over Moses's face, which he took off before he went into the tent to speak with God, a veil over our minds hinders us from communication with God—and in Israel's case, from perceiving the *telos* of what God was communicating to them in the law (2 Cor 3:13).[42] "But when one

---

38. As the chiastic structure in Ezek 11:19 and 36:26 (see chapter 2 of our study) suggests, the transformation of the heart is through the presence of the Spirit inside the person's heart (v. 27)."

39. Seifrid, *Corinthians*, 176.

40. The presence of the Spirit, Owen helps us see, is the "author or principal efficient cause of" subjective revelation or illumination (John Owen, *Causes, Ways, and Means of Understanding the Mind of God*, vol. 4 of *The Works of John Owen*, ed. William Goold [1850–1853; repr., Edinburgh: Banner of Truth, 1967], 135; hereafter cited as *Works* 4:135).

41. Seifrid, *Corinthians*, 114, argues, "the Corinthians are so 'written' implies an unqualified remaking, a rewriting of their person and life by God the Creator. As Paul later says expressly, 'If someone is in Christ, there is a new creation. ... the Spirit establishes an active, saving *communication* between the fallen human being and God, a communication that does not end, not even with death itself (vv. 17–18)."

42. Harris, *Corinthians*, 302. R. Penna, "L'évolution de l'attitude de Paul envers les Juifs," in *L'apôtre Paul: Personnalité, Style et Conception du Ministère*, ed. A. Vanhoye (Leuven: Leuven

turns [ἐπιστρέψῃ] to the Lord [who is the Spirit], the veil is removed" (2 Cor 3:16).[43] The unveiling of the Spirit frees us for communion with God in covenant union with Christ (2 Cor 3:14–16).[44] "Now the Lord is the Spirit, and where the Spirit of the Lord is, there is freedom" (2 Cor 3:17 NRSV). Here, "[f]reedom is not a freedom of autonomy, as it is usually understood, but a freedom of communication."[45] In the presence of the Spirit, there is freedom from sin for communication with God in Christ (John 8:32–36; Rom 6:18; 8:2; Gal 5:1, 13).[46]

The presence of the Spirit frees us from sin and falsehood with "truth" by uniting us to Christ who is "the truth" and "the light" (John 8:12, 31–32; 14:6).[47] "Indeed, to this very day, when they hear the reading of the old covenant, that same veil is still there, since only in Christ [ἐν Χριστῷ] is it set aside" (2 Cor 3:14 NRSV). The Spirit makes the truth and presence of the risen Christ "real" in his presence because he is the "Spirit of Christ"

University Press, 1986), 405–6, argues that what Paul wants to say is not that the law is abolished, but that by grace through faith in Christ, the old covenant can be understood in a profounder way.

43. While the word, ἐπιστρέφω, as mentioned above, could mean a variety of things, the modification from εἰσεπορεύετο (LXX Exod 34:34) to ἐπιστρέψῃ πρός (2 Cor 3:16), Murray Harris points out, "was doubtless prompted by Paul's desire to express spiritual rather than physical movement ... a spiritual 'turning to the Lord' (or, to God) in heartfelt repentance (e.g., 1 Kgdms. 7:3; Hos. 5:4; 6:1; Amos 4:6)" (Harris, *Corinthians*, 307). The indicative εἰσεπορεύετο simply means to enter, so Paul's use of ἐπιστρέψῃ seems to aim at invoking more than a physical turning. The spiritual sense of ἐπιστρέψῃ finds its support among these exegetes: Samuel Amsler, *L'Ancien Testament dans L'Eglise* (Paris: Delachaux & Niestlé, 1960), 48; Rudolf Bultmann, *The Second Letter to the Corinthians*, trans. Roy A. Harrisville (Minneapolis: Augsburg Publishing House, 1985), 89; J. F. Collange, *Enigmes de le deuxième Épître de Paul aux Corinthiens* (London: Cambridge University Press, 1972), 103; Richard B. Hays, *Echoes of Scripture in the Letters of Paul* (New Haven: Yale University Press, 1989), 146, Norbert Hugedé, *La métaphore du miroir dans les épîtres de saint Paul aux Corinthiens* (Neuchâtel: Delachaux & Niestlé, 1957), 26; and Seifrid, *Corinthians*, 172. The Old Testament Pseudepigrapha often uses ἐπιστρέφω to denote conversion (Apocr. Ezek. 2:1; 5:1; Apoc. Sedr. 12:5–6; 14:5; T. Jud. 23:5; T. Iss. 6:3–4; T. Zeb. 9:7–8; T. Dan 5:9, 11; Apoc. Ab. 10:14; T. Ab. 12:13; Pr. Man. 1:17). Paul uses this verb two other times, in both cases it means to change direction in life (Gal 4:9; 1 Thess 1:9).

44. John Webster, "Illumination," *Journal of Reformed Theology* 5 (2011): 325, argues that the unveiling of the Spirit causes, preserves, and directs the "operation of creaturely intelligence ... by divine light, whose radiance makes creatures to know: 'that light is what enables [the soul] to understand whatever is within the range of its powers.'"

45. Seifrid, *Corinthians*, 177.

46. Seifrid, *Corinthians*, 176. Max-Alain Chevallier, *Esprit de Dieu, Paroles d'hommes: Le rôle de l'esprit dans les ministères de la parole selon l'apôtre Paul* (Neuchâtel: Delachaux & Niestlé, 1966), 99, similarly argues that it is a relational knowledge: "C'est un esprit de relation. It établit une relation parfaite . . . avec le Kyrios (v. 17)." Furnish, *Corinthians*, 242, calls this freedom, an "unhindered participation in the splendor of the new covenant."

47. The presence of the Spirit enables us to be "taught in [Christ], as the truth is in Jesus" (Eph 4:21 ESV).

(Rom 8:9; cf. 2 Cor 3:17; John 16:13).[48] The presence of Jesus with the Father in heaven is with us here and now on earth by the presence of the Spirit (John 14:23).[49] Jesus going to the Father, John tells us, is at the same time his coming into our hearts through the presence of the Holy Spirit. "I am going away, and I will come to you" (John 14:28).[50] No longer physically close in proximity, Jesus becomes closer still, in our innermost, through the indwelling presence of the Spirit—God who was with us is now *in* us (John 14:16–17).[51]

The presence of the Spirit makes the word of God *effective*, causing what God says concerning his Son to take root in our heart and transform us (Eph 3:17; Col 3:16), because through the presence of the Spirit, Christ is in us[52] and we are in Christ[53]—the "true light, which gives light to everyone" (John 1:9, cf. John 1:5, 14–18; 3:17). So "when we are enlightened in the Spirit, it is Christ who enlightens us in him" to the Father (Athanasius, *Ep. Serap.* 1.19.4). To have the light of new creation shine into our heart is to be renewed by the knowledge of the Father in the Son through the presence of the Spirit, a renewing of our heart that directs our minds and actions—our whole being—to God (Col 3:10).

---

48. Grant Macaskill, *Union with Christ in the New Testament* (Oxford: Oxford University Press, 2013), 300, argues similarly, "As the gift of the new covenant, the Spirit makes real to (and in) believers 'the truth as it is in Jesus.' The terms of the covenant are written in their hearts, minds are enabled to grasp the Christoform revelation, and their persons are conformed to his. What this means is that our selves are defined by and, indeed, *in* another. This is not simply formal but real, because of the Spirit's presence."

49. So "the real gift of the post-resurrectional period was a union with Jesus that was not permanently dependent on bodily presence" (Brown, *John*, 646). Craig S. Keener, *The Gospel of John: A Commentary* (Grand Rapids: Baker Academic, 2003), 2:972, writes, "The disciples, ready to lament Jesus' departure, would in fact obtain his continuing presence by the Spirit once he was glorified! ... 14:17 assigns the Spirit's presence wholly to believers in Jesus, excluding 'the world.' In the context of the Fourth Gospel, 'the world' is all those outside Jesus' following ...."

50. John tells us that, when the Spirit comes, Jesus will be *in* them and they will be *in* him, a mutual indwelling between Christ and the church, the body of Christ. "In that day [when the Father pours out the Spirit] you will know that I am in my Father, and you in me, and I in you" (John 14:20 ESV).

51. While the Spirit was abiding (μένει) with the disciples during Jesus' ministry, the Spirit will be (ἔσται) in them forever after Jesus's glorification (v. 17). The "*promised Spirit ... will mediate the presence and self-revelation of Father and Son*" (Max Turner, "Holy Spirit," in *NDBT* [Downers Grove, IL: InterVarsity Press, 2000], 556; emphasis his).

52. Cf. 2 Cor 13:5; Rom 8:10; Gal 2:20; 4:19; Eph 3:17; Col 1:27; 2 Thess 1:10.

53. Cf. John 15:4–5; Rom 6:8–11; 8:1; 1 Cor 1:30; Gal 3:14; Eph 1:4–10; Phil 3:9.

THE TRINITARIAN OPERATION OF LIGHTING

The Father, Son, and Spirit who are one in essence as light operate inseparably as three distinct lights *ad extra*. Gregory of Nazianzus likens Paul's experience of the economy of illumination as "a flash of ... light which is both one and three" (*Or.* 39.11) because the economy of illumination is an outflow of God's being, "three in properties, or indeed in hypostases ... or ... 'persons' ... and one with regard to the concept of substance, or indeed divinity" (*Or.* 39.11; cf. 32.9). The three divine persons are one light but relate to us as three lights because each relates to us in a distinct way.[54] The Father is light because he is the light of our sight, allowing us to see what he sees in his Son from all eternity. The Son is light because he is the radiance of the Father's glory and the exact imprint of his essence (Heb 1:3), so he enables us to see the Father in himself as the image of the Father by nature. The Spirit is the ray and warmth of light because he is the presence and the power of light, imparting divine sensibility in us to see the truth of the Son from the perspective of the Father and the truth of the Father in the image of the Son through the gospel (Calvin, Edwards, Owen). Together, the three persons of God work as one in the economy of illumination to open the eyes of our hearts to see the "image" of the Son (Irenaeus, Tertullian) by the presence of the Spirit (Origen, Clement, Athanasius) from the eternal "sight" of the Father (Edwards). The image, presence, and sight of light are inseparable in the experience of illumination, beholding light in light via light.

CONCLUSION

This chapter presented the economy of illumination as a means by which the triune God applies redemption accomplished by Christ to us in covenant union with him. Instead of focusing on the operation of the Holy Spirit, I followed the ante-Nicene and pro-Nicene fathers and construed Paul's personal experience of light from his encounter with Christ in a trinitarian framework. The economy of illumination, I proposed, is the trinitarian operations of God, the Father opening the eyes of our heart to behold the Son, the image of light, through the Spirit, the presence of light, from his perspective, the

---

54. Our theologians from the second moment refer to all three as light because the "paternal light" comes to us from the "resplendent flesh" of the Son (Irenaeus, *Haer.* 4.20.2) through the enlightenment of the Spirit (Athanasius, *Ep. Serap.* 1.19.4).

sight of light. Each divine operation of light is distinct, yet inseparable from the other two operations of light; together the three operations of light bring us into fellowship with light.

In Acts 9, Luke's account of Paul's encounter narrates the economy of illumination as a movement of light: "God comes to us by enlightening us; and we go to him by thinking of him: *come to him and be enlightened* (Ps 33:6)" (*In Ioan.* 14.6 §1945). All Scripture points to Jesus, the Messiah who fulfills all righteousness (Isa 53:11; Matt 3:15) to restore fellowship with God in himself for us as the head of new humanity (Luke 24:26–27; John 5:39; Rom 1:2; 1 Cor 15:3–4). Paul was in the dark to who Jesus was. He was zealous for God, but he was not enlightened because he was blind to who the Messiah was (Rom 10:2). On the road to Damascus, Paul came into light because the light of God met him in the face of Jesus, the Messiah. The Father shines into Paul's heart his light in the Son through the Spirit to move Paul from darkness to light (2 Cor 4:6; Col 1:12–13; 1 Thess 5:5). What the Father shines in the Son is his eternal intention in the covenant of redemption because the Son, whom the Father sent, has actualized and revealed the Father's eternal decree perfectly in his life, death, and resurrection by the Spirit.

If darkness (ignorance) is the absence of fellowship with God, then light (knowledge of God) is fellowship with God, a share in the mind and will of God (John 17:3).[55] To share the mind and will of God, revealed in the cross and resurrection of Jesus Christ, we need a new heart and mind in Christ (Ezek 11:19; 18:31; 36:26) because the cross is nonsensical to our fallen minds (1 Cor 1:23–24; 2:14–16) and does not affect our hardened hearts (Eph 4:18). The economy of illumination is both a cognitive and cardiac process, involving knowledge and transformation to draw us into light. It is the dual process by which the triune God transforms us *with* the knowledge of God *for* the knowledge of God in covenant union with Christ (Col 3:10; 1 John 3:2). As the ray from the sun changes a dark and cold room with its brightness and warmth, the light of new creation turned Paul's heart of stone into a heart of flesh with "the knowledge of the glory of God in the face of Jesus Christ" to respond and know God as covenant Lord (2 Cor 4:6). The light of the gospel

55. Ramm, *The Witness of the Spirit*, 32, similarly argues: "The knowledge of God intends a fellowship and communion of God with man. Knowledge of God merely as theological information is unknown to Scripture. The knowledge of God is *always* the instrument of God to create worship and fellowship with the creature."

changed Paul with the knowledge of Christ his Lord (Phil 3:8, 10). Paul's life became a pattern of the gospel, a letter of Christ written by the Spirit on the tablet of his new heart and read by all (2 Cor 3:2–3).

The economy of illumination led Paul into new covenant fellowship with God because it united him to Christ, from whom fellowship with God and all blessings from God flow (John Owen, *Works* 2:8–9). In covenant union with Christ, we receive the mind of Christ to know the Father and have Christ dwell in our hearts as the object of faith and love, which is to be "taught by God," hearing the Father speak into our hearts to share his perspective and see what he sees in the Son through the Spirit from eternity (John 6:44–45). Jesus mediates communion with God because he has entered heaven to be with God on our behalf (Heb 6:18–20; Eph 2:6) and he is with us on earth on the Father's behalf through the Spirit (Matt 28:20; John 14:28). So, we communicate with the Father in the Son who has entered heaven for us, and the Father communicates to us with his Word who dwells in our hearts through the Spirit (Eph 2:22; John 14:23; 17:23). Each day the sun breaks the night to fill our world with light so we may be in light. In the same way, the Father shines the light of the gospel of Jesus Christ through the Spirit into our hearts to bring us into his life of light and love from glory to glory.

9

BEING TRANSFORMED FROM GLORY TO GLORY

This chapter concludes the constructive moment of the study with the reciprocal and ongoing nature of the cardiac and cognitive processes in the economy of illumination, through which God deepens the church's communion with God in contemplative union with Christ from glory to glory. What we have in contemplative union with Christ is not a still image of God, but an ever-deepening beholding of the heart and mind of God in the Son through the Spirit. In this ongoing lighting of the economy of illumination, the Father unveils us to contemplate the Son (the image of light) through the Spirit (the presence of his light) from his perspective (the sight of light), so we may see what the Father eternally sees in the Son, the fullness of his divine heart (or will) and mind in bodily form.

While God is the one who unveils us through the Spirit to behold the Son and transforms us into the image of Christ, we are not inanimate objects but are called to partake in the work of light. Our progress in knowledge and transformation to the image of Christ involves both God's action of lighting and our action in light. Observe, for example, Paul's words in 2 Cor 3:18: "we all, with unveiled face, looking as in a mirror at the glory of the Lord, are being transformed into the same image from glory to glory" (NASB). The participle, *κατοπτριζόμενοι*, for *knowledge* and the verb, *μεταμορφούμεθα*, for *transformation* are neither in the active nor the passive voice, but the middle voice. In the middle voice, the "subject intimately participates in the results of the action."[1] Our actions of beholding and being transformed are in the middle voice because, through these actions, we actively participate in the

1. Richard A. Young, *Intermediate New Testament Greek: A Linguistic and Exegetical Approach* (Nashville: Broadman & Holman, 1994), 134.

result of the concerted action of the triune God in the economy of illumination that unveils our face and transforms us in contemplative union with Christ for new covenant fellowship with God (Col 3:10; Eph 4:20–24).[2] God's concerted action authors and perfects our participatory action in the ongoing process of knowing and being transformed into God's likeness in contemplative union with Christ.

The body, I want to stress, is as significant as the heart and mind in contemplative union with Christ. As Tertullian and Irenaeus have taught us, our body not only expresses what is in our heart and mind but also enables our heart and mind to experience and behold Christ through our actions. This goes against the understanding of contemplation inherited from Plato and Aristotle who separated the active life from the contemplative life, the "knowledge of reality itself, as opposed to knowing how: the kind of know-how involved in getting things done."[3] In the retrieval moment, we observed the impact of this view of contemplation on Origen and Athanasius from the East, who understood the body as the point of departure to the mind's contemplation on God. This view also impacted Augustine and Aquinas from the West, who viewed the journey of the mind to God as a movement from following what Jesus has done in the flesh by faith to contemplating the eternal truth and wisdom of the Son from the light grace to the light of glory (cf. *ST* II-II, q.182, a.1–4). In this view, the body is something we leave behind to go deeper into the knowledge of God. I hope to remedy this perception of the body by demonstrating that our embodiment of faith is essential to communion with God in contemplative union with Christ because our embodiment of faith allows our hearts and minds to see and experience God's truth and wisdom more profoundly, personally, and tacitly (John 8:32). God is not

2. To conform to the word of God, for instance, is to participate in what God does with his word in our lives. So, in our participatory action of working out our salvation, we enter "the action begun by another, [our] creating and saving Lord, and find [ourselves] participating in the results of the action" (Eugene H. Peterson, *The Contemplative Pastor: Returning to the Art of Spiritual Direction* [Grand Rapids: Eerdmans, 1993], 104). With regard to illumination, Kevin J. Vanhoozer, "Effectual Call or Causal Effect?: Summons, Sovereignty and Supervenient Grace," *Tyndale Bulletin* 49.2 (1998): 248, writes something similar: "One who has been illumined is both passive and active: being made to understand, one understands."

3. Andrew Louth, "Theology, Contemplation and the University," *Studies in Christian Ethics* 17 (2004): 71, helps us understand that the "distinction between the active life and the contemplative life" is "the distinction between the life of worldly activity—the world of business and commerce, the world of farming and manufacture, the world of everyday life—and, in contrast, the world of thought. ... the contemplative life is concerned with beholding things."

a reality of ideas but of persons, so knowledge of God requires us to learn how to live with God in new covenant fellowship.

To reflect on the interplay between God's concerted action and our participatory action in the ongoing cardiac and cognitive processes of the economy of illumination, I begin with God's concerted action in the *ordo salutis* and then end with our participatory actions in God's action through reading, praying, obeying, partaking, and singing Scripture.

DIVINE ILLUMINATION IN THE *ORDO SALUTIS*

In 2 Cor 3:18, Paul compared our communication with God in the new covenant to Moses' face-to-face communication with God in the old covenant. As Moses unveiled his face to enter God's presence (Exod 33:11; 34:30–35), God unveils our face (πρόσωπον) through the Spirit to the presence of Christ. Both communications take place in God's presence and transform the beholder in God's glory, but while the glory of the old covenant fades, the glory of the new covenant goes on from glory to glory. The transformation of the new covenant is the transformation of the image of God within us. The *imago Dei*, Augustine said, is "both given and yet to come."[4] It is given because it is our *capax Dei*, capacity for God, bestowed on us at creation. Augustine located this capacity in our mind (*Trin.* 14.8.11),[5] but I have argued in chapter 7 that it is the capacity of our heart, mind, and body for God because God has made us to know and love him with our whole being (Deut 6:5).[6] It is yet to come because we mature into the likeness of God as the activities of our hearts, minds, and bodies conform to the mind and will of God (cf. *Trin.* 14.18.24). Like a mirror, we become and reflect what we behold, the object in front of our hearts, minds, and lives. After the fall, however, we no longer behold God

---

4. A. N. Williams, "Contemplation," in *Knowing the Triune God: The Work of the Spirit in the Practice of the Church*, ed. James J. Buckley and David S. Yeago (Grand Rapids: Eerdmans, 2001), 128.

5. For discussion on Augustine's concept of the *imago Dei as* the *capax Dei* in the mind, see Jason McMartin, "The Theandric Union as Imago Dei and Capax Dei," in *Christology: Ancient and Modern*, ed. Oliver D. Crisp and Fred Sanders (Grand Rapids: Zondervan, 2013), 136–50.

6. In Scripture, our hearts and body are capable for God because God is able to dwell in our hearts (Eph 3:17) and make our body his temple (1 Cor 6:19). The deeds of our body allow us to reflect God's light (Matt 5:16) and represent God (who is spirit) physically to the world. In a similar way, Richard E. Averbeck, "A Literary Day, Inter-Textual, and Contextual Reading of Genesis 1–2," in *Reading Genesis 1–2: An Evangelical Conversation*, ed. J. Daryl Charles (Peabody, MA.: Hendrickson, 2013), 26, argues, "[w]e stand before God to serve as his authoritative representative on this earth 'in his image as his likeness.'"

because sin has darkened our minds by hardening our hearts from living for God (Eph 4:18). To behold God again, God needs to illumine (unveil and transform) us in contemplative union with Christ, to turn us from sin to behold Christ as the object of our knowledge and love by faith.

The order of salvation in Rom 8:29–30 details the different stages that the ongoing cardiac (transforming) and cognitive (unveiling) processes of the economy of illumination in 2 Cor 3:18 bring us into from glory to glory: "For those whom he foreknew he also predestined to be conformed to the image of his Son, in order that he might be the firstborn among many brothers. And those whom he predestined he also called, and those whom he called he also justified, and those whom he justified he also glorified."[7] To put it another way, the order of salvation details the benefits of union with Christ, whose completed work has actualized redemption for us.[8] We receive the benefits of the work of Christ in union with him by *faith*. "Faith," argued Herman Bavinck, "is the only way [salvation] can be appropriated, the only form in which it can take shape. Indeed, all benefits (forgiveness, regeneration, sanctification, perseverance, the blessedness of heaven) exist for us only by faith. We enjoy them only by faith."[9] The role of faith in the different links of the

---

7. Commentators have long recognized the connection between the order of salvation in Rom 8:29–30 and the process of being transformed from glory to glory in 2 Cor 3:18. For example, Paul W. Barnett, *The Message of 2 Corinthians*, ed. John R. W. Stott, BST (Downers Grove, IL: InterVarsity Press, 1988), 75, argues that 2 Cor 3:18 "should be read alongside Romans 8:29–30 which refers to God's great plan, stretching from eternity to eternity, by which we are 'predestined', ... justified, ... glorified.'" See also Ralph P. Martin, *2 Corinthians*, 2nd ed., WBC 40 (Grand Rapids: Zondervan, 2014), 215; and Murray J. Harris, *The Second Epistle to the Corinthians: A Commentary on the Greek Text*, NIGTC (Grand Rapids: Eerdmans, 2005), 316–17.

8. For example, aorist *ἐδόξασεν* is used to indicate that glorification is completed in Christ (Rom 8:30): "When Paul proclaims that those whom God justified 'he also gloried (8:30, Gk. *Kai edoxasen*), the aorist tense views our glorification as completed. God's purpose was fulfilled when Christ was glorified and in him our glorification has already been accomplished. The future for those who trust in Christ has already been decided" (David Peterson, *Possessed by God: A New Testament Theology of Sanctification and Holiness*, NSBT [Grand Rapids: Eerdmans, 1995], 120).

9. Herman Bavinck, *Holy Spirit, Church, and New Creation*, vol. 4 of *Reformed Dogmatics*, ed. John Bolt and trans. John Vriend (Grand Rapids: Baker Academic, 2008), 103. Unlike Buddhists, who view "'unconscious' salvation" as "the pinnacle of being," Herman Bavinck argues, "to the Christian the highest state of being is to know God and by that knowledge to have eternal life. ... Of what benefit would the forgiveness of sins, regeneration, and complete renewal by the Holy Spirit, the glories of heaven, be to us if we did not know about them? They could not exist. They presuppose and require consciousness, knowledge, enjoyment, and in these confer salvation. God saves by causing himself to be known and enjoyed in Christ. But since on earth the benefits of the covenant of grace are only granted to us in part; since communion with God, regeneration, and sanctification are still incomplete; and since our knowledge is imperfect, has

ordo salutis offers a way to reflect on the initial and ongoing lighting in the economy of illumination that brings the church from faith to sight in Christ.

Before we look at these links, a word on the general illumination of Hebrews 6:4 will allow us to understand the nature of the initial and ongoing lighting of the economy of illumination that draws us into union with Christ. General illumination of faith, John Owen said (*Works* 3:231–33), is the same for both "those who have once been enlightened" (φωτισθέντας), but fall away (Heb 6:4), and those who have been enlightened and persevere to sight (Heb 10:32, 39). The experience of the light for both groups is the same in the beginning: both taste (γευσαμένους) the "heavenly gift," the "goodness" of God's word, and the "power of the age to come," and have a share (μετόχους) in the Spirit (Heb 6:4–5). Like those in the Gospel of John who only followed Jesus for a "season" (John 6:66–71; 8:31–59),[10] the first group stays at embryonic faith[11] and eventually falls away (Heb 6:6), never reaching an Abrahamic faith that justifies and raises us from the dead (Rom 4:17).[12] General illumination offers a glimmer of light but does not prevent a person from returning to darkness. This is the illumination that both the apostates with temporary faith (*fides temporaria*) and believers with justifying faith (*fides iustificans*) experience in the beginning through the Spirit who dwells *with* them but not *in* them (John 14:17; Rom 8:9–11).[13]

---

invisible things for its object, and is bound to Scripture, our knowledge of God on earth is 'a knowledge of faith'" (Bavinck, *Holy Spirit*, 103).

10. Andreas J. Köstenberger, *John*, BECNT (Grand Rapids: Baker Academic, 2004), 261.

11. In John, we find various types of faith; not all faith, however, leads to salvation or eternal life with God (e.g., 2:23; 7:31; 10:42; 11:45; 12:11, 42). See, for example, John 8:31–32, which took place after many people placed their faith in Jesus through what he had said: "So Jesus said to the Jews who had believed him, 'If you abide in my word, you are truly my disciples, and you will know the truth, and the truth will set you free.'" They understood Jesus's word and believed in part but did not understand its truth to the extent of experiencing the freedom that it brings from sin to partake in communicative relationship with God. They have not yet truly come to the Son because they have not heard and learned from the Father (6:45) and did not belong to him (8:42, 47, 55), but still to their father, the devil (vv. 38, 41, 44).

12. See Simon Gathercole, "The Doctrine of Justification in Paul and Beyond: Some Proposals," in *Justification in Perspective*, ed. Rutherford House and Bruce L. McCormack (Grand Rapids: Baker Academic, 2006), 219–42, who argues that justification comes from a resurrection faith like Abraham who was as good as dead, but because of his faith was able to perform what God had promised, the birth of his son Isaac (Rom 4:19–25).

13. The indwelling of the Spirit is the exclusive experience of those who love Jesus and remain in his word: "If you love me, you will keep my commandments. And I will ask the Father, and he will give you another Helper, to be with you forever, even the Spirit of truth, whom the

Turning to the order of salvation, the first and the last links of the chain are fixed in eternity because, as I mentioned in chapter 7, the covenant of redemption is the principal *cause* (Eph 1:5) and the glorification of the church is the *telos* (Rom 8:17–23).[14] Those whom God foreknew (προέγνω) are those whom he has elected to be his covenant partners before time (Rom 8:29a; Eph 1:4–5; 1 Pet 1:20; Rev 13:8), so they may be conformed into the image of his Son (συμμόρφους τῆς εἰκόνος τοῦ υἱοῦ αὐτοῦ, Rom 8:29).[15] The purpose of conformity, indicated by εἰς τὸ εἶναι,[16] is so Jesus could be the "firstborn" (πρωτότοκον) among God's covenant family (Rom 8:29).[17] As Israel was God's firstborn in the old covenant (Exod 4:22; Jer 2:3), Jesus is now God's firstborn in the new covenant, the head of the church who brings her to glory (Col 1:18; 1 Cor 15:20–23; Heb 1:6; 2:10–12). The glorification of the church is her consummation in union with Christ for communion with God, a share in God's glory, the oneness of love and knowledge between the Father and the Son in Spirit (John 17:22–26).

The link that actualizes God's eternal decree into the history of believers is the effectual call of God (cf. 2 Tim 1:9).[18] Effectual call is a gospel call that

---

world cannot receive, because it neither sees him nor knows him. You know him, for he dwells with you and will be in you" (John 14:15–17).

14. See John Murray, *Redemption, Accomplished, and Applied* (Grand Rapids: Eerdmans, 1955), 95–97.

15. In the Old Testament, for God to know a people refers to God knowing them covenantally. For example, God said to the nation of Israel, "You only have I known of all the families of the earth; therefore I will punish you for all your iniquities" (Amos 3:2). If God is omniscient (2 Chr 16:9; Prov 15:3), he would certainly have known all the people of the world; but God knew Israel in a covenantal way, so he will punish them for their disobedience as a Father would a son. See Douglas J. Moo, *The Epistle to the Romans*, NICNT (Grand Rapids: Eerdmans, 1996), 532–33; and Thomas R. Schreiner, *Romans*, BECNT (Grand Rapids: Baker, 1998), 451–52. Grant Macaskill, *Union with Christ in the New Testament* (Oxford: Oxford University Press, 2013), 272, is right that election should be "explicated covenantally along nascent Trinitarian lines" because it is the Father who foreknew his covenant partners to be transformed into the image of His Son through the Spirit.

16. In Romans, εἰς τὸ εἶναι always denotes a purpose or result cause (Rom 1:20; 3:26; 4:11, 16; 8:29; 15:16).

17. In Col 1:18, for example, Paul parallels Jesus' identity as the "firstborn" of new creation with his identity as the "head" of the body, his church (cf. 1 Cor 15:20–23)

18. That the call is effectual is further indicated by Rom 8:30 because "there Paul says that 'those whom he called (ἐκάλεσεν, *ekalesen*) he also justified. It fuses the called and justified together so that those who have experienced calling have also inevitably received the blessing of justification. Now if all those who are called are also justified, then calling must be effectual and must create faith, for 'all' those who are called are justified and justification cannot occur without faith (3:21–22, 28; 5:1)" (Thomas R. Schreiner, *Romans*, BECNT [Grand Rapids: Baker, 1998], 451).

has become effective through illumination.[19] Karl Barth wrote that a man "is called and becomes a Christian as he is illuminated."[20] As I've mentioned from Saul's encounter in the last chapter, the initial lighting of the economy of illumination is the efficient cause[21] that enables a person to hear the One who "calls nonbeing into being" and raises her from death to life (Rom 4:17; John 3:3–8; 5:25; 11:43).[22] The effect of the call, in other words, is regeneration, the renewal of our image of God's nature as mind and will. Richard Muller defines regeneration, for example, as "the rebirth of mind and will accomplished by the gracious work of the Holy Spirit at the outset of the *ordo salutis*."[23] Though, in Rom 8:30, regeneration and sanctification are not mentioned in the order of salvation, they are implied by the verb, ἐδόξασεν, which likely includes regeneration as the first moment and sanctification as the ongoing process to glorification.[24] The move from being

19. "Indeed," writes Calvin, "the Word of God is like the sun, shining upon all those to whom it is proclaimed, but with no effect among the blind. Now, all of us are blind by nature in this respect. Accordingly, it cannot penetrate into our minds unless the Spirit, as the inner teacher, through his illumination makes entry for it" (*Institutes*, 3.2.34). In light of Matt 22:14, Calvin argues that illumination causes the gospel call to be effective: "by the inward illumination of his Spirit he causes the preached Word to dwell in their hearts" (*Institutes*, 3.24.8).

20. *CD* IV.3.2., p. 508.

21. Efficient cause is what Aristotle called "the *source of motion*" (*Metaph.* 5.2.4 [Tredernnick, LCL). For example, the source that puts the production of a bronze statue into motion is the sculptor. Illumination is the efficient cause of the gospel call because it is the *movement* of God that produces change, bringing those in the darkness of ignorance to the light of knowledge, covenant fellowship with him (1 Pet 2:9).

22. Jonathan Hoglund, *Called by Triune Grace: Divine Rhetoric and the Effectual Call*, ed. Daniel Treier and Kevin J. Vanhoozer (Downers Grove, IL: IVP Academic, 2016), 111, argues, "Calling and illumination refer to the same reality but in different ways. To say that one is enlightened is to focus on one's renewed abilities to perceive as a result of God's action, something not encompassed in 'calling' itself. God's call is his summons, which comes with all the power of his address and tailored for the individual." My take on the relationship between effectual call and illumination is slightly different because I see illumination as the process, which makes the call effective. To put otherwise, the gospel call is ineffective if divine light is not turned on in the hearer's heart because the hearer would remain in the domain of darkness, where the god of this world blinds the minds of the unbelievers (2 Cor 4:4). Without the light of new creation to renew our hearts and the inner testimony of the Spirit in illumination, the person would not hear and respond to the Word of God's call.

23. Richard A. Muller, *Dictionary of Latin and Greek Theological Terms: Drawn Principally from Protestant Scholastic Theology* (Grand Rapids: Baker, 1985), 259

24. C. E. B. Cranfield, *The Epistle to the Romans*, ICC (Edinburgh: T. & T. Clark, 1975), 1:433, for example, points out, "[Paul] may perhaps have felt that ἐδόξασεν covered sanctification a beginning of glorification (cf. 2 Cor 3.18—μεταμορφούμεθα ἀπὸ δόξης εἰς δόξαν, and also the way in which—if our interpretation was right—the words συμμόρφους τῆς εἰκόνος τοῦ υἱοῦ αὐτοῦ in v. 29 referred not only to conformity to Christ's glory hereafter but also to being conformed to

called to being justified in the verse requires regeneration, a begetting of a person with justifying faith (*fides iustificans*) in Christ.[25]

The question is, Does faith or regeneration come first in union with Christ? Faith is the cognitive effect of illumination, arising from the knowledge of God's glory in Christ, and regeneration is the cardiac effect of illumination, the renewal of our heart and mind in Christ. To have faith we need a new heart and mind in Christ, but to be in Christ, we need faith. So, which is first? Regeneration and faith, I argue, happen simultaneously in Christ because the two mutually affect one another, when a person hears the gospel call through the economy of illumination. The initial lighting of the economy of illumination produces "true faith," which the Heidelberg Catechism says, "is not only a sure knowledge by which I hold as true all that God has revealed to us in Scripture; it is also a wholehearted trust, which the Holy Spirit *creates* in me by the gospel, that God has freely granted, not only to others but to me also, forgiveness of sins, eternal righteousness, and salvation ... granted solely by Christ's merit" (emphasis mine). We cannot have true faith without regeneration, but we cannot be regenerated without true faith.[26] The two go hand in hand at the first moment of being transformed through beholding, when the triune God shines the light of the knowledge of his glory into our heart. This cognitive effect of faith and cardiac effect of regeneration form the moment of germination, when the seed of the gospel call (1 Pet 1:23) and the Spirit come together to conceive a new person with true faith in union with Christ (2 Cor 3:14, 17; 5:17).[27] The gospel is the seed of faith, containing

Him here and now in sufferings and obedience)." Harris, *Corinthians*, 316–17, also sees a similar point from Paul in the phrase "glory to glory" (2 Cor 3:18): "Justified at regeneration, believers are progressively sanctified until their final glorification at the consummation (Rom. 8:29–30; 12:2; Eph. 4:23; Col. 3:10)."

25. In Titus 3:4–7, for example, Paul reveals that God "saved us," which Paul equates to "being justified by his grace," "not because of works done by us in righteousness, but according to his own mercy, by the washing of regeneration and renewal of the Holy Spirit" (cf. 1 Cor 6:11). A person, in other words, is saved in general and justified in particular through the regeneration of the Spirit. See Robert W. Yarbrough, *The Letters to Timothy and Titus*, PNTC (Grand Rapids: Eerdmans, 2018), 548–50, who offers a comparison from the occurrences of δικαιόω and σῴζω in Paul's corpus to show, "being "justified" and "saved" can be virtually synonymous in Paul."

26. Perhaps, we can say that God engenders faith to renew the person's heart and mind, and the person with a new heart and mind sees and so receives Christ by faith (Rom 4:25).

27. Max Turner, "Holy Spirit," in *Dictionary of Jesus and the Gospels* (Downers Grove, IL: InterVarsity Press, 1992), 348, also sees a parallel and writes thus: "It is the combination of revelatory 'word' and Spirit together that is the 'living water' (cf. 1QS 4:21–22) which effects the 'birth from above.'"

the spiritual DNA structure (the narrative pattern of Jesus' life, death, and resurrection) for the elect to become who she is in Christ. The economy of illumination is the efficient cause of the germination process in union with Christ that cultivates the right condition and provides light for the seed of the gospel to take root (via the cognitive process) and grow in the heart (via the cardiac process), to form a person in the pattern of Christ by faith.

Unlike embryonic faith, which can wither and die during germination, faith conceived through the economy of illumination flourishes to sight, seeing Jesus as he is in glory (1 John 3:2; cf. John 17:24; 1 Cor 13:12). This faith is the "substance" (ὑπόστασις) of what is hoped for (Heb 11:1)[28] because it allows us to participate in covenant union with Christ, the substance of our new covenant fellowship with God (John 3:16; 5:24; 17:3). It is the faith of the elect, which arises from the effectual call. The answer to question 68 of the Westminster Larger Catechism, "*Are the elect only effectually called?*," similarly states: "All the elect, and they only, are effectually called; although others may be, and often are, outwardly called by the ministry of the Word, and have some common operations of the Spirit; who, for their willful neglect and contempt of the grace offered to them, being justly left in their unbelief, do never truly come to Jesus Christ." The elects are effectually called because the truth of the gospel concerns them and their union with Christ in God's eternal decree (Eph 1:4–10). Calvin wrote that God "illumines those whom he has predestined to salvation" (*Inst.* 3.24.17), but those whom God has not elected are not affected because illumination has no truth to affect them with.

Those who are effectually called are justified because faith, the proper response, is awakened. This faith justifies because it allows us to see Christ and ourselves no longer according to the flesh, but the Spirit (2 Cor 5:16–17). The illuminating rays of the Spirit in Christ,[29] Jonathan Edwards argued, infuse us with "spiritual sensation" that allows us to taste the sweetness

28. According to "ὑπόστασις," BDAG, 1040: Ἔστιν δὲ πίστις ἐλπιζομένων ὑπόστασις can mean, "*in faith things hoped for become realized,* or *things hoped for take on . . . reality.*" I side with the later rendering.

29. John Owen, *Causes, Ways, and Means of Understanding the Mind of God*, vol. 4 of *The Works of John Owen*, ed. William Goold (1850–1853; repr., Edinburgh: Banner of Truth, 1967), 135, believes the Spirit is the "author or principal efficient cause of" illumination. According to Cyril, "the Spirit transfers those in whom he comes and dwells into a new disposition and transforms them into newness of life" (*In Jo.* 16.7 [2.620]).

of Christ and enjoy what is ours in him.[30] Our spiritual sensations are the experience of having the eyes of our hearts opened to understand Scripture as the word of God (1 Thess 2:13), so we may see Christ as the Word of God (John 1:14).[31] The elect who see Christ as he is by faith are made right with God on account of Christ. They have a new sense of God and themselves in Christ because they see their old self in Adam crucified with Christ and their new self made alive in Christ to God (Gal 2:20). They are justified before God because God now sees them *in* Christ, who has become for them "wisdom from God, righteousness and sanctification and redemption" (1 Cor 1:30). The gospel call, which produces regeneration through new creation light, justifies a person because this light produces in a person a new heart and mind to see Christ as he is (via a cardiac process) and so receive him as he is by faith (via a cognitive process), as the one "who was delivered up for our trespasses and raised for our justification" (Rom 4:24).

Sanctification comes after and on the basis of justification. Sanctification is the renewed mind and will assimilating more and more into the object of faith. Through the ongoing lighting of the economy of illumination, God forms us with the knowledge after the image of Christ (cognitive process, Col 3:10), so Christ may be formed in us (cardiac process, Gal 4:19).[32] The cardiac and cognitive processes in the economy of illumination are reciprocal to each other in sanctification: to behold more is to become more like what we behold (1 John 3:2).[33] The economy of illumination is the process by which

30. Edwards, *Affections*, 205–6. The holy inhabitation of the Spirit, Aquinas and Owen similarly intimate, infuses a new habit or principle of grace that imparts a new disposition and affection for God, attuning and rewiring our heart and mind in Christ. With a new heart and mind in Christ, we enjoy new covenant fellowship with God, knowing and loving God as we are known and loved by God.

31. It is similar to what C. Stephen Evans, *Natural Signs and Knowledge of God: A New Look at Theistic Arguments* (Oxford: Oxford University Press, 2010), has said of natural signs, which can be external sensations (e.g., cosmological argument for God) or internal sensations (e.g., our moral structure from God) that enable us to experience God's general presence in creation.

32. Paul uses the same word, μεταμορφόω, for transformation in both 2 Cor 3:18 and Rom 12:2 to denote an inward transformation that flows out into the person's life.

33. Although according to David G. Peterson, *Possessed by God: A New Testament Theology of Sanctification and Holiness*, NSBT (Downers Grove, IL: InterVarsity, 1995), the main focus of the New Testament is on "positional sanctification," there are places where the process of sanctification is also stressed. For the NT view on the process of sanctification, see 1 Thess 5:23 and 2 Thess 2:13, along with these verses the commentaries from Jeffrey A. D. Weima, *1–2 Thessalonians*, BECNT (Grand Rapids: Baker Academic, 2014), 417–20; F. F. Bruce, *1 & 2 Thessalonians*, WBC 45 (Waco: Word Books, 1982), 129, 191, and Charles A. Wanamaker, *The Epistles to the Thessalonians*,

God sanctifies us by unveiling us to Christ from glory to glory, so we may be transformed into his image from glory to glory (2 Cor 3:18).

Finally, God glorifies and perfects us through the ongoing lighting of the economy of illumination because God unveils us to behold Christ as he is in *glory*, when beholding Christ by faith dimly in the mirror of Scripture turns into sight. In the light of glory (*lumen gloria*), believers not only behold and enjoy "unending fellowship" with God in Christ (see Gregory of Nyssa; John 17:22–24),[34] but also share in the light of Christ and become as he is for we see him as he is (1 John 3:2; cf. Col 3:3–4; Rom 8:18–19; 1 Cor 13:12; Phil 3:21).[35] So, the initial and ongoing lighting from the economy of illumination brings us from faith to faith (Rom 1:17), from divine faith (*fides divina*) engendered by God to actualization of faith (*actus fidei*) through God (Phil 1:6), the moment when faith turns to sight (1 John 3:2),[36] by transforming and perfecting us in contemplative union with Christ for deeper and deeper communion with God.

In contemplative union with Christ, we behold Christ as the object of our knowledge and love, so Christ dwells in us as "the known in the knower and the loved in the lover" (*ST* I, q. 43, a.3, *resp.*), and we are united to him (the object of our knowledge and love) through knowing and loving him. In beholding Christ as the object of our knowledge and love, we come deeper into communion with God because we come to share God's mind and will in the Son through the Spirit. We share the mind of God because we see what God sees in the Son from eternity, and we share the will of God because we love the Son whom God loves in the Spirit from eternity. The economy of illumination is the dual process by which God unveils us to behold (cognitive process) and to be transformed (cardiac process) into the image of Christ

---

NIGTC (Grand Rapids: Eerdmans, 1990), 266–67. The process is through sanctified believing in the truth (2 Thess 2:13) and sanctified living in response to the truth (1 Thess 5:13), living more and more to the truth that they were called to and beheld in the gospel.

34. G. K. Beale, *The Book of Revelation*, NIGTC (Grand Rapids: Eerdmans, 1999), 1120. Concerning the fulfillment of all things in Christ, John said, "night will be no more. They will need no light of lamp or sun, for the Lord God will be their light, and they will reign forever and ever" (Rev 22:5). And Habakkuk said similarly to Isaiah, "the earth will be filled with the knowledge of the glory of the Lord as the waters cover the sea" (Hab 2:14; cf. Isa 11:9).

35. As Owen writes, "The true nature of saving illumination is this, that it gives the mind such a direct intuitive insight and prospect into spiritual things as that, in their own spiritual nature, they suit, please, and satisfy it, so that it is transformed into them, cast into the mould of them, and rests in them, Rom. vi. 17, xii. 2; 1 Cor. ii. 13–15; 2 Cor. iii. 18, iv. 6" (*Works* 3:238).

36. Muller, *Latin and Greek*, 21–23, 116.

from glory to glory because we come to see and receive from one spiritual blessing to another what God desires to give and communicate to us in the Son through the Spirit, the blessings of regeneration, justification, sanctification, and glorification. The economy of illumination stretches us into unending glory, drawing us into ever-increasing closeness with God in Christ, but always at a distance, neither absorbed nor mixed into God. The beholder never becomes the beheld in essence, but only in likeness from glory to glory.

PUTTING ON AND WORKING OUT THE LIFE OF LIGHT IN GOD

God is the one who illumines us in Christ through the Spirit from glory to glory, but we are not passive in the process. We are called to participatory actions, to come to light, put on light, work out light, and become a light of the light (John 3:21; Gal 3:27; Phil 2:12; 1 John 1:7). We participate in God's concerted action in the economy of illumination by reading, praying, obeying, partaking, and singing Scripture. In these actions, we participate in the result of God's concerted action to unveil, shine light, and transform us into light. We perform all these actions with God's "energy that ... powerfully works within" us (Col 1:29). So, in the end, we confess and acknowledge, "O LORD, ... you have indeed done for us all our works" (Isa 26:12) because we perform all our actions in and through God's action working in us both to will and to act (Phil 2:13).

We perform these actions of faith with our body, so we may gain a heart and mind of Christ, the wisdom of God (1 Cor 1:24; Col 2:3). To perform and embody faith is messy and even gray at times, but it yields "a fuller and greater illumination" and understanding in the end (*Haer.* 4.29.1; 4.20.5; 4.38.3). Take Rahab, for example, who embodied faith with her questionable action in a thorny situation (Heb 11:31). A prostitute faced with a choice between her people and foreign spies. She chose the spies and lied to the authorities (Josh 2:10). As unorthodox as her action may be, it was her enactment of faith. Her act of faith made her right with God (Jas 2:25; Heb 11:31), permitted her to behold the power of God (Josh 6:20–21), and allowed her to experience the salvation of God (Josh 6:22–23; Matt 1:5). Rahab had heard of the Lord and his mighty deeds in Egypt (Josh 2:10–11), but now she saw for herself and experienced God by what she had done (Josh 6:20–25). To embody faith yields a deeper and more personal understanding of faith because to embody is to flesh out the details, make a choice, and get involved with our whole being, so we may participate in the truth of what we have heard and behold the reality of this truth personally.

Let us now consider how the embodiment of faith in the actions of reading, praying, obeying, partaking, and singing Scripture allow us to participate in God's concerted action of light. Our embodiment of faith in the economy of illumination is a process from knowledge to transformation and back. To understand and enact God's word requires transformation. We need to change our old ways of thinking and doing to follow Christ and conform our hearts, minds, and actions to the logic of the gospel: the first will be last (Matt 20:16) and power made perfect in weakness (2 Cor 12:9). As we change, we will see more; as we see more, we will change more. We may not always know how to read, pray, obey, partake, and sing Scripture as we enter the valley of the shadow of death (Ps 23:4), but we will come out of it more illumined, knowing that God is closer, more awesome, and greater than what we have thought or imagined. These actions of ours in light intertwine and mutually affect each other in contemplating God in Christ through the Spirit. But for the sake of clarity, let us consider them one by one.

BEING ILLUMINED IN READING SCRIPTURE

To perform faith, we need a script. The script, which God gives, to perform in the theater of his glory is the Bible. The Bible is the word of God,[37] breathed out into human languages, God speaking his Son through his Spirit who moved the prophets and apostles to put God's word into the written form of Scripture (1 Cor 2:12–13; 2 Tim 3:16; 2 Pet 1:21).[38] God uses the Bible to speak, call, and make covenant with us.[39] We hear God speak and call us in the Bible

37. "The Bible," Kevin J. Vanhoozer, *Remythologizing Theology: Divine Action, Passion, and Authorship* (Cambridge: Cambridge University Press, 2010), 208, writes, "is God's word (i.e., a triune communicative work) because the ultimate speaking voice in Scripture is God's, but this no more makes God an attribute of Scripture than of a burning bush. The speaking subject is in, but not exhausted by, the speech act." Fred Sanders, *The Deep Things of God: How the Trinity Changes Everything*, 2nd ed. (Wheaton, IL: Crossway, 2017), 202, adds, "Trinitarian inspiration of the text underwrites Trinitarian encounter through the text."

38. When Jesus was on earth, for example, he spoke the word of God in the word of man because he is fully man and fully God (John 7:16; 8:26–28; 12:49; 14:10, 24; 17:8). Jean-Luc Marion, *God without Being* 2nd ed. (Chicago: University of Chicago Press, 2012), 142, shows that human language can speak the unspeakable because the triune God has ordained it in the incarnation of the Word.

39. See John Webster, *Holy Scripture: A Dogmatic Sketch* (Cambridge: Cambridge University Press, 2003), 32, who presents Scripture as merely the instrumental means of God for covenant

through the economy of illumination. Reading the Bible is our participatory action in God's concerted action of light because we participate in God's speaking presence. "'God is present where God speaks, and God's saving communication is the modality of God's being with God's people.'"[40] If the Bible is the word of God, then to read the Bible is to attend to the speaking presence of God, hearing God speak *to* us in Christ through the Spirit.[41] This way of reading, however, goes against the grain of certain circles in biblical studies.

According to John H. Walton, for example, "the Bible is written *for* us (indeed, for everyone), it is not written *to* us. In its context, it is not communicated in our language; it is not addressed to our culture; it does not anticipate the questions about the world and its operations that stem from our modern situations and issues."[42] Since the Bible is not written directly to us and our context, we should first understand the message of the Bible to its intended readers before we apply it to our situation today. Walton's concern is important to keep in mind: "If we read modern ideas into the text, we skirt the authority of the text and in effect compromise it, arrogating authority to ourselves and our ideas. This is especially true when we interpret the text as if it is making reference to modern science, of which the author and audience had no knowledge. The text cannot mean what it never meant."[43] Walton wants us to avoid an eisegesis of Scripture, putting our modern ideas and agendas into the text. A proper

---

fellowship; and Timothy Ward, *Words of Life: Scripture as the Living and Active Word of God* (Downers Grove, IL: InterVarsity, 2009), 76–77, who balances Webster's position by affirming that Scripture is the word of God: "An 'instrument' for the declaration of a covenant by the covenant-making God of Scripture will inevitably share in some of the 'nature' and 'properties' of that God." I take the view that Scripture *is* the word of God, and we hear God speak his word in Scripture, when we are illumined by God.

40. Quoted in Vanhoozer, *Remythologizing Theology*, 238. "Revelation," John Webster, "Perfection and participation," in *The Analogy of Being: Invention of the Antichrist or Wisdom of God*, ed. Thomas J. White (Grand Rapids: Eerdmans, 2011), 382, would add, "is God's communicative and intelligible presence, and this presence disciples theological reason, commanding its attention and directing it to the place where God's majestic condescension is to be found: in the external works of God."

41. According to J. Todd Billings, *The Word of God for the People of God: An Entryway to the Theological Interpretation of Scripture* (Grand Rapids: Eerdmans, 2010), xiii, Christians "are people who interpret Scripture 'in Christ,' as those united to the living Christ by the Holy Spirit's mediation and power."

42. John H. Walton, *The Lost World of Adam and Eve: Genesis 2–3 and the Human Origins Debate* (Downers Grove, IL: IVP Academic, 2015), 19 (emphasis mine).

43. Walton, *The Lost World*, 19.

exegesis of the text would be first to understand what the text meant to its intended readers in the original context and then see how the message of the text applies for us today.

What Walton laid out is necessary, but not sufficient for reading Scripture[44] because it leaves out the speaking presence of the divine Author and so leaves the meaning and application of Scripture for modern readers to figure out on their own.[45] The meaning and application of Scripture, I argue, rest on

44. That is why Peter Stuhlmacher, *Biblische Theologie und Evangelium* (Tübingen: Mohr Siebeck, 2002), 164, argues that historical critical exegesis is not enough to understand the spiritual depth of the gospel message: "Bei der biblischen Exegese bleibt die methodisch überlegte historische Kritik in Geltung, weil und insofern sie dazu befähigt, den Ursprungssinn des biblischen Schriftzeugnisses zu erschließen. Aber sie is kein Instanz, auch noch die geistliche Tiefendimension und Tragweite dieses Schriftzeugnisses zu beurteilen." To be sure, he is not arguing that historical critical exegesis does not have a place in the proper understanding of the gospel; only that historical critical exegesis is not the key to faith, but a human means that should be placed in the "service of faith." What Stuhlmacher is pointing out is the proper understanding of the gospel requires the interpreter to accept and obey it as God's word: "Evangelium in seiner biblisch gefüllten Sprachgestalt gemäß 1Thess 2,13 als Wort Gottes anzunehmen und ihm gehorsam auf den Grund zu gehen" (Stuhlmacher, *Biblische Theologie*, 165–66). Thus only interpreters in the body of Christ could have a proper understanding of Scripture by virtue of the gift of the Spirit (Stuhlmacher, *Biblische Theologie*, 165). The gift of the Spirit enables interpreters to know the mystery that has been disclosed in Christ and what they have in him: "Kraft der Gabe des Geistes (den sie alle in der Taufe empfangen haben, vgl. 1Kor 12,13) gewinnen die Glaubenden Einsicht in die Geheimnisse der Offenbarung und können ermessen, was es mit den ihnen von Gott in Christus geschenkten Gnadengaben auf sich hat" (Stuhlmacher, *Biblische Theologie*, 158). This spiritual knowledge from the Spirit is deepened in conversation and mutual encouragement of brothers and sisters within the community of believers: "Die geistliche Erkenntnis hat ihren natürlichen Ort in der Gemeinschaft der Glaubenden und gedeiht am besten per mutuum colloquium et consolationem fratrum" (Stuhlmacher, *Biblische Theologie*, 165).

45. In Walton's view, the text seems like an artifact, where we excavate the meaning of the text by decoding the structure and wording of the text in its original language and through uncovering the parallels of the text to other ancient texts and neighboring cultures in its original context. Language also seems to serve only as a function of information transferring. But to limit language in this way would go against the multi-functional nature of language. Walton's take on language reminds me of the younger Ludwig Wittgenstein in *Tractatus Logico-Philosophicus*. The young Wittgenstein believed that words and syntax offer a logical snapshot of the state of affairs in the world, so we are to decipher words and syntax to get the meaning they are referring to. In *Philosophical Investigations*, 4th ed., trans. G. E. M. Anscombe, et al. (Oxford: Blackwell Publishing, 2009), Wittgenstein shifted from this picture theory view of meaning in language to a "use" theory of meaning in language. He coined the term, "language game," to illustrate that there are a variety of ways in which we use language in the various activities of life. In this later work, he offers a list of language games, which I summarize here: making a request; making a promise, believing a promise; giving a lecture, asking questions in a lecture; coming up with a joke, telling a joke; giving orders, obeying orders; describing and prescribing something; creating a story, telling and acting it out; instructing a child; proposing a hypothesis; translating one language to another, singing, worshiping, praying, and the list goes on (Wittgenstein, *Investigations*, 15). However, if there is a primary function of language for God the divine Author of Scripture, then I believe it is not to transfer information, but to make covenant with us.

God who speaks to us in Scripture[46] and makes us alive in Christ to hear him speak (John 6:45; 2 Cor 4:6; 5:16–17).[47] The goal of reading Scripture is to participate in God's speaking presence—to be illumined by God and hear him speak to us in the Son (Eph 4:20–21; cf. Isa 54:13; John 6:45; Matt 23:10) through the presence of the Spirit (1 John 2:27; cf. John 14:26; 15:26; 16:12–15; 1 Thess 4:9). In reading Scripture, we are not left to ourselves with our exegetical tools and methods to figure out what Scripture meant and how it should be applied to our situation today. We read Scripture to hear God speak to us.

In Scripture, God speaks truth directly to us because the truth of Scripture is *about* us. Christians are in the story of Adam and the story of Christ: we all died in Adam by virtue of sin and are made alive in Christ by faith (1 Cor 15:22; Rom 5:14; 8:11; Eph 2:5; Col 2:13). In Christ, we are the intended audience of Scripture because Scripture is about us. To properly exegete Scripture, which bears witness to Christ (John 5:39; cf. Luke 24:27, 44), is also to see ourselves in the story of Christ because God chose us in Christ before the foundation of the world (Eph 1:3–14). In his story, we should see our story, our whole existence in him, because God has chosen us in Christ who came in the fullness of time to live, die, and rise again for us.

But how would we see ourselves in a particular story, such as the one with the Samaritan woman at the well (John 4)? The insight of Balthasar is worth reading,

> To be sure, Jesus addresses a particular Samaritan woman at the well, but, at the same time, in her, he also addresses every sinner, woman or man. When Jesus sits, tired, at the well's edge, it is not for this one person alone: "quaerens *me* sedisti lassus"! Therefore it is not a mere

46. In general hermeneutics, George Steiner, *Real Presences* (Chicago: University of Chicago Press, 1989), 3, puts "forward the argument that the experience of aesthetic meaning in particular, that of literature, of the arts, of musical form, infers the necessary possibility of this 'real presence' of God." In his book *Is There a Meaning in This Text?*, Vanhoozer offers a Christian theological counterpart of Steiner's book on general hermeneutics and argues against the postmodern sentiment of the death of the author. Instead, he believes that the divine Author of Scripture is alive and well, and it is because of his presence that there is meaning in this text (Kevin J. Vanhoozer, *Is There a Meaning in This Text?: The Bible, the Reader, and the Morality of Literary Knowledge* [Grand Rapids: Zondervan, 1998], 198–99).

47. To be made in God's image means that we are "communicative agents in covenantal relations" (Vanhoozer, *Meaning*, 6). Hans Urs von Balthasar, *Prayer*, trans. Graham Harrison (San Francisco: Ignatius Press, 1986), 22–23, similarly said, "Man was created to be a hearer of the word, and it is in responding to the word that he attains his true dignity. His innermost constitution has been designed for dialogue."

> "pious exercise" when, in spirit, I put myself beside this woman and enter into her role. Not only may I play this part: I must play it, for I have long been involved in this dialogue without being consulted. I am this dried-up soul, running after the earthly water every day because it has lost its grasp of the heavenly water it is really seeking. Like her I give the same obtuse, groping response to the offer of the eternal wellspring; in the end, like her, I have to be pierced by the Word as it wrings from me the confession of sin. And even then I cannot make this confession in plain language; it has to be supplemented by the grace of the eternal Word and Judge, which—so incomprehensible is his mercy!—actually justifies me and puts me in the right: "You are right in saying, 'I have no husband'; for you have had five husbands, and he whom you now have is not your husband; this you said truly" (Jn 4:17–18). So it is not at all enough to see the dialogues and encounters presented in the gospel as mere "examples", like the instances of valor in a heroic tale, which a boy reads and feels inspired to emulate. For the Word which became flesh at that particular point in order to speak to us, on whatever particular occasion he addresses us, is concerned with every particular, unique occasion; in addressing this repentant sinner he addresses every sinner; in speaking to this woman listening at his feet he is speaking to every listener. Since it is God who is speaking, there can be no historical distance from his word; hence too our attitude to it cannot be merely historical. Instead there is that utter directness which confronted those who met him on the roads of Palestine: "Follow me!", "Go and sin no more!", "Peace be with you!"[48]

The Samaritan woman is a concrete-specific person in history, but she represents us and the way God speaks to us in Christ. To read ourselves into her story is not to put our ideas and agendas into it, but to see ourselves in her as a human experience and hear God addressing us in her concrete-specific situation with the universal truth of his word because the word of God is not bound by space and time, but speaks to his people always, everywhere.[49]

---

48. Balthasar, *Prayer*, 17–18.

49. If the word of God in Scripture is eternal, then should we discard the historical aspect of Scripture? By no means. On the contrary, to understand ourselves and hear God speak to us in the biblical narrative is to attend to the *literal sense* of the text. The *literal sense* is what God intends to say and do by the way he puts his words together in the text in a particular context

In reading Scripture, we hear God speak to us, illumined through the concrete-specific events and people in history to the truth of who God is to us, caught up in the world of the text as our world made new in Jesus Christ.

BEING ILLUMINED IN PRAYING SCRIPTURE

Prayer is another participatory action in the concerted action of God through the economy of illumination. In prayer, we participate in the prayer of God and are illumined to who we are in God. Prayer is faith, awakened by the gospel and the Spirit in Christ, seeking God for further understanding.[50] We cannot know and be illumined to God without prayer. To pray, Clement of Alexandria said, is to relate rightly to God who gives us light to his "eternal rest" (*Paed.* 1.13.102). Prayer involves reading and listening to the words of God in Scripture, so we can learn to speak well and relate properly to God with the words of Scripture. As children learn to speak and relate to others by listening to their parents speak and relate to them, we learn to speak and relate to God by listening to God speak and relate to us in Scripture.

Prayer is not a monologue, but a dialogical union with Christ[51] who dwells in our hearts by faith (*Conf.* 10.40.65; cf. *Mag.* 11.38; Eph 3:17).[52] In prayer, we come into communication with the Father in the Son because the Son has made a place in himself for us in heaven through his death and resurrection (John 14:2–3, 6, 23; Heb 10:20). Through prayer, we come and stand in the place of the Son to speak to the Father, joining the prayer of the Son through the Spirit of adoption (Rom 8:14–15; Gal 4:6), "Our Father in heaven, hallowed be

---

of history (Kevin Vanhoozer, "Augustinian Inerrancy: Literary Meaning, Literal Truth, and Literate Interpretation in the Economy of Biblical Discourse," in *Five Views on Biblical Inerrancy* [Grand Rapids: Zondervan, 2013], 220).

50. Karl Barth, *Anselm: Fides Quaerens Intellectum*, trans. Ian W. Robertson (Virginia: John Knox Press, 1960), 101–2.

51. Prayer is union because we pray in the name of Jesus (John 14:13–14; 15:16; 16:23–26). Brown, *John*, 636, writes, "A Christian prays in Jesus' name in the sense that he is in union with Jesus. ... because the Christian is in union with Jesus and Jesus is in union with the Father, there can be no doubt that the Christian's requests will be granted. ... the requests of the Christians are now no longer thought of as requests concerning the petty things of life—they are requests of such a nature that when they are granted the Father is glorified in the Son" (13).

52. From the desert fathers and mothers, Henri Nouwen, *The Way of the Heart: The Spirituality of the Desert Fathers and Mothers* (New York: HarperOne, 1981), 76, learned: "Prayer is standing in the presence of God with the mind in the heart; that is, at that point of being where there are no divisions or distinctions and there the great encounter takes place. There heart speaks to heart, because there we stand before the face of the Lord, all seeing, within us."

your name" (Matt 6:9).[53] Prayer illumines and "opens [us] up to an eternal Trinitarian vista. There is always already a conversation going on among Father, Son, and Holy Spirit. When we pray, we are joining that conversation. We have been invited to call on God as Father, invited by a Spirit of sonship that cries out, 'Abba, Father,' as the eternal Son does."[54]

Prayer is our proper posture and response to the concerted action of God in the economy of illumination. Pride, Augustine said, blinds us from God, but humility is the balm and medicine for the blindness of pride because humility allows us to acknowledge and see our blindness and our need for God (*Trin.* 8.4.7). To pray is to practice humility, which illumines us to see that there is nothing that we have, which we did not receive, even our very self (1 Cor 4:7).[55] To pray is to listen, receive the word of God, trust it as truth, and accept it as wisdom. To listen is to love because it is to attend to what God has to say with care, "cherishing every comma and semicolon, relishing the oddness of this preposition, delighting in the surprising placement of this noun."[56] Prayers open our hearts to hear, so we may receive from God what is ours in Christ through his words in Scripture by the Spirit (Eph 1:18–19).

Lastly, prayer illumines us to who we are in Christ: a *prayer*. The author of Hebrews reveals that Jesus, our High Priest who lives forever, always prays for us (Heb 7:23–25). So, we are in prayer, even when we are not praying, because we are always in the prayer of God. In Romans 8, the intercessions of the Spirit in verses 26–27 and the Son in verse 34b encapsulate our whole existence:

---

53. N. T. Wright, "The Lord's Prayer as a Paradigm of Christian Prayer," in *Into God's Presence: Prayer in the New Testament* (Grand Rapids: Eerdmans, 2001), 132, writes, "For the Lord's Prayer is ... an invitation to share in the prayer-life of Jesus himself. ... with trinitarian perspective—the Lord's Prayer becomes an invitation to share in the *divine* life itself. ... the baptized and believing Christian is (1) incorporated into the inner life of the triune God *and* (2) intended not just to believe that this is the case, but actually to experience it," and again, in "the Lord's Prayer we are meeting the beginnings of trinitarian soteriology: the Son is inviting his followers to share the intimacy of his own life with the Father."

54. Sanders, *Deep Things*, 223. "Prayer," Eugene H. Peterson, *Tell It Slant: A Conversation on the Language of Jesus in His Stories and Prayers* (Grand Rapids: Eerdmans, 2008), 165, similarly writes, prayer "is the language of the Trinity, intimately personal language. When we pray, we embrace the language of Jesus as our language."

55. There are many ways to pray; being silent, listening, asking, talking, and crying are a few forms of prayer, but in all forms of prayer is a sort of struggle to let God be God.

56. Eugene H. Peterson, *Eat This Book: A Conversation in the Art of Spiritual Reading* (Grand Rapids: Eerdmans, 2006), 55. See also Scott R. Swain, *Trinity, Revelation, and Reading* (London: Bloomsbury, 2011), 127–28.

> We know that all things work together for good for those who love God, who are called according to his purpose. For those whom he foreknew he also predestined to be conformed to the image of his Son, in order that he might be the firstborn within a large family. And those whom he predestined he also called; and those whom he called he also justified; and those whom he justified he also glorified. What then are we to say about these things? If God is for us, who is against us? He who did not withhold his own Son, but gave him up for all of us, will he not with him also give us everything else? Who will bring any charge against God's elect? It is God who justifies. Who is to condemn? (Rom 8:28–34a NRSV)

The *inclusio*, formed by the prayers of the Spirit and the Son "for us," suggests that our whole life is in God's prayer (Luke 22:31–32).[57] From before our first breath and long after our last on this side of glory, we live in the prayer of God who knows and loves us from eternity to eternity. Since God always prays for us, we are called to participate and "pray without ceasing" (1 Thess 5:17 NRSV). When we pray, we participate in the dialogue of the Trinity (Eph 6:18) and are illumined and become who we are, people who pray in, with, and like Christ. Prayer is the heart of who we are in Christ.

BEING ILLUMINED IN OBEYING SCRIPTURE

To obey is to be illumined, "understanding in action."[58] George Steiner argues that a consummate interpreter is not a critic, but a performer.[59] The performer embodies the work, so she feels, experiences, and participates in the meaning of the work more immediately and profoundly than the critic. To embody requires a person to ingest the work with her mind, know it by heart, and understand it personally and tacitly with her body through

---

57. To drive this point home, Paul asked, "Who shall separate us from the love of Christ? Shall tribulation, or distress, or persecution, or famine, or nakedness, or danger, or sword?" (Rom 8:35). Paul's answer further solidifies his rhetorical questions: "For I am sure that neither death nor life, nor angels nor rulers, nor things present nor things to come, nor powers, nor height nor depth, nor anything else in all creation, will be able to separate us from the love of God in Christ Jesus our Lord" (Rom 8:38–39).

58. Steiner, *Real Presences*, 7–8.

59. "The 'dramatic critic' *par excellence* is the actor and the producer who, with and through the actor, tests and carries out the potentialities of meaning in the play" (George Steiner, *Real Presences* [Chicago: University of Chicago Press, 1989], 8).

movements and actions.[60] In obedience, likewise, we are illumined more profoundly and personally to God's love and truth, which surpass understanding (John 17:3; Eph 3:19), because we enact God's truth with our very being—heart, mind, and body. To obey is to walk by the Spirit, so we may bear the fruit of the Spirit, a deeper, more tacit, and personal sense and experience of truth, love, joy, peace, patience, kindness, goodness, faithfulness, gentleness, and self-control (Gal 5:22–23; cf. John 15:5, 7–8). Unlike an actor who is required to act out and become who he is not on stage, Christians are called to act out and become who we are in Christ on the stage of the world.

To follow Jesus is to be illumined and conformed to the will and mind of God because "to follow the light is to perceive [and reflect] the light" (*Haer.* 4.14.1; 4.29.1; 4.20.5; 4.38.3). In Scripture, truth is not abstract, but personal and covenantal because God is truth, and we know God in covenant fellowship. Jesus said, "I am ... the truth" (John 14:6). We "learned Christ ... as the truth is in Jesus" by putting off our "old self" to renew our "minds" and put on our "new self" in Christ (Eph 4:20–24). To know Christ who is truth, we need to obey him and work out what is ours in him, our truth. The knowledge that God desires to illumine us to in Scripture is not merely cognitive, but tacit and personal. It is a personal and tacit knowledge that we receive from God over time through the practice and habits of faith. What we do with our body affects what we know with our hearts and minds (recall Irenaeus and Tertullian in chapter 3). Without picking up our cross to follow Christ, we would not be illumined and experience the love, power, and wisdom of God for ourselves in the cross of Jesus Christ. As Paul said in Phil 3:8–10 that he suffered the loss of all things, so that he "may gain Christ" and "know him and the power of His resurrection and the fellowship of His sufferings" (NASB).

BEING ILLUMINED IN PARTAKING SCRIPTURE

In *On Christian Teaching* 3.9.13, Augustine describes the eucharist and baptism as "sacred signs" that illumine us to partake in God's invisible grace.[61] Jesus instituted the sacraments as signs to point and enable us to taste

---

60. Steiner writes, "To learn by heart is to afford the text or music an indwelling clarity and life-force. ... What we know by heart becomes an agency in our consciousness, a 'pace-maker' in the growth and vital complication of our identity" (Steiner, *Real Presences*, 9).

61. "Sacraments," in *Augustine through the Ages: An Encyclopedia*, ed. Allan D. Fitzgerald (Grand Rapids: Eerdmans, 1999), 741.

the reality of our life hidden with him in God (1 Cor 11:24; Matt 28:18–20).[62] The sacraments point us to this reality in the event of the cross and resurrection of Jesus Christ.

The event of the cross and resurrection is a critical part of the gospel narrative, and so our narrative identity. Why do certain events make it into the narrative of history while others do not? Paul Ricoeur argues that certain "events, which are said to be 'epoch-making,' draw their specific meaning from their capacity to found or reinforce the community's consciousness of its identity, its narrative identity, as well as the identity of its members."[63] These events form the narrative identity of the community through memory; the community that continues to commemorate these events is formed by them. To remember our past is to know who we are, our identity.[64]

> As Hannah Arendt points out, the meaning of human existence is not just the power to change or master the world, but also the ability to be remembered and recollected in narrative discourse, to be *memorable*. These existential and historical implications of narrativity are very far-reaching, for they determine what is to be "preserved" and rendered "permanent" in a culture's sense of its past, of its own "identity."[65]

The church has preserved, or perhaps been preserved by, the event of the cross and resurrection, which has formed her identity from the beginning.[66] Understanding her past allows her to project herself meaningfully into the

---

62. I think Augustine's concept of signs is reminiscent of Thomas Reid's concept of "natural signs." According to C. Stephen Evans, *Natural Signs and Knowledge of God: A New Look at Theistic Arguments* (Oxford: Oxford University Press, 2010), 34, "natural sign for Reid is something … that has a causal connection (in the 'loose' sense of causality) 'upstream' with what the sign signifies and also plays a causal role (again in the loose sense) 'downstream' in generating a characteristic judgement."

63. Paul Ricoeur, *Time and Narrative*, trans. Kathleen McLaughlin Blamey and David Pellauer [Chicago: University of Chicago Press, 1984–1988], 3:187.

64. Memory is essential to identity because, without memory, we would forget who we are. Augustine connected our memory with our self: "O my God, profound, infinite complexity, what a great faculty memory is, how awesome a mystery! It is the mind, and this is nothing other than my very self" (*Conf.* 10.17.26).

65. Richard Kearney, *On Paul Ricoeur: The Owl of Minerva* (Burlington, VT: Ashgate, 2004), 127–28.

66. See Michael P. Jensen, *Martyrdom and Identity: The Self on Trial* (London: T. & T. Clark, 2010), who argues that the cross and martyrdom were closely connected to the identity of the early Christians.

future.[67] So in remembering Christ in the Eucharist, the church projects herself to her future in him: "For as often as you eat this bread and drink the cup, you proclaim the Lord's death until he comes" (1 Cor 11:26).[68]

To be illumined in the Eucharist is to allow the elements to transcend themselves and point us to their reference, the real presence of Jesus Christ, on whom we feed for life with God.[69] It is in hearing the words, "Take and eat; this is my body," that we come to *remember* (Matt 26:26b); it is in seeing the words enacted, "took the bread and blessed and broke it and gave it," that the eyes of our hearts are opened to understand how Jesus was broken and poured out for us (Luke 24:30). And it is in partaking the elements, "drink of it" and "take and eat," that we are conscious of our life hidden with Christ in God (Col 3:3), desiring and waiting for our life to be revealed with Christ in glory at the great banquet in God's kingdom (Col 3:4; Matt 26:29; Rev 19:7–9). By growing in these activities with our heart, mind, and body, the *imago Dei* within us is refashioned by God: "Let me remember you, let me understand you, let me love you. Increase these things in me until you refashion me entirely" (*Trin.* 15.28.51). When we hear, see, and partake in the word of God enacted in the Eucharist, we hear the *vox Verbum Dei* again through the voice of his messenger, the pastor, the priest. We hear, see, and taste the nearness of the Word in the sacraments, and at that moment, we are reminded again and experience the reality of Jesus as Ἐμμανουήλ, God with us and now in us through the Holy Spirit.

When we undergo baptismal water, we are illumined to the reality of our union with Christ and our communion with the triune God (Matt 28:18–20).

67. Concerning the retelling of the past, Kearney, *Ricoeur*, 131, writes, "The structure of narrativity demonstrates that it is by trying to put order on our past, by retelling and recounting what has been, that we acquire an identity. … As Heidegger himself points out, the notion of 'repeating' (*Wiederholung*) the past is inseparable from the existential projection of ourselves towards our possibilities. To 'repeat' our story, to retell our history, is to recollect our horizon of possibilities in a resolution and responsible manner. In this respect, one can see how the retrospective character of narration is closely linked to the prospective horizon of the future. … narration preserves the meaning that is behind us so that we can have meaning before us. There is always *more* order in what we narrate than in what we have actually already lived; and this narrative excess (*surcroît*) of order, coherence and unity, is a prime example of the creative power of narration."

68. Grant Macaskill, *Living in Union with Christ: Paul's Gospel and Christian Moral Identity* (Grand Rapids: Baker Academic, 2019), 96, puts it this way, "Like baptism, the Lord's Supper dramatically performs the past of Jesus in a way that directs us toward his future and affirms that this future will be ours as well."

69. See Jean-Luc Marion, *God without Being* 2nd ed. (Chicago: University of Chicago Press, 2012), 151. Elements, as we have mentioned, are signs, which point us beyond themselves.

Clement of Alexandria and other patristic theologians believed baptism is illumination because we are baptized into triune Light, the name of the Father, Son, and Holy Spirit (*Paed.* 1.6.26; cf. Eph 5:13–14). Tertullian helped us see that baptismal water is indispensable to our experience of spiritual baptism because we experience the latter in the former (*Res.* 8). What we experience physically in the water allows us to sense in our heart and mind the spiritual reality of our union with Christ. "We were buried therefore with him by baptism into death, in order that, just as Christ was raised from the dead by the glory of the Father, we too might walk in newness of life" (Rom 6:4; Col 3:3). We are illumined to our life with Christ in God, awakened to our communion with the triune God, a communion of knowledge and love between the Father and Son in the Spirit from eternity.

Baptism and the eucharist are two modes of participation in the death and resurrection of Jesus Christ. The repetitive *habitus* of the Eucharist illumines us to our constant dependence on the cross and resurrection of Jesus Christ for new covenant fellowship with God. The singular experience of baptism allows us to experience "the non-identical repetition of the substitutionary self of Jesus Christ," reminding us that our life and identity in Christ come from God alone once for all (Heb 7:27; 9:12, 26; 10:10).[70]

BEING ILLUMINED IN SINGING SCRIPTURE

God calls his church out of the dead to sing because her dew, which is her song, is light that gives life. "You who dwell in the dust, awake and sing for joy! For your dew is a dew of light, and the earth will give birth to the dead" (Isa 26:19; cf. Eph 5:14). To sing Scripture to the Lord is to "be filled with the Spirit," illumined to "what the will of the Lord is" in Christ (Eph 5:17–19), because it is to have the word of Christ dwell richly in our hearts (Col 3:16–17) and participate in God's work of light by bringing light into darkness, filling fragmented time with eternity, the coherent whole of God's eternal decree to unite all things in Christ (Eph 1:10).

In Scripture, worship of God consists of every form and activity under the sun (Rom 12; 1 Cor 10:31; Deut 6:5; Matt 22:37; Luke 10:27). The language of worship, which we find most in Scripture, is singing. Singing is

70. David F. Ford, *Self and Salvation: Being Transformed* (Cambridge: Cambridge University Press, 1999), 164.

the crescendo of all the different forms of worship.[71] It is the worship language of the end of time.[72] "Then I heard what seemed to be the voice of a great multitude, like the roar of many waters and like the sound of mighty peals of thunder, crying out, 'Hallelujah'" (Rev 19:6)! It is the language of how much more, the language of inclusion, drawing an individual believer outside of herself into the community of the redeemed to sing a "new song" (Rev 5:9). In singing, the individual and community are illumined to find their voice, place, and identity in space and time before the face of the divine Other, *"remembering, taking to heart, indwelling and communicating" what God has done, is doing, and will do for us in Christ.*[73]

The confluence of different tongues from the community come together in unison to transform space and time with eternity.[74] What might have once been hostile voices, which desecrated the land with war, corruption, and lies, now harmonize to create sacred space, a sanctuary of the Spirit for the praise of God in Christ (Eph 5:15–20; cf. 2:14–18).[75] These voices redeem time, wasted and consumed with selfish pleasure, ambition, and vainglory, with "psalms and hymns and spiritual songs" to God (Eph 5:16, 19). Time is transformed by the community's word of thanks to God's Word of grace.[76] In singing, the community is free for a moment in time from sin and suffering to God and hope. The participants transcend their situation in that moment to be illumined and taste God's future promise that death and sin, which are so present and real, will be no more, but life, light, and love with God will

---

71. In the Magnificat, for example, Mary sang and poured out her soul to the Lord (Luke 1:46–55), after she believed and accepted the word of the Lord (vv. 38, 45).

72. To all eternity, we will join with all the redeemed, the heavenly hosts, and everything that has breath to sing a new song to the Lamb who was slain (Rev 5:9–14; 15:3).

73. David F. Ford, *Christian Wisdom: Desiring God and Learning in Love* (Cambridge: Cambridge University Press, 2007), 250 (emphasis original).

74. Ford, *Salvation*, 121, puts it like this, "Sounds do not have exclusive boundaries—they can blend, harmonise, resonate with each other in endless ways. In singing there can be a filling of space with sound in ways that draw more and more voices to take part, yet with no sense of crowding. It is a performance of abundance, as new voices join in with their own distinctive tones. There is an 'edgeless expansion' (Begbie), an overflow of music, in which participants have their boundaries transformed. The music is both outside and within them, and it creates new vocal, social space of community in song."

75. Reflecting on Ephesians, Ford writes, "The community is pictured being joined together ('harmonised together'—*sunarmologoumene*) into 'a holy temple,' the space which above all is filled with psalms and hymns, 'a dwelling place of God in the Spirit'" (Ford, *Salvation*, 121).

76. Ford, *Salvation*, 123.

last forevermore (Rev 21:4). To sing is to stretch ourselves toward eternity, transcending our situation and circumstance for that moment in time, to be illumined to eternity. In eternity, we will still sing because we will know more than ever the love of God—all that we are and have we owe to the love of God in Christ. "To him who sits on the throne and to the Lamb be blessing and honor and glory and might forever and ever" (Rev 5:13)!

Praise is a harmonious cry of the community to the Trinity, resembling the harmony within the Trinity, the giving and receiving of the Father and Son in the Spirit. To praise God is to enjoy fellowship with God because it allows us to receive God as we offer ourselves to God in return with praise. To praise is to breathe out with gratitude what we breathed in, a gift from God. In praising God, we pour ourselves out to God as a thank-offering to be made whole in God because our praise turns the cacophonic cries of our fragmented heart (which pulls us in every direction, tearing us apart from within) into melody in the Lord (Eph 5:20; Jer 33:11; Ps 107:22; Rom 1:21). In singing to the Lord, we find rest for our soul, filled with joy, uncontainable and inexpressible, because we are overwhelmed with God's immensity, his goodness and love that never ends everywhere we turn. All the goodness of creation no longer pulls us in multifarious directions due to sin but illumines and directs us to the goodness of God, pointing us as *signa* to the *res*, the goodness and love of God. The singing of a new song renews and perfects our nature with God's grace because it allows our hearts and minds through our mouths to participate with awe and wonder in the reality that God has made all things new in Jesus Christ, even us.

CONCLUSION

According to the Reformed tradition, we participate in Christ by faith, and faith is a gift of God through the effectual call. If we come into God through God's call, then how do we continue to be in God from glory to glory? Building on what I have said in the last chapter concerning the economy of illumination as both a cardiac and cognitive process, I focus on the reciprocal and continuous nature of this dual process to show the ongoing lighting of the economy of illumination that stretches and draws us into God from glory to glory. The cardiac and cognitive processes mutually affect each other in drawing us from faith to sight because the knowledge of God transforms us, and we are transformed with a new heart and mind in Christ to know God further in new covenant fellowship with God. The Father shines into our heart the light of new creation in the Son through the holy inhabitation of the Spirit to make us new. With a new heart and disposition, our mind and body turn to God as the object of our knowledge and love—moving our whole person (heart, mind, and body) to God as the weight of our love.

If God shines light, so we may come into light, then our coming into light involves both God's action and our actions. Our actions are in the middle voice because they are our participation in the result of God's concerted action that produces the light of his knowledge in our hearts and minds to transform us into his likeness. Our actions of reading, praying, obeying, partaking, and singing Scripture with our bodies enable our hearts and minds to experience and feel the truth of faith more (John 8:32). To experience and feel more is to be illumined to know the lordship of God more personally, tacitly, and profoundly. "[T]o those who believe in Him and follow Him," Irenaeus writes, "He grants a fuller and greater illumination of mind" (*Haer.* 4.29.1; 4.20.5; 4.38.3). In contemplative union with Christ through the economy of illumination, we are united to Christ with our whole person, heart, mind, and body, because we are one with Christ through loving, knowing, and doing what is in the mind and will of God in Christ.

CONCLUSION

"... no one knows the Son except the Father, and no one knows the Father except the Son and anyone to whom the Son chooses to reveal him."

—Matt 11:27

"No one can come to me unless the Father who sent me draws him. ... It is written in the Prophets, 'And they will all be taught by God.' Everyone who has heard and learned from the Father comes to me ..."

—John 6:44–45

From eternity, the Trinity, the Father, Son, and Spirit, "dwells in unapproachable light, whom no one has ever seen or can see" (1 Tim 6:16 ESV). In the fullness of time, the Father shines his light in the face of his Son, the radiance of his glory, through the presence of his Spirit, the ray of his light, to draw sinners into light, so we may see light. "For with you," the psalmist said, "is the fountain of life; in your light do we see light" (Ps 36:9 ESV). By participating in God who is light, we are illumined to see God in light because, outside of God, there is only darkness. That's why patristic and medieval theologians often wed illumination and participation together to ponder our life with God. Still, contemporary theology has put the two themes asunder, separating discussion on participation from illumination. My book came out of this divorce because I believe contemporary discussions on these themes have left something on the table.

SEVEN THESES: THE BROAD STROKES

The seven theses lay out the broad strokes for my book, which retrieves the teachings of theologians from the patristic to the modern era in the Orthodox, Roman Catholic, and Reformed traditions to construct a dogmatic account of the economy of illumination, an account of God, the Father, personally rolling up his sleeves to bring us from darkness to light with his two hands, God, the Son, and God, the Holy Spirit.

1. The economy of illumination is the trinitarian operations of the Father, Son, and Holy Spirit.
2. The economy of illumination is a means of participation in God.
3. The economy of illumination is a manner of participation in God.
4. The economy of illumination is a mark of participation in God.
5. The economy of illumination opens and draws us into the heart and mind of the Trinity in glory.
6. The economy of illumination produces an integral and reciprocal effect of knowledge and transformation to participants in divine light.
7. In the economy of illumination, participants are not passively receiving light but are called to work out their salvation in light.

SEVEN THESES: THE FINER POINTS

1. THE ECONOMY OF ILLUMINATION IS THE TRINITARIAN OPERATIONS OF THE FATHER, SON, AND SPIRIT.

According to Carl Trueman, Augustine has made a profound impact "on pre-Enlightenment Protestantism with respect to grace," but not so much with his doctrine of illumination because Protestant theologians have viewed illumination as the operation of the Spirit rather than Christ, our divine teacher.[1] In chapter 6, I argued that, in the case of John Calvin, it was not so much a shift as it was a development of Augustine's divine illumination and an emphasis on the Spirit's work to unite us to Christ, our inner teacher, who "daily illuminates us by his doctrine and his Spirit" (*Comm. Mal.* 4:2). This emphasis on the Spirit, however, has become so pronounced in our theological landscape that Reformed theology now identifies illumination

1. Carl R. Trueman, "Illumination," in *Dictionary for Theological Interpretation of the Bible*, ed. Kevin J. Vanhoozer (Grand Rapids: BakerAcademic, 2005), 317.

with the Spirit's internal witness to convince us of what God has revealed in Scripture. I stand firm on the Reformed understanding of illumination that, without Scripture, the Spirit has nothing to illumine us, and without the Spirit, we are blind to what Scripture reveals, but I believe there is more to be said. So in the spirit of "always reforming" (*semper reformanda*), I turn to Scripture and the early church to expand my Reformed understanding of illumination as follows:

The economy of illumination is not simply the operation of the Spirit, but the trinitarian operations of the Father, Son, and Spirit that transfer us from darkness to light. As object, light, and sight are three distinct, but inseparable components of seeing, the operations of the Father, Son, and Spirit are distinct, but inseparable in our beholding of God's glory. The Father shines in our hearts, so we may see the "image" of his glory in the Son through the "luminous presence" of the Holy Spirit from his "sight," the way the Father sees his Son from eternity. In John 6:45, Jesus said that those who come to see and believe in him have "heard and learned from the Father." What happens when we hear and learn from another person is we come to see from his perspective. To see the Son from the Father's perspective also means we see the Father himself as Jesus said, "Whoever has seen me has seen the Father" (John 14:9 ESV). Through the economy of illumination, we participate in the Father's knowledge of the Son and Son's knowledge of the Father in the Spirit[2] because "no one knows the Son except the Father, and no one knows the Father except the Son and anyone to whom the Son chooses to reveal" (Matt 11:27 ESV) and illumine through the Spirit (1 Cor 2:13).

2. *THE ECONOMY OF ILLUMINATION IS A MEANS OF PARTICIPATION IN GOD.*

As the sun brings us into its light by shining its rays on us, God brings us into his light by the economy of illumination. Aquinas said, "God comes to us by enlightening us; and we go to him by thinking of him: *come to him and be enlightened* (Ps 33:6)" (*In Ioan.* 14.6 §1945). God shines on us by giving us

2. Building on the work of Ike Miller, *Seeing in the Light: Illumination in Augustine's and Barth's Reading of John* (Downers Grove, IL: IVP Academic, 2020), 3, I argue that *the economy of illumination is "human participation [not only] in the Son's knowledge of the Father," but also in the Father's knowledge of the Son because it is seeing the Son from the perspective of the Father "by the power of the Holy Spirit."*

the gospel, and we come into his light by receiving the gospel. The act of giving and receiving, which Athanasius construed as participation in chapter 4, is easy to see with physical items. For example, a friend hands us a new book, and we open our hands to receive it. But how do we receive the gospel, which offers God himself (John 3:16), his work in Christ to reconcile us (2 Cor 5:19), and all his spiritual blessings in Christ (Eph 1:3), such as forgiveness of sin, adoption, justification, sanctification, and glorification? We receive the gospel not with our hands, but with our hearts and minds by faith, understanding, trusting, submitting, and accepting what God says and gives us in the gospel as truth and reality. No matter how bright the light of the gospel is, a spiritually blind person remains in darkness until the economy of illumination opens the eyes of his heart to see. The economy of illumination is the means of participation in God because it turns the gospel call of God into an effectual call, to call us out of the darkness in Adam to God's marvelous light in Christ (Col 1:13; 1 Pet 2:9–10). Through this economy of triune light, we are transferred from the headship of Adam to the headship of Christ, so what Christ has accomplished as our head (in his life, death, and resurrection) becomes ours by faith.

3. *THE ECONOMY OF ILLUMINATION IS A MANNER OF PARTICIPATION IN GOD.*

If effectual call through illumination brings us into covenant union with Christ by faith, then how do we continue our participation in Christ from faith to sight? The manner, in which we participate in God through union with Christ, is the economy of illumination because it unveils us continually in contemplative union with Christ for communion with God from glory to glory. "And we all, who with unveiled faces contemplate the Lord's glory, are being transformed into his image with ever-increasing glory" (2 Cor 3:18 NIV). The economy of illumination uncovers our darkness with light to unite us to Christ as a beholder is united to the object beheld through beholding, so Christ can dwell in our hearts and minds as the object of our faith, hope, and love. Our contemplative union with Christ draws us into deeper communion with God from glory to glory because, in beholding God in Christ, we love him, and in loving him in Christ, we desire to behold him more.

4. *THE ECONOMY OF ILLUMINATION IS A MARK OF PARTICIPATION IN GOD.*

There are people, relationships, and events that have left a mark on us, affecting the way we think, feel, and even live. A mark is an impression or effect something or someone has left on us. The economy of illumination is not only a means and manner by which God brings and sustains us in light but also a mark of participation in God who is light because we cannot see God outside of God, but we cannot be in God without becoming more like God. God dwells in unapproachable light because he is beyond all creaturely reality and comprehension. So, to see God is to be in God—illumined. In the presence of Jesus Christ through the Spirit, we behold the Father in the face of his Son, the radiance of his glory and the exact imprint of his essence (Heb 1:3), and are transformed into the image of his Son from glory to glory (2 Cor 3:18), conforming more and more to the heart and mind of Christ to know and love the Father more like him (1 Cor 2:16; Phil 2:5). Illumination and participation are distinct, but inseparable in communion with God. Like two sides of a coin, we cannot have one without the other in our life with God. They are interconnected because illumination is a means, a manner, and a mark of participation in God.

5. *THE ECONOMY OF ILLUMINATION OPENS AND DRAWS US INTO THE HEART AND MIND OF THE TRINITY IN GLORY.*

In his hour of glory with his eyes to heaven and his face towards the cross, Jesus said to his Father and perhaps also to remind himself of eternal life, which he has come to give those whom the Father has given him. "And this is eternal life, that they know you, the only true God, and Jesus Christ whom you have sent" (John 17:3 ESV). What is this knowledge, which Jesus said is eternal life? It's the knowledge of the Father, Son, and Spirit share in their glory. "The glory that you have given me I have given to them, that they may be one even as we are one, I in them and you in me ... I made known to them your name, and I will continue to make it known, that the love with which you have loved me may be in them, and I in them" (John 17:22–23, 26 ESV). This glory, which Jesus gives to allow us to be one with God, is the knowledge and love the Father and Son share in the Spirit from eternity. The Father fully knows and loves and is fully known and loved by the Son in the Spirit because the Father, Son, and Spirit share one essence, one mind and will. God shares his glory, so we may have communion with him, know him even as we are known by him. In communion, we participate in the ocean of knowledge and love between the Father, Son, and Spirit, who share one mind and will.

How does the economy of illumination bring us into this communion between the three persons of God who share one mind and will by nature? Does it draw us into the mind and will (essence) of God through the light of glory (Roman Catholic tradition)? Or enable us to participate in God's uncreated energies, whereby God acts in history or works in us to will and to act (Phil 2:13), so we may become like God (Orthodox tradition)? Or rather does it allow us to participate in God through the gospel, by which God communicates, offers, and brings elect sinners into covenant union with Christ for communion with God (Reformed tradition)? All three to a certain extent.

The economy of illumination allows us to participate in God's heart and mind as God *communicates* himself to us in the Son through the gospel and *moves* in our hearts and minds, both to receive and follow his Son, so he may dwell in our hearts and minds by faith as the object of our knowledge and love. God draws us into his glory by opening himself to us in the Son. As we open ourselves up to each other with our words, the Father opens himself to us with his Word. The Word became flesh and dwelt among us, opening the Father's innermost being— "his glory ... full of grace and truth" (John 1:14). "No one has ever seen God; the only God, who is at the Father's side [or heart], he has made him known" (John 1:18 ESV). In the incarnation, Jesus disclosed the heart and mind of the Father by enacting the Father's will with his word, work, and way of life (John 6:38–40). Jesus enacted and actualized the mind and will of God from eternity in the *pactum salutis* (covenant of redemption), where the Father, Son, and Spirit agreed within themselves to become God for us and appointed the Son as our covenant surety. So, the nature of our communion with God is new covenant fellowship with God, the source or principle cause of our communion is the covenant of redemption in eternity, and the substance of communion is the person and work of the Son in the history of redemption because Jesus has become the perfect effect of God's principal cause of redemption, conforming perfectly to the will of God's eternal decree in his life, death, and resurrection.

The gospel bears witness to Jesus and "a secret and hidden wisdom of God, which God decreed before the ages for our glory" (1 Cor 2:7 ESV), "things into which angels long to look" (1 Pet 1:12 ESV). But those in darkness cannot comprehend the light of the gospel because they do the will of their father, the devil (John 8:44)—who blinded their minds to keep "them from seeing the light of the gospel the glory of Christ, who is the image of God" (2 Cor 4:4 ESV). Knowledge of God is personal and relational arising from new covenant fellowship with God, so the transformation of our minds, wills, and affections are required. In the economy of illumination, the Father causes the knowledge of himself (his heart and mind) revealed objectively in the Son to be subjectively ours by opening our hearts and minds to what he is communicating in the Son through the Spirit with the gospel. God communicates his Son with the gospel, and we receive his Son into our hearts as the object of our faith through being taught by the Father in the Spirit and respond to God with our hearts, minds, and life because the economy of illumination transforms and makes our hearts and minds alight with the knowledge of his glory in the face of Jesus Christ through the gospel (2 Cor 4:6).

6. *THE ECONOMY OF ILLUMINATION PRODUCES AN INTEGRAL AND RECIPROCAL EFFECT OF KNOWLEDGE AND TRANSFORMATION TO PARTICIPANTS IN DIVINE LIGHT.*

Transformation and knowledge are integral and reciprocal to each other in the economy of illumination because the light, which God shines in our heart, is the light of new creation in Christ Jesus, "the long awaited light of the eschaton, heralding a new creation,"[3] so "receiving this light produces cognitive and cardiac effects."[4] The knowledge through illumination is the new covenant knowledge of God, which the Old Testament prophets foretold, that comes through the transformation of our hearts and minds (Jer 31:33; Ezek 11:19; 36:26) because, in Adam, our hearts were unresponsive to God, and our minds were unable to think God's thoughts (Eph 4:18). The economy of illumination is not only the initial act of God to bring us into covenantal union with Christ through the Spirit, but also the ongoing process of God to draw us into contemplative union with Christ, transforming us in the knowledge of Christ for the knowledge of God from glory to glory (2 Cor 3:18). God renews us in the knowledge of Christ (Col 3:10), and we are renewed and

3. Timothy B. Savage, *Power through Weakness: Paul's Understanding of the Christian Ministry in 2 Corinthians* (Cambridge: Cambridge University Press, 1996), 126.

4. This comment from Kevin Vanhoozer clarifies what I sought to express.

transformed to know God more because, without holiness, no one sees God (Heb 12:14). This reciprocal process between knowledge and transformation in beholding Christ goes on from one degree of glory to another until we see God face to face in glory.

7. IN THE ECONOMY OF ILLUMINATION, PARTICIPANTS ARE NOT PASSIVELY RECEIVING LIGHT BUT ARE CALLED TO WORK OUT THEIR SALVATION IN LIGHT.

While God authors and perfects our lives hidden with Christ in him (Col 3:3), we are not passive in the process but are called to participatory actions. Our actions are in the middle voice because they allow us to participate in God's concerted action in the economy of illumination. In our act of following and conforming to Christ, we are putting off our "old self" to put on our "new self, which is being renewed in knowledge after the image of its creator" (Col 3:9–10). Our bodies are as significant as our hearts and minds in the process of contemplating God in Christ. What we do with our bodies by faith allows our hearts and minds not only to see God's heart and mind in the person and work of the Son but also to understand *how* to relate to God in the Son. God is not a thing, but persons. So, to know God is to know how to relate to God who exists eternally in three persons. Knowledge of God is fellowship with God (John 17:3), so it involves a personal, tacit, and covenantal knowledge that we develop over time by doing, feeling, and forming habits of faith, hope, and love with our bodies for the sake of the light of Christ in the body of Christ.

IN CLOSING

This book began its life from the desire to understand what happens when a person is brought from darkness (our life in Adam) to light (our new life in Christ) and the transformation that ensues. As the book closes, my desire grows to what will happen when our faith becomes sight. David said, "As for me, I shall behold your face in righteousness; when I awake, I shall be satisfied with your likeness" (Ps 17:15). Similarly, John said, "They will see his face, and his name will be on their foreheads. And night will be no more. They will need no light of lamp or sun, for the Lord God will be their light" (Rev 22:3–4). Will we still need the economy of illumination for the beatific vision of God?

The beatific vision is the blessed and happy vision of God. God has made us with himself as our highest good, so we are restless and unhappy until we see him face to face. The beatific vision is this sight of God in the end, the one that we will see in the new heaven and earth, so we may become like Christ as we see him as he is (1 John 3:2; cf. Pss 17:15; 27:4; 1 Cor 13:12; Rev 22:4). Theologians from our three Christian traditions disagree on whether it is the vision of the Father or the Son, whether it is static or ever-increasing, and whether it is physical or spiritual.[5] My account of the economy of illumination implies that it is both the vision of the Father and the Son because they are one essence (so, we see the Father in the Son [image] and the Son in the Father [sight] through the Spirit [presence of light], Matt 11:27; Luke 10:22; John 14:9–11); static and ever-increasing because God's fully actual light and love never ends (1 Cor 13:8); and physical and spiritual because we will know God spiritually with our resurrected body (Rom 12:1; cf. Tertullian, *An.* 18.8). But does the economy of illumination continue to open the eyes of our hearts to behold the face of God in what Aquinas refers to as, the light of glory, *lumen gloria*? Will God continue to impart the capacity and the vision of him for all eternity? I can only conjecture that we will continue to see God's eternal glory in the "face of Jesus Christ" in the world without end because the light of God's glory will always and forever come from the lamp of the Lamb through the Spirit (Rev 21:23–24; 22:4–5; 2 Cor 4:6; 1 John 3:2). And then "the earth will be filled with the knowledge of the glory of the LORD as the waters cover the sea" (Hab 2:14). Amen.

5. See Hans Boersma, *Seeing God: The Beatific Vision in Christian Tradition* (Grand Rapids: Eerdmans, 2018); Marc Cortez, "The Body and the Beatific Vision," in *Being Saved: Explorations in Human Salvation*, ed. Marc Cortez, Joshua R. Farris, and S. Mark Hamilton (London: SCM Press, 2018), 326–43, and Simon F. Gaine, "Thomas Aquinas and John Owen on the Beatific Vision: A Reply to Suzanne McDonald," *NBf* 97 (2016): 432–46.

AFTERWORD

In talking with Paul Uyen—a man with an extraordinary conversion story—I have often reached the point during our lunches where I find tears running down my face, tears of joy. I am naturally an emotional person, but the reader of Paul's book will understand why these tears flow. It is because Paul is not simply a theologian; he is a faith-filled Christian who has experienced God in Jesus Christ through the Spirit. He not only writes about the "economy of illumination"; he has experienced the cardiac and cognitive transformation in which, as he says in his book, "the trinitarian operations of the Father, Son, and Spirit... [make] a person's heart alight with the knowledge of God's glory in the face of Jesus as reflected in the mirror of Scripture." His spirit is open to sharing this knowledge and love with others, both in personal conversation and in this wonderful book.

Paul Uyen discovered in the church fathers, the medieval theologians, and the Reformers a host of fellow Christians. They, too, rejoice in the economy of illumination. Like Uyen, they have experienced the Trinitarian light, to which Scripture testifies, as when the apostle Paul asks rhetorically, "Will not the dispensation of the Spirit be attended with greater splendor?" (2 Cor 3:8).

In a recent book titled *Imitating Christ: The Disputed Character of Christian Discipleship*, the prolific biblical scholar and theologian Luke Timothy Johnson praises Christian teachers who exhibit "fidelity to a vision of discipleship that is more demanding, and more beautiful, than that peddled by Christ-huskers and timeservers." Paul Uyen is definitely no "Christ-husker" or "timeserver"! Everything for Uyen is about real participation in and union with Christ. He yearns to be caught up still more into the Trinitarian life. As a believer seeking the face of the Lord, he is utterly dependent on God's mercy and grace. The economy of illumination is not a Pelagian achievement.

I read this book in its earlier dissertation form some years ago. Now that I look back on it, the years that have followed have involved me in projects that I can see were inspired by Paul's mediation of light. For example, I have been working on baptism as illumination, focusing on how Thomas Aquinas takes up this theme. With respect to baptism as illumination, Paul in his book delves deeply into Clement of Alexandria, Tertullian, Origen, and the Cappadocians. He shared with me the illumination that these church fathers proclaimed. His book directed me to the light of Christ; he shared his (intellectual and spiritual) light with me in conversation and through this book. I have no doubt that many other scholars will find themselves similarly illuminated, brought more deeply into the economy of light, by this important book. Paul has tapped into a crucial stream of biblical and theological wisdom.

Let me add that most recently, I have been writing on the theme of "knowing Jesus," and again I now see Paul's light behind this project, illuminating me with the light of Christ. In addition to reading Scripture, there are various modes in which we are configured to Jesus so as to know him from *inside* our union with him in the body of Christ. These participatory modes are suffering out of love for others (bearing our cross, dying with Christ), doing the works of mercy ("as you did it to one of the least of these my brethren, you did it to me" [Mt 25:40]), prayer (the Lord's Prayer), and the Eucharist (the Lord's Supper). All these make possible the light-filled communion with Christ that Uyen describes as the salvific economy of illumination.

In sum, as a theologian and as a Christian, I have been illuminated by Paul Uyen's marvelous book, with its testimony to the Trinitarian economy of illumination. This sharing of light is what Christians may expect from each other, as friends of Christ through the Spirit. The apostle Paul tells his flock, "Be imitators of me, as I am of Christ" (1 Cor 11:1). The apostle reflects and refracts the Lord Jesus' light, and we must imitate this sharing. All light comes from "the Father of lights" (Jas 1:17). Therefore, Christ calls his church as the Spirit-filled "body of Christ" (1 Cor 12:27) to communicate this Trinitarian light in wisdom and love. Indeed "we all, with unveiled face, beholding the glory of the Lord, are being changed into his likeness from one degree of glory to another" (2 Cor 3:18). I am grateful to Paul Uyen for sharing this transforming light thought his ecumenically and spiritually powerful book, the fruit of his life as a man bathed in Christ's light. "At one time you were darkness, but now you are light in the Lord" (Eph 5:8).

Matthew Levering

BIBLIOGRAPHY

Aalen, Sverre. *Die Begriffe Licht und Finsternis Im Alten Testament*. Oslo: J. Dybwad, 1951.

Alexander, T. Desmond, et al., eds. *New Dictionary of Biblical Theology*. Downers Grove, IL: InterVarsity Press, 2000.

Allen, Leslie C. *Ezekiel 1–19*. WBC 28. Dallas: Word, 1994.

Allen, Michael and Scott R. Swain. *Reformed Catholicity: The Promise of Retrieval for Theology and Biblical Interpretation*. Grand Rapids: Baker Academic, 2015.

Alpers, Christiane. *A Politics of Grace: Hope for Redemption in a Post-Christendom Context*. London: Bloomsbury Academic, 2018.

Amsler, Samuel. *L'Ancien Testament dans L'Eglise*. Paris: Delachaux & Niestlé, 1960.

Anatolios, Khaled. *Athanasius: The Coherence of His Thought*. New York: Routledge, 1998.

———. *Deification through the Cross: An Eastern Christian Theology of Salvation*. Grand Rapids: Eerdmans, 2020.

———. "The Immediately Triune God: A Patristic Response to Schleiermacher." *Pro Ecclesia* 10 (2001): 159–78.

———. *Retreiving Nicaea: The Development and Meaning of Trinitarian Doctrine*. Grand Rapids: Baker Academic, 2011.

———. "The Soteriological Significance of Christ's Humanity in St. Athanasius." *St. Vladimir's Theological Quarterly* 40.4 (1996): 265–86.

Aquinas, Thomas. *Commentary on the Gospel of John*. Translated by Fabian R. Larcher and edited by Aquinas Institute. Lander, WY: Aquinas Institute for the Study of Sacred Doctrine, 2013.

———. *Commentary on the Letters of Saint Paul to the Corinthians*. Edited by J. Mortensen and E. Alarcón. Translated by Fabian R. Larcher, Beth Mortensen, and Daniel Keating. Lander, WY: Aquinas Institute for the Study of Sacred Doctrine, 2012.

———. *Summa Theologiae,* Vol.3. Edited and translated by Herbert McCabe. London: Blackfriars, 1964.

———. *Summa Theologiae.* Vol.7. Translated by T. C. O'Brien. London: Blackfriars, 1976.

———. *Summa Theologiae.* Vol.13. Edited and translated by Edmund Hill. London: Blackfriars, 1964.

———. *Summa Theologiae.* Vol.14. Edited and translated by T. C. O'Brien. London: Blackfriars, 1975.

Arbesmann, Rudolph, Emily Joseph Daly, and Edwin A. Quain, trans. *Tertullian: Apologetical Works.* FC 10. Washington, DC: Catholic University of America Press, 1950.

Aristotle. *Metaphysics.* Translated by Hugh Tredernnick. LCL. Cambridge: Harvard University Press, 1933.

Arnold, Clinton E. *Ephesians.* ZECNT. Grand Rapids: Zondervan, 2010.

Ashley, Timothy R. *The Book of Numbers.* NICOT. Grand Rapids: Eerdmans, 1993.

Ashwin-Siejkowski, Piotr. *Clement of Alexandria: A Project of Christian Perfection.* London: T & T Clark, 2008.

Athanasius. *Contra Gentes and De Incarnatione.* Edited and translated by Robert W. Thomson. London: Oxford, 1971.

———. *On the Incarnation.* Translated and edited by C.S.M.V. Crestwood, NY: St. Vladimir's Seminary Press, 1996.

Athanasius and Didymus the Blind. *Works on the Spirit.* Translated by Mark DelCogliano, Andrew Radde-Gallwitz, and Lewis Ayres. Yonkers, NY: St. Vladimir's Seminary Press, 2011.

Augustine. *Augustine: Earlier Writings.* Edited and translated by J. H. S. Burleigh. Louisville: Westminster John Knox, 2006.

———. *Enchiridion on Faith, Hope, and Love.* Translated by Thomas S. Hibbs. Washington, D.C.: Regnery, 1996.

———. *The Confessions.* 2nd ed. Translated by Maria Baulding. Hyde Park, NY: New City Press, 2012.

———. *Confessions.* Translated by Henry Chadwick. Oxford: Oxford University Press, 1991.

———. *Confessions.* Vol. 1. Translated by Carolyn J. B. Hammond. LCL 26. Cambridge: Harvard University Press, 2014.

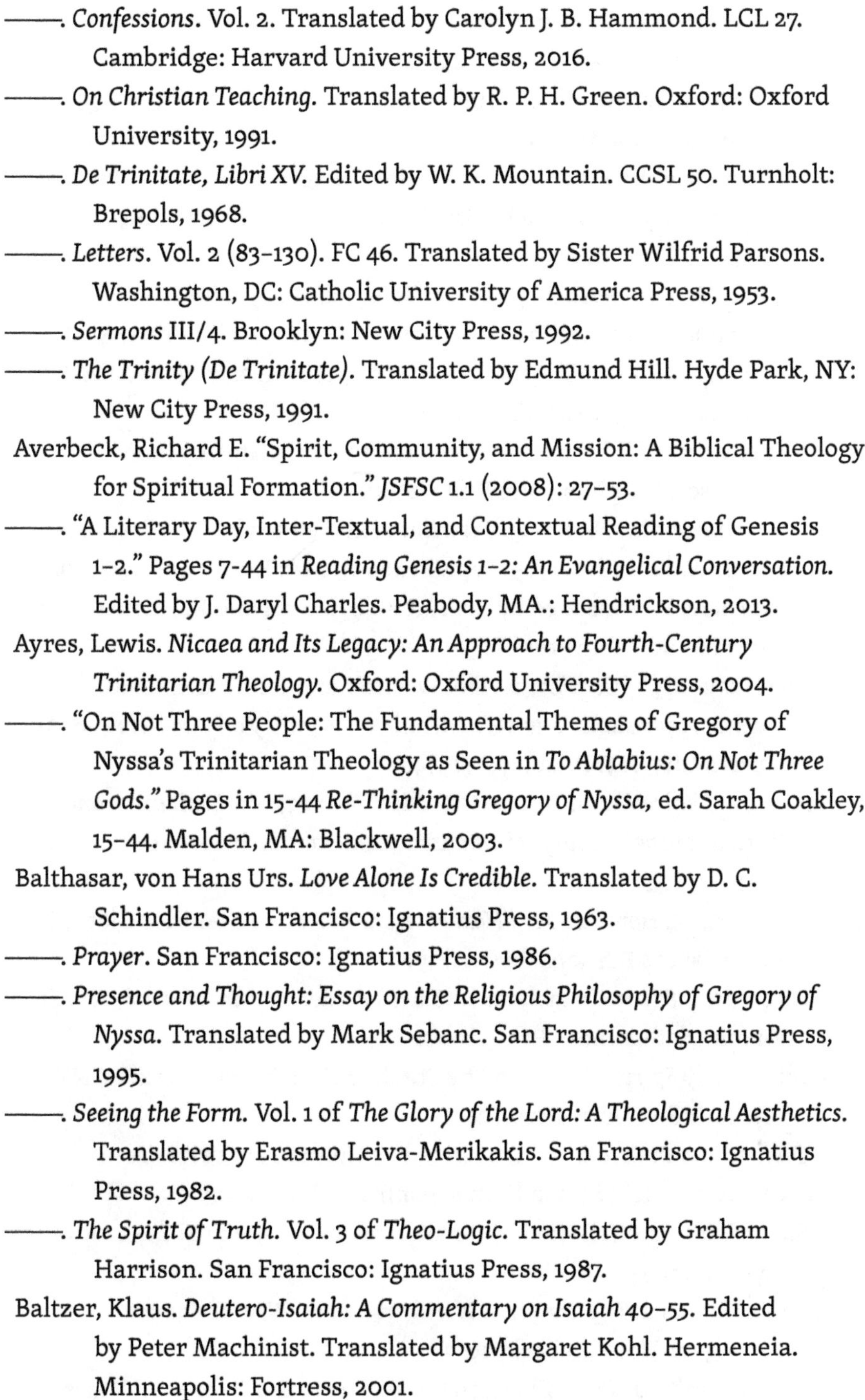

———. *Confessions*. Vol. 2. Translated by Carolyn J. B. Hammond. LCL 27. Cambridge: Harvard University Press, 2016.

———. *On Christian Teaching*. Translated by R. P. H. Green. Oxford: Oxford University, 1991.

———. *De Trinitate, Libri XV*. Edited by W. K. Mountain. CCSL 50. Turnholt: Brepols, 1968.

———. *Letters*. Vol. 2 (83–130). FC 46. Translated by Sister Wilfrid Parsons. Washington, DC: Catholic University of America Press, 1953.

———. *Sermons* III/4. Brooklyn: New City Press, 1992.

———. *The Trinity (De Trinitate)*. Translated by Edmund Hill. Hyde Park, NY: New City Press, 1991.

Averbeck, Richard E. "Spirit, Community, and Mission: A Biblical Theology for Spiritual Formation." *JSFSC* 1.1 (2008): 27–53.

———. "A Literary Day, Inter-Textual, and Contextual Reading of Genesis 1–2." Pages 7-44 in *Reading Genesis 1–2: An Evangelical Conversation*. Edited by J. Daryl Charles. Peabody, MA.: Hendrickson, 2013.

Ayres, Lewis. *Nicaea and Its Legacy: An Approach to Fourth-Century Trinitarian Theology*. Oxford: Oxford University Press, 2004.

———. "On Not Three People: The Fundamental Themes of Gregory of Nyssa's Trinitarian Theology as Seen in *To Ablabius: On Not Three Gods*." Pages in 15-44 *Re-Thinking Gregory of Nyssa*, ed. Sarah Coakley, 15–44. Malden, MA: Blackwell, 2003.

Balthasar, von Hans Urs. *Love Alone Is Credible*. Translated by D. C. Schindler. San Francisco: Ignatius Press, 1963.

———. *Prayer*. San Francisco: Ignatius Press, 1986.

———. *Presence and Thought: Essay on the Religious Philosophy of Gregory of Nyssa*. Translated by Mark Sebanc. San Francisco: Ignatius Press, 1995.

———. *Seeing the Form*. Vol. 1 of *The Glory of the Lord: A Theological Aesthetics*. Translated by Erasmo Leiva-Merikakis. San Francisco: Ignatius Press, 1982.

———. *The Spirit of Truth*. Vol. 3 of *Theo-Logic*. Translated by Graham Harrison. San Francisco: Ignatius Press, 1987.

Baltzer, Klaus. *Deutero-Isaiah: A Commentary on Isaiah 40–55*. Edited by Peter Machinist. Translated by Margaret Kohl. Hermeneia. Minneapolis: Fortress, 2001.

Barnes, Michel René. "Augustine in Contemporary Trinitarian Theology." *Theological Studies* 56 (1995): 237–250.

———. "De Régnon Reconsidered." *Augustinian Studies* 26–2 (1995): 51–79.

———. "Divine Unity and the Divided Self: Gregory of Nyssa's Trinitarian Theology in its Psychological Context." Pages 45–66 in *Re-Thinking Gregory of Nyssa*. Edited by Sarah Coakley. Malden, MA: Blackwell, 2003.

Barnett, Paul W. *The Message of 2 Corinthians*. Edited by John R. W. Stott. Bible Speaks Today. Downers Grove, IL: InterVarsity Press, 1988.

Barrett, C. K. *A Critical and Exegetical Commentary of the Acts of the Apostles*. Vol. 1. ICC. Edinburgh: T&T Clark, 1994.

Barth, Karl. *Anselm: Fides Quaerens Intellectum*. Translated by Ian W. Robertson. Virginia: John Knox, 1960.

———. *Church Dogmatics*, Vol. 1–15. Translated and edited by T. F. Torrance and G. W. Bromiley. 1965. Repr. Peabody, MA: Hendrickson, 2010.

———. *God in Action*. Translated by E. G. Homrighausen and K. J. Ernst. New York: Round Table Press, 1936.

———. *The Humanity of God*. Louisville: Westminster John Knox, 1960.

Barth, Markus. *Ephesians: Translation and Commentary on Chapters 4–6*. AB. Garden City, NY: Doubleday, 1974.

Bartos, Emil. *Deification in Eastern Orthodox Theology: An Evaluation and Critique of the Theology of Dumitru Staniloae*. Carlisle: Paternoster, 1999.

Basile de Césarée. *Homélies sur l'Hexaéméron*. Edited by Stanislas Giet. SC 26. Paris: Les Éditions du Cerf, 1968.

———. *On the Holy Spirit*. Translated by David Anderson. Crestwood, NY: St. Vladimir's Seminary Press, 1980.

———. *On the Holy Spirit*. Translated by Stephen Hildebrand. Yonkers, NY: St Vladimir Seminary Press, 2011.

———. *On the Human Condition*. Translated by Nonna Verna Harrison. Crestwood, NY: St. Vladimir's Seminary Press, 2005.

———. *Sur le Saint-Esprit*. Edited by Benoît Pruche. SC 17. Paris: Les Éditions du Cerf, 2013.

Bauckham, Richard. *The Christian World around the New Testament*. Tübingen: Mohr Siebeck, 2017.

———. "The Divinity of Jesus Christ in the Epistle to the Hebrews." Pages

15–36 in *The Epistle to the Hebrews and Christian Theology*. Edited by Richard Bauckham et al., Grand Rapids: Eerdmans, 2009.

———. *God Crucified: Monotheism and Christology in the New Testament*. Grand Rapids: Eerdmans, 1999.

———. *Gospel of Glory: Major Themes in Johannine Theology*. Grand Rapids: Baker Academic, 2015.

———. *Jude, 2 Peter*. Word Bible Commentary 50. Waco, TX: Word, 1983.

Bavinck, Herman. *Holy Spirit, Church, and New Creation*. Vol. 4 of *Reformed Dogmatics*. Edited by John Bolt. Translated by John Vriend. Grand Rapids: Baker Academic, 2008.

———. *Prolegomena*. Vol. 1 of *Reformed Dogmatics*. Edited by John Bolt. Translated by John Vriend. Grand Rapids: Baker Academic, 2003.

Beale, G. K., *The Book of Revelation*. NIGTC. Grand Rapids: Eerdmans, 1999.

———. "The Old Testament Background of Reconciliation in 2 Corinthians 5–7 and Its Bearing on the Literary Problem of 2 Corinthians 6.14–7.1." *New Testament Studies* 35 (1989): 550–81.

Beale, G. K. and Mitchell Kim. *God Dwells Among Us: Expanding Eden to the Ends of the Earth*. Downers Grove, IL: InterVarsity Press, 2014.

Beasley-Murray, George R. *John*. WBC 36. Waco, TX: Word, 1987.

Beeley, Christopher A. *Gregory of Nazianzus on the Trinity and the Knowledge of God: In Your Light We Shall See Light*. Oxford: Oxford University Press, 2008.

Bender, Wolfgand. *Die Lehre über den heiligen Geist bei Tertullian*. Munich: Hueber, 1961.

Behr, John. *Asceticism and Anthropology in Irenaeus and Clement*. Oxford: Oxford University Press, 2000.

———. *The Way to Nicaea*. Vol. 1 of *Formation of Christian Theology*. Crestwood, N.Y.: St. Vladimir's Seminary Press, 2001.

Billings, J. Todd. *Calvin, Participation, and the Gift: The Activity of Believers in Union with Christ*. Oxford: Oxford University Press, 2007.

———. *The Word of God for the People of God: An Entryway to the Theological Interpretation of Scripture*. Grand Rapids: Eerdmans, 2010.

Bissen, J. M. *L'Éxemplarisme Divin selon saint Bonaventure*. Paris: J. Vrin, 1929.

Blackwell, Ben C. *Christosis: Pauline Soteriology in Light of Deification in Irenaeus and Cyril of Alexandria*. Tübingen: Mohr Siebeck, 2011.

Blankenhorn, Bernhard. *The Mystery of Union with God: Dionysian Mysticism in Albert the Great and Thomas Aquinas*. Washington: The Catholic University of America Press, 2015.

Blass, F., A. Debrunner, and R. W. Funk. *A Greek Grammar of the New Testament and Other Early Christian Literature*. Chicago: University of Chicago Press, 1961.

Block, Daniel I. *The Book of Ezekiel: Chapters 1–24*. NICOT. Grand Rapids: Eerdmans, 1997.

———. *The Book of Ezekiel: Chapters 25–48*. NICOT. Grand Rapids: Eerdmans, 1998.

———. *Deuteronomy*. NIVAC. Grand Rapids: Zondervan, 2012.

———. *The Triumph of Grace: Literary and Theological Studies in Deuteronomy and Deuteronomic Themes*. Eugene, OR: Cascade, 2017.

Bockmuehl, Markus N. A. *Revelation and Mystery in Ancient Judaism and Pauline Christianity*. Tübingen: Mohr Siebeck, 1990.

Boersma, Hans. *Embodiment and Virtue in Gregory of Nyssa: An Analogical Approach*. Oxford: Oxford University Press, 2013.

———. *Seeing God: The Beatific Vision in Christian Tradition*. Grand Rapids: Eerdmans, 2018.

Bonaventure. *Breviloquium*. Vol. 9 of *Works of St. Bonaventure*. St. Bonaventure, NY: Franciscan Institute Publications, 2005.

———. *Collations of the Seven Gifts of the Holy Spirit*. Vol. 14 of *Works of St. Bonaventure*. St. Bonaventure, NY: Franciscan Institute Publications, 2008.

———. *Collations on the Six Days*. Translated by José de Vinck. Paterson, NJ: St. Anthony Guild Press, 1970.

———. *Commentary on the Gospel of John*. Vol. 11 of *Works of St. Bonaventure. St.* Bonaventure, NY: Franciscan Institute Publications, 2007.

———. *Disputed Questions on the Knowledge of Christ*. Vol. 4 of *Works of St. Bonaventure*. St. Bonaventure, NY: Franciscan Institute Publications, 2005.

———. *Itinerarium Mentis in Deum*. Vol. 2 of *Works of St. Bonaventure*. St. Bonaventure, NY: Franciscan Institute Publications, 2002.

———. *On the Reduction of the Arts to Theology*. Vol. 1 of *Works of St. Bonaventure*. St. Bonaventure, NY: Franciscan Institute Publications, 1996.

———. *What Manner of Man?: Sermons on Christ by St. Bonaventure*. Translated

by Zachary Hayes. Chicago: Franciscan Herald Press, 1974.
Bordeianu, Radu. *Dumitru Staniloae: An Ecumenical Ecclesiology*. London: Bloomsbury, 2011.
Brady, Ignatius. "St. Bonaventure's Doctrine of Illumination: Reactions Medieval and Modern Author(s)." *Southwestern Journal of Philosophy* 5.2 (1974): 27–37.
Briggman, Anthony. *Irenaeus of Lyons and the Theology of the Holy Spirit*. Oxford: Oxford University Press, 2012.
Brown, Peter. *Augustine of Hippo: A Biography*. Berkeley: University of California Press, 2000.
Brown, Raymond E. *The Gospel According to John II, 13–21*. AB. Garden City, NY: Doubleday, 1970.
Bruce, F. F. *1 & 2 Thessalonians*. WBC 45. Waco, TX: Word, 1982.
———. *The Epistle to the Colossians, to Philemon, and to the Ephesians*. NICNT. Grand Rapids: Eerdmans, 1984.
———. *The Gospel of John: Introduction, Exposition and Notes*. Grand Rapids: Eerdmans, 1983.
Brueggemann, Walter. *Genesis*. IBC. Atlanta: John Knox, 1982.
Bultmann, Rudolf. *The Second Letter to the Corinthians*. Translated by Roy A. Harrisville. Minneapolis: Augsburg, 1985.
Burns, J. Patout, trans. and ed. *Theological Anthropology*. Philadelphia: Fortress, 1981.
Burger, Hans. *Being in Christ: A Biblical and Systematic Investigation in a Reformed Perspective*. Eugene, OR.: Wipf & Stock, 2009.
Caldwell, Robert W, III. *Communion in the Spirit: The Holy Spirit as the Bond of Union in the Theology of Jonathan Edwards*. Eugene, OR: Wipf & Stock, 2007.
Calvin, John. *Calvin's First Catechism: A Commentary*. Edited by I. John Hesselink. Louisville: Westminster John Knox, 1997.
———. *Commentary on the Book of the Prophet Isaiah*. Translated by William Pringle. Calvin Translation Society, 1849–1850. Repr. Grand Rapids: Baker, 1999.
———. *Commentaries on the Book of the Prophet Jeremiah and the Lamentations*. Translated by John Owen. Calvin Translation Society, 1849–1850. Repr. Grand Rapids: Baker, 1999.
———. *Commentary on the Book of Psalms*. Translated by James Anderson.

Calvin Translation Society, 1849–1850. Repr. Grand Rapids: Baker, 1999.

———. *Commentaries on the Catholic Epistles*. Translated by John Owen. Calvin Translation Society, 1849–1850. Repr. Grand Rapids: Baker, 1999.

———. *Commentary on the Epistles of Paul the Apostle to the Galatians and Ephesians*. Translated by William Pringle. Calvin Translation Society, 1849–1850. Repr. Grand Rapids: Baker, 1999.

———. *Commentary on the Epistle of Paul the Apostle to the Hebrews*. Translated by John Owen. Calvin Translation Society, 1849–1850. Repr. Grand Rapids: Baker, 1999.

———. *Commentary on the Epistle of Paul the Apostle to the Philippians, Colossians, and Thessalonians*. Translated by John Pringle. Calvin Translation Society, 1849–1850. Repr. Grand Rapids: Baker Books, 1999.

———. *Commentary on the Epistle of Paul the Apostle to the Romans*. Translated by John Owen. Calvin Translation Society, 1849–1850. Repr. Grand Rapids: Baker, 1999.

———. *Commentaries on the Four Last Books of Moses*. Translated by Charles W. Bingham. Calvin Translation Society, 1849–1850. Repr. Grand Rapids: Baker, 1999.

———. *Commentary on the Gospel According to John*. Translated by William Pringle. Calvin Translation Society, 1849–1850. Repr. Grand Rapids: Baker, 1999.

———. *Commentary on a Harmony of the Evangelists*. Translated by William Pringle. Calvin Translation Society, 1849–1850. Repr. Grand Rapids: Baker, 1999.

———. *Commentaries on the Twelve Minor Prophets*. Vol. 4. Translated by John Owen. Calvin Translation Society, 1849–1850. Repr. Grand Rapids: Baker, 1999.

———. *Commentary upon the Acts of the Apostles*. Translated by Henry Beveridge. Calvin Translation Society, 1849–1850. Repr. Grand Rapids: Baker, 1999.

———. *The Commentaries of John Calvin on the First Epistle of Paul the Apostle to the Corinthians*. Translated by John Pringle. Calvin Translation Society, 1849–1850. Repr. Grand Rapids: Baker, 1999.

———. *The Commentaries of John Calvin on the Second Epistle of Paul the Apostle to the Corinthians*. Translated by John Pringle. Calvin Translation Society, 1849–1850. Repr. Grand Rapids: Baker, 1999.

———. *Institutes of the Christian Religion*. Edited by John T. McNeill. Translated by Ford Lewis Battles. 2 vol. Louisville: Westminster John Knox, 1960.

Campbell, Constantine R. *Paul and Union with Christ: An Exegetical and Theological Study*. Grand Rapids: Zondervan, 2012.

Canlis, Julie. *Calvin's Ladder: A Spiritual Theology of Ascent and Ascension*. Grand Rapids: Eerdmans, 2010.

Carasik, Michael, ed. *The Commentator's Bible: Exodus*. The JPS Miqra'ot Gedolot. Philadelphia: Jewish Publication Society, 2005.

Carson, D. A. *The Gospel According to John*. PNTC. Grand Rapids: Eerdmans, 1991.

———. "The Function of the Paraclete in John 16:7–11." *Journal of Biblical Literature* 98.4 (1979): 547–66.

Carson, D. A., and Douglas J. Moo. *An Introduction to the New Testament*. 2nd ed. Grand Rapids: Zondervan, 2005.

Casidy, Augustine. "Church Fathers and the Shaping of Orthodox Theology." Pages 167–87 in *Cambridge Companion to Orthodox Christian Theology*. Edited by Mary B. Cunningham and Elizabeth Theokritoff. Cambridge: Cambridge University Press, 2008.

Cassuto, Umberto. *A Commentary on the Book of Genesis I – V18: Part I From Adam to Noah*. Jerusalem: Magnes, 1961.

Chevallier, Max-Alain. *Esprit de Dieu, Paroles d'hommes: Le rôle de l'esprit dans les ministères de la parole selon l'apôtre Paul*. Neuchâtel: Delachaux & Niestlé, 1966.

Childs, Brevard S. *Isaiah*. OTL. Louisville: Westminster John Knox, 2001.

Chadwick, Henry. *East and West: The Making of a Rift in the Church: From Apostolic Times until the Council of Florence*. Oxford: Oxford University Press, 2003.

Clement of Alexandria, *Christ the Educator*. Translated by Simon Wood. FC 23. Washington, DC: Catholic University of America Press, 1953.

———. *Exhortation to the Greeks, The Rich Man's Salvation, and To the Newly Baptized*. Translated by G. W. Butterworth. LCL 92. Cambridge: Harvard University Press, 1919.

———. *Le Pédagogue, livre 1*. Edited and translated by Henri-Irénée Marrou and Marguerite Harl. Sources Chretiennes 70. Paris: Les Éditions du Cerf, 1960.

———. *Les Stromates IV.* Edited and translated by Annewies van den Hoek and Claude Mondésert. SC 463. Paris: Les Éditions du Cerf, 2001.

———. *Stromateis: Books One to Three.* FC 85. Translated by John Ferguson. Washington, DC: Catholic University of America Press, 1991.

Clines, D. J. A., "The Tree of Knowledge and the Law of Yahweh (Psalm XIX)." *Vestus Testamentum* 24 (1974): 8–14.

Collange, J. F. *Enigmes de le deuxième Épître de Paul aux Corinthiens.* London: Cambridge University Press, 1972.

Cooper, John W. *Panentheism: The Other God of the Philosophers.* Grand Rapids: Baker Academic, 2006.

Cortez, Marc. "The Body and the Beatific Vision." Pages 326–43 in *Being Saved: Explorations in Human Salvation.* Edited by Marc Cortez, Joshua R. Farris, and S. Mark Hamilton. London: SCM, 2018.

Craigie, Peter C. *Psalms 1–50.* WBC 19. Grand Rapids: Zondervan, 1983.

Cranfield, C. E. B. *The Epistle to the Romans.* Vol. 1. ICC. Edinburgh: T&T Clark, 1975.

Crawford, Matthew R. *Cyril of Alexandria's Trinitarian Theology of Scripture.* Oxford: Oxford University Press, 2014.

Crisp, Oliver D. *Approaching the Atonement: The Reconciling Work of Christ.* Downers Grove, IL: InterVarsity Press, 2020.

———. Divinity and Humanity: The Incarnation Reconsidered. Cambridge: Cambridge University Press, 2007.

———. *Jonathan Edwards on God and Creation.* Oxford: Oxford University Press, 2012.

Crouzel, Henri. *Origen*, Translated by A. S. Worrall. San Francisco: Harper & Row, 1989.

Cullen, Christopher M. *Bonaventure.* Oxford: Oxford University Press, 2006.

———. "Bonaventure's Philosophical Method." In A Companion to Bonaventure. Edited by Jay H. Hammond, J. A. Wayne Hellmann, and Jared Goff. Leiden: Brill, 2014.

Cyril of Alexandria. *Commentary on John.* 2 volumes. Edited and translated by David R. Maxwell and Joel C. Elowsky. IVP Academic, 2013, 2015.

———. *Commentary on the Twelve Prophets.* Vol. 1. Translated by Robert C. Hill.

FC 115. Washington, DC: Catholic University of America Press, 2007.
———. *On the Unity of Christ*. Translated by John Anthony McGuckin. Crestwood, NY: St. Vladimir's Seminary Press, 1995.
Daley, Brian E. *Gregory of Nazianzus*. New York: Routledge, 2006.
Dalferth, Ingolf U. *Becoming Present: An Inquiry into the Christian Sense of the Presence of God*. Leuven: Peeters, 2006.
Danaher, William. *The Trinitarian Ethics of Jonathan Edwards*. Louisville: Westminster John Knox, 2004.
———. *Platonisme et théologie mystique*. Paris: Aubier, 1944.
Davidson, Ivor J. "Atonement and Incarnation." Pages 35–56 in *T&T Clark Companion to Atonement*. Edited by Adam J. Johnson. New York: Bloomsbury T&T Clark, 2017.
Davison, Andrew. *Participation in God: A Study in Christian Doctrine and Metaphysics*. Cambridge: Cambridge University Press, 2019.
de Andia, Ysabel. *Homo vivens*. Paris: Études augustinennes, 1986.
De Vries, Simon John. *1 Kings*. WBC 12. Grand Rapids: Zondervan, 1985.
Dillenberger, John, ed. *John Calvin: Selections from His Writings*. Missoula, MT: Scholars Press, 1975.
Dodd, C. H. *The Interpretation of the Fourth Gospel*. Cambridge: Cambridge University Press, 1953.
Dolezal, James E. *God without Parts: Divine Simplicity and the Metaphysics of God's Absoluteness*. Eugene, OR: Pickwick, 2011.
Doyle, Patrick James. "The Disintegration of Divine Illumination Theory in the Franciscan School, 1285–1300: Peter of Trabes, Richard of Middleton, William of Ware." PhD diss., Marquette University, 1984.
Dumbrell, William J. *Covenant and Creation: A Theology of the OT Covenants*. Grand Rapids: Baker, 1984.
Dunn, Geoffrey D. *Tertullian*. London: Routledge, 2004.
Dunn, James D. G. Romans 1-8. WBC 38A. Dallas: Word, 1988.
———. *Romans 9–16*. WBC 38B. Dallas: Word, 1988.
———. *The Theology of Paul the Apostle*. Grand Rapids: Eerdmans, 1998.
Dupont, Jacques. *Essais sur la christologie de saint Jean: Le Christ, parole, lumière et vie: La glorie du Christ*. Bruges: Éditions de l'Abbaye de Saint-André, 1951.
Edwards, Jonathan. *The Works of Jonathan Edwards*. 26 vols. New Haven: Yale University Press, 1957–2008.

———. *Works of Jonathan Edwards Online.* Vols. 17–73 of the Works of Jonathan Edwards. Jonathan Edwards Center, Yale University, 2008—. Online: http://edwards.yale.edu

Edwards, Mark, and Elena Ene D-Vasilescu, eds. *Visions of God and Ideas on Deification in Patristic Thought.* London: Routledge, 2017.

Emery, Gilles. "Holy Spirit." In *Cambridge Companion to the Summa Theologiae.* Edited by Philip McCosker and Denys Turner. New York: Cambridge University Press, 2016.

———. *The Trinitarian Theology of Saint Thomas Aquinas.* Translated by Francesca A. Murphy. Oxford: Oxford University Press, 2007.

———. *The Trinity: An Introduction to Catholic Doctrine on the Triune God.* Translated by Matthew Levering. Washington, DC: Catholic University of America Press, 2011.

Evans, C. Stephen. *Natural Signs and Knowledge of God: A New Look at Theistic Arguments.* Oxford: Oxford University Press, 2010.

Evans, Ernest. *Tertullian's Homily on Baptism.* London: SPCK, 1964.

———. *Tertullian's Treatise on the Resurrection.* London: SPCK, 1960.

Fairbairn, Donald. *Grace and Christology in the Early Church.* Oxford: Oxford University Press, 2003.

Faro, Ingrid. "A Lexical, Exegetical, Conceptual, and Theological Study of Evil in Genesis." PhD diss., Trinity Evangelical Divinity School, 2013.

Ferguson, Everett. *Baptism in the Early Church: History, Theology, and Liturgy in the First Five Centuries.* Grand Rapids: Eerdmans, 2009.

———. "Paradosis and Traditio: A Word Study." Pages 3–29 in *Tradition and the Rule of Faith in the Early Church: Essays in Honor of Joseph T. Lienhard.* Washington, DC: Catholic University of America Press, 2010.

Fesko, J. V. *Adam and the Covenant of Works.* Fern: Mentor, 2021.

———. *The Covenant of Redemption: Origins, Development, and Reception.* Göttingen: Vandenhoeck & Ruprecht, 2016.

Festugière, A. J. *Contemplation et vie contemplative selon Platon.* 3rd ed. Paris: Vrin, 1967.

Fitzgerald, Allan D. *Augustine through the Ages: An Encyclopedia.* Grand Rapids: Eerdmans, 1999.

Fitzmyer, Joseph A. *The Acts of the Apostles.* AB. New Haven: Yale University Press, 1998.

Ford, David F. *Self and Salvation: Being Transformed.* Cambridge: Cambridge University Press, 1999.

Furnish, Victor P. *II Corinthians.* AB 32A. New York: Doubleday, 1984.

Gaine, Simon F. "Thomas Aquinas and John Owen on the Beatific Vision: A Reply to Suzanne McDonald." *NBf* 97 (2016): 432–46.

Garcia, Mark A. *Life in Christ: Union with Christ and Twofold Grace in Calvin's Theology*. Studies in Christian History and Thought. Colorado Springs: Paternoster, 2008.

Garland, David. *1 Corinthians.* BECNT. Grand Rapids: Baker Academic, 2003.

Garrett, Stephen M. *God's Beauty-in-Act: Participating in God's suffering Glory.* Eugene, OR: Wipf & Stock, 2013.

Gathercole, Simon. "The Doctrine of Justification in Paul and Beyond: Some Proposals." Pages 219–42 in *Justification in Perspective.* Edited by Rutherford House and Bruce L. McCormack. Grand Rapids: Baker Academic, 2006.

Gaventa, Beverly Roberts. *From Darkness to Light: Aspects of Conversion in the New Testament.* Philadelphia: Fortress, 1986.

Gentry, Peter J., and Stephen J. Wellum. *Kingdom through Covenant: A Biblical-Theological Understanding of the Covenants.* Wheaton, IL: Crossway, 2012.

Georgi, Dieter. *Die Gegner des Paulus im 2. Korintherbrief: Studien zur Religiösen Propaganda in der Spätantike.* WMANT. Neukirchen-Vluyn: Neukirchener Verlag, 1964.

Gilson, Etienne. *The Philosophy of St. Bonaventure.* Translated by Dom Illtyd Trethowan and F. J. Sheed. London: Sheed & Ward, 1940.

Goldingay, John. *Psalms*. BCOT. Grand Rapids: Baker Academic, 2008.

Goldingay, John and David Payne. *Isaiah 40–55.* ICC. London: T & T Clark, 2006.

Green, Garret. *Imagining God: Theology and the Religious Imagination.* San Francisco: Harper & Row, 1989.

Green, Joel B. "Learning Theological Interpretation from Luke." Pages 55–78 in eading Luke: Interpretation, Reflection, Formation. Edited by Craig G. Bartholomew, Joel B. Green, and Anthony C. Thiselton.; Grand Rapids: Zondervan, 2005.

Green, Joel B, and Scot McKnight. *Dictionary of Jesus and the Gospels.* Downers Grove, IL: InterVarsity Press, 1992.

Grant, Robert M. *Irenaeus of Lyons*. London: Routledge, 1997.

Gregory of Nyssa. *Contra Eunomium II*. Edited by Lenka Karfíková, Scot Douglass and Johannes Zachhuber. Translated by Stuart George Hall. Leiden: Brill, 2007.

———. *Contra Eunomium III*. Edited by Johan Leemans and Matthieu Cassin. Translated by Stuart George Hall. Leiden: Brill, 2010.

———. *From Glory to Glory: Texts from Gregory of Nyssa's Mystical Writings*. Edited and translated by Herbert Musurillo. Crestwood, NY: St. Vladimir's Seminary Press, 2001.

———. *Homilies on the Song of Songs*. Translated by Richard A. Norris Jr. Atlanta: Society of Biblical Literature, 2012.

———. *La Vie de Moïse*. Edited by Jean Daniélou. Sources Chretiennes 1 bis. Paris: Les Éditions du Cerf, 2007.

———. *The Life of Moses*. Translated by Abraham J. Malherbe and Everett Ferguson. New York: Paulist, 1978.

———. *The Lord's Prayer, the Beatitudes*. Translated by Hilda C. Graef. New York: Newman Press, 1954.

———. *On the Soul and the Resurrection*. Translated by Catharine P. Roth. Crestwood, NY: St. Vladimir's Seminary Press, 1993.

Grégoire de Nazianze. *Discours 27–31*. Edited by Paul Gallay. SC 250. Paris: Les Éditions du Cerf, 2008.

———. *Discours 38–41*. Edited by Paul Gallay. SC 358. Paris: Les Éditions du Cerf, 1990.

———. *Festal Orations*. Translated by Nonna Verna Harrison. Crestwood, NY: St. Vladimir's Seminary Press, 2008.

Grégoire Palamas. *Défense des saints hésychastes*. 2 vols. Edited by Jean Meyendorff. Louvain: "Spicilegium Sacrum Lovaniense" Admistration, 1959.

———. *The Triads*. Edited by John Meyendorff. Translated by Nicholas Gendle. New York: Paulist, 1983.

Hafemann, Scott J. *Suffering and the Spirit: An Exegetical Study of II Cor. 2:14–3:3 within the Context of the Corinthians Correspondence*. WUNT 19. Tübingen: Mohr Siebeck, 1986.

Hahn, Scott W. *Kinship by Covenant: A Canonical Approach to the Fulfillment of God's Saving Promises*. New Haven: Yale University Press, 2009.

Hallo, William W, and K. Lawson Younger Jr., eds. *Canonical Compositions,*

Monumental Inscriptions, and Archival Documents from the Biblical World. Vol. 2 of *The Context of Scripture*. Leiden: E. J. Brill, 2000.

Hamilton, Victor P. *The Book of Genesis Chapters 1–17*. NICOT. Grand Rapids: Eerdmans, 1990.

Hammond, Jay M., J. A. Wayne Hellmann, and Jared Goff, eds. *A Companion to Bonaventure*. Leiden: Brill, 2014.

Hansen, G. Walter. *The Letter to the Philippians*. PNTC. Grand Rapids: Eerdmans, 2009.

Hanson, Anthony T. *The New Testament Interpretation of Scripture*. London: SPCK, 1980.

Hardy, Edward R., and Cyril C. Richardson, trans. and eds. *Christology of the Later Fathers*. Philadelphia: Westminster, 1954.

Harris, Murray J. *The Second Epistle to the Corinthians*. NIGTC. Grand Rapids: Eerdmans, 2005.

Harrison, Carol. *Rethinking Augustine's Early Theology: An Argument of Continuity*. Oxford: Oxford University Press, 2006.

Hartsock, Chad. *Sight and Blindness in Luke-Acts: The Use of Physical Features in Characterization*. Leiden: Brill, 2008.

Hastings, W. Ross. *Jonathan Edwards and the Life of God: Toward an Evangelical Theology of Participation*. Minneapolis: Fortress, 2015.

Hays, Richard B. *Echoes of Scripture in the Letters of Paul*. New Haven: Yale University Press, 1989.

———. "What is 'Real Participation in Christ'?: A Dialogue with E. P. Sanders on Pauline Soteriology." Pages 336–51 in *Redefining First-Century Jewish and Christian Identities: Essays in Honor of Ed Parish Sanders*. Edited by Fabian E. Udoh, Susannah Heschel, Mark Chancey, and Gregory Tatum. Notre Dame: University of Notre Dame Press, 2008.

Heine, Ronald E. *Gregory of Nyssa's Treatise on the Inscriptions of the Psalms*. Oxford: Clarendon, 1995.

Helm, Paul, and Oliver D. Crisp, eds. *Jonathan Edwards: Philosophical Theologian*. Burlington: Ashgate, 2003.

Hildebrand, Stephen M. *Basil of Caesarea*. Grand Rapids: Baker Academic, 2014.

———. *Basil of Caesarea*. New York: Routledge, 2018.

Hill, Jonathan. *The History of Christian Thought*. Downers Grove, IL: IVP Academic, 2003.

Hill, Kevin Douglas. *Athanasius and the Holy Spirit: The Development of His Early Pneumatology.* Minneapolis: Fortress, 2016.

Hoglund, Jonathan. *Called by Triune Grace: Divine Rhetoric and the Effectual Call.* Edited by Daniel Treier and Kevin J. Vanhoozer. Downers Grove, IL: IVP Academic, 2016.

Holladay, William L. *Jeremiah 2.* Hermeneia. Minneapolis: Fortress, 1989.

Horton, Michael. *Covenant and Salvation: Union with Christ.* Louisville: Westminster John Knox, 2007.

Hossfeld, Frank-Lothar, and Erich Zenger. *Psalms: A Commentary on Psalms 101–150.* Translated by Linda M. Maloney. Hermeneia. Minneapolis: Fortress, 2011.

Hugedé, Norbert. *La métaphore du miroir dans les épîtres de saint Paul aux Corinthiens.* Neuchâtel: Delachaux & Niestlé, 1957.

Hunsinger, George. *How to Read Karl Barth: The Shape of His Theology.* New York: Oxford University Press, 1991.

Hurley, M. "Illumination according to S. Bonaventure." *Gregorianum* 32.3 (1951): 388–404.

Irenaeus of Lyons. *Against the Heresies, Book 1.* Translated by D. J. Unger. ACW 55. New York: Newman Press, 1992.

———. *Against the Heresies, Book 2.* Translated by D. J. Unger. ACW 65. New York: Newman Press, 2012.

———. *Against the Heresies, Book 3.* Translated by D. J. Unger. ACW64. New York: Newman Press, 2012.

———. *Contre les heresies, Livre* 1. Edited by A. Rousseau and L. Doutreleau. SC 264. Paris: Les Éditions du Cerf, 2008.

———. *Contre les heresies, Livre* 4. Edited by A. Rousseau and L. Doutreleau. SC 100. Paris: Les Éditions du Cerf, 1965.

———. *Proof of the Apostolic Preaching.* Translated by Joseph P. Smith. New York: Newman Press, 1952.

Itter, Andrew C. *Esoteric Teaching in the Stromateis of Clement of Alexandria.* Leiden: Brill, 2009.

Jensen, Michael P. *Martyrdom and Identity: The Self on Trial.* London: T& T Clark, 2010.

Jobes, Karen H. *1, 2, and 3 John.* ZECNT. Grand Rapids: Zondervan, 2014.

Jüngel, Eberhard. *God's Being is in Becoming: The Trinitarian Being of God in the Theology of Karl Barth.* Translated by John Webster. Grand

Rapids: Eerdmans, 2001.

Kapic, Kelly M. *Communion with God: The Divine and the Human in the Theology of John Owen.* Grand Rapids: Baker Academic, 2007.

Kantzer, Kenneth S. "John Calvin's Theory of the Knowledge of God and the Word of God." PhD diss., Harvard University, 1950.

Karavites, Peter (Panayiotis). *Evil, Freedom, and the Road to Perfection in Clement of Alexandria.* Leiden: Brill, 1999.

Kautzsch, E. ed. *Gesenius' Hebrew Grammar.* Translated by A. E. Cowley. 2d. ed. Oxford: Oxford, 1910.

Keating, Daniel A. *The Appropriation of Divine Life in Cyril of Alexandria.* Oxford: Oxford University Press, 2004.

———. "Divinization in Cyril: The Appropriation of Divine Life." Pages 148–86 in *The Theology of St. Cyril of Alexandria.* Edited by Thomas G. Weinandy and Daniel A. Keating. London: T & T Clark, 2003.

Kearney, Richard. *On Paul Ricoeur: The Owl of Minerva.* Burlington, VT: Ashgate, 2004.

Keener, Craig S. *The Gospel of John: A Commentary.* Vol. 2. Grand Rapids: Baker Academic, 2003.

———. *The Mind of the Spirit: Paul's Approach to Transformed Thinking.* Grand Rapids: Baker Academic, 2016.

Keown, Gerald L., Pamela J. Scalise, and Thomas G. Smothers. *Jeremiah 26–52.* WBC 27. Grand Rapids: Zondervan, 1995.

Kim, Seyoon. *The Origin of Paul's Gospel.* Grand Rapids: Eerdmans, 1981.

Kidner, Derek. *Proverbs: An Introduction and Commentary*, TOTC 17. Downers Grove, IL: InterVarsity Press, 1964.

Knierim, Rolf P., and George W. Coats. *Numbers.* Forms of Old Testament Literature 4. Grand Rapids: Eerdmans, 2005.

Köstenberger, Andreas J. *John.* BECNT. Grand Rapids: Baker Academic, 2004.

Kuhn, Thomas S. *The Essential Tension.* Chicago: University of Chicago Press, 1977.

———. *The Structure of Scientific Revolutions.* 3d ed. Chicago: University of Chicago Press, 1992.

Lafond, Yves. "Corinthus/Corinth." BNP 3:798–804.

Laird, Martin. *Gregory of Nyssa and the Grasp of Faith: Union, Knowledge and Divine Presence.* Oxford: Oxford University Press, 2006.

Lashier, Jackson. *Irenaeus on the Trinity*. Leiden: Brill, 2014.

Le Blond, J.-M. *Les conversions de s. Augustin*. Paris: Aubier, 1950.

Legge, Dominic. *Trinitarian Christology of St. Thomas Aquinas*. Oxford: Oxford University Press, 2017.

Leslie, Andrew M. *The Light of Grace: John Owen on the Authority of Scripture and Christian Faith*. Göttingen: Vandenhoeck & Ruprecht, 2015.

Letham, Robert. *Union with Christ: In Scripture, History, and Theology*. Phillipsburg, NJ: P & R, 2011.

Levering, Matthew. *Participatory Biblical Exegesis: A Theology of Biblical Interpretation*. Notre Dame: University of Notre Dame Press, 2008.

———. *Paul in the Summa Theologiae*. Washington, DC: Catholic University of America Press, 2014.

———. *Scripture and Metaphysics: Aquinas and the Renewal of Trinitarian Theology*. Oxford: Blackwell, 2004.

Lewis, C. S. *Surprised by Joy: The Shape of My Early Life*. Orlando: Harcourt, 1955.

Lilla, Salvatore R. C. *Clement of Alexandria: A Study in Christian Platonism and Gnosticism*. Oxford: Oxford University Press, 1971.

Lincoln, Andrew T. *Ephesians*. WBC 42. Grand Rapids: Zondervan, 1990.

Lossky, Vladimir. *The Mystical Theology of the Eastern Church*. Crestwood, NY: St. Vladimir's Seminary Press, 1976.

Locke, John. *An Essay Concerning Human Understanding*. Edited by Peter H. Nidditch. Oxford: Clarendon, 1975.

Louth, Andrew. "The Concept of the Soul in Athanasius' Contra Gentes—De Incarnatione." *Studia Patristica* 13 (1975): 227–231.

———. *Introducing Eastern Orthodox Theology*. Downers Grove, IL: IVP Academic, 2013.

———. *The Origins of the Christian Mystical Tradition: From Plato to Denys*. 2nd ed. Oxford: Oxford University Press, 2007.

———. "Theology, Contemplation and the University." *Studies in Christian Ethics* 17 (2004): 69–79.

Lundbom, Jack R. *Deuteronomy: A Commentary*. Grand Rapids: Eerdmans, 2013.

Macaskill, Grant. *Living in Union with Christ: Paul's Gospel and Christian Moral Identity*. Grand Rapids: Baker Academic, 2019.

———. *Union with Christ in the New Testament*. Oxford: Oxford University

Press, 2013

Malina, Bruce J., and John J. Pilch. *Social-Science Commentary on the Book of Acts*. Minneapolis: Fortress, 2008.

Marion, Jean-Luc. *God without Being*. 2nd ed. Chicago: University of Chicago Press, 2012.

———. *In the Self's Place: The Approach of Saint Augustine*. Translated by Jeffrey L. Kosky. Stanford: Stanford University Press, 2012.

Martens, Peter W. *Origen and Scripture: The Contours of the Exegetical Life*. Oxford: Oxford University Press, 2012.

Martin, Ralph P. *2 Corinthians. 2nd ed.* WBC 40. Grand Rapids: Zondervan, 2014.

Mateo-Seco, Lucas Francisco, and Giulio Maspero, eds. *The Brill Dictionary of Gregory of Nyssa*. Leiden: Brill, 2010.

Mauss, Marcel. *The Gift: The Form and Reason for Exchange in Archaic Societies*. Translated by W. D. Halls. New York: Norton, 1990.

Mayer, P. Augustinus. *Das Gottesbild im Menschen: Nach Clemens von Alexandrien*. Rome: Pontificium Institutum S. Anselmi, 1942.

McClymond, Michael J., and Gerald R. McDermott. *The Theology of Jonathan Edwards*. Oxford: Oxford University Press, 2012.

McConnell, Timothy P. *Illumination in Basil of Caesarea's Doctrine of the Holy Spirit*. Minneapolis: Fortress, 2014.

McComiskey, Thomas E. *The Covenants of Promise: A Theology of the Old Testament Covenants*. Grand Rapids: Baker, 1985.

McCormack, Bruce L. *Orthodox and Modern: Studies in the Theology of Karl Barth*. Grand Rapids: Baker Academic, 2008.

McMartin, Jason. "The Theandric Union as Imago Dei and Capax Dei." Pages 136–50 in *Christology: Ancient and Modern*. Edited by Oliver D. Crisp and Fred Sanders. Grand Rapids: Zondervan, 2013.

Meyendorff, John. *A Study of Gregory Palamas*. Edited by George Lawrence. Leighton Buzzard: Faith Press, 1964.

Meadors, Edward P. *Idolatry and the Hardening of the Heart: A Study in Biblical Theology*. New York: T & T Clark, 2006.

Meister, Chad, ed. *The Oxford Handbook of Religious Diversity*. Oxford: Oxford University Press, 2011.

Miller, Ike. *Seeing in the Light: Illumination in Augustine's and Barth's Reading of John*. Downers Grove, IL: IVP Academic, 2020.

Milbank, John. *Being Reconciled: Ontology and Pardon*. London: Routledge, 2003.

———. "Can a Gift be Given?: Prolegomena to a Future Trinitarian Metaphysic." *Modern Theology* 11.1 (1995): 119–161.

———. *The Future of Love: Essays in Political Theology*. Eugene, OR: Cascade, 2009.

———. *Theology and Social Theory*. 2nd ed. Oxford: Blackwell, 2006.

Milbank, John, and Catherine Pickstock. *Truth in Aquinas*. London: Routledge, 2001.

Moltmann, Jürgen. *Crucified God*. New York: HarperCollins, 1974.

———. *God in Creation: A New Theology of Creation and The Spirit of God*. San Francisco: Harper & Row, 1985.

———. *Theology of Hope*. Minneapolis: Fortress, 1993.

Moo, Douglas J. *The Epistle to the Romans*. NICNT. Grand Rapids: Eerdmans, 1996.

———. *The Letters to the Colossians and to Philemon*. PC. Grand Rapids: Eerdmans, 2008.

Morgna-Wynne, John Eifion. *Holy Spirit and Religious Experience in Christian Literature ca. AD 90–200*. Waynesboro, GA: Paternoster, 2006.

Motyer, J. Alec. *Isaiah: An Introduction and Commentary*. TOTC 20. Downers Grove, IL: InterVarsity Press, 1999.

———. *The Prophecy of Isaiah: An Introduction and Commentary*. Downers Grove, IL: InterVarsity Press, 1993.

Muller, Richard A. *Calvin and the Reformed Tradition: On the Work of Christ and the Order of Salvation*. Grand Rapids: Baker Academic, 2012.

———. *Dictionary of Latin and Greek Theological Terms: Drawn Principally from Protestant Scholastic Theology*. Grand Rapids: Baker, 1985.

Muraoka, Takamitsu. *A Greek-English Lexicon of the Septuagint*. Louvain: Peeters, 2009.

Murphy, Roland E. *Proverbs*. WBC 22. Grand Rapids: Zondervan, 1998.

Murray, John. *Redemption, Accomplished, and Applied*. Grand Rapids: Eerdmans, 1955.

Neder, Adam. *Participation in Christ: An Entry into Karl Barth's Church Dogmatics*. Louisville: Westminster John Knox, 2009.

Nichols, Aidan. "The Theo-logic." In *Cambridge Companion to Hans Urs von*

Balthasar. Edited by Edward T. Oakes and David Moss. Cambridge: Cambridge University Press, 2004.

Nock, A. D. *Conversion: The Old and the New in Religion from Alexander the Great to Augustine of Hippo*. Baltimore: Johns Hopkins University Press, 1998.

Nouwen, Henri. *The Way of the Heart: The Spirituality of the Desert Fathers and Mothers*. New York: HarperOne, 1981.

O'Brien, Peter T. *Colossians–Philemon*. WBC 44. Nashville: Nelson, 1982.

O'Brien, Peter T. "Was Paul Converted." In *Justification and Variegated Nomism*. Edited by D. A. Carson, Peter T. O'Brien, and Mark A. Seifrid. Grand Rapids: Baker, 2004.

O'Donovan, Oliver. *Self, World, and Time: Ethics as Theology 1*. Grand Rapids: Eerdmans, 2013.

Origen. *Commentary on the Epistle to the Romans Books 1–5*. FC 103. Translated by Thomas P. Scheck. Washington, DC: Catholic University of America Press, 2001.

———. *Commentary on the Gospel of John Books 13–32*. FC 89. Translated by Ronald E. Heine. Washington, DC: Catholic University of America Press, 1993.

———. *Commentaire sur saint Jean, Livre* 1–5. Edited by Cécile Blanc. SC 120. Paris: Les Éditions du Cerf, 1996.

———. *Contra Celsum*. Edited by M. Marcovich. Leiden: Brill, 2001.

———. *Homélies sur la Genèse*. Edited by Louis Doutreleau. SC 7 bis. Paris: Les Éditions du Cerf, 2011.

———. *Homilies on Genesis and Exodus*. FC 71. Translated by Ronald E. Heine. Washington, DC: Catholic University of America Press, 1981.

———. *Homilies on Judges*. FC 119. Translated by Elizabeth A. Dively Lauro. Washington, DC: Catholic University of America Press, 2010.

———. *Homilies on Luke*. FC 95. Translated by Joseph T. Lienhard. Washington, DC: Catholic University of America Press, 2009.

———. *On First Principles*. Translated by G. W. Butterworth. Notre Dame: Ave Maria Press, 2013.

———. *The Song of Songs Commentary and Homilies*. Translated by R. P. Lawson. ACW 26. New York: Newman Press, 1956.

———. *Traité des principes, Livres* 1–2. Edited by Henri Crouzel and Manlio Simonetti. SC 252. Paris: Les Éditions du Cerf, 1978.

Osborn, Eric. *Clement of Alexandria*. Cambridge: Cambridge University Press, 2005.

———. *Irenaeus of Lyons*. Cambridge: Cambridge University Press, 2001.

———. *Tertullian: First Theologian of the West*. Cambridge: Cambridge University Press, 1997.

Oswalt, John N. *The Book of Isaiah: Chapters 40–66*. NICOT. Grand Rapids: Eerdmans, 1998.

Oulton, John E. L., and Henry Chadwick, trans. and eds. *Alexandrian Christianity*. Philadelphia: Westminster, 1954.

Owen, John. *Causes, Ways, and Means of Understanding the Mind of God*, vol. 4 of *The Works of John Owen*. Edited by William Goold. 1850–1853. Reprint. Edinburgh: Banner of Truth, 1967.

———. *Communion with God*. Vol. 2 of *The Works of John Owen*. Edited by William H. Goold. 1850–1853. Repr. Edinburgh: Banner of Truth, 1965.

———. ΠΝΕΥΜΑΤΟΛΟΓΙΑ or *A Discourse Concerning the Holy Spirit*. Vol. 3 of *The Works of John Owen*. Edited by William H. Goold. 1850–1853. Repr. Edinburgh: Banner of Truth, 1965.

Pao, David W. *Acts and the Isaianic New Exodus*. Grand Rapids: Baker Academic, 2002.

Paul, Shalom M. *Isaiah 40–66: Translation and Commentary*. ECC. Grand Rapids: Eerdmans, 2012.

Penna, R. "L'évolution de l'attitude de Paul envers les Juifs." Pages 390–421 in *L'apôtre Paul: Personnalité, Style et Conception du Ministère*. Edited by A. Vanhoye. Leuven: Leuven University Press, 1986.

Peterson, David G. *The Acts of the Apostles*. PNTC. Grand Rapids: Eerdmans, 2009.

———. *Possessed by God: A New Testament Theology of Sanctification and Holiness*. NSBT. Grand Rapids: Eerdmans, 1995.

———. *Transformed by God: New Covenant Life and Ministry*. Downers Grove, IL: InterVarsity Press, 2012.

Peterson, Eugene H. *The Contemplative Pastor: Returning to the Art of Spiritual Direction*. Grand Rapids: Eerdmans, 1993.

———. *Eat This Book: A Conversation in the Art of Spiritual Reading*. Grand Rapids: Eerdmans, 2006.

———. *Tell It Slant: A Conversation on the Language of Jesus in His Stories and*

Prayers. Grand Rapids: Eerdmans, 2008.

Pitkin, Barbara. *What Pure Eyes Could See: Calvin's Doctrine of Faith in Its Exegetical Context*. New York: Oxford University Press, 1999.

Puckett, David L. *John Calvin's Exegesis of the Old Testament*. Columbia Series in Reformed Theology. Louisville: Westminster John Knox, 1995.

Pusey, P. E. *Sancti patris nostril Cyrilli Archiepiscopi Alexandrini in d. Joannis Evangelium*. 3 vols. Oxford: Clarendon, 1872.

Ramm, Barnard. *The Witness of the Spirit: An Essay on the Contemporary Relevance of the Internal Witness of the Holy Spirit*. Grand Rapids: Eerdmans, 1960.

Reid, Thomas. *Essays on the Intellectual Powers of Man: A Critical Edition*. Edited by Derek R. Brookes. University Park, PA: Pennsylvania State University Press, 2002.

Ricoeur, Paul. *Time and Narrative*. Vol. 1. Translated by Kathleen Blamey and David Pellauer. Chicago: University of Chicago Press, 1983.

———. *Time and Narrative*. Vol. 3. Translated by Kathleen Blamey and David Pellauer. Chicago: University of Chicago Press, 1988. .

Russell, Norman. *Cyril of Alexandria*. London: Routledge, 2000.

———. *The Doctrine of Deification in the Greek Patristic Tradition*. Oxford: Oxford University Press, 2004.

Ryken, Leland, James C. Wilhoit, and Tremper Longman III, eds. *Dictionary of Biblical Imagery*. Downers Grove: IL: InterVarity Press, 1998.

Salladin, James R. *Jonathan Edwards and Deification: Reconciling Theosis and the Reformed Tradition*. Downers Grove, IL: InterVarsity Press, 2022.

Sanders, E. P. *Paul and Palestinian Judaism: A Comparison of Patterns of Religion*. Philadelphia: Fortress, 1977.

Sanders, Fred. *The Triune God*. Grand Rapids: Zondervan, 2016.

———. *The Deep Things of God: How the Trinity Changes Everything*. 2nd ed. Wheaton, IL: Crossway, 2017.

Sarna, Nahum M. *Genesis*. JPS Torah Commentary. Philadelphia: Jewish Publication Society, 1989.

Savage, Timothy B. *Power through Weakness: Paul's Understanding of the Christian Ministry in 2 Corinthians*. Cambridge: Cambridge University Press, 1996.

Schnabel, Eckhard J. *Acts*. ZECNT. Grand Rapids: Zondervan, 2012.

Schreiner, Thomas R. *Covenant and God's Purpose for the World*. Wheaton,

IL: Crossway, 2017.

———. *Romans*. ZECNT. Grand Rapids: Baker, 1998.

Schumacher, Lydia. *Divine Illumination: The History and Future of Augustine's Theory of Knowledge*. Oxford: Wiley-Blackwell, 2011.

Scobie, Charles H. H. "A Canonical Approach to Interpreting Luke: The Journey Motif as a Hermeneutical Key." Pages 327–49 in *Reading Luke: Interpretation, Reflection, Formation*. Edited by Craig G. Bartholomew, Joel B. Green, and Anthony C. Thiselton. Grand Rapids: Zondervan, 2005.

Scott, James M. *2 Corinthians*. New International Biblical Commentary 8. Peabody, MA: Hendrickson, 1998.

Seaman, Mark X. *Illumination and Interpretation: The Holy Spirit's Role in Hermeneutics*. Eugene, OR: Wipf & Stock, 2013.

Seifrid, Mark A. *The Second Letter to the Corinthians*. PNTC. Grand Rapids: Eerdmans, 2014.

Spawforth, Antony J. S. "Corinth." OCD, 390–91.

Staniloae, Dumitru. *Revelation and Knowledge of the Triune God*. Vol. 1 of *The Experience of God: Orthodox Dogmatic Theology*. Translated and edited by Ioan Ionita and Robert Barringer. Brookline, MA: Holy Cross Orthodox, 1998.

———. *The Church: Communion in the Holy Spirit*. Vol. 4 of *The Experience of God: Orthodox Dogmatic Theology*. Translated and edited by Ioan Ionita. Brookline, MA: Holy Cross Orthodox, 2012.

———. *The Fulfillment of Creation*. Vol. 6 of *The Experience of God: Orthodox Dogmatic Theology*. Translated and edited by Ioan Ionita. Brookline, MA: Holy Cross Orthodox, 2013.

———. *Theology and the Church*. Translated by Robert Barringer. Crestwood, NY: St. Vladimir's Seminary Press, 1997.

———. *The Person of Jesus Christ as God and Savior*. Vol. 3 of *The Experience of God: Orthodox Dogmatic Theology*. Translated and edited by Ioan Ionita. Brookline, MA: Holy Cross Orthodox, 2011.

———. *The Sanctifying Mysteries*. Vol. 5 of *The Experience of God: Orthodox Dogmatic Theology*. Translated and edited by Ioan Ionita and Robert Barringer. Brookline, MA: Holy Cross Orthodox, 2012.

———. *The World: Creation and Deification*. Vol. 2 of *The Experience of God: Orthodox Dogmatic Theology*. Translated and edited by Ioan Ionita

and Robert Barringer. Brookline, MA: Holy Cross Orthodox, 2000.
Steenberg, M. C. *Irenaeus on Creation*. Leiden, Brill, 2008.
Steiner, George. *Real Presences*. Chicago: University of Chicago Press, 1989.
Stendahl, Krister. *Paul Among Jews and Gentiles*. Philadelphia: Fortress, 1976.
Still, Todd D. and David E. Wilhite *Tertullian and Paul*. New York: Bloomsbury, 2013.
Stott, John R. W. *The Cross of Jesus Christ*. Downers Grove, IL: InterVarsity Press, 2021.
———. *The Letter of John: An Introduction and Commentary*. TNTC 19. Downers Grove, IL: InterVarsity Press, 1988.
Stuhlmacher, Peter. *Biblische Theologie und Evangelium*. Tübingen: Mohr Siebeck, 2002.
Stump, Eleonore. *Atonement*. Oxford: Oxford University Press, 2018.
Swain, Scott. "Covenant of Redemption." Pages 107–25 in *Christian Dogmatics: Reformed Theology for the Church Catholic*. Edited by Michael Allen and Scott R. Swain, 107–125. Grand Rapids: Baker Academic, 2016.
———. *Trinity, Revelation, and Reading*. London: Bloomsbury, 2011.
Tate, Michael J., Kevin J. Vanhoozer, and Constantine R. Campbell, eds. *'In Christ' in Paul: Exploration in Paul's Theology of Union and Participation*. Tübingen: Mohr Siebeck, 2014.
Thielman, Frank. *Ephesians*. BECNT. Grand Rapids: Baker Academic, 2010.
Thiselton, Anthony C. *The First Epistle to the Corinthians: A Commentary on the Greek Text*. NIGTC. Grand Rapids: Eerdmans, 2000.
Thompson, J. A. *The Book of Jeremiah*. NICOT. Grand Rapids: Eerdmans, 1980.
Thrall, Margaret E. *A Critical and Exegetical Commentary on the Second Epistle to the Corinthians*. 2 vol. ICC. Edinburgh: T&T Clark, 1994–2001.
Tremblay, Réal. *La manifestation et la vision de Dieu selon saint Irénée de Lyon*. Münster: Aschendorff, 1978.
Trueman, Carl R. "Illumination." Pages 316–18 in*Dictionary for Theological Interpretation of the Bible*, edited by Kevin J. Vanhoozer, 316–18. Grand Rapids: Baker Academic, 2005.
Turcescu, Lucian. *Gregory of Nyssa and the Concept of Divine Persons*. Oxford: Oxford University Press, 2005.

———. "'Person' versus 'Individual,' and Other Modern Misreadings of Gregory of Nyssa." Pages 97–110 in *Re-Thinking Gregory of Nyssa*, . Edited by Sarah Coakley, 97–110. Malden, MA: Blackwell, 2003.

Vanhoozer, Kevin J. "Augustinian Inerrancy: Literary Meaning, Literal Truth, and Literate Interpretation in the Economy of Biblical Discourse." Pages 199–235 in *Five Views on Biblical Inerrancy*. Edited by J. Merrick and Stephen M. Garrett, 199–235. Grand Rapids: Zondervan, 2013.

———. "Effectual Call or Causal Effect?: Summons, Sovereignty and Supervenient Grace," *Tyndale Bulletin* 49.2 (1998): 213–51.

———. *Is There a Meaning in This Text?: The Bible, the Reader, and the Morality of Literary Knowledge*. Grand Rapids: Zondervan, 1998.

———. "Lost in Interpretation?: Truth, Scripture, and Hermeneutics." *Journal of Evangelical Theological Society* 48/1 (2005): 89–114.

———. *Remythologizing Theology: Divine Action, Passion, and Authorship*. Cambridge: Cambridge University Press, 2010.

Vanhoozer, Kevin J. and Daniel J. Treier. *Theology and the Mirror of Scripture: A Mere Evangelical Account*. Downers Grove, IL: IVP Academic, 2015.

Vogels, Walter. "Like One of Us, Knowing Ṭôḇ and Raʿ" (Gen 3:22)." *Semeia* 81 (1998): 145–157.

Wallace, Daniel B. *Greek Grammar Beyond the Basics: An Exegetical Syntax of the New Testament*. Grand Rapids: Zondervan, 1996.

Wallace, Howard M. *The Eden Narrative*. Atlanta: Scholars Press, 1985.

Waltke, Bruce K., *The Book of Proverbs: Chapter 1–15*. NICOT. Grand Rapids: Eerdmans, 2004.

Waltke, Bruce K., and Michael P. O'Connor, *An Introduction to Biblical Hebrew Syntax*. Winona Lake, IN: Eisenbrauns, 1990.

Waltke, Bruce K., and Cathi J. Fredricks. *Genesis: A Commentary*. Grand Rapids: Zondervan, 2001.

Walton, John H. *Genesis*. NIVAC. Grand Rapids: Zondervan, 2001.

———. *The Lost World of Adam and Eve: Genesis 2–3 and the Human Origins Debate*. Downers Grove, IL: IVP Academic, 2015.

Wanamaker, Charles A. *The Epistles to the Thessalonians*. NIGTC . Grand Rapids: Eerdmans, 1990.

Ward, Timothy. *Words of Life: Scripture as the Living and Active Word of God*.

Downers Grove, IL: InterVarsity Press, 2009.
Ware, Timothy. *The Orthodox Church: An Introduction to Eastern Christianity.* 3rd ed. London: Penguin, 2015.
Warfield, Benjamin Breckinridge. *Calvin and Augustine.* Philadelphia: Presbyterian & Reformed, 1956.
Way, Sister Agnes Clare, trans. *St. Basil: Exegetic Homilies.* FC 46. Washington, DC: Catholic University of America Press, 1963.
Webb, Barry G. *The Message of Isaiah.* Bible Speaks Today. Downers Grove, IL: Intervarsity Press, 1996.
Webster, John. *Holy Scripture: A Dogmatic Sketch.* Cambridge: Cambridge University Press, 2003.
———. "Illumination." *JRT* 5 (2011): 325–340.
———. *The Domain of the Word: Scripture and Theological Reason.* London: T & T Clark, 2012.
Weima, Jeffrey A. D. *1–2 Thessalonians.* BECNT. Grand Rapids: Baker Academic, 2014.
Wenham, Gordon J. *Genesis 1–15.* WBC 1. Grand Rapids: Zondervan, 1987.
———. *Numbers: An Introduction and Commentary.* TOTC. Downers Grove, IL: InterVarsity Press, 1981.
Westcott, B. F. *The Epistles of St. John.* Grand Rapids: Eerdmans, 1966.
Whidden III, David L. *Christ the Light: The Theology of Light and Illumination in Thomas Aquinas.* Minneapolis: Fortress, 2014.
———. *The Trinity: On the Nature and Mystery of the One God.* Washington, DC: Catholic University of America Press, 2022.
Williams, A. N. "Contemplation." Pages 121–46 in *Knowing the Triune God: The Work of the Spirit in the Practice of the Church.* Edited by James J. Buckley and David S. Yeago. Grand Rapids: Eerdmans, 2001.
———. *The Divine Sense: The Intellect in Patristic Theology.* Cambridge: Cambridge University Press, 2007.
———. *The Ground of Union: Deification in Aquinas and Palamas.* New York: Oxford University Press, 1999.
Williams, Rowan. *On Augustine.* New York: Bloomsbury, 2016.
Williamson, Paul R. *Sealed with an Oath: Covenant in God's Unfolding Purpose.* Downers Grove, IL: InterVarsity Press, 2007.
Wilson, R. McL. *A Critical and Exegetical Commentary on Colossians and Philemon.* ICC. London: T & T Clark, 2005.

Wingren, Gustaf. *Man and the Incarnation: A Study in the Biblical Theology of Irenaeus*. Trans. Ross Mackenzie. Edinburgh: Oliver & Boyd, 1959.

Witherington, Ben, III. *The Acts of the Apostles: A Socio-Rhetorical Commentary*. Grand Rapids: Eerdmans, 1998.

Wittgenstein, Ludwig. *Philosophical Investigation*. Translated by G. E. M. Anscombe, P. M. S. Hacker, and Joachim Schulte. 4th ed. Oxford: Blackwell, 2009.

———. *Tractatus Logico-Philosophicus*. Translated D. F. Pears and B. F. McGuinness. New York: Routledge & Kegan Paul, 1961.

Wright, N. T. *Colossians and Philemon: An Introduction and Commentary*. TNTC. Downers Grove, IL: InterVarsity Press, 1986.

———. "The Lord's Prayer as a Paradigm of Christian Prayer." Pages 132–54 in *Into God's Presence: Prayer in the New Testament*. Edited by Richard N. Longenecker, 132–154. Grand Rapids: Eerdmans, 2001.

———. *Paul: A Biography*. San Francisco: HarperOne, 2018.

———. *Resurrection and the Son of God*. Minneapolis: Fortress, 2003.

Wyrwa, Dietmar, and Kyriakos Savvidis, eds. *Athanasius Werke 1.1*. Vol. 4 of *Die Dogmatischen Schriften: Epistulae I-IV ad Serapionem*. Berlin: de Gruyter, 2010.

Yarbrough, Robert W. *The Letters to Timothy and Titus*. PNTC. Grand Rapids: Eerdmans, 2018.

Young, Richard A. *Intermediate New Testament Greek: A Linguistic and Exegetical Approach*. Nashville: Broadman & Holman, 1994.

Zachman, Randall C. *Image and Word in the Theology of John Calvin*. Notre Dame: University of Notre Dame Press, 2007.

Zuber, Kevin D. "What Is Illumination? A Study in Evangelical Theology Seeking a Biblically Grounded Definition of the Illuminating Work of the Holy Spirit." PhD diss., Trinity Evangelical Divinity School, 1996.

SUBJECT & AUTHOR INDEX

—

SCRIPTURE & OTHER ANCIENT WITNESSES INDEX

Old Testament

Proverbs

Ecclesiastes

Isaiah

New Testament

Acts

Ancient Near Eastern Texts

Dead Sea Scrolls

Philo